XML

Pocket Consultant

William R. Stanek

PUBLISHED BY
Microsoft Press
A Division of Microsoft Corporation
One Microsoft Way
Redmond, Washington 98052-6399

Library of Congress Cataloging-in-Publication Data
XML Pocket Consultant / William R. Stanek.
p. cm.
Includes index.
ISBN 0-7356-1183-1
1. XML (Document markup language) I. Title.

QA76.76.H94 S735 2002
005.7'2--dc21 2001055873

Printed and bound in the United States of America.

1 2 3 4 5 6 7 8 9 QWE 7 6 5 4 3 2

Distributed in Canada by Penguin Books Canada Limited.

A CIP catalogue record for this book is available from the British Library.

Microsoft Press books are available through booksellers and distributors worldwide. For further information about international editions, contact your local Microsoft Corporation office or contact Microsoft Press International directly at fax (425) 936-7329. Visit our Web site at www.microsoft.com/mspress. Send comments to *mspinput@microsoft.com*.

Acquisitions Editor: Juliana Aldous Atkinson
Project Editor: Jean Trenary

Body Part No. X08-04469

Contents at a Glance

Table of Contents

Tables

Acknowledgements

The *XML Pocket Consultant* represents a dramatic shift—an additional direction—for the *Pocket Consultant* series I began back in 1999. While previous *Pocket Consultants* have focused on administration techniques, this latest endeavor focuses on technology solutions. This new direction for a *Pocket Consultant* required a great deal of thought to plan and a lot of hard work to implement. Still, I think the result is a good book that will help any technologist learn XML and its related technologies.

Once again, I was fortunate enough to team up with a great group of individuals from Microsoft Press. I must say that the editorial team was very patient with me, even as I revised the outline and structure for the umpteenth time, which is great news for readers because the result is much clearer in focus and more detailed in coverage. Indeed, one of the goals was to present the most concise yet thorough coverage of XML and its related technologies available anywhere. (You'll be the judge as to whether this goal was achieved.)

As always, it is gratifying to see techniques I've used time and again to solve problems put into a printed book so that others may benefit from them. But no man is an island, and this book couldn't have been written without help from some very special people. I owe huge Thank Yous to the team at Microsoft Press, both for recognizing the potential of my practical and useful approach to the *Pocket Consultant* series and for their willingness to run with it. Juliana Aldous handled acquisitions and helped make sure I had the tools I needed to write this book. Jean Trenary managed the editorial process from the Microsoft Press side, with Erin Connaughton heading up the editorial process for nSight, Inc. They both helped the writing/editorial process run very smoothly!

Unfortunately for the writer (but fortunately for readers), writing is only one part of the publishing process. Next came editing and author review. Special thanks to Julie and Jean. Toby Andrews was the technical editor for the book. Thank you, Toby, for checking all those examples and details! I'd also like to thank Joseph Gustaitis for his careful attention to detail while copy editing the book. Good copy editors are hard to find!

Hopefully I haven't forgotten anyone, but if I have, it was an oversight. *Honest.* ;-)

Introduction

XML Pocket Consultant is the authoritative quick reference guide to the eXtensible Markup Language (XML) and related technologies that empower Microsoft .NET solutions, including SQL Server, BizTalk Server, and Commerce Server. Unlike many other XML books, this one covers the official World Wide Web Consortium (W3C) recommendations rather than beta versions of various XML technologies. In this book you'll find concise and precise coverage of

- XML as based on XML 1.0 2nd Edition, W3C Recommendation, October 2000
- XML Schemas as based on XML Schema, W3C Recommendation, May 2001
- XML Namespaces as based on Namespaces in XML, W3C Recommendation, January 1999
- XML Links as based on XLink and XBase, W3C Recommendation, June 2001
- Extensible Stylesheet Language (XSL) Transformations as based on XSL Transformations (XSLT) Version 1.0 W3C Recommendation, November 16, 1999, and extended by XSL Transformations (XSLT) Version 1.1
- XML Path as based on the XML Path Language (XPath) Version 1.0 W3C Recommendation, November 16, 1999

Because the focus is on giving you maximum value in a pocket-sized guide, you don't have to wade through hundreds of pages of extraneous information to find what you're looking for. Instead, you'll find exactly what you need to get the job done.

In short, this book is designed to be the one resource you turn to whenever you have questions about XML. To this end, it zeroes in on key technologies that you'll use every day, whether you're a developer implementing XML solutions or an administrator maintaining XML-based solutions.

Inside this book's pages, you'll find comprehensive overviews, step-by-step procedures, frequently used tasks, documented examples, and options that are representative, although not necessarily inclusive. One of the goals is to keep the content so concise that the book remains compact and easy to navigate while at the same time ensuring that the book is packed with as much information as possible—making it a valuable resource. Thus, instead of a hefty 1,000-page tome or a lightweight 100-page quick reference, you get a valuable resource guide that can help you quickly and easily perform common tasks, solve problems, and implement everyday solutions.

Who Is This Book For?

XML Pocket Consultant focuses on the essentials of the XML standard and provides detailed discussions of key related technologies that you'll need to be successful with XML. The book is designed for

- Developers creating XML-based solutions
- Administrators who support XML-based solutions
- Technologists working with XML who want to understand how the technology works

To pack in as much information as possible, I had to assume that you have basic technology skills and a basic understanding of the Internet, the World Wide Web, and markup languages, such as Hypertext Markup Language (HTML). With this in mind, I don't devote entire chapters to understanding the World Wide Web, markup languages, or how structured documents can be used on the Web. You should already know this material or have resources to study. I do, however, provide a detailed introduction to XML and its related technologies that serves as the start of your foray into the world of XML. I also provide an introduction covering the structure of XML documents. After that, the book delves into each of the key technologies that you'll need to understand and use in your daily work, including document type definitions (DTDs), XML namespaces, XML Schema, and XSL Transformations.

As I stated, I assume that you're familiar with the Internet and the Web. For example, I might talk about transfer protocols, such as Hypertext Transfer Protocol (HTTP), in various contexts and assume that you know that HTTP is used to transfer information over the Web. I might also discuss documents that use HTML and compare them to documents that use XML. Again, I'll assume that you know the basics of HTML and the Web. If you don't (or have forgotten what you previously learned), I'd recommend getting a book that covers the basics of the Internet and the basics of Web publishing.

How Is This Book Organized?

XML Pocket Consultant is designed to be studied as a resource guide and used as a quick reference to meet your everyday needs whether you're a developer implementing XML technologies or an administrator maintaining XML-based solutions. Speed and ease of reference is an essential part of this hands-on guide. The book has an expanded table of contents and an extensive index for finding answers to problems quickly. Many other quick reference features have been added as well. These features include quick step-by-step instructions, lists, tables with fast facts, and extensive cross-references. The book is broken down into both parts and chapters. Each part contains an opening paragraph or two about the chapters contained in that part.

Part I, "XML Essentials," covers the fundamental concepts you need to be successful with XML. Chapter 1 provides a background on the development of XML, a review of XML-based technologies, and a brief discussion on creating XML-based solutions. In Chapter 2 you'll learn XML naming rules, how XML documents are organized, and how to work with key XML structures, including elements, attributes, entities, processing instructions, and comments.

In Part II, "DTDs and Namespaces," you'll find the essential tasks for working with DTDs and XML namespaces. DTDs provide a way to describe the structure of XML documents in terms of the elements, attributes, and contents they can contain. You use XML namespaces to prevent naming conflicts when like-named elements and attributes are associated with different types of data structures and used in the same document. Chapter 3 discusses techniques you can use to create DTDs. Chapters 4 through 6 delve into the details of how you can define elements, attributes, entities, and notations in DTDs. Chapter 7 zeroes in on XML namespaces and explains how namespaces are defined and referenced in documents that use DTDs. Because many XML-based technologies, including XML Schemas, are implemented through DTDs, a solid understanding of DTDs and how they work is essential to your success—even if you don't plan to use DTDs.

Part III, "XML Schemas," focuses on the XML Schema language. XML Schemas provide an alternative way to describe the structure of XML documents in terms of the elements, attributes, and contents they can contain. The chapters in part III discuss the XML Schema language defined by the W3C and referred to as XML Schema Definition (XSD). XSD is more advanced than early schema implementations referred to as XML Data Reduced (XDR) schemas. Chapter 8 introduces the XML Schema language and its related concepts. The chapter also discusses how namespaces are used with schemas. Chapters 9 to 11 cover the details of the XML schema language. Chapter 12 provides a resource guide to schema declarations that is designed to clarify schema usage.

To round out the coverage of XML, the final part of the book, Part IV "XSLT and XPath," examines techniques you can use to transform XML structures dynamically. An understanding of transformation is essential if you want to implement or support an end-to-end XML solution. Typically, you'll use transformations to structure information dynamically after extracting the information from a database. Chapter 13 introduces XSL Transformations and related technologies, including XSL Formatting Objects (used to provide formatting and style) and XML Path (XPath) (used to identity parts of documents). Chapter 14 provides a detailed discussion of XPath operators and expressions that you can use to locate specific parts of XML documents. Chapter 15 examines structures that you can use to conditionally process a part of a document based on the value of an expression.

The advanced discussion of XSLT and XPath continues with Chapters 16-18. Chapter 16 explores techniques you can use to pass values into templates and hold values temporarily during processing. Chapter 17 delves into techniques you can use to manipulate the text content of elements and attributes. You'll learn how to extract substrings, convert strings to number, format strings, and much more. Chapter 18 completes the discussion of XSLT and XPath by explaining how to restructure input documents and manipulate document subsets. You'll learn how to merge sets of documents, how to manipulate document structures, and how to define sort keys.

Conventions Used in This Book

I've used a variety of elements to help keep the text clear and easy to follow. You'll find code terms and listings in monospace type, except when I tell you to actually type a command. In that case, the command appears in **bold** type. When I introduce and define a new term, I put it in *italics*.

Other conventions include

Note To provide details on a point that needs emphasis

Tip To offer helpful hints or additional information

Caution To warn you when there are potential problems you should look out for

More Info To provide more information on the subject

Real World To provide real-world advice when discussing advanced topics

I truly hope you find that XML Pocket Consultant provides everything you need to use XML successfully. You're welcome to send your thoughts to me at xml@tvpress.com. Thank you.

Support

Every effort has been made to ensure the accuracy of this book. Microsoft Press provides corrections for books through the World Wide Web at the following address:

http://mspress.microsoft.com/support/

If you have comments, questions, or ideas about this book, please send them to Microsoft Press using either of the following methods:

Postal Mail:

Microsoft Press
Attn: *XML Pocket Consultant* Editor
One Microsoft Way
Redmond, WA 98052-6399

E-mail:

MSPINPUT@MICROSOFT.COM

Please note that product support isn't offered through the mail addresses. For support information visit Microsoft's Web site at *http://support.microsoft.com/*.

Part I

XML Essentials

Part I covers the fundamental concepts you need to be successful with XML. Chapter 1 provides a background on the development of XML, a review of XML-based technologies, and a brief discussion on creating XML-based solutions. Chapter 2 explores XML document structures. In it, you'll learn XML naming rules, how XML documents are organized, and how to work with key XML structures, including elements, attributes, entities, processing instructions, and comments.

Chapter 1

Introducing XML

Working groups within the World Wide Web Consortium (W3C) started developing eXtensible Markup Language (XML) in 1996. Their goal was simple: develop a version of the Standard Generalized Markup Language (SGML) that could be used efficiently on the Web, and this is exactly what was done. By November 1996, the W3C working groups had drafted a document that outlined XML's basic structure and functionality. Throughout 1997, the W3C and its member groups continued to develop and expand XML. XML got a lot of praise in certain circles, especially within the SGML community. However, few people in the mainstream knew much about XML—and mainstream awareness is what XML needed to really take off.

That all began to change around the time XML was formalized as a proposed recommendation. By this time it was December 1997 and XML was being used as the basis of many technologies. These applications of XML helped make the technology less abstract and more real. Suddenly lots of people were starting to take a closer look at XML. Before you knew it, XML had a very public—and enthusiastic—following. More and more books about XML started to appear on bookstore shelves. A buzz began to build. People started to wonder what XML was all about, and they had many questions. They wanted to know how XML would affect the Web and whether XML would replace Hypertext Markup Language (HTML). They wanted to know how XML worked and, more importantly, what XML could do for them.

Answering these and other important questions about XML is what this chapter is all about. It starts with a look at how XML works and how you can use XML, and then it examines extensions to XML.

XML Basics

XML is a metalanguage. That is, it's a language that can be used to describe other languages. Although XML and HTML may seem to have a lot in common, in reality the difference between them is like the difference between night and day. HTML is used to format information, but it isn't very useful when it comes to describing information. For example, you can use HTML to format a table, but you can't use HTML to describe the data elements within the table. The reason for this is that you can't really depict something as abstract as a distributor or a customer with HTML, which is where XML comes into the picture. XML can be, and is, used to define the structure of data rather than its format.

What makes XML so powerful is that any type of data—even abstract data concepts—can be given form and structure. You give data concepts—such as distributor, purchase order, and inventory—form by describing their components and the relationship between those components. Instead of the abstract concept of a distributor, you have a specified structure that describes the distributor-related information, such as distributor name, contact name, and address. You could define the structure of an inventory item handled by the distributor with components such as item number, name, description, unit cost, and suggested retail price.

XML gets this power and versatility from SGML, but it does so without the complexities that make SGML difficult to implement and use on the Web. With this solution, you get the best aspects of SGML without the overhead, which makes XML practical for transmission and use in cyberspace. A key difference between XML and other similar technologies is that XML is used to define the structure of data rather than its format. This means you can use XML to describe the individual data components in a document. For example, using XML you could define the structure of an employee record with components such as employee ID number, full name, contact information, and position within the company. These components could then be further broken down to their basic level.

Although XML can give data structure, you can't use XML to detail how the content is to be rendered. To do this, you have to rely on another technology to format the information. One way to format XML data structures is to combine them with HTML. Here, you create so-called XML islands within standard HTML documents. You use HTML to format the contents of the document, including the data, and you use XML to define the structure of the data. Another formatting solution for XML is to create a style sheet detailing how each piece of the data structure should be formatted. Although a special style sheet language called Extensible Stylesheet Language (XSL) is designed specifically for this purpose, you could also use the cascading style sheet language (CSS).

Generally, XML-only documents end with the .xml extension. You can use this extension to tell the application reading the document that it contains XML data. To interpret the data structures within the document, the application relies on an XML processor. Two types of XML processors are used: those that validate documents and those that don't. A validating XML processor checks the structure of documents; a nonvalidating XML processor doesn't.

Note In practice, XML-only documents created for Web browser display should end with the .xml extension. If you're developing for a different environment, the extension doesn't really matter. The XML parser classes that you use to interpret the document don't need the extension. However, for consistency, it's best to use the .xml extension for files that contain XML. This ensures that other developers (including yourself at a later date) know what the files contain.

Most XML processors are implemented as extension modules for existing applications. In this context, the XML processor is used within the application to extract information from the XML document and display it in an application window. This window could be in your Web browser or in a stand-alone application.

XML processors are also implemented in programming languages like Java and C#. Here, you use the processor classes to help you extract information from an XML document and display it in an application or applet window.

Tip Another name for a processor is a parser. Not only are there XML parsers, but there are XSL parsers as well. XSL parsers are used to process style sheet definitions in XML documents and render the documents according to those definitions.

Using XML

Using XML is a lot easier than you might think. That's because with XML you're in control. Unlike HTML, XML doesn't rely on predefined tags and attributes. This allows you to structure the data in an XML document any way you like. You define the tags for components within the document. You add attributes to these tags as necessary, and you decide how the components fit together.

The general set of rules for a document's tags and attributes is defined in a document type definition (DTD). XML processors can use the DTD to determine if the document is constructed properly and the processor can pass this information along to the application rendering the document. Keep in mind that documents don't have to have DTDs. However, if they do have a DTD, they should be structured to conform to the DTD.

Once the DTD for a particular type of data is created, you can use the DTD either by inserting it directly into the document, or by referencing the DTD so that it can be imported into the document by the XML processor. Next, you need to create the body of the XML document. There are several ways to do this, and the method you choose depends primarily on how the data is used.

If you're working with fixed data records that change infrequently, you may want to create the necessary data structures using an authoring tool. Here, you insert the data directly into a document and save the result to a file so that it can be viewed directly in an application or compatible browser. You could then publish the document on the Web where others could access it. When you need to update the document, you'd load the document into the authoring tool's editor, make the necessary changes, and then publish the updated document.

If you're working with data that changes frequently, you probably need a more dynamic solution, and rather than creating static documents you could create documents on the fly. To do this, you'd use a document publishing or content management system. These systems are usually integrated with a database. The database stores data records so they can be retrieved on demand. The management system reads in the data and converts it to the appropriate structure based on the DTD and then passes this data off to an application or browser for viewing. Users accessing the dynamic document don't know all this is happening in the background, and they can still access the document using a Uniform Resource Locator (URL).

Extensions to XML

As with most Web technologies, the XML specification is only a starting point. The specification describes XML's core functionality, such as how XML documents are to be defined, and the necessary grammar that enables documents to comply with this definition.

Beyond the core language, several extensions have been defined, including XML Linking Language, XML Pointer Language, Extensible Stylesheet Language (XSL), XML Namespaces, and XML Schema. These technologies are direct extensions of XML that are defined in XML.

Another technology that you'll learn about in this book is XPath. XPath isn't defined in XML—that is, it's a non-XML language. It is, however, a useful technology that is used with XML.

XLink and XPointer

The XML Linking Language (XLink) and the XML Pointer Language (XPointer) are related. XLink defines the relationship between objects—think hypertext reference. XPointer details how to reference specific structures within a document—think internal links within pages. Together, you can use these technologies to create hypertext links for XML documents.

Unlike the simple unidirectional links defined in HTML, XML links are much more sophisticated. Because XML links can be multidirectional, a single XML link can point to multiple resources and you can move through these resources in any order. For example, in an index, a link could point to all references to the word "hypertext" and you could access these resources in any order and then go back to the index using the single link. XML links are also *self-describing*, meaning a link can contain text that describes the resources it relates to.

XSL

XSL provides rich formatting for XML documents. Using XSL, you can define rules that specify how to extract information from an XML document and how to format this information so that it can be viewed. Often, XML data is transformed into another format, such as HTML—as is the case for Microsoft's XSL processor. Because XSL uses XML as its syntax, you don't need to learn yet another markup language.

Real World Applications that extract information from XML documents need an XML parser. Applications that extract information from documents and display their contents using XSL style sheets need an XML parser and an XSL parser. While many Web browsers, including Microsoft Internet Explorer, have a built-in XML and XSL parser, applications written in Java or C# must use XML and XSL parser classes to handle the extraction and presentation tasks.

XML Namespaces

XML Namespaces provide easy access to document structures and prevent namespace conflicts within documents that may use like-named structures. By giving each structure a universal name, a document can use markup defined in multiple namespaces, which is pretty cool when you think about it.

XML Schema

With XML Schema, you can create schemas that describe the characteristics of data structures within documents. For example, in the schema you can define how structures are used, how they're grouped together, and how different structures are related. If you're familiar with XML DTDs, you might be thinking that schemas sound a lot like DTDs—and you'd be right. Schemas provide the same functionality as DTDs. However, because XML schemas are written in XML, they're easy to use and completely extensible, making them much more powerful than DTDs.

XPath

XPath is a non-XML language used to identify specific parts of XML documents. Using XPath, you can write expressions that refer to specific structures in a document. These expressions can be used to match and select elements in an input document and copy it into an output document or to process the elements further. XPointer uses the concept of using XPath to identify specific parts of a document to identify the location to which an XLink links. XPath also supports simple arithmetic, string manipulation, and Boolean expressions.

Creating XML-Based Solutions

To create effective XML solutions, developers need many tools. The key tools they may want to use include authoring tools, application development environments, and database and data integration solutions.

Authoring Tools

Creating XML documents isn't easy. Before you get started, you need to decide how to structure data within documents, and, unfortunately, each project typically is different. The reason for this is that the way you might structure inventory data is very different from the way you might structure customer account data. To make matters worse, you may need to define the data structures in a DTD, and DTDs aren't exactly user-friendly.

Enter XML authoring tools, the easy way to define data structures and create documents using those structures. Most XML authoring tools on the market are actually integrated XML/SGML authoring tools. The reason for this is that XML is a subset of SGML and it's very logical to extend existing SGML tools so they're compatible with XML.

Application Development Environments

Application development environments provide a toolkit that can help you implement XML solutions. Because most of these toolkits come complete with XML parsers, conversion utilities, and more, you can be sure that you'll be able to start and finish an XML-based project.

Database and Data Integration Solutions

Databases can use XML to structure information extracted from the database so that it can be distributed and published. Data integration solutions take this concept a few steps further by using XML to automate the exchange of data. Generally speaking, with an integration solution XML serves as an interface layer or wrapper for data being passed between data sources. This makes it possible for a wide variety of applications, legacy systems, and databases to exchange information.

Chapter 2

XML Document Structure

XML documents, like HTML documents, contain text and can be written using any text editor or word processor, such as Microsoft Notepad. For ease of reference, XML documents normally are saved with the .xml extension. The .xml extension ensures that the document is easily recognized as containing XML and that applications, such as Microsoft Internet Explorer, view the document as such.

XML documents are built using text content marked up with tags. For a document describing items in an inventory, these tags could be `<item>`, `<item_number>`, `<item_name>`, and `<item_description>`. In addition to tags, XML documents can contain other types of markup, including attributes, processing instructions, entity references, comments, and character data. Each of these types of markup is discussed in this chapter.

XML Naming Rules

XML uses the same building blocks as HTML. Because of this, XML documents can contain elements, attributes, and values. Elements are the most basic parts of XML documents. They can contain other elements and text.

The names of elements, attributes, and other structures in XML must conform to a specific naming convention. They may include alphanumeric characters (the letters a-z and A-Z, as well as the numerals 0-9), syllabic base characters, and ideographic characters, such as α, β, χ, and δ. They may also include three punctuation characters:

- Underscore (_)
- Hyphen (-)
- Period (.)

Note The only other punctuation character allowed in the names for XML structures is colon (:). The colon character is reserved for XML namespaces, as discussed in Chapter 7, "XML Namespaces."

Names for XML structures may not contain white space, and they may not begin with a hyphen, a period, or a number. They may, however, begin with the letters a-z, A-Z, ideograms, and the underscore character. This means that although the following are invalid element names:

```
<.inventory></.inventory>
< item26></ item26>
<product^inventory></product^inventory>
```

the following are valid names:

```
<_inventory></_inventory>
<item26></item26>
<product-inventory></product-inventory>
```

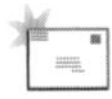

Note Names beginning with the letters xml are reserved and should not be used. XML and applications of XML, such as XML Namespaces, often use the xml prefix to identify structures they define.

Working with Root, Parent, and Child Elements

XML documents are processed a bit differently than other types of documents. With XML, documents should be structured as a tree that processors can navigate easily using method or function calls. Because of this, every XML document has a root element, which is the basis or starting point of the tree hierarchy.

Understanding Root Elements

The root element is the first element in a document, and it contains all other elements. In the following example, `inventory` is the root element and all other elements are contained within it:

```
<inventory>
 <item tracking_number="459323" manufacturer="Not listed">
  <item_type>3 1/2" Floppy Disk Drive</item_type>
  <description>Standard 3 1/2" floppy drive</description>
 </item>
 <item tracking_number="459789" manufacturer="Not listed">
  <item_type>5 1/4" Floppy Disk Drive</item_type>
  <description>Standard 5 1/4" floppy drive</description>
 </item>
</inventory>
```

Every well-formed XML document has one, and only one, root element. In the example, the `inventory` element is the parent of the `item` elements. That is, the `inventory` element contains the `item` elements. Every element, except the root element, has exactly one parent element.

Understanding Parent and Child Elements

Parent elements, such as the `item` elements in the previous example, can contain other elements. These elements are called child elements. In the previous example, the child elements of `item` are `item_type` and `description`. Tags at the same level in a tree hierarchy, such as `item_type` and `description`, are referred to as siblings.

Nesting Parent and Child Elements

In XML you can't overlap tags. The opening and ending tags of child elements must be inside the parent element and can't overlap with the tags of siblings.

The following code is improperly formatted:

```
<item>
 <item_type><description>Standard 3 1/2" floppy drive
 </item_type></description>
</item>
```

To properly format the example, the `item_type` and `description` elements can't overlap. This means the code should be written as:

```
<item>
 <item_type>Standard 3 1/2" floppy drive</item_type>
 <description></description>
</item>
```

Adding Root Elements to Documents

To add a root element to a document, follow these steps:

1. Open an XML document for editing, or create a new document.
2. At the beginning of the document, type **<*name*>**, where *name* is the name of the element that will contain the rest of the elements in the document. The name must conform to the XML naming rules discussed in the previous section.
3. Enter other structures as necessary (using the techniques discussed later in this chapter).
4. Type **</*name*>**, ensuring that *name* exactly matches the name used in Step 2.

Note Although no other elements are allowed outside the root element, other XML structures, such as processing instructions and schemas, can be placed before the start of the root element. You'll find a discussion of processing instructions later in this chapter. Schemas are discussed in Part III, "XML Schemas."

Defining XML Elements and Tags

XML has no predefined elements. You can create any elements you like in XML documents. In most cases you use element names that identify the content and make it easier to process the information later. XML elements are written in one of two forms; either with beginning and ending tags, or as empty tags. Each form can have a special meaning.

The sections that follow examine the key element types and how elements are used in XML documents.

Using Elements with Beginning and Ending Tags

All elements have an opening tag and an ending tag. In the opening tag, the element name is written between less than (<) and greater than (>) signs, such as `<item>`. In the ending tag, the element name is written between a less than symbol followed by a slash (</) and a greater than (>) sign. For example, inventory item could have an opening tag of `<item>` and an ending tag of `</item>`.

Caution XML is used to define data structures and not formatting. With this in mind, it's important to remember that the names of XML elements reflect the type of content inside the element and not how that content will be formatted on the screen.

Everything between an element's opening tag and its ending tag is the element's content. In a document the item element could be used as follows:

```
<item>3 1/2" Floppy Disk Drive</item>
```

Here, the element's content is the text string:

```
3 1/2" Floppy Disk Drive
```

Although any white space between the opening and ending tag is part of the content, most applications, including Web browsers, choose to ignore it. This means the element's content could be entered into the document as:

```
<item>
3 1/2" Floppy Disk Drive
</item>
```

or even:

```
<item>
  3 1/2" Floppy Disk Drive
</item>
```

and it'll be handled the same way. In the example, `<item>` and `</item>` are markup and the text string `3 1/2" Floppy Disk Drive`—and any white space around it—is character data.

The only characters you can't use in content are the less than symbol (`<`) and the ampersand symbol (`&`). These characters are reserved by XML and must not be used as part of the normal text in a document. Instead of using the `<` or `&` symbol, you must use an escaped value called a *predefined entity reference*. When an XML parser sees this escaped value, it replaces the value with the actual character. (For more information, see the "Using Predefined Entity References" section of this chapter.)

Unlike HTML, XML is case-sensitive. This means that you must enter elements in the same case throughout a document or set of documents and that the case must match the one used in a document's document type definition (DTD)—if one is provided. For example, if you defined an element called employee, the matching tags are `<employee>` and `</employee>`. The opening tags `<Employee>` and `<EMPLOYEE>` would refer to different elements, as would the ending tags `</Employee>` and `</EMPLOYEE>`.

Tip Although you can't start a tag using one case, such as `<employee>`, and end with a different case, such as `</Employee>`, you can use lower, upper, or mixed cases in element names. The key is that the case must be consistent within any one element.

To add an element with beginning and ending tags to a document, follow these steps:

1. Open an XML document for editing. If the document doesn't have a root element, add one following the steps outlined in the "Working with Root, Parent, and Child Elements" section of this chapter. Afterward, move the insertion point after the opening tag for the root element, making sure to follow the nesting rules as appropriate.
2. Type the opening tag for the element you want to specify, such as **<item>**. Be sure to follow the naming rules defined in the "XML Naming Rules" section of this chapter.
3. Enter any content after the opening tag, such as descriptive text. Afterward, enter the ending tag for the element, such as **</item>**. The name must match exactly the name used previously.

Using Empty Elements

Not all elements have content. In XML you can define an element without content as an *empty element*. Unlike other elements that have an opening and ending tag, empty elements only have an opening tag, which is specially formatted to indicate that no ending element follows.

Empty elements begin with the less than symbol (`<`) and end with a slash followed by a greater than symbol (`/>`). For example, you could write a symbol element as `<symbol />`. Writing `<symbol />` is the same as writing `<symbol>` `</symbol>`. In XML you can, in fact, use either technique to write empty elements. You can't, however, write only an opening or ending tag. Doing so would result in the document being improperly structured.

Empty elements can be created as top-level elements just below the root element in the tree hierarchy or as child elements of existing elements. As with other types of elements, empty elements must be properly nested. This means that you could use:

```
<employee>
 <name first="William" initial="R" last="Stanek" />
 <id empnum="123" />
</employee>
```

or

```
<employee>
 <name first="William" initial="R" last="Stanek"></name>
 <id empnum="123"></id>
</employee>
```

However, you could not use:

```
<employee>
 <name first="William" initial="R" last="Stanek">
 </id empnum="123">
</employee>
```

or

```
<employee>
 <name first="William" initial="R" last="Stanek">
 <id empnum="123">
</employee>
</name></id>
```

To add an empty element with a single tag to a document, follow these steps:

1. Open an XML document for editing and then move the insertion point to where you want to insert the empty element. Be sure to follow the proper nesting rules.
2. Type the element you want to specify using the form **<*name* />**, such as **<item />**. Be sure to follow the naming rules defined in the "XML Naming Rules" section of this chapter.

To add an empty element with separate opening and ending tags to a document, follow these steps:

1. Open an XML document for editing and then move the insertion point to where you want to insert the empty element. Be sure to follow the proper nesting rules.
2. Type the opening tag for the element you want to specify, such as **<item>**.
3. Immediately after the opening tag, enter the ending tag for the element, such as **</item>**.

Using XML Attributes

As with elements, attributes are an important part of XML documents. You use attributes to describe characteristics of the data structure you're building.

Defining Attributes

Attributes, which can be contained within an element's opening tag, have quotation-mark delimited values that further describe the data structure that the element represents. For example, the `item` element could have an attribute called `tracking_number`, which serves as a tracking number for each item in the inventory. If the tracking number for a 3 1/2" floppy disk drive were 459323, then you could write the `item` element with the attribute as:

```
<item tracking_number="459323">
3 1/2" Floppy Disk Drive
</item>
```

Note Note that the equals sign is being used to assign the value to the attribute. The value assigned to the attribute can have white space around the equals sign. Here, the white space would be added purely to make the value easier to read when viewed in a text editor.

Because either single quotation marks or double quotation marks are acceptable, the element could also be written as:

```
<item tracking_number='459323'>
3 1/2" Floppy Disk Drive
</item>
```

Tip Switching between single quotation marks and double quotation marks is required when the attribute value itself contains either single or double quotation marks. If an attribute value contained single quotation marks, you could use double quotation marks to enclose it. If an attribute value contained double quotation marks, you could use single quotation marks to enclose it.

As shown in the previous examples, attribute values are defined using text strings enclosed by quotation marks. As with element content, attribute values may not use the less than symbol (<) or the ampersand (&). Instead, you should replace these values with the appropriate predefined entity reference. Predefined entity references are also provided for single and double quotation marks to eliminate any confusion that may be caused by having quotation marks inside attribute values.

Elements can have multiple attributes, provided that each attribute has a unique name. If you need to specify an attribute several times, you'll need to create separate elements. For example, you'd write:

```
<employee>
 <name first="William" initial="R" last="Stanek" />
 <job role="software engineer" />
 <job role="IT administration" />
</employee>
```

instead of:

```
<employee>
 <name first="William" initial="R" last="Stanek" />
 <job role="software engineer" role="IT administration" />
</employee>
```

When to Use Attributes

Because both elements and attributes can be used to hold information, you may be wondering which to use when. For example, is it better to write:

```
<item>
 <item_type>3 1/2" Floppy Disk Drive</item_type>
 <tracking_number>459323</tracking_number>
 <manufacturer>Not listed</manufacturer>
 <description>
 Standard 3 1/2" floppy drive for use with new computers
 </description>
</item>
```

or

```
<item tracking_number="459323" manufacturer="Not listed">
 <item_type>3 1/2" Floppy Disk Drive</item_type>
 <description>
 Standard 3 1/2" floppy drive for use with new computers
 </description>
</item>
```

Unfortunately, there's no clear answer, and different people would have different arguments as to which is correct. Officially, attributes are name-value pairs used with elements (that can contain information about the data or contain actual data). Still, there are some who argue that information contained in attributes is metadata, meaning it's only information about the data rather than being data itself. In the school of thought where attribute values are metadata, you could have attributes, such as `lang`, used to describe the language used for the element's content, but you wouldn't have attributes that contained actual values, such as an item's description or type.

As you set out to use attributes in XML, you'll probably find that it's better to think of attribute values as both metadata and data. In this way you can use an attribute in a way that makes sense for a specific situation rather than being tied to one school of thought.

You'll often find that the application you're using to display the data will help determine how attributes are used. In some cases applications may be able to process attribute values more easily than they can process the raw contents of elements. In other cases you may want to hide certain types of information from viewers until they perform a specific action that causes the values to be displayed or processed.

Adding Attributes to Elements

Attributes specify additional information for data structures. Elements can have zero or more attributes. The order of attributes doesn't matter as long as the attributes are entered before the closing > of the opening tag.

To add an attribute to an element, follow these steps:

1. After the name of the element in the opening tag and before the closing >, type ***attribute*=**, where *attribute* is the name of the attribute you're adding to the tag. Each attribute name for a given element must be unique. If the element already has an attribute of the same name, the name used for the new attribute must be different.
2. Specify the value for the attribute using either single or double quotation marks, such as "value" or 'value'.

Note Either form of quotation marks is acceptable, as long as the same type of quotation mark is used at the beginning and ending of the value. If the value contains a double quotation mark, however, you should enclose the value in single quotation marks. Similarly, if the value contains a single quotation mark, you should enclose the value in double quotation marks.

Working with Entity References, Character Data, Comments, and Processing Instructions

In addition to defining elements, attributes, and values, XML documents can contain entity references, character data sections, comments, and processing instructions. These structures are examined in the sections that follow.

Using Predefined Entity References

Entity references are placeholders for other values or other types of content. XML predefines several entity references that allow you to enter text containing characters that are otherwise reserved in the language or that may be misinterpreted.

The two reserved characters in the language are the less than symbol (<) and the ampersand symbol (&). Characters that can easily be misinterpreted are the greater than symbol (>), the single quotation mark ('), and the double quotation mark ("). This means there are five predefined entity references:

- **<** The less than symbol; reserved for the opening bracket of elements
- **>** The greater than symbol; normally used for the closing bracket of elements
- **&** The ampersand symbol; reserved to specify the beginning of an entity reference
- **"** The straight, double quotation mark; normally used to enclose attribute values
- **'** The apostrophe or straight single quotation mark; normally used to enclose attribute values

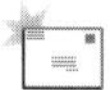

Note ` ` isn't a predefined entity for XML. However, this entity frequently is used in HTML to force whitespace characters. To use this character in XML without resulting in an error, you have to use the actual character code, such as ` ` or define the ` ` entity yourself in the DTD. You'll find detailed information on defining and using encoded characters in the "Using Encoded Characters" section of Chapter 6, "XML Entities and Notations in DTDs."

You can use the predefined entity references as part of an element's content, as shown here:

```
<business>Stanek &amp; Associates</business>
```

With attributes, you can use predefined entity references, as shown here:

```
<business name="Stanek &amp; Associates"></business>
```

Entity references, such as `"` and `'`, are considered to be markup. When an application processes an XML document containing these references, it replaces the entity reference with the actual character to which it refers. This means that in both cases, `Stanek & Associates` is replaced with Stanek & Associates when it's displayed.

To add an entity reference to a document, follow these steps:

1. Open an XML document for editing and then locate the text that contains a value you need to replace with an entity reference or move the pointer to the position where the value should be inserted.
2. Delete the character you're replacing (if any) and then type the entity reference you want to use, such as **&**.

Using Character Data Sections

Character data sections allow you to specify areas within an XML document that contain raw character data and aren't to be processed by XML parsers. You'll find that character data sections are useful when you want to include XML, HTML, or other examples containing markup in a document without replacing all the reserved or possibly misinterpreted values with entity references. You can, for example, insert an entire snippet of markup within a character data section.

Character data sections have beginning and ending designators. The beginning designator is `<![CDATA[` and the ending designator is `]]>`. Everything within these designators is handled as raw character data and isn't processed. This means the `&` and `<` characters can appear within the character data section and they won't be interpreted as markup. The only value that can't appear within a character data section is the end designator `]]>`.

Here's an example of a character data section in an XML document:

```
<book title="XHTML Pocket Consultant">
 <chapter number="3" title="XHTML Essentials">
  <page>
  <![CDATA[ <p> A text paragraph </p>
    <br /> for line breaks
    <hr /> for horizontal rules
  ]]>
  </page>
  <main_text></main_text>
 </chapter>
</book>
```

Character data sections can appear anywhere in a document, as long as they're between the opening and ending tags for the root element. To add a character data section to an XML document, follow these steps:

1. Open an XML document for editing and then move the pointer to the position where the character data section should be inserted.
2. Type **<![CDATA[**.
3. Enter the text containing markup or other structures that you want to display but don't want to be parsed.
4. Type **]]>**.

Note The only use for the `]]>` designator is to end the character data section. Although this prevents you from nesting character data sections within other character data sections, you can insert multiple character data sections into a single document. To do this, you must start and end one section before beginning another section.

Using Comments

Comments are useful in any programming or markup language, and XML is no exception. You can use comments to annotate sections of an XML document or to add general notes for the XML document overall. As with HTML, XML comments begin with `<!--` and end with `-->`. Here's an example:

```
<!-- Still working to get the example structures in correct
  sequence -->
```

No spaces are required between the double hyphens and the comment text. This allows you to write:

```
<!--Still working to get the example structures in correct
  sequence-->
```

The double hyphen can't appear anywhere else within the comment text. This prevents you from writing:

```
<!-- Still working -- example structures aren't in correct
  sequence -->
```

and

```
<!-- Still working on example structures --->
```

Comments are best used to specify information that may be useful to other document authors as they set out to work with a document. Comments aren't displayed in applications, such as Internet Explorer, by default but can be viewed if the document's source code is available. However, a document's parsed contents may or may not contain the hidden comments. The reason for this is that XML parsers may choose to ignore the comments and not pass them along with the document's contents.

Real World You shouldn't rely on comments being available in an application. If you need to pass on information in a document, you may want to use processing instructions. Processing instructions provide special instructions or additional information to the application rendering a document.

Because comments aren't parsed, they can occur anywhere in the text of a document. This means they could occur before the opening root tag or after the ending root tag as well. To add a comment to a document, follow these steps:

1. Open an XML document for editing and then move the pointer to the position where the comment should be inserted.
2. Type **<!--**.
3. Enter the text for the comment.
4. Type **-->**.

Using Processing Instructions

Processing instructions are used to pass information to applications. The application processing the document can use the instructions to perform special tasks or simply as a source of additional information regarding a document.

Processing instructions begin with <? and end with ?>. The most commonly used processing instructions are those that specify a style sheet attached to a document and those that set the XML version, encoding, and mode for a document. An example instruction that sets a style sheet is:

```
<?xml-stylesheet href="corp.css" type="text/css"?>
```

An example of a processing instruction that sets version, encoding, and mode follows:

```
<?xml version="1.0" encoding="US-ASCII" standalone="yes"?>
```

Documents don't have to have either type of processing instruction. However, if they do, certain rules apply:

- If a document has a processing instruction that specifies a style sheet, the style sheet is used to format elements in the document. When multiple style sheets are used, the style sheet definitions applied last take precedence over those applied earlier. If you don't declare style definitions for every element in the document, the default font settings are applied.
- If a document has a processing instruction that declares the XML version, encoding, and mode, the instruction must be the first line of the document. It can't be preceded by comments, white space, or other processing instructions. (For more information on this type of instruction, see the following section, "Specifying XML Declarations.")

To add a processing instruction to a document, follow these steps:

1. Open an XML document for editing and then move the pointer to the position where the processing instruction should be inserted.
2. Type **<?**.
3. Type the instruction name immediately after the open instruction tag, such as **<?xml** or **<?xml-stylesheet**. Don't use a space between the instruction name and the start of the tag.
4. Enter the body of the instruction.
5. Type **?>**.

Specifying XML Declarations

An XML declaration is a processing instruction that sets the version, encoding, and mode for an XML document. Declarations aren't required in documents. However, as stated previously, if they're present, they must be the first line of the document and they must not be preceded by comments, white space, or other processing instructions.

XML declarations can specify three attributes: `version`, `encoding`, and `standalone`, as shown in the following example:

```
<?xml version="1.0" encoding="ISO-8859-1" standalone="yes"?>
```

These attributes have special meaning and are discussed in the sections that follow.

Using the Version Attribute

The `version` attribute in an XML declaration sets the version of XML used in the document. Currently, the only version of XML available is 1.0. Although it's plausible that future versions of XML will be developed, most of the current enhancements to XML have been implemented as extensions to the language.

If you use an XML declaration, the `version` attribute is mandatory. The other attributes, however, are optional. Because of this, the following XML declaration is valid:

```
<?xml version="1.0"?>
```

Using the Encoding Attribute

XML parsers assume documents are encoded using either UTF-8 or UTF-16. UTF is the Unicode Transformation Format. Because UTF-8 allows variable length characters, parsers use the first few characters in a document to deduce the number of bytes used to express characters. If necessary, you can set the document encoding using the optional `encoding` attribute for an XML declaration. In the following example the encoding is ISO-8859 Latin 1:

```
<?xml version="1.0" encoding="ISO-8859-1"?>
```

If a document is written in UTF-8 or UTF-16, the document encoding can be omitted. When any other encoding is specified, the parser reading the document translates characters from the document's native encoding (as set in the encoding attribute of the XML declaration) into Unicode.

UTF-8 and UTF-16 are implementations of the international standard character set, Unicode. XML parsers are required to support both the UTF-8 and UTF-16 implementations of Unicode. Support for other character encoding is optional. Nevertheless, the recommended set of supported encoding includes:

EUC-JP	ISO-8859-4
ISO-10646-UCS-2	ISO-8859-5
ISO-10646-UCS-4	ISO-8859-6
ISO-2022-JP	ISO-8859-7
ISO-8859-1	ISO-8859-8
ISO-8859-2	ISO-8859-9
ISO-8859-3	

Using the Standalone Attribute

The `standalone` attribute in an XML declaration sets the mode for the document and is optional. You can use two values:

- `standalone="no"` If standalone is set to `no`, the document may have to read an external DTD to determine the validity of the document's structures and to determine values for parts of the document that use entities or other references defined in the DTD.
- `standalone="yes"` If standalone is set to `yes`, the document doesn't rely on an external DTD. This doesn't mean the document doesn't have a DTD. The document may have an internally specified DTD. (For more information on DTDs, see Part II, "DTDs and Namespaces.")

When the `standalone` attribute isn't set in the XML declaration, the value `standalone="no"` is assumed. This allows the parser to retrieve a DTD if one is referenced.

Creating Well-Formed Documents

Regardless of whether XML documents have a DTD, they must be well formed. If a document is well formed, it can be said that the document conforms to specific rules of the XML 1.0 specification, including these rules:

- A document must have exactly one root element.
- Every start tag must have a matching end tag (or use the empty element format).
- Elements can't be nested improperly so that they overlap.
- Attribute values must be enclosed within single or double quotation marks.
- Attribute names within elements must be unique; elements can't have two attributes with the same name.
- Unescaped `<` and `&` signs can't appear as part of an element's content or as part of an attribute's value.
- Comments and processing instructions can't appear inside tags.

Although the list isn't exhaustive, you can see that there are many rules that determine whether a document is well-formed. The most basic well-formed document is one that contains a single element, such as:

```
<inventory>
 100 3 1/2" floppy drives
</inventory>
```

This basic document can be read and understood by XML parsers. It meets all the constraints of the previous rules. However, most documents you'll work with will be considerably more complex and it'll be much more difficult to determine if the document is well-formed. In fact, if you create an XML document by hand, you can almost be assured that it'll contain some type of well-formedness error.

One way to determine if a document is well-formed is to load the document into a Web browser that includes an XML parser, such as Internet Explorer 5.0 or later. If there are problems with the document, the browser should display an error message. As you correct each error, additional errors may be displayed when you reload the document. When the document is finally free of errors, the document should load into the browser and display using the default style sheet as shown in Figure 2-1.

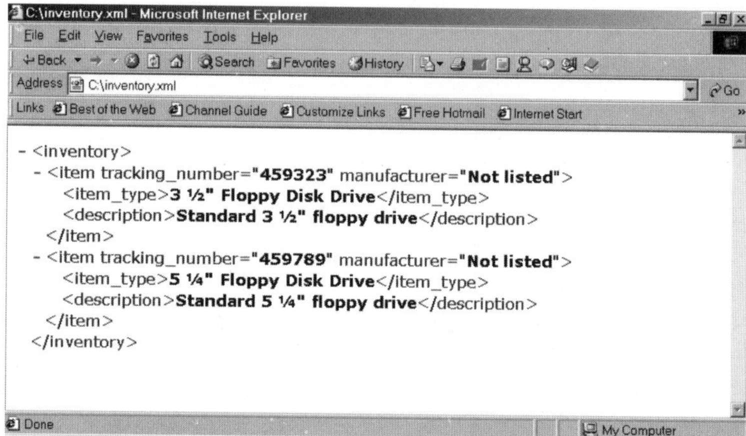

Figure 2-1. *A well-formed document displayed in Internet Explorer using the default style sheet.*

Of course, using Internet Explorer to check documents isn't the most sophisticated technique you can use. If you like, you can use the parser classes from an application programming interface (API). The Simple API for XML (SAX) provides a class that you can use to check documents called sax.SAXCount. Several capable XML parsers written in Java use SAX, including Xerces from the Apache XML Project.

Once you've installed Java and Xerces on your system, you can check files from the command line by typing:

```
java sax.SAXCount filename
```

where *filename* is the actual name of the XML file, such as:

```
java sax.SAXCount inventory.xml
```

The good news about Xerces and other parsers written in programming languages is that they'll print a complete list of errors in a document (rather than having to fix errors one by one in Internet Explorer). Once you fix the errors that the parser reports, you can publish the document or pass it off to a database program or other application that you can use to process it.

Part II

DTDs and Namespaces

In Part II, you'll find the essential tasks for working with document type definitions (DTDs) and XML namespaces. DTDs provide a way to describe the structure of XML documents in terms of the elements, attributes, and contents they can contain. You use XML namespaces to prevent naming conflicts when like-named elements and attributes are associated with different types of data structures and are used in the same document.

Chapter 3

Creating DTDs

In the previous chapter you learned about the basic structures for creating XML documents. As mentioned previously, XML documents can contain many different types of markup, including elements, attributes, and entity references. Whether you generate documents manually in an editor, programmatically in an application, or automatically using a document management system, you'll often need to ensure that documents conform to a specific set of rules. That is, you'll want to ensure that not only are the data structures in the documents formatted correctly, but also that the documents can be understood by the applications that will process them. What you need is a way of expressing the necessary data structures as a set of rules and ensuring conformity. What you need is a custom application of XML. Enter document type definitions (DTDs) and schemas.

Both DTDs and schemas allow you to create XML applications. An XML application defines a custom markup language that describes specific types of data and uses the rules set out in the associated DTD or schema. The DTD/schema rules specify items that are allowed or required in compliant documents. Once you create an XML application using a DTD or schema, you can write documents that conform to your custom markup language. Application software, database systems, and other programs can use the DTD/schema to interpret compliant documents and ensure conformity to the rule set. DTDs are the focus of this chapter. You'll learn more about schemas in Part III, "XML Schemas."

Understanding DTDs

DTDs have a formal—fairly rigid—syntax that precisely describes the elements and entities that may appear in a document, as well as the contents and attributes for acceptable elements. In a DTD you could specify that a purchase order must have one and only one order number but can have one or more requested products. You could go on to specify that each purchase order must have one order date and one customer identifier but no more. These details in the DTD would allow programs to determine if purchase orders are valid.

Validity is an important concept when DTDs are used. If a document is valid, it can be said that it conforms to its DTD. If a document is invalid, the document doesn't conform to its DTD. However, keep in mind that validation is an optional step in processing XML. Programs that use validating parsers can compare documents to their DTD and list places where the document differs from the DTD specification. The programs can then determine actions to take regarding noncompliance with the DTD. Some programs may mark the document as invalid and stop processing it. Other programs may try to correct problems in the document and reprocess it.

Although DTDs can help you specify constraints for documents, DTDs don't specify every nuance of a document's format. Among other things, a DTD doesn't control allowed values, the denotation of elements (explicit meaning), the connotation of elements (figurative meaning), or the character data that can be associated with elements. This allows for flexibility in the document structure so that you can create many types of documents using the same set of rules.

All valid documents include a reference to the DTD to which they conform. DTDs aren't mandatory, however. When a document lacks a DTD, the XML processor can't verify that the data format is appropriate, but it can still attempt to interpret the data.

Note A document that is well-formed but doesn't have a DTD wouldn't be considered valid. The reason for this is that the document doesn't have a DTD, and, as a result, the document can't be said to comply with the DTD. The document, however, is still a well-formed XML document.

DTDs can be specified in several different ways. An internal DTD is one that is defined within a document. An external DTD is one that is defined in a separate document and is imported into the document. Both types of DTDs have their advantages and disadvantages.

Internal DTDs are convenient when you want to apply constraints to an individual document and then easily distribute the document along with its DTD. They're also convenient when you're developing a complex DTD and want to test an example document against the DTD. Putting the DTD and the related markup in the same file makes it easy to modify the DTD and the example document as often as necessary during testing.

With an external DTD, you place a reference to a DTD in a file rather than the DTD itself. This makes it easy to apply the DTD to multiple documents. Because the DTD is referenced rather than included, you can make changes to the DTD later and you don't need to edit the DTD definition in each and every document to which it's applied. Two types of external DTDs are used:

- **Public** Public DTDs are DTDs that have been standardized and provide a publicly available set of rules for writing specific types of XML documents, such as those used by the airlines or insurance industries.
- **Nonpublic** Nonpublic DTDs are DTDs created by private organizations or individuals. Generally speaking, these DTDs aren't publicly available (or haven't become a public standard).

When you use an external DTD, you should set the `standalone` attribute of the XML declaration to `no`, such as:

```
<?xml version="1.0" encoding="US-ASCII" standalone="no"?>
```

Real World Validating parsers are required to read the external DTD you specify when you set `standalone` to `no`. Nonvalidating parsers, however, may read the external DTD but aren't required to—even if `standalone` is set to `no`. This is important to note because a nonvalidating parser that reads an external DTD would be able to replace DTD-defined entity references with their actual values. However, a nonvalidating parser that doesn't read an external DTD wouldn't know what to do with DTD-defined entity references that occur in a document. To improve parsing times, developers sometimes set `standalone` to `yes` so that external DTDs aren't read. If you choose not to read an external DTD, you should be certain that the DTD doesn't contain definitions (such as entity references) that are needed in the document.

Working with Internal DTDs

You specify internal DTDs using the `DOCTYPE` assignment. The `DOCTYPE` assignment is one of the most basic elements in an XML document. Similar to the document type element, which is a container for all other elements, the `DOCTYPE` declaration is a container for all DTD assignments.

Declaring Internal DTDs

Internal DTD declarations are formatted as follows:

```
<!DOCTYPE root_name [ assignments ]>
```

The declaration begins with the `DOCTYPE` keyword, followed by the name of the root element for the document. Typically, the name of the root element serves as a descriptor for the type of information the document contains. The root name is followed by an open bracket, which signifies the beginning of the declaration assignments. Because there's usually a large group of declarations, assignments are normally entered on separate lines following the document type declaration. The last entry in the document type declaration is always the closing bracket for the `DOCTYPE` keyword.

Following this, if you wanted to structure a set of purchase orders, you might define the document type as follows:

```
<?XML version="1.0" ?>
<!DOCTYPE purchase_order [

]>
```

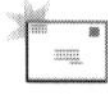

Note The `DOCTYPE` declaration follows the XML declaration. In a document with a DTD, the `DOCTYPE` declaration must be between the XML declaration and the root element.

Within the DTD for the `purchase_order` document, you could then define elements, such as:

```
<!DOCTYPE purchase_order [
 <!ELEMENT purchase_order (customer)>
 <!ELEMENT customer (account_id, name)>
 <!ELEMENT account_id (#PCDATA)>
 <!ELEMENT name (first, mi, last)>
 <!ELEMENT first (#PCDATA)>
 <!ELEMENT mi (#PCDATA)>
 <!ELEMENT last (#PCDATA)>
]>
```

The example DTD declares seven elements (`purchase_order`, `customer`, `account_id`, `name`, `first`, `mi`, and `last`) and sets the order in which those elements may be entered in a document. The line breaks used aren't relevant to the DTD, and neither is the order in which the elements are listed. Although the elements are entered from the highest level to the lowest level, you could also enter them in this order:

```
<!DOCTYPE purchase_order [
 <!ELEMENT last (#PCDATA)>
 <!ELEMENT mi (#PCDATA)>
 <!ELEMENT first (#PCDATA)>
 <!ELEMENT name (first, mi, last)>
 <!ELEMENT account_id (#PCDATA)>
 <!ELEMENT customer (account_id, name)>
 <!ELEMENT purchase_order (customer)>
]>
```

or this order:

```
<!DOCTYPE purchase_order [
 <!ELEMENT account_id (#PCDATA)>
 <!ELEMENT customer (account_id, name)>
 <!ELEMENT first (#PCDATA)>
 <!ELEMENT last (#PCDATA)>
 <!ELEMENT mi (#PCDATA)>
 <!ELEMENT name (first, mi, last)>
 <!ELEMENT purchase_order (customer)>
]>
```

As these examples show, the order of DTD declarations isn't important. What is important are the declaration, the declaration name, and the associated values.

In the case of elements, the values in parentheses set the order in which the elements must be used. Here, customer elements must contain exactly one account_id element followed by exactly one name element. The name element must contain exactly one first element followed by exactly one mi element followed by exactly one last element. The first, mi, and last elements must contain parsed character data (#PCDATA), which is raw text that could contain entity references, such as > or < but don't contain other markup or child elements.

The spacing between the declaration name and other elements is also important. The following declaration is improperly formatted:

```
<!ELEMENTaccount_id (#PCDATA)>
```

as is the following declaration:

```
<!ELEMENT account_id(#PCDATA)>
```

The correct format is:

```
<!ELEMENT account_id (#PCDATA)>
```

Listing 3-1 provides the source for a basic document with an internal DTD. As you can see, the internal DTD definition follows the XML declaration and is in turn followed by the document's contents. The opening tag for the root element, purchase_order, is the first tag in the body of the document. It's followed by other elements in the order prescribed in the DTD. The closing tag for the root element is that last item in the document.

Listing 3-1. An XML Document with an Internal DTD

```
<?xml version="1.0" ?>
<!DOCTYPE purchase_order [
 <!ELEMENT purchase_order (customer)>
 <!ELEMENT customer (account_id, name)>
 <!ELEMENT account_id (#PCDATA)>
 <!ELEMENT name (first, mi, last)>
 <!ELEMENT first (#PCDATA)>
 <!ELEMENT mi (#PCDATA)>
 <!ELEMENT last (#PCDATA)>
]>

<purchase_order>
 <customer>
  <account_id>10-487</account_id>
  <name>
   <first> William </first>
   <mi> R </mi>
   <last> Stanek </last>
  </name>
  </customer>
</purchase_order>
```

Adding Internal DTDs to Documents

To declare an internal DTD in an XML document, follow these steps:

1. Open your XML document for editing. At the top of the document following the XML declaration, type **<!DOCTYPE *root_name* [**, where *root_name* is the name of the document's root element.
2. Enter a few blank lines, in which you'll later enter your declarations as discussed in Chapter 4, "XML Elements in DTDs," Chapter 5, "XML Attributes in DTDs," and Chapter 6, "XML Entities and Notations in DTDs."
3. Type **]>** to complete the DTD.

The result should look similar to the following example:

```
<?XML version="1.0" ?>
<!DOCTYPE purchase_order [

]>
```

Working with External DTDs

You specify external DTDs using a `DOCTYPE` assignment that contains a Uniform Resource Identifier (URI). The URI in the assignment identifies the location of the DTD. Because URIs are a superset of Uniform Resource Locators (URLs) and Uniform Resource Names (URNs), XML documents can reference both a URL and a URN.

The `DOCTYPE` declaration must occur after the XML declaration but before the root element. Officially, the part of the XML document before the root element start tag is called the prolog. You can think of the prolog as a header, much like the header in HTML documents.

As discussed previously in this chapter, there are two types of external DTDs: public and nonpublic. The sections that follow examine each type of external DTD.

Declaring Public External DTDs

Standard, publicly accessible DTDs are specified using the keyword `PUBLIC` in the `DOCTYPE` declaration. A public DTD can have a public ID, officially referred to as a formal public identifier (FPI). The idea is that an XML parser could use the public ID to find the latest version of the DTD on a public server. In practice, however, most XML parsers rely on the public ID to locate and validate documents.

The following document type declaration refers to the version 2.0 DTD specification for XML 1.0:

```
<!DOCTYPE spec PUBLIC "-//W3C//DTD Specification V2.0//EN"
    "/XML/1998/06/xmlspec-v20.dtd">
```

By examining the previous declaration, you can learn many things about how declarations are defined and used. The example declaration says that the root element is `spec` and then specifies information about the DTD's owner and location. The owner information is supplied first as a URN:

```
-//W3C//DTD Specification V2.0//EN
```

The double slashes (//) separate categories of information regarding the DTD and its owner:

- **- (Minus)** Indicates that the DTD isn't a recognized standard. A plus (+) here would have meant that the DTD *is* a recognized standard.

Note Wondering how something could be a public standard but not a recognized standard? Consider the case where a DTD is standard throughout your organization and used by associated vendors and contractors but isn't an official standard recognized by a standards body, such as the International Organization for Standardization (ISO). Here, your DTD would be a public, unrecognized standard.

- **W3C** Specifies the owner of the DTD as the World Wide Web Consortium (W3C). This means that the W3C wrote and maintains the DTD. The owner can be a person or an organization.
- **DTD Specification V2.0** Sets a descriptive label for the DTD. The label can contain any standard characters except double slashes (//).
- **EN** A two-letter abbreviation for the language of the XML documents to which the DTD applies. In this case the language is U.S. English. A complete list of two-letter language abbreviations is specified in ISO 639-1.

Unlike the URN, which allows the DTD to be located by a publicly identified name, the next section of the declaration refers to a static URL:

```
"/XML/1998/06/xmlspec-v20.dtd"
```

In this example the URL is relative to a location on a specific server but could also have been an absolute URL that pointed to a specific location on a remote server, such as:

```
"http://www.w3.org/XML/1998/06/xmlspec-v20.dtd"
```

The important thing to note about the URL is the DTD file name, which is `xmlspec-v20.dtd`. As with XML file names, the extension for DTDs doesn't have to be .dtd, as shown. However, the .dtd extension does make it easier for you and other developers to locate your DTDs.

Listing 3-2 provides the source for a basic document with an external DTD that is public. As with an internal DTD definition, an external DTD definition declares the root element, which in this case is `purchase_order`. The document type declaration is in turn followed by the document's contents.

Listing 3-2. An XML Document with a Public External DTD

```
<?xml version="1.0" standalone="no"?>
<!DOCTYPE purchase_order PUBLIC "-//Stanek//PO Specification//EN"
 "http://www.tvpress.com/pospec.dtd">
<purchase_order>
 <customer>
  <account_id>10-487</account_id>
  <name>
   <first> William </first>
   <mi> R </mi>
   <last> Stanek </last>
  </name>
 </customer>
</purchase_order>
```

Adding Public External DTDs to Documents

To add a public external DTD to an XML document, follow these steps:

1. Open your XML document for editing. In the XML declaration, add **standalone="no"** (or replace an existing value of yes with no).
2. Type **<!DOCTYPE *root_name***, where *root_name* is the name of the document's root element.
3. Type **PUBLIC** to indicate that the external DTD is publicly accessible. Be sure there's a space before and after the keyword.
4. Type the public ID of the external DTD between quotation marks, such as: **"-//Stanek//PO Specification//EN"**.

Note The initial character within the quotation marks can be a + or – sign, which indicates that the DTD is or isn't a recognized standard, respectively. Note also that the final two letters of the public ID are the language identifier for documents written to conform to the DTD.

More Info ISO 639-1 provides two-letter language abbreviations and can be found online at *http://lcweb.loc.gov/standards/iso639-2/bibcodes.html*.

5. Type the URL for the public DTD between quotation marks, such as: **"http://www.microsoft.com/pospec.dtd"**.
6. Type **>** to complete the declaration.

The result should look similar to the following:

```
<!DOCTYPE purchase_order PUBLIC "-//Stanek//PO Specification//EN"
 "http://www.microsoft.com/pospec.dtd">
```

Declaring Nonpublic External DTDs

DTDs that organizations and individuals create for their own purposes are personal DTDs and are declared with the keyword `SYSTEM` rather than `PUBLIC`. With nonpublic DTDs, the standard declaration usually looks like this:

```
<!DOCTYPE purchase_order SYSTEM
 "http://www.microsoft.com/pospec.dtd">
```

In this example:

- **purchase_order** The designator for the root element, which is the name of the root of the XML tree.
- **SYSTEM** Identifies an external DTD that isn't public and generally is created by an organization or individual for their own purposes.
- **http://www.microsoft.com/pospec.dtd** Sets the URL for the DTD, which could be relative to a specific location or an absolute URL to a specific location on a remote server.

Listing 3-3 provides the source for a basic document with an external DTD that isn't public. Again, the document type declaration is followed by contents of the document. Note that the DTD location reflects only a file name, which means the file is in the same directory as the associated XML document.

Listing 3-3. An XML Document with a Nonpublic External DTD

```
<?xml version="1.0" standalone="no"?>
<!DOCTYPE purchase_order SYSTEM "pospec.dtd">
<purchase_order>
 <customer>
  <account_id>10-487</account_id>
  <name>
   <first> William </first>
   <mi> R </mi>
   <last> Stanek </last>
  </name>
 </customer>
</purchase_order>
```

Adding Nonpublic DTDs to Documents

To add a nonpublic DTD to an XML document, follow these steps:

1. Open your XML document for editing. In the XML declaration, add **standalone="no"** (or replace an existing value of yes with no).
2. Type **<!DOCTYPE *root_name***, where *root_name* is the name of the document's root element.
3. Type **SYSTEM** to indicate that the external DTD is nonpublic and nonstandardized. Be sure there's a space before and after the keyword.

4. Type the URL for the DTD between quotation marks, such as: **"pospec.dtd"**.
5. Type > to complete the declaration.

The result should look similar to the following:

```
<!DOCTYPE purchase_order SYSTEM "pospec.dtd">
```

Resolving Errors with Externally Referenced DTDs

The XML parser processing a document must be able to locate external DTDs using the URI you've provided. If the parser is unable to locate the DTD, the error you'll see usually specifies that the system can't locate the resource specified or that there was an error processing the resource DTD.

If this occurs, check the accuracy and syntax of the URL you're using. Keep in mind that URLs in the form `dir_name/file.dtd` are located relative to the current directory but URLs in the form `/dir_name/file.dtd` are located relative to the root directory for the server or current file system. Further, if only a filename is specified as the URL, the DTD is expected to be in the same directory as the associated XML document.

Combining Internal and External DTDs

XML documents can have an internal and an external DTD. To do this, you add the internal DTD declarations after specifying the location of the external DTD. As before, the internal declarations begin with the open bracket (`[`) and end with the closing bracket and the greater than sign (`]>`).

Listing 3-4 shows an example document with an internal DTD and a nonpublic external DTD. Note the reference to the external nonpublic DTD (pospec.dtd) as well as the internal DTD declarations.

Listing 3-4. An XML Document with an Internal and External DTD

```
<?xml version="1.0" standalone="no"?>
<!DOCTYPE purchase_order SYSTEM "pospec.dtd"[
 <!ELEMENT purchase_order (customer)>
 <!ELEMENT customer (account_id, name)>
 <!ELEMENT account_id (#PCDATA)>
 <!ELEMENT name (first, mi, last)>
 <!ELEMENT first (#PCDATA)>
 <!ELEMENT mi (#PCDATA)>
 <!ELEMENT last (#PCDATA)>
]>
```

(continued)

Listing 3-4. *(continued)*

```
<purchase_order>
 <customer>
  <account_id>10-487</account_id>
  <name>
   <first> William </first>
   <mi> R </mi>
   <last> Stanek </last>
  </name>
 </customer>
</purchase_order>
```

If you decide to create documents with an internal and external DTD, you should ensure that the two DTDs are compatible. When determining compatibility, keep in mind these basic rules:

- Neither DTD can override the element or attribute declarations of the other. This also means that the DTDs can't contain the same element or attribute declarations.
- Entity declarations can be declared as external and can be redefined in an internal DTD. If there are conflicting entity declarations, the first declaration has precedence. Because internal DTDs are read first, internal declarations have precedence over identically named external references. However, when the external reference is read, its definition is still applied.

Note As with most things in XML, there are, of course, other compatibility rules that apply. These, however, are the key rules you should keep in mind.

Adding Internal and External DTDs to Documents

To add an internal and external DTD to an XML document, follow these steps:

1. Open your XML document for editing. In the XML declaration, add **standalone="no"** (or replace an existing value of yes with no).
2. Type **<!DOCTYPE *root_name***, where *root_name* is the name of the document's root element.
3. Type **PUBLIC** or **SYSTEM** as appropriate. The PUBLIC keyword indicates a public, standard DTD. The SYSTEM keyword indicates a nonpublic, nonstandard DTD.
4. If you're specifying a public external DTD, type the public ID of the external DTD between quotation marks, such as: **"-//Stanek//PO Specification//EN"**.
5. Type the URL for the public DTD between quotation marks, such as: **"http://www.microsoft.com/pospec.dtd"**.
6. Type **[**.

7. Enter a few blank lines, in which you'll later enter your declarations as discussed in Chapters 4, 5, and 6.
8. Type **]>** to complete the DTD.

The result should look similar to the following example:

```
<?XML version="1.0" standalone="no"?>
<!DOCTYPE purchase_order PUBLIC "-//Stanek//PO Specification//EN"
      "http://www.microsoft.com/pospec.dtd" [

]>
```

Writing External DTD Files

DTD files are standard Unicode or ASCII text files that contain the definitions you're declaring externally. In the DTD file, you don't enter the `DOCTYPE` declaration or any formatting characters other than those required for the definitions being declared. Although the file can be named with any valid system name, it's better to name the file with the .dtd extension. The .dtd extension makes it easy to recognize that the file contains a DTD.

Listing 3-5 provides the contents of an external DTD file and shows how the file could be referenced in a conforming document.

Listing 3-5. An External DTD File with an Associated XML Document File

Filename: pospec.dtd

```
<!ELEMENT purchase_order (customer)>
<!ELEMENT customer (account_id, name)>
<!ELEMENT account_id (#PCDATA)>
<!ELEMENT name (first, mi, last)>
<!ELEMENT first (#PCDATA)>
<!ELEMENT mi (#PCDATA)>
<!ELEMENT last (#PCDATA)>
```

Filename: purchase.xml

```
<?xml version="1.0" standalone="no"?>
<!DOCTYPE purchase_order SYSTEM "pospec.dtd">
<purchase_order>
 <customer>
  <account_id>10-487</account_id>
  <name>
   <first> William </first>
   <mi> R </mi>
   <last> Stanek </last>
  </name>
 </customer>
</purchase_order>
```

Although DTD files can contain blank lines and properly formatted comments, they shouldn't contain XML or DOCTYPE declarations. Additionally, XML elements aren't allowed inside a DTD. An example DTD file with properly formatted comments follows:

```
<!-- Purchase Order Specification V2.1 -->
<!-- Author: William Stanek -->
<!-- Last modified: 12/15/01 -->
<!ELEMENT purchase_order (customer)>
<!ELEMENT customer (account_id, name)>
<!ELEMENT account_id (#PCDATA)>
<!ELEMENT name (first, mi, last)>
<!ELEMENT first (#PCDATA)>
<!ELEMENT mi (#PCDATA)>
<!ELEMENT last (#PCDATA)>
```

Note that DTD comments use the same syntax as standard XML comments, beginning with `<!--` and ending with `-->`.

Chapter 4

XML Elements in DTDs

Every element used in a valid document must be declared in the document's document type definition (DTD). Element declarations specify the markup tags that can appear in a conforming document and how those tags can be used. If a DTD doesn't declare elements that are used in a document, the document can't be said to be valid.

Note As you read this chapter, keep in mind that XML is case-sensitive. This means you must use the exact case for keywords and declarations specified. There are no exceptions.

Defining Elements in DTDs

Five types of elements are used in XML documents:

- Those with standard content
- Those with only character data
- Those with mixed content
- Those with any type of content allowed
- Those with no content allowed

You declare each of these element types using the `ELEMENT` declaration, which consists of an element name followed by a description of the element's contents in the form:

```
<!ELEMENT element_name (element_content)>
```

where *element_name* is the name of the element and *element_content* specifies the child elements, text, or both, that the element will contain. If an element declaration has contents, those contents are always enclosed in the opening and closing parentheses. I'll discuss the exceptions shortly.

Each and every element that you allow in the body of an XML document must be declared. Techniques for declaring the various types of elements are discussed in the sections that follow.

Note The name of an element can be any legal XML name, as discussed in the "XML Naming Rules" section of Chapter 2, "XML Document Structure." This means you could name an element describing purchase orders as `purchase-order`, `purchase_order`, or `purchase.order`. Once it's declared in the DTD, you could use the element describing purchase orders in the body of the XML document.

Declaring Elements with Standard Content

Most element declarations define one or more child elements that an element must contain as its standard content. The most basic type of element declaration is one that specifies that an element must have exactly one child of a certain type. In the following example, the `purchase_order` element must contain exactly one `customer` element:

```
<!ELEMENT purchase_order (customer)>
```

Note This declaration is only for `purchase_order`. Although I don't declare it here, the `customer` element still must be declared before it can be used. The examples that follow assume that this declaration is made somewhere in the DTD.

Based on this declaration, the `purchase_order` element must have a single `customer` element. It may not contain any other elements or text, and it may not contain multiple `customer` elements. This means you could use the element in the body of the document like this:

```
<purchase_order>
 <customer>Microsoft Corp.</customer>
</purchase_order>
```

but you couldn't use the element like this:

```
<purchase_order>
 <customer>Microsoft Corp.</customer>
 <customer>MSN</customer>
</purchase_order>
```

Tip As you might imagine, you can extend the standard content model with various structures to allow for multiple child elements and text. You can also specify that child elements are to be used in a specific sequence or as choices where an element may contain one kind of child in one instance and a different kind of child in another instance. For details, see the "Structuring Elements" section of this chapter.

Element declarations can occur anywhere in a DTD and no specific order is necessary. With internal DTDs, the declaration must follow the DOCTYPE declaration that marks the start of the DTD. With external DTDs, the declaration can be placed anywhere in the DTD file.

To add an element declaration with standard content to a DTD, follow these steps:

1. In the document's DTD, type **<!ELEMENT *element_name***, where *element_name* is the name of the element you wish to define.
2. Type an open parenthesis, followed by the name of the child element(s) you want the element to contain.

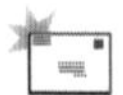

Note Usually multiple child elements are entered in the exact sequence in which they must be used, with each entry separated by a comma. For details on sequencing and other element structure indicators, see the "Structuring Elements" section of this chapter.

3. Type a closing parenthesis and the greater than symbol to complete the element declaration.

The result should look like the following:

```
<!ELEMENT parent (child)>
```

or

```
<!ELEMENT parent (child1, child2, ..., childN)>
```

Declaring Elements with Character Data Only

Although top-level elements are usually containers for other elements, low-level elements in a document won't contain other elements. Instead, they'll contain parsed character data. In XML, #PCDATA is a keyword that describes basic elements that contain parsed character data, which is raw text that could contain entity references, such as > or < but doesn't contain other markup or child elements. For example, the customer element declared as a child of purchase_order in the previous section could be defined as:

```
<!ELEMENT customer (#PCDATA)>
```

This declaration says that the customer element may contain text but may not contain child elements.

To add an element declaration with text content to a DTD, follow these steps:

1. In the document's DTD, type **<!ELEMENT *element_name***, where *element_name* is the name of the element you wish to define.
2. Type **(#PCDATA)**, making sure to use the open and close parentheses. This specifies that the element allows only text.
3. Type > to complete the element declaration.

The result should look like the following:

```
<!ELEMENT element_name (#PCDATA)>
```

Declaring Elements with Mixed Content

Often you'll want a way to declare that elements can contain mixed content—that is, that the element contains both text and other elements. For example, you may want to declare that an `inventory` element can contain `item` elements as well as text, and, if so, the declaration would look like this:

```
<!ELEMENT inventory (#PCDATA | item)*>
```

This declaration specifies that the `inventory` element can contain text and any number of `item` elements (which also have their own declaration). The pipe symbol (|) in the declaration indicates that there's a choice between text and `item` elements, which is further qualified by the asterisk (*) to indicate that text and `item` elements can be repeated.

The declaration doesn't specify an order that the text or `item` elements must use, and it doesn't specify how many `item` elements can be used. This means you could use the element in the body of the document like this:

```
<inventory>
 This is an inventory item.
 <item>3 1/2" Floppy Disk Drive</item>
</inventory>
```

or even like this:

```
<inventory>
 <item>3 1/2" Floppy Disk Drive</item>
 This is an inventory item.
 <item>5 1/4" Disk Drive </item>
 This is an inventory item also.
 <item>Zip Disk Drive </item>
 This is an inventory item as well.
</inventory>
```

When you want an element to contain mixed content, you must use this declaration technique. You can't try to restrict the number of `item` elements allowed or the amount of text that can be entered. You can't specify the order for text and `item` elements. You can't try to group the declaration within a larger group using additional sets of parentheses. This means the following are incorrect mixed content declarations:

```
<!ELEMENT inventory (#PCDATA | item)>
<!ELEMENT inventory (#PCDATA, item)>
```

Additionally, when you use mixed content, the `#PCDATA` keyword must be listed first. This means the following is an incorrect mixed content declaration:

```
<!ELEMENT inventory (item | #PCDATA)*>
```

When you use mixed content, however, you can specify additional child elements. To do this, simply enter the names of the elements you want to use, separating each element name with the choice indicator (|), such as:

```
<!ELEMENT inventory (#PCDATA | item | orig_cost | weight |
 color)*>
```

This declaration says that the `inventory` element may contain text and any number of `item`, `orig_cost`, `weight`, and `color` elements.

To add an element declaration with mixed content to a DTD, follow these steps:

1. In the document's DTD, type **<!ELEMENT *element_name***, where *element_name* is the name of the element you wish to define.
2. Type **(#PCDATA |**, making sure to use the open parenthesis and the choice indicator (|).
3. Type the child elements you want to allow, separating each child element with the choice indicator (|).
4. Type **)>** to complete the declaration.

The result should look like the following:

```
<!ELEMENT element_name (#PCDATA | child1 | child2 | ... | childN)>
```

Declaring Elements with Any Content Allowed

Occasionally, you may want to allow an element to contain any type of content. To do this, you use the keyword `ANY` in the element declaration, such as:

```
<!ELEMENT main ANY>
```

This declaration specifies that the main element can contain any type of content, including standard content, text, and mixed content. Because any type of content is allowed, the main element may even contain instances of the main element. As shown, you don't use parentheses with the `ANY` keyword. Further, you can't follow the `ANY` keyword with other declarations for the element. This means the following declarations are incorrect:

```
<!ELEMENT main (ANY) >
<!ELEMENT main ANY (#PCDATA | para)*>
```

Caution The `ANY` keyword doesn't allow you to use undeclared elements. You must still declare the elements you plan to use.

To add an element that allows any type of content to a DTD, follow these steps:

1. In the document's DTD, type **<!ELEMENT *element_name***, where *element_name* is the name of the element you wish to define.
2. Type **ANY**, and then type **>** to complete the declaration.

The result should look like the following:

```
<!ELEMENT element_name ANY>
```

Real World In practice, the ANY keyword is useful when you're developing new DTDs and aren't sure of the exact document structure that you want to use. However, by the time the DTD is in final form, the ANY keyword should be long gone. You rarely want to allow an element to contain any type of content. If you do, you won't be able to control the data structure in documents that used the DTD for validation—and structure is what XML is all about.

Declaring Elements with No Content Allowed

In Chapter 2, "XML Document Structure," you learned about elements that are used as a single tag containing an extra slash, such as `<br />`, instead of a pair of tags. These elements are called empty elements, which means that they don't have, nor do they allow, content.

You declare empty elements with the EMPTY keyword. Like the ANY keyword, you don't use parentheses in the element declaration and you can't specify other contents for the element. This means you could declare the br element in the DTD as follows:

```
<!ELEMENT br EMPTY>
```

However, the following are incorrect declarations:

```
<!ELEMENT br (EMPTY)>
```

```
<!ELEMENT br EMPTY (#PCDATA)>
```

Note Just because an element is empty, it doesn't mean that the element doesn't have attributes. Empty elements can, and often do, have attributes that specify additional information. For example, the `<br>` tag in Extensible HyperText Markup Language (XHTML) has a clear attribute that allows the line break to clear the left or right margins, or both.

To add an empty element to a DTD, follow these steps:

1. In the document's DTD, type **<!ELEMENT *element_name***, where *element_name* is the name of the element you wish to define.
2. Type **EMPTY**, and then type > to complete the declaration.

The result should look like the following:

```
<!ELEMENT element_name EMPTY>
```

Structuring Elements

To gain precise control over how elements are used in documents, you need to structure the element declarations very carefully. As you learned in the previous section, you can use the `#PCDATA`, `ANY`, and `EMPTY` keywords to allow elements to be used in various contexts. In this section you'll learn about additional structures that allow you to gain more control over how elements are used. These structures are called order indicators and qualifiers.

Understanding Element Order Indicators and Qualifiers

Order indicators and qualifiers specify element order and requirements by describing how often and in what context elements occur. In the following example, the pipe symbol (|) is an order indicator:

```
<!ELEMENT purchase_order (purchase | customer)>
```

Here, the pipe symbol (|) is a choice statement, which means that the `purchase_order` element would occur with one of the named child elements, either `purchase` or `customer`, but not both.

As shown in Table 4-1, several different types of order indicators and qualifiers are available. Order indicators determine grouping, sequencing, or choices. Qualifiers indicate how many instances of a child element are permitted.

Note This naming and typing for XML symbols is my own. The DTD specification may refer to these symbols by other names. However, I think it's easier to refer to the symbols as described in this table—it has certainly helped me remember how these symbols are used.

Table 4-1. Order Indicators and Qualifiers for Elements

Type	Value	Context	Description
Order	|	Choice	Either one child element or another can occur (grouping and qualifiers can modify).
	( )	Group	Groups related elements together.
	,	Sequence	Element must follow another element (grouping and qualifiers can modify).
Qualifier	?	Optional	Element appears once or not at all.
	*	Optional and repeatable	Element appears zero or more times.
	+	Required and repeatable	Element appears one or more times.

Order indicators and qualifiers have specific uses. When multiple child elements are specified, you define whether the elements are sequences or choices. For example, you could specify that elements appear in an exact sequence, such as:

```
<!ELEMENT contact_details (account_id, name)>
```

Here the `contact_details` contain an `account_id` followed by a `name`. This means that in the body of the document you'd use the elements like this:

```
<contact_details>
 <account_id>55384</account_id>
 <name>Microsoft Corp.</name>
</contact_details>
```

You could also specify that the `account_id` and `name` are choices for child elements that could be used within the `contact_details` element, such as:

```
<!ELEMENT contact_details (account_id | name)>
```

Here the `contact_details` contain an `account_id` or a `name` but not both. This means in the body of the document you'd use the elements like this:

```
<contact_details>
 <account_id>55384</account_id>
</contact_details>
```

or

```
<contact_details>
 <name>Microsoft Corp.</name>
</contact_details>
```

To combine a set of choices or sequences, you can use the grouping indicators. You could, for example, group a set of choices as part of a sequence. In the following example, the `contact_details` can contain an `account_id` and one of the choice elements, either `name`, `phone`, or `email`:

```
<!ELEMENT contact_details (account_id, (name | phone | email))>
```

This means that you'd have several different ways of using the elements in a document. You could use:

```
<contact_details>
 <account_id>55384</account_id>
 <name>Microsoft Corp.</name>
</contact_details>
```

or

```
<contact_details>
 <account_id>55384</account_id>
 <phone>555-1212</phone>
</contact_details>
```

or

```
<contact_details>
 <account_id>55384</account_id>
 <email>customer@microsoft.com</email>
</contact_details>
```

You can add qualifiers to individual elements as well as grouped elements. For example, you could follow the `name`, `phone`, and `email` grouping with ? to indicate that the choice element is optional, such as:

```
<!ELEMENT contact_details (account_id, (name | phone | email)?)>
```

Here, you could have an `account_id` child element by itself, such as:

```
<contact_details>
 <account_id>55384</account_id>
</contact_details>
```

Or the `account_id` element could be followed by a `name`, `phone`, or `email` element, such as:

```
<contact_details>
 <account_id>55384</account_id>
 <email>customer@microsoft.com</email>
</contact_details>
```

Specifying Sequences

If you've worked with HTML documents, you know that elements often are entered in a haphazard manner where the element order and structure isn't as important as the proper document display. In XML, however, the structure and order of elements are often critically important. The reason for this is that the data often must be structured so that it can be easily interpreted or processed by an application.

Most elements declarations specify that an element can contain one or more child elements. When you want the child elements to appear in a specific sequence, you separate them with commas. The comma specifies an exact sequence that must be followed. For example, if you want the `contact_details` element to have an `account_id` followed by a `name`, `phone`, and `email` address in that specific order, you'd declare the element as follows:

```
<!ELEMENT contact_details (account_id, name, phone, email)>
```

Give this declaration, the contact details element must be used like this:

```
<contact_details>
 <account_id>55384</account_id>
 <name>Microsoft Corp.</name>
 <phone>555-1212</phone>
 <email>customer@microsoft.com</email>
</contact_details>
```

However, the following element is incorrect because the order defined in the declaration isn't followed:

```
<contact_details>
 <name>Microsoft Corp.</name>
 <phone>555-1212</phone>
 <email>customer@microsoft.com</email>
 <account_id>55384</account_id>
</contact_details>
```

Sequences must be followed exactly as specified; you can't skip elements unless an optional qualifier (?) or an optional and repeatable qualifier (*) is used. Because of this, the following element examples are invalid:

```
<contact_details>
 <name>Microsoft Corp.</name>
 <phone>555-1212</phone>
 <email>customer@microsoft.com</email>
</contact_details>
```

and

```
<contact_details>
 <account_id>55384</account_id>
 <email>customer@microsoft.com</email>
</contact_details>
```

The first example omits the `account_id` element, and the second example omits the `name` and `phone` elements.

You can't repeat elements in a sequence unless an optional and repeatable qualifier (*) or a required and repeatable qualifier (+) is used. This means the following example is invalid because it repeats the name element:

```
<contact_details>
 <account_id>55384</account_id>
 <name>Microsoft Corp.</name>
 <name>MSN</name>
 <phone>555-1212</phone>
 <email>customer@microsoft.com</email>
</contact_details>
```

Finally, you can't add elements that aren't in the sequence defined in the declaration. This means the following example is incorrect because it adds a `website` element:

```
<contact_details>
 <account_id>55384</account_id>
 <name>Microsoft Corp.</name>
 <phone>555-1212</phone>
 <email>customer@microsoft.com</email>
 <website>www.microsoft.com</website>
</contact_details>
```

Specifying Choices

You won't want elements to occur in an exact sequence all the time. Sometimes, you'll want to allow an element to contain one kind of child or another given the current situation. To do this, you use the choice indicator (|). The choice indicator is used as a separator in a list of elements that an element may contain. You could use the choice indicator to provide a list of choices for the `contact_details` element as follows:

```
<!ELEMENT contact_details (account_id | name)>
```

This element declaration specifies that the `contact_details` element can contain either an `account_id` or `name`. Unless the element entries are further qualified, only one of the choices can be used and that choice can't be repeated.

The following element usage is correct, because only one of the choices is used:

```
<contact_details>
  <account_id>55384</account_id>
</contact_details>
```

However, the following example is incorrect because it uses both of the choices and there's no qualifier:

```
<contact_details>
  <account_id>55384</account_id>
  <name>Microsoft Corp.</name>
</contact_details>
```

You can specify as many choices as you want, as long as the choices are separated with the choice indicator (|) and declared in the DTD somewhere. This means you could add `phone`, `name`, and `website` as choices like this:

```
<!ELEMENT contact_details (account_id | name | phone | email |
 website)>
```

Specifying Groups

Choices and sequences don't have to be used by themselves. Often you'll want to combine the two concepts to allow you to specify a choice within a sequence or a set of choices that contain specific sequences of elements.

To group choices or sequences, you use the open and close parentheses. The parentheses allow you to nest choices in sequences and sequences in choices. In addition, as with individual elements, these grouped sets can be qualified with the ?, *, or + suffixes to indicate the exact usage permitted.

Using Grouping to Specify Choices Within Sequences

To use the parentheses to specify a choice within a sequence, you could declare the element like this:

```
<!ELEMENT contact_details (account_id, name, (phone | email |
 website))>
```

This declaration specifies that the `contact_details` element must contain an `account_id` followed by a `name`, followed by a `phone`, `email`, or `website` element. Based on this declaration, you could use the element as follows:

```
<contact_details>
 <account_id>55384</account_id>
 <name>Microsoft Corp.</name>
 <phone>555-1212</phone>
</contact_details>
```

or

```
<contact_details>
 <account_id>55384</account_id>
 <name>Microsoft Corp.</name>
 <email>customer@microsoft.com</email>
</contact_details>
```

or

```
<contact_details>
 <account_id>55384</account_id>
 <name>Microsoft Corp.</name>
 <website>www.microsoft.com</website>
</contact_details>
```

However, you couldn't use the element like this:

```
<contact_details>
 <account_id>55384</account_id>
 <name>Microsoft Corp.</name>
</contact_details>
```

or this:

```
<contact_details>
 <account_id>55384</account_id>
 <name>Microsoft Corp.</name>
 <email>customer@microsoft.com</email>
 <website>www.microsoft.com</website>
</contact_details>
```

In the first example, the choice element is omitted. In the second example, two of the choices are used without a qualifier permitting this.

Using Grouping to Specify Sets of Choices with Specific Sequences

To use the parentheses to designate sets of choices with specific sequences, you could declare the element like this:

```
<!ELEMENT contact_details ((account_id, name) | (name, email, phone))>
```

This declaration specifies that the `contact_details` element must contain an `account_id` followed by a `name`; or it could contain a `name` followed by an `email`, followed by a `phone`. Based on this declaration, you could use the element as follows:

```
<contact_details>
 <account_id>55384</account_id>
 <name>Microsoft Corp.</name>
</contact_details>
```

or

```
<contact_details>
 <name>Microsoft Corp.</name>
 <email>customer@microsoft.com</email>
 <phone>555-1212</phone>
</contact_details>
```

However, you couldn't use the element like this:

```
<contact_details>
 <account_id>55384</account_id>
 <name>Microsoft Corp.</name>
 <email>customer@microsoft.com</email>
</contact_details>
```

or this:

```
<contact_details>
 <name>Microsoft Corp.</name>
 <email>customer@microsoft.com</email>
 <website>www.microsoft.com</website>
</contact_details>
```

In the first example, an `email` element is used when one isn't allowed as part of the first choice. In the second example, a `website` element is used when it isn't part of the second choice.

Specifying the Number of Child Elements

Qualifiers are an important part of the element declaration in that they allow you to specify the number of child elements allowed or required. Three qualifiers are defined:

- ? The question mark specifies that the element is optional and should occur once or not at all.
- * The asterisk specifies that the element is optional and can be repeated if it's used.
- + The plus sign indicates that the element is required and must occur at least once.

Both child elements and groups of choices or sequences enclosed in parentheses can have qualifiers. Although there's no direct way to use qualifiers to define specific quantities, you can define specific minimum requirements. Techniques for using qualifiers with child elements and groups and for setting specific minimum requirements are examined in the sections that follow.

Qualifying Child Elements

In the following example, the `contact_details` element contains a mandatory `account_id` and an optional `name`:

```
<!ELEMENT contact_details (account_id, name?)>
```

This means the element could be used as:

```
<contact_details>
 <account_id>55384</account_id>
 <name>Microsoft Corp.</name>
</contact_details>
```

or it could have only an `account_id`, as shown in this example:

```
<contact_details>
  <account_id>55384</account_id>
</contact_details>
```

The same rules about sequences, choices, and grouping apply when qualifiers are used. This means that the following example is invalid because it doesn't follow the sequence defined in the declaration:

```
<contact_details>
 <name>Microsoft Corp.</name>
 <account_id>55384</account_id>
</contact_details>
```

and the following example is invalid because the `name` element is repeated:

```
<contact_details>
 <account_id>55384</account_id>
 <name>Microsoft Corp.</name>
 <name>MSN</name>
</contact_details>
```

To allow multiple names in the `contact_details`, you'd have to declare the element like this:

```
<!ELEMENT contact_details (account_id, name*)>
```

Now the `contact_details` element can have multiple occurrences of the `name` element. The `name` element, however, isn't required—it's optional. To make the `name` element required and repeatable, you'd have to use the plus qualifier, such as:

```
<!ELEMENT contact_details (account_id, name+)>
```

Qualifying Groups of Sequences or Choices

If you want to add a qualifier after a group of sequences or choices, you must be sure that you add the qualifier to the inner parentheses for the group and not the outer parentheses that enclose the declaration. For example, if you want to allow the `phone`, `email`, and `website` choices to be optional and repeatable, you could declare the element like this:

```
<!ELEMENT contact_details (account_id, name, (phone | email |
 website)*)>
```

Here, the `contact_details` must contain an `account_id` followed by a `name`, followed by zero or more occurrences of `phone`, `email`, and `website` in any order. This means the following is valid:

```
<contact_details>
 <account_id>55384</account_id>
 <name>Microsoft Corp.</name>
</contact_details>
```

as is this example:

```
<contact_details>
 <account_id>55384</account_id>
 <name>Microsoft Corp.</name>
 <phone>555-1212</phone>
 <email>customer@microsoft.com</email>
 <website>www.microsoft.com</website>
</contact_details>
```

and this example:

```
<contact_details>
 account_id>55384</account_id>
 <name>Microsoft Corp.</name>
 <phone>555-1212</phone>
 <phone>555-3456</phone>
 <email>customer@microsoft.com</email>
</contact_details>
```

However, the following example is incorrect because it omits the `name` element, which is required as part of the defined sequence:

```
<contact_details>
 <account_id>55384</account_id>
 <phone>555-1212</phone>
 <email>customer@microsoft.com</email>
</contact_details>
```

Using Qualifiers to Specify Minimum Requirements

In XML there's no direct way to specify that an element must contain at least four of this and at least five of that. You can't set these types of requirements. You can only specify that something is

- Required, meaning that there must be one and only one of this item
- Optional, meaning there will be zero or one of this item
- Optional and repeatable, meaning there will be zero or more of this item
- Required and repeatable, meaning there will be one or more of this item

Although you can't control specific requirements, you can use these rules to specify minimum requirements. For example, if you wanted to ensure that a purchase order included three or more items, you could do this by declaring the element as follows:

```
<!ELEMENT purchase_order (item, item, item+)>
```

Now the `purchase_order` element must have three or more `item` elements. If it doesn't, the document won't be valid and the processing application could reject the order. This means the body of the document must define `purchase_order` elements like this:

```
<purchase_order>
 <item>3 1/2" Floppy Disk Drive</item>
 <item>5 1/4" Disk Drive</item>
 <item>Zip Disk Drive</item>
</purchase_order>
```

or there could be more than three `item` elements, such as:

```
<purchase_order>
 <item>3 1/2" Floppy Disk Drive</item>
 <item>5 1/4" Disk Drive</item>
 <item>Zip 100 Disk Drive</item>
 <item>Zip 250 Disk Drive</item>
</purchase_order>
```

However, the following usage is incorrect because there are only two `item` elements:

```
<purchase_order>
 <item>3 1/2" Floppy Disk Drive</item>
 <item>5 1/4" Disk Drive</item>
</purchase_order>
```

You can extend this technique as necessary to set higher minimums. In the following example, at least four `items` are required:

```
<!ELEMENT purchase_order (item, item, item, item+)>
```

This means the `purchase_order` element must have at least four `item` elements or the document won't be considered valid.

Chapter 5

XML Attributes in DTDs

Like HTML elements, XML elements can have attributes. Because a document's elements are completely configurable, you're free to create as many attributes as necessary. However, all attributes used in a valid document must be declared in the document type definition (DTD). Otherwise the document can't be said to be valid.

Defining Attributes in DTDs

The following sections examine the fundamental concepts you'll need to define attributes in DTDs. You'll learn how to

- Make attribute assignments
- Specify attribute names, types, and default usages
- Assign values to attributes in DTDs

After these sections you'll find a complete discussion on declaring the five standard types of attributes in DTDs.

Making Attribute Assignments

You define a list of attributes for an element with the `ATTLIST` assignment. Using the `ATTLIST` assignment, you could declare a shipping attribute for the `purchase_order` element used previously like this:

```
<!ATTLIST purchase_order shipping CDATA #REQUIRED>
```

This declaration says the `shipping` attribute is required and contains character data.

You can assign multiple attributes to an element using a single assignment as well. In the following example, `shipping`, `prepaid`, and `type` are defined as possible attributes for the `purchase_order` element:

```
<!ATTLIST  purchase_order shipping CDATA #REQUIRED
           prepaid CDATA #REQUIRED
           type CDATA #REQUIRED
>
```

The declaration specifies that the `shipping`, `prepaid`, and `type` attributes are required. It also specifies that the attributes contain character data. The spacing used in the example is added for readability and isn't required. You could also have entered:

```
<!ATTLIST purchase_order shipping CDATA #REQUIRED prepaid CDATA
#REQUIRED type CDATA #REQUIRED>
```

or you could have used a separate attribute declaration for each attribute, such as:

```
<!ATTLIST purchase_order shipping CDATA #REQUIRED>
<!ATTLIST purchase_order prepaid CDATA #REQUIRED>
<!ATTLIST purchase_order type CDATA #REQUIRED>
```

As you can see from the examples, the `ATTLIST` assignment uses the following syntax:

```
<!ATTLIST element_describing attrib_name attrib_type
default_usage>
```

What this means is that when you create attributes, you must complete the following steps:

1. Start the assignment by typing **<!ATTLIST**.
2. Specify the element the attribute relates to. In previous examples this was `purchase_order`.
3. Give the attribute a name. In the examples the attributes are named `shipping`, `prepaid`, and `type`.

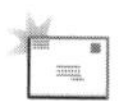

Note Attribute names must be valid XML names, meaning that they must conform to the XML naming rules discussed in Chapter 2, "XML Document Structure."

4. Set the attribute type, such as `CDATA` or `ENTITY`.
5. Set the default usage, such as `#REQUIRED` or `#FIXED`.
6. Complete the assignment by typing >.

Specifying Attribute Names, Types, and Default Usages

Most attribute declarations have an attribute name, an attribute type, and a default usage. The following sections examine these concepts and then provide an overview of how you can use names, types, and default usages in DTDs.

Defining Attribute Names

Attribute names are for the most part arbitrary and you can assign any valid XML name. This means the attribute name must follow the naming rules discussed in the "XML Naming Rules" section of Chapter 2.

Additionally, each attribute name for a given element must be unique. If the element already has an attribute of the same name, the name used for the new attribute must be different.

Defining Attribute Types

While attribute names are arbitrary, attribute types have specific values that you must use in order to properly declare the attribute. Table 5-1 summarizes the available attribute types. As shown in the table, attribute types fall into one of three categories: string types, tokenized types, and enumerated types.

Note This chapter examines all the attribute types except `ENTITY`, `ENTITIES`, and `NOTATION`. These attribute types are discussed in Chapter 6, "XML Entities and Notations in DTDs."

Table 5-1. Attribute Types

Attribute Type	Category	Description
`CDATA`	String type	Contains character data.
`ENTITY`	Tokenized type	Contains the name of an unparsed entity.
`ENTITIES`	Tokenized type	Contains names of multiple unparsed entities.
`ID`	Tokenized type	Contains an XML name that's a unique identifier.
`IDREF`	Tokenized type	Contains a reference to a unique identifier.
`IDREFS`	Tokenized type	Contains a list of references to unique identifiers.
`NOTATION`	Enumerated type	Contains the name of a notation declared in the DTD.
`NMTOKEN`	Tokenized type	Contains an XML name token.
`NMTOKENS`	Tokenized type	Contains a list of XML name tokens.
`ENUMERATION`	Enumerated type	Contains a list of possible values for an attribute. `ENUMERATION` isn't an actual XML keyword. Rather, it's a type.

Defining Attribute Default Usages

In addition to attribute types, you can also specify an attribute's default usage. For string and tokenized attributes, the default usage can be set with the keywords shown in Table 5-2. For enumerated types, the default value for the attribute must follow the permissible values set when creating the enumerated types. In all cases, if you define a default value for an attribute in the DTD but don't assign one explicitly in the related document, the XML parser will add the default value to the document automatically.

Table 5-2. Attribute Keywords

Keyword	Attribute Usage	Default Value	Description
#IMPLIED	Optional attributes	No default value is assigned or allowed.	A value is optional. When no value is set, the document can still be considered valid. However, the parser might return a warning.
#FIXED	Fixed-value attributes	Default value is assigned as provided and necessary.	The value is fixed and immutable. The value doesn't need to be included on individual instances. However, the value must match the fixed value if assigned. Otherwise, the document won't be considered valid.
#REQUIRED	Mandatory attributes	No default value is assigned or allowed.	A value is mandatory. If no value is set, the document isn't valid and a validating parser will return an error.
-	Literal value attributes	Default value is assigned as provided and necessary.	A value is assigned as a quoted string. If no value is set, the value is implicitly assigned.

Using Attribute Types and Default Usages in DTDs

Using attribute types and default usages is easier than it might seem—I promise. Let's start by creating attributes for the `purchase_order` element we've been using:

```
<!ELEMENT purchase_order (date, item+, contact_details)>
<!ATTLIST purchase_order id ID #REQUIRED
          cust_rep CDATA #IMPLIED
          shipping CDATA #REQUIRED
          prepaid CDATA #FIXED "yes"
          type (walkin | phone | catalog) "walkin"
          store NMTOKEN "Seattle"
>
```

Here, the `id` attribute is defined as an `ID` attribute type, which could be used to track a unique identifier for each purchase order. Because the `id` attribute is required, it must be present in the purchase order. If it isn't, the document can't be considered valid.

The next attribute is called `cust_rep`. The attribute contains character data and is implied. Because no specific values have been set for the attribute, any value is considered valid. This allows you to assign any customer representative's name to the purchase order without having to define a list of all customer representatives. If the value isn't filled in, however, the document is still considered valid. The reason for this is that implied attributes are optional.

The third attribute is called `shipping`. Here, the `shipping` attribute could be used to determine the type of shipping the customer has requested. Because all orders must have some type of shipping information, the `shipping` attribute is required. The value of the attribute, however, isn't prespecified and must be entered by the customer representative processing the order.

The fourth attribute, called `prepaid`, has a fixed value. If the `prepaid` attribute is used with a value other than `"yes"`, the document is considered invalid and the order could be rejected. One reason for forcing the attribute to have a fixed value could be that all orders must be prepaid. Thus, if the value were `"pending"` or `"no"` instead of `"yes"`, the order wouldn't be processed.

Note Fixed values set a specific default that's a constant. If a value isn't specified, the fixed value is assigned implicitly. The reason for this is that fixed values don't have to be specified on individual instances. With this in mind, a purchase order that doesn't specify a `prepaid` attribute would still be considered valid.

The fifth attribute, called `type`, uses enumeration. The `type` attribute has three name tokens that define the valid values for the attribute. From these tokens you can determine that purchase orders are defined as walk-in orders, telephone orders, or catalog orders. The default value, walkin, is assigned as a literal value enclosed in quotation marks. If no value is specified, the purchase transaction is assumed to be a walk-in order.

The final attribute, `store`, is assigned literally as a name token. If the literal value isn't assigned explicitly, the value is implicitly assigned.

Tip To see that your default values are assigned to a document, create a DTD that specifies defaults and then create a document based on the DTD that doesn't use the defaults. Next, display the document in Microsoft Internet Explorer. You'll find that the default values were added during processing.

You could use these attributes in a document, as shown in the following example:

```
<purchase_order id="s553"
     cust_rep="William Stanek"
     shipping="USPS Ground"
     prepaid="yes"
     type="phone">
...
</purchase_order>
```

Here, specific `id`, `cust_rep`, `shipping`, `prepaid`, and `type` values are assigned to the purchase order. The literal attribute `store`, however, is assigned implicitly as `"Seattle"` during processing. If you wanted, you could allow the fixed and type values to be assigned automatically as well, such as:

```
<purchase_order id="s553"
    cust_rep="William Stanek"
    shipping="USPS Ground">
...
</purchase_order>
```

Here, the fixed `prepaid` value of `"yes"` and the default `type` of `"walkin"` are used without their being manually assigned. Again, the literal attribute `store` is assigned implicitly as `"Seattle"`, but you can also assign the value explicitly if desired, such as:

```
<purchase_order id="s553"
    cust_rep="William Stanek"
    shipping="USPS Ground"
    store="Seattle">
...
</purchase_order>
```

or you could set a different value for `store` all together, such as:

```
<purchase_order id="s553"
    cust_rep="William Stanek"
    shipping="USPS Ground"
    store="Atlanta">
...
</purchase_order>
```

Assigning Values to Attributes in DTDs

Values can be assigned to attributes in DTDs. When you assign a default value, you must enclose it in quotation marks. As shown in previous examples, the value assignment for a fixed or literal attribute is the last item specified in the assignment, such as:

```
<!ATTLIST purchase_order prepaid CDATA #FIXED "yes">
```

or

```
<!ATTLIST purchase_order store NMTOKEN "Seattle">
```

With enumerated attributes that use a literal value as a default, the value assignments take the form of choices enclosed in parentheses followed by a default choice enclosed in quotation marks, such as:

```
<!ATTLIST purchase_order type (walkin | phone | catalog)
 "walkin">
```

Although the examples use double quotation marks, DTD attribute assignments can use either single or double quotation marks. Whatever type of quotation mark you start with, however, you must finish with. For example, you could rewrite the previous examples using single quotation marks as follows:

```
<!ATTLIST purchase_order prepaid CDATA #FIXED 'yes'>
<!ATTLIST purchase_order store NMTOKEN 'Seattle'>
<!ATTLIST purchase_order type (walkin | phone | catalog)
 'walkin'>
```

However, the following example that mixes single and double quotation marks is incorrect:

```
<!ATTLIST purchase_order prepaid CDATA #FIXED "yes'>
<!ATTLIST purchase_order store NMTOKEN 'Seattle">
<!ATTLIST purchase_order type (walkin | phone | catalog)
 "walkin'>
```

Values assigned to attributes in a DTD can be any string of text. The only characters you can't use are the less than symbol (<) and the ampersand symbol (&). These characters are reserved by XML and must escaped using a predefined entity reference: either `&` for `&` or `<` for <. Further, if an attribute value contains either single or double quotation marks, you have to use a different type of quotation mark to enclose the value or escape the single or double quotation marks using `'` or `"`, respectively.

Examples using escaped values and quotation marks follow:

- Escaped ampersand:

```
<!ATTLIST purchase_order prepaid CDATA #FIXED "B&amp;A">
```

- Single quotation marks within double quotation marks:

```
<!ATTLIST purchase_order type "type 'not specified'">
```

- Escaped double quotation marks:

```
<!ATTLIST purchase_order type "error &quot;not
 specified&quot;">
```

Declaring Standard Attribute Types in DTDs

Attribute assignments that you'll use most often in DTDs are:

- Character data
- Name tokens
- Enumeration
- Unique identifiers
- Unique identifier references

These attribute assignments are discussed in the following sections.

Defining CDATA Attribute Types

Character data is the most basic type of attribute assignment. A CDATA attribute value can contain any acceptable string value, as discussed in the "Assigning Values to Attributes in DTDs" section of this chapter. You'll use the CDATA attribute type when you want to assign general values to an attribute, which can include text and entity references.

A CDATA attribute can be declared as #IMPLIED, #FIXED, or #REQUIRED, such as:

```
<!ATTLIST purchase_order cust_rep CDATA #IMPLIED>
<!ATTLIST purchase_order prepaid CDATA #FIXED "yes">
<!ATTLIST purchase_order shipping CDATA #REQUIRED>
```

You can also assign a literal value as a default, such as:

```
<!ATTLIST purchase_order prepaid CDATA "yes">
```

When you use a fixed value, you must assign a default. When values are implied and required, you can't assign a default value. Because of this, these assignments are incorrect:

```
<!ATTLIST purchase_order cust_rep CDATA #IMPLIED "William">
<!ATTLIST purchase_order prepaid CDATA #FIXED>
<!ATTLIST purchase_order shipping CDATA #REQUIRED "USPS Ground">
```

To add a CDATA attribute type to a DTD, follow these steps:

1. Start the assignment by typing **<!ATTLIST** and then specify the name of the element the attribute relates to.
2. Enter the name of the attribute. The name must be a valid XML name.
3. Type **CDATA**.
4. Set the default usage as #IMPLIED, #REQUIRED, or #FIXED. If you use a fixed type, you must also enter a default value in quotation marks. Or simply assign a literal value as a default.
5. Complete the assignment by typing >.

The result should follow this format:

```
<!ATTLIST element_describing attrib_name CDATA default_usage>
```

Restricting Attribute Values Using Name Tokens

DTDs don't allow you to specify data types that are permitted or not permitted to be assigned as attribute values. For example, you can't specify that one attribute value must be a date type and another must be an integer type. The only way that you can restrict attribute values is to specify that they must be valid XML name tokens.

XML name tokens are similar to XML names, which were discussed in Chapter 2. They may include alphanumeric characters (the letters a-z and A-Z as well as the numerals 0-9), syllabic base characters, and ideographic characters, such as α, β, χ, and δ. They may also include the punctuation characters underscore (_), hyphen (-), and period (.). Although they may not contain white space, they may begin with alphanumber characters, syllabic base characters, and ideographic characters. They may also begin with a hyphen, period, or underscore character. This means that although the following are *valid* name tokens:

```
store12
_store
store
12store
.store
-store
```

the following are *invalid* name tokens:

```
store 12
store$12
#store
12 store
```

To restrict an attribute so that its values must be valid name tokens, declare the attribute as the `NMTOKEN` type. A `NMTOKEN` attribute can be declared as `#IMPLIED`, `#FIXED`, or `#REQUIRED`, such as:

```
<!ATTLIST purchase_order store NMTOKEN #IMPLIED>
<!ATTLIST purchase_order store NMTOKEN #FIXED "Seattle">
<!ATTLIST purchase_order store NMTOKEN #REQUIRED>
```

When you use a fixed value, you must assign a default. When values are implied and required, you can't assign a default value. Because of this, these assignments are incorrect:

```
<!ATTLIST purchase_order store NMTOKEN #IMPLIED "Seattle">
<!ATTLIST purchase_order store NMTOKEN #FIXED>
<!ATTLIST purchase_order store NMTOKEN #REQUIRED "Seattle">
```

`NMTOKEN` attributes can be assigned as literal values as well, such as:

```
<!ATTLIST purchase_order store NMTOKEN "Seattle">
```

If you later specify a different value for the literally assigned attribute, the value must still be a valid name token. If a value isn't assigned explicitly, the literal value is implicitly assigned.

To restrict an attribute value using name tokens, follow these steps:

1. Start the assignment by typing **<!ATTLIST** and then specify the name of the element the attribute relates to.
2. Enter the name of the attribute. The name must be a valid XML name.

3. Type **NMTOKEN**.
4. If the name token will have a literal value, enter the value in quotation marks and then complete the assignment by typing >.
5. If the name token is implied, fixed, or required, type **#IMPLIED**, **#REQUIRED**, or **#FIXED** as appropriate, making sure to add a default value in quotation marks for the fixed type. Afterward, complete the assignment by typing >.

The result should follow this format:

```
<!ATTLIST element_describing attrib_name NMTOKEN default_usage>
```

Defining Enumerated Attribute Types

Enumeration allows you to specify a predefined set of values for attributes. Each of the possible values is entered as a choice separated by the choice indicator (|) and must be legal XML name tokens. One of the most common types of enumerated attribute values uses a literally assigned default value, such as:

```
<!ATTLIST purchase_order type (walkin|phone|catalog) "walkin">
```

Here the possible values for the `type` attribute are: walkin, phone, and catalog. The default value, walkin, is assigned automatically if no explicit value is assigned.

An enumerated attribute can be declared as `#IMPLIED` or `#REQUIRED` as well. As before, you can't assign a default value. This means that correct declarations should look similar to the following:

```
<!ATTLIST purchase_order type (walkin|phone|catalog) #IMPLIED>
<!ATTLIST purchase_order type (walkin|phone|catalog) #REQUIRED>
```

and that the following are incorrect declarations:

```
<!ATTLIST purchase_order type (walkin|phone|catalog) #IMPLIED
"walkin">
<!ATTLIST purchase_order type (walkin|phone|catalog) #REQUIRED
"walkin">
```

To add an enumerated attribute type to a DTD, follow these steps:

1. Start the assignment by typing **<!ATTLIST** and then specify the name of the element the attribute relates to.
2. Enter the name of the attribute. The name must be a valid XML name.
3. Type an open parenthesis followed by a | delimited list of possible values for the attribute, and then type a close parenthesis.
4. Optionally, set the default usage as `#IMPLIED` or `#REQUIRED`.
5. If you didn't specify an implied or required type, enter a literal value in quotation marks that will serve as the default.
6. Complete the assignment by typing >.

The result should follow this format:

```
<!ATTLIST element_describing attrib_name (choice1|choice2| ... |
choiceN) default_usage>
```

Note You can add white space around the choices if you want. The white space is only used to improve readability for you or others looking at the DTD. However, because the values must be valid name tokens, you can't include white space within the enumerated value. For example, you can't use "walk in" but could use "walkin" or "walk_in".

Defining Attributes with Unique Values

The ID attribute type allows you to specify that an attribute value must be unique within a particular document. What this means is that no other ID attribute in the same document can have the same value as any other ID attribute, which ensures that all ID attribute values are unique. Several other conventions apply:

- When setting the value of an ID attribute, you must use the rules for valid XML names (and not the rules for valid XML name tokens). Among other things, this means that ID values can't begin with a number.
- Each element can have one and only one ID attribute. No element can have more than one ID attribute.
- Although the attribute's name doesn't have to be id, it's commonly named this so that it's easy for others to interpret what the attribute is used for.

An ID attribute must be declared as #IMPLIED or #REQUIRED and no default value should be assigned. This means that correct declarations should look similar to the following:

```
<!ATTLIST purchase_order id ID #REQUIRED>
<!ATTLIST purchase_order id ID #IMPLIED>
```

and that the following are incorrect declarations:

```
<!ATTLIST purchase_order id ID #REQUIRED "t107">
<!ATTLIST purchase_order id ID #IMPLIED "t107">
```

Because identifiers must be unique, you can't declare default literal or fixed values. This means the following declarations are incorrect as well:

```
<!ATTLIST purchase_order id ID #FIXED "t107">
<!ATTLIST purchase_order id ID "t107">
```

Real World Often you'll want your unique identifier to be a numeric value when entered in the body of a document. However, because the values must be valid XML names, you can't use a value that consists only of numbers. The workaround that most people use is to begin the identifier with an underscore or an alphabetic character. This means that instead of using an ID of "102", you'd use an ID of "_102" or "s102".

To add an ID attribute type to a DTD, follow these steps:

1. Start the assignment by typing **<!ATTLIST** and then specify the name of the element the attribute relates to.
2. Enter the name of the attribute. The name must be a valid XML name.
3. Type **ID**.
4. Set the default usage as #IMPLIED or #REQUIRED.
5. Complete the assignment by typing >.

The result should follow this format:

```
<!ATTLIST element_describing attrib_name ID default_usage>
```

Referencing Attributes with Unique Values

In XML you can reference the unique values specified in ID attributes using an IDREF or IDREFS attribute type. These references are used to constrain an attribute's value so that it matches the values used previously for unique identifiers in the document. Although there's no way to specify that a particular reference must match a particular identifier, you can use references to ensure that each referenced value is appropriate and has a corresponding unique identifier somewhere in the document.

Using an IDREF Attribute Type

An IDREF attribute type refers to the ID type attribute of another element in the current document. The purpose of the reference is to establish a many-to-many relationship between one element in a document and another element in a document. You use the IDREF type to constrain the value of the IDREF attribute type so that it matches the value of an ID attribute somewhere in the document. Consider the case of a document that contains entries for each day's purchase orders from a particular branch office that must be processed and input into the company's central database. The document has four sections:

- A section containing all purchase orders for the branch office on that day
- A section that lists purchased items currently in stock at the branch office
- A section that lists purchased items on back order at the branch office
- A section that lists purchased items no longer sold

Since each in stock, back order, or no longer sold list can contain items from multiple purchase orders, you need a convenient way to reference back to previous purchase orders while ensuring that only items in an actual purchase order get processed. To do this, you decide to reference the ID attribute for items in purchase orders as well as the purchase order number itself. This ensures that any item listed in the in stock, back order, or no longer sold sections has a related purchase order. However, it doesn't ensure that the correct purchase order is referenced—there's no way to do this using DTDs.

Following this, the document could look similar to the following:

```
<master_list store="123 Main Denver">
 <purchases>
  <purchase_order po_num="d1">
    <item id="d890">3 1/2" Floppy Disk Drive</item>
    <item id="d891">5 1/4" Floppy Disk Drive</item>
    <item id="d892">Zip Drive</item>
  </purchase_order>
  <purchase_order po_num="d2">
    <item id="d893">Zip Drive</item>
    <item id="d894">3 1/2" Floppy Disk Drive</item>
  </purchase_order>
 </purchases>
 <in-stock>
  <inventory_item ref_num="d892" orig_po="d1" />
  <inventory_item ref_num="d893" orig_po="d2" />
 </in-stock>
 <back-order>
  <inventory_item ref_num="d890" orig_po="d1" />
  <inventory_item ref_num="d894" orig_po="d2" />
 </back-order>
 <no-longer-sold>
  <inventory_item ref_num="d891" orig_po="d1" />
 </no-longer-sold>
</master_list>
```

In this example, the `po_num` and `id` attributes should be declared as `ID` attribute types. Since the `ref_num` attribute references the `id` attribute, it should be declared as an `IDREF`. Similarly, the `orig_po` attribute references the `po_num` attribute and should be declared as an `IDREF`. These declarations could look like this:

```
<!ATTLIST  purchase_order po_num ID #REQUIRED>
<!ATTLIST  item id ID #REQUIRED>

<!ATTLIST  inventory_item ref_num IDREF #REQUIRED>
<!ATTLIST  inventory_item orig_po IDREF #REQUIRED>
```

or like this:

```
<!ATTLIST  purchase_order po_num ID #REQUIRED>
<!ATTLIST  item id ID #REQUIRED>

<!ATTLIST  inventory_item ref_num IDREF #REQUIRED
           orig_po IDREF #REQUIRED>
```

These declarations constrain the `ref_num` and `orig_po` attributes of the `inventory_item` element so that their values must match a unique identifier listed elsewhere in the document. The declaration doesn't ensure that `ref_num` attributes reference `id` attributes or that `orig_po` attributes reference `po_num` attributes. These attribute references could be mixed up so that an `orig_po` attribute references an `id` value and a `ref_num` attribute references a `po_num`. The `ref_num` and `orig_po` attributes could also reference the wrong purchase order or the wrong purchase item. The only thing you can guarantee is that the unique identifiers are in the document.

To add an `IDREF` attribute type to a DTD, follow these steps:

1. Start the assignment by typing **<!ATTLIST** and then specify the name of the element the attribute relates to.
2. Enter the name of the `IDREF` attribute. The name must be a valid XML name.
3. Type **IDREF** and then set the default usage as `#REQUIRED`. The required type is best in most cases.
4. Complete the assignment by typing **>**.

The result should follow this format:

```
<!ATTLIST element_describing attrib_name IDREF #REQUIRED>
```

Using an IDREFS Attribute Type

An `IDREFS` attribute type allows one attribute to reference multiple unique identifiers. The purpose of the reference is to establish a many-to-many relationship between one element in a document and multiple elements in the same document. You use the `IDREFS` type to constrain the value of the `IDREFS` attribute type so that its values match the values of `ID` attributes somewhere in the document.

In the previous example we could add a section that allowed us to quickly reference all purchase orders that had items on back order or items that were no longer sold. The revised document might look like this:

```
<master_list store="123 Main Denver">
 <purchases>
  <purchase_order po_num="d1">
    <item id="d890">3 1/2" Floppy Disk Drive</item>
    <item id="d891">5 1/4" Floppy Disk Drive</item>
    <item id="d892">Zip Drive</item>
  </purchase_order>
  <purchase_order po_num="d2">
    <item id="d893">Zip Drive</item>
    <item id="d894">3 1/2" Floppy Disk Drive</item>
  </purchase_order>
 </purchases>
 <in-stock>
  <inventory_item ref_num="d892" orig_po="d1" />
  <inventory_item ref_num="d893" orig_po="d2" />
 </in-stock>
 <back-order>
  <inventory_item ref_num="d890" orig_po="d1" />
  <inventory_item ref_num="d894" orig_po="d2" />
 </back-order>
```

(continued)

(continued)

```
  <no-longer-sold>
    <inventory_item ref_num="d891" orig_po="d1" />
  </no-longer-sold>
  <flagged_orders>
    <store_purchase purchase_refs="d1 d2" />
  </flagged_orders>
</master_list>
```

The attribute declaration that allows us to reference multiple unique identifiers would look like this:

```
<!ATTLIST store_purchase purchase_refs IDREFS #REQUIRED>
```

The declaration constrains the `purchase_refs` attribute of the `store_purchase` element so that its values must match a unique identifier listed elsewhere in the document. As with an `IDREF`, the `IDREFS` declaration doesn't ensure that identifiers used match only `po_num` attribute values. Other unique identifiers could be referenced. However, if an identifier is referenced and the document is validated without error, you can guarantee that the unique identifiers referenced are in the document.

To add an `IDREFS` attribute type to a DTD, follow these steps:

1. Start the assignment by typing **<!ATTLIST** and then specify the name of the element the attribute relates to.
2. Enter the name of the `IDREFS` attribute. The name must be a valid XML name.
3. Type **IDREFS** and then set the default usage as `#REQUIRED`. The required type is the best in most cases.
4. Complete the assignment by typing >.

The result should follow this format:

```
<!ATTLIST element_describing attrib_name IDREFS #REQUIRED>
```

Chapter 6

XML Entities and Notations in DTDs

In addition to elements and attributes, document type definitions (DTDs) can contain entity and notation declarations. In this chapter you'll learn how to declare and use both of these declaration types. Since encoded characters are similar to entities, this chapter also discusses encoded characters.

Getting Started with Entities and Notations

In its basic form, an entity is a component, based on a declaration, that can be substituted into a document. The component can be a text string or any type of file. Because entities allow text and files to be substituted into a document, you can use entities to replace values when a document is displayed. Notations are used with certain types of entities to specify external identifiers that are used to help process entity contents. This could be a Multipurpose Internet Mail Extension (MIME) type that specifies the media type of an entity, a Uniform Resource Locator (URL) to an external application that can handle the entity content, or anything else that you want to notate about an entity.

Entities are the most complex structures you'll work with when creating DTDs. As Figure 6-1 shows, entities are organized into two broad categories:

- **General entities** Shortcut references to text or data that should be substituted into a document. They're defined in a DTD and are used in the body of an XML document or in DTD text that'll be used in the body of an XML document.
- **Parameter entities** Shortcut references to parts of a DTD that should be substituted into a DTD. They're defined in a DTD and used in a DTD.

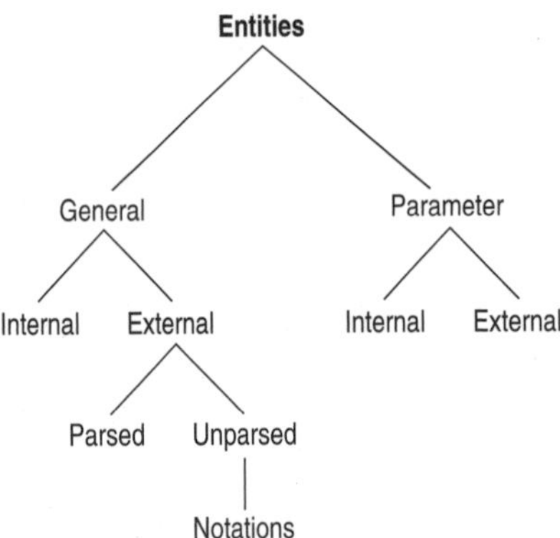

Figure 6-1. *Overview of available entity types.*

General entities have two categories as well: internal and external. Internal general entities are always text values and are always defined in a DTD. They provide shortcut references to text that should be substituted into a document. On the other hand, external general entities can be text or another type of data, such as the source for an image, and they're always stored in an external file. They provide shortcut references to data files that should be substituted into a document.

Note In previous chapters you worked with predefined entities where an escaped value, such as `&`, is replaced with its actual value when the document is processed. Predefined entities are examples of internal general entities—although they're built in and don't need to be declared, unlike all other entities, which must be declared.

External general entities can be either parsed or unparsed. The XML processor analyzes parsed entities as the document is processed. Unparsed entities are passed to the application handling the document without parsing. In most cases parsed entities will point to text, including markup or other entities, that must be processed, and unparsed entities will point to nontext data, such as an image file.

Parameter entities can also be internally or externally defined. Internal parameter entities provide shortcuts to commonly referenced parts of a DTD so that it can be substituted where needed without having to reenter the same values repeatedly. External parameter entities provide shortcuts to external DTD subsets so that you can include a DTD in another DTD. You'll find that parameter entities come in handy when you're creating new DTDs or working to incorporate existing DTDs into your organization's DTDs. Unlike general entities, which can be either parsed or unparsed, parameter entities are always parsed.

Table 6-1 provides a quick reference for the five entity types. You define entities using the `ENTITY` assignment. The basic format of an `ENTITY` assignment is:

```
<!ENTITY entity_name entity_content>
```

where *`entity_name`* is the entity's name and *`entity_content`* is the entity's content.

Table 6-1. Entity Types in DTDs

Category	Type	Description
General	Internal parsed	DTD-defined text values that should be substituted into a document
	External parsed	Externally defined text that should be substituted into a document
	External unparsed	Nontext data that should be substituted into a document without processing by the XML parser
Parameter	Internal parsed	A shortcut reference to part of the current DTD so that it can be substituted without having to reenter a value
	External parsed	A shortcut reference to an external DTD subset that should be substituted into the current DTD

Another structure that you can use with entities is called a *notation*. Notations provide additional information about the format of a document's unparsed contents and, as such, are most commonly used with external unparsed general entities. You can also use notations with processing instructions and some attribute values.

XML parsers don't use notations. Instead, notations are passed on to the application handling the document so that the application can use the information to properly interpret unparsed contents. Notations used with entities follow this general format:

```
<!NOTATION notation_name SYSTEM "content_descriptor">
```

where *`notation_name`* is the notation's name, `SYSTEM` is a reserved keyword that indicates the entity is defined in another document, and *`content_descriptor`* describes the content you're embedding. In most cases the descriptor is a MIME type that specifies the content media type so that an application can process the data appropriately.

Notations by themselves don't guarantee that an application will know how to handle the unparsed data or that the application will process the data in any way. The application must be designed to handle the referenced data type and it must be running in a mode where handling that data makes sense. If an application is running in an automated mode or there's no display of the data to a user, processing a data file containing an image may not make any sense.

As you set out to work with entities and notations, keep in mind that entities and notations that are part of an internal DTD will be read by both validating and nonvalidating parsers. However, only validating parsers are guaranteed to read external files. This means that a nonvalidating parser may or may not read externally specified entities.

Tip You can create external DTD files that contain only entity references. If so, name the DTD files with the .ent file extension and then import the entities into a document using an external parameter entity reference. For an example, see the "Creating Entities to Reference Characters" section of this chapter.

Working with General Entities in DTDs

As discussed previously, three types of general entities are available:

- Internal parsed general entities
- External parsed general entities
- External unparsed general entities

Techniques for using these entity types are discussed in the following sections.

Using Internal General Entities

Internal general entities provide replacement text or markup that can be substituted into a document and are designed to make document maintenance easier. You should use internal general entities to define common elements for sets of documents. For example, you could define the organization's name, address, and phone number using internal general entities. Then if this information ever changed, you'd only need to update the DTD to ensure that all documents using the DTD reflected the changes.

Defining Substitution Text

Entity references are declared with an `ENTITY` declaration in the DTD. The declaration gives the entity's name and the entity's replacement text. The entity name must be a valid XML name and the replacement text must be enclosed in quotation marks. Following this, the declarations for an organization's name, address, and phone number might look like this:

```
<!ENTITY companyName "Microsoft Corporation">
<!ENTITY companyAddress
 "One Microsoft Way, Redmond, WA 98052-6399">
<!ENTITY companyPhone "(425) 882-8080">
```

Once these declarations are made, you can use the entities anywhere within the DTD or the document itself instead of typing in the actual value. To do this, you precede the entity name with an ampersand (&) and add a semicolon (;) to the end of the entity name. For example, you'd enter:

- **&companyName;** for the company name
- **&companyAddress;** for the company address
- **&companyPhone;** for the company phone number

If you use an internal general entity in a DTD, the entity must be placed in a location where it'll eventually be placed in the body of the document. This means you could use an internal general entity to set an attribute's value, such as:

```
<!ATTLIST origin CDATA #FIXED "&companyName;">
```

However, you can't use it as part of the content model for an element or any other part of the DTD that won't be placed in the body of the document. This means the following usage is incorrect:

```
<!ELEMENT contact_info
 (&companyName;,&companyAddress;,&companyPhone;)>
```

To use an entity in this way, you must define an internal parameter entity.

Defining Markup for Replacement

Because internal general entities are parsed, they can also contain markup. You could, for example, use an entity to create a common header and footer for documents. A common document header may look like this:

```
<!ENTITY header '<h1>XML Pocket Consultant</h1>
<p>written by William R. Stanek</p>
<hr size="2" />
'>
```

and the footer may look like this:

```
<!ENTITY footer '<hr size="2" />
<p align="center">Copyright 2001 William R. Stanek,
 Microsoft Corporation.</p>
<p align="center">All Rights Reserved</p>
<p>If you have any questions, please send mail to One Microsoft
 Way, Redmond, WA 98052-6399 or phone (425) 882-8080.</p>
'>
```

These entities would be referenced as `&header;` and `&footer;`, respectively, in the body of a document.

The key to using markup with entities is to remember that the markup must be a well-formed unit that contains the necessary beginning and ending tags, or is represented as an empty element. This is the case even when you're using HTML tags that aren't normally closed. For example, in standard HTML you can use the `<p>` and `<br>` tags to represent a paragraph and line break respectively without having to complete either tag. In XML (and in Extensible HyperText Markup Language [XHTML]), the paragraph tag must be used with the begin tag `<p>` and the end tag `</p>`, and the line break tag must be represented using the empty tag `<br />`. Additionally, you can't place the begin tag of an element in one entity and the end tag of the element in another entity.

Note Requiring that markup be a well-formed unit doesn't mean that the markup must have a root element. The document has its own root element.

Internal General Entities Dos and Don'ts

If the text or markup contains quotation marks, you must be sure that the entity declaration uses a different quotation mark style—either single quotation marks or double quotation marks as appropriate—or you must replace the in-text quotation marks with the appropriate predefined entity reference. Because the header and footer created previously use double quotation marks when assigning values to the HTML attributes, I used single quotation marks to mark the start and end of the entity text.

The replacement text an entity defines can contain entity references. When the document is parsed, these entity references will be replaced with their actual values as well. For example, I could have referenced the company name, address, and phone number entities in the footer entity. If so, the new declaration for the footer would look like this:

```
<!ENTITY footer '<hr size="2" />
<p align="center">Copyright 2001 William R. Stanek,
 &companyName;.</p>
<p align="center">All Rights Reserved</p>
<p>If you have any questions, please send mail to
 &companyAddress;
 or phone &companyPhone;.</p>
'>
```

Keep in mind that circular or self-referencing declarations are forbidden. This means that you should not define the footer declaration as:

```
<!ENTITY footer '<hr size="2" />
<p align="center">Copyright 2001 William R. Stanek,
 &companyName;.</p>
<p align="center">All Rights Reserved</p>
 &footer;
'>
```

It also means that you can't reference an entity that references another entity that eventually references the same entity, such as:

```
<!ENTITY companyContactInfo "&companyName; &companyData;>
<!ENTITY companyName "Microsoft Corporation">
<!ENTITY companyData "&companyContactInfo; &companyAddress;">
<!ENTITY companyAddress
 "One Microsoft Way, Redmond, WA 98052-6399">
```

Here, the company contact information entity references the `companyName` and `companyData` entities. The `companyData` entity in turn references back to the `companyContactInfo` entity, creating an illegal circular reference.

Defining the Internal General Entity in a DTD

To define an internal general entity in a DTD, follow these steps:

1. Start the assignment by typing **<!ENTITY** and then specify the name of the entity. The entity name must follow the rules for valid XML names as specified in Chapter 2, "XML Document Structure."
2. Type the entity text, making sure to enclose the text in single or double quotation marks as appropriate.
3. Complete the assignment by typing >.

The result should follow this format:

```
<!ENTITY entity_name "text">
```

To use the entity in the body of a document, type an ampersand, followed by the name of the entity, and then type a semicolon. The result should follow this format:

```
&entity_name;
```

Using External Parsed General Entities

When you want to substitute lengthy sections of text or markup into a document, the best way to do this is to use an external parsed general entity. With this type of entity, the necessary text or markup is stored in an external file that's loaded when the page is processed by the application handling the document. In most cases this means that a client machine rather than a server is responsible for getting all the document components and putting them together.

External Parsed General Entity Dos and Don'ts

External parsed general entities follow the same rules as internal parsed general entities. This means that

- Markup must be a well-formed unit that contains the necessary beginning and ending tags. You can't place the begin tag of an element in one entity and the end tag of the element in another entity. It doesn't mean, however, that the markup must have a root element. The document has its own root element.
- If the text or markup contains quotation marks, you must be sure that the entity declaration uses a different quotation mark style—either single quotation marks or double quotation marks as appropriate or you must replace the in-text quotation marks with the appropriate predefined entity reference.
- The replacement text can contain entity references. When the document is parsed, these entity references will be replaced with their actual values as well.

- Circular or self-referencing declarations are forbidden. This means that you can't reference an entity within its own text and you can't reference an entity that references another entity that eventually references the same entity.

Declaring External Parsed General Entities

External parsed general entities are declared using the `ENTITY` declaration. However, instead of using the actual replacement text, the declaration uses the `SYSTEM` keyword and provides a Uniform Resource Indicator (URI) to an external file containing the replacement text. In most cases, the URI is an absolute URL that specifies the complete server path to the file, such as:

```
<!ENTITY substData SYSTEM "http://www.microsoft.com/data/sub.xml">
```

or a relative URL, such as:

```
<!ENTITY substData SYSTEM "/data/sub.xml">
```

To use the entity in a document, you'd reference it as `&substData;`, and a validating parser processing the document would replace the entity reference with the contents of the external file you specified in the DTD. A nonvalidating parser, however, may or may not retrieve the externally specified file. No substitution is made when a nonvalidating parser doesn't retrieve the file.

Creating the External File for the Entity

Files used with external parsed general entities can't contain an XML declaration or a `DOCTYPE` declaration. They can contain only the text or markup that will be substituted into the document and a text declaration that specifies their encoding. The optional text declaration allows you to use various encoding types for external files.

In most cases the text declaration uses the following form:

```
<?xml encoding="enc_type">
```

but you can also use this form:

```
<?xml version="version" encoding="enc_type">
```

This means the following example is a correctly formatted text declaration:

```
<?xml encoding="ISO-8859-1">
```

as is this text declaration:

```
<?xml version="1.0" encoding="ISO-8859-1">
```

However, the following declaration is incorrect because it includes the `standalone` attribute:

```
<?xml version="1.0" encoding="ISO-8859-1" standalone="no"?>
```

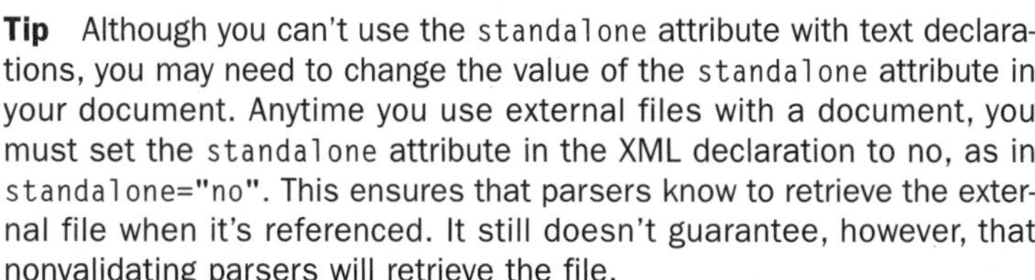

Tip Although you can't use the `standalone` attribute with text declarations, you may need to change the value of the `standalone` attribute in your document. Anytime you use external files with a document, you must set the `standalone` attribute in the XML declaration to no, as in `standalone="no"`. This ensures that parsers know to retrieve the external file when it's referenced. It still doesn't guarantee, however, that nonvalidating parsers will retrieve the file.

If included, the text declaration should be on the first line of the external file and should be followed by the contents of the file, as shown in the following example:

```
<?xml  encoding="ISO-8859-1">
<!ENTITY footer '<hr size="2" />
<p align="center">Copyright 2001 William R. Stanek,
 Microsoft Corporation.</p>
<p align="center">All Rights Reserved</p>
'>
```

Defining the External Parsed General Entity in a DTD

To define an external parsed general entity in a DTD, follow these steps:

1. Start the assignment by typing **<!ENTITY** and then specify the name of the external entity. The entity name must follow the rules for valid XML names as specified in Chapter 2.
2. Type **SYSTEM** and then type the URI to the external file containing the substitution markup or text. Be sure to enclose the URI in single or double quotation marks.
3. Complete the assignment by typing >.

The result should follow this format:

```
<!ENTITY entity_name SYSTEM "URI">
```

To use the entity in the body of a document, type an ampersand, followed by the name of the entity, and then type a semicolon. The result should follow this format:

```
&entity_name;
```

Using External Unparsed General Entities

Whenever you need to insert nontext or non-XML content into an XML document, you can use external unparsed general entities. With this type of entity, the data is passed directly to the application, bypassing the XML parser. This means the XML parser doesn't look at the data and instead relies on the application to handle the data appropriately. Keep in mind that the application must be able to handle the data, or else the data won't be displayed or interpreted in any way.

Real World As you set out to use external unparsed general entities, you'll find that they're complex and confusing. Don't worry, they aren't the only way to insert unparsed content into XML documents. You can link in content in other ways as well. One way to do this would be to use a URL associated with an *Xlink*. XLink is a language specification that defines methods for creating relationships between document instances or document elements. You can think of an XLink as a very advanced hypertext reference.

Declaring External Unparsed General Entities

External unparsed general entities are often used to reference data sources, such as GIF or JPEG images, that should be embedded in a document. They could also reference plain text that's to be embedded in a document without parsing. Although these data sources are part of the document, the XML parser doesn't process them—the XML parser wouldn't know what to do with the data anyway.

Two declarations are necessary to fully specify an external unparsed general entity. The first declaration is a notation that provides additional information about the unparsed contents and will be referenced in the actual entity declaration. The notation follows the form:

```
<!NOTATION notation_name SYSTEM "content_descriptor">
```

The second declaration specifies the entity itself. The format for the entity declaration is:

```
<!ENTITY entity_name SYSTEM "URI" NDATA notation_name>
```

To put this together, consider the case where you have a corporate logo that you want to include with all images. The corporate logo is created as a GIF image and stored in a file called corp_logo.gif. Knowing this, you could create a notation called `gif` that provides the image MIME type as the content descriptor. The notation would look like this:

```
<!NOTATION gif SYSTEM "image/gif">
```

You could then declare an entity called `corp_logo` that references the logo file and the related notation:

```
<!ENTITY corp_logo SYSTEM "../images/corp_logo.gif" NDATA gif>
```

To specify unparsed content in a DTD, follow these steps:

1. In the DTD, start the entity assignment by typing **<!ENTITY** and then specify the name of the external entity. The entity name must follow the rules for valid XML names as specified in Chapter 2.
2. Type **SYSTEM** and then type the URI to the external file containing the unparsed content. Be sure to enclose the URI in single or double quotation marks.

3. Type **NDATA** and then enter the name of the notation that will describe the unparsed contents. The notation name must follow the rules for valid XML names.
4. Complete the entity assignment by typing >.
5. On the next line in the DTD, start the notation assignment by typing **<!NOTATION** and then specify the name of the notation. This name must be the same as specified earlier.
6. Type **SYSTEM** and then type the content descriptor that identifies the data you're embedding. Be sure to enclose the descriptor in single or double quotation marks.
7. Complete the notation assignment by typing >.

The result should follow this format:

```
<!ENTITY entity_name SYSTEM "URI" NDATA notation_name>
<!NOTATION notation_name SYSTEM "content_descriptor">
```

Embedding Unparsed Content in Documents

After you define an entity for your unparsed contents, you can embed it in your XML document. Unparsed entities don't have entity references. This means you don't enter them in the form `&entity_name;`. Instead, you reference the unparsed entity as part of a specially declared attribute. This type of attribute is called an entity attribute.

Entity attributes have two different declaration keywords: `ENTITY` and `ENTITIES`. You use the first form when you want to reference a single unparsed data source. You use the second when you want to reference multiple unparsed data sources.

Declaring ENTITY Attributes You specify a single data source using the `ENTITY` declaration keyword as part of the attribute declaration. In the following example, you declare a source attribute for an image element and provide an entity attribute:

```
<!ELEMENT image EMPTY>
<!ATTLIST image source ENTITY #REQUIRED>
```

The corresponding entity and notation declarations are:

```
<!ENTITY corp_logo SYSTEM "../images/corp_logo.gif" NDATA gif>
<!NOTATION gif SYSTEM "image/gif">
```

Once you've made these declarations, you can specify the image in a document. To do this, you set the entity name as the value for the source attribute, such as:

```
<image source="corp_logo" />
```

You could declare an entity attribute as `#IMPLIED` or `#FIXED` as well. The `#IMPLIED` value indicates the attribute is optional and has no default value. The `#FIXED` value indicates the attribute has a fixed default value that's specified in the DTD (but can be overridden by providing a new value). Following this, here's another way to make the declarations that display a corporate logo:

```
<!ELEMENT logo EMPTY>
<!ATTLIST logo source ENTITY #FIXED "corp_logo">
```

You would also use these declarations:

```
<!ENTITY corp_logo SYSTEM "../images/corp_logo.gif" NDATA gif>
<!NOTATION gif SYSTEM "image/gif">
```

In the document, you could declare the `logo` element as:

```
<logo />
```

or

```
<logo source="corp_logo" />
```

To declare an `ENTITY` attribute to reference unparsed content, follow these steps:

1. In the DTD, make the entity and notation assignments as specified in the "Declaring External Unparsed General Entities" section of this chapter. Afterward, define the element that will contain the attribute used to reference the unparsed content.
2. Type **<!ATTLIST** and then specify the name of the element declared in Step 1.
3. Enter the attribute's name. The name must be a valid XML name as specified in Chapter 2.
4. Type **ENTITY** to indicate that this attribute can contain references to unparsed contents.
5. Optionally, set the default usage as `#IMPLIED`, `#FIXED`, or `#REQUIRED`.
6. If you didn't specify an implied or required type, enter a literal value in quotation marks that will serve as the default.
7. Complete the assignment by typing >.

The result should follow this format:

```
<!ATTLIST element_name attrib_name ENTITY usage>
```

You can then embed the content in a document by adding the attribute to the related element. To add the entity attribute to an element, follow these steps:

1. After the name of the element in the opening tag and before the closing >, type ***attribute=***, where *attribute* is the name of the entity attribute you're adding to the tag.
2. Specify the value for the attribute using either single or double quotation marks, such as "value" or 'value'. Be sure to use the value assigned to the entity reference.

The result should look like this:

```
<element_name attrib_name="value"></element_name>
```

or

```
<element_name attrib_name="value" />
```

Declaring ENTITIES Attributes In some cases you'll want to reference multiple data sources instead of a single data source as part of the unparsed content you want to add to documents. To do this, you use the ENTITIES declaration keyword as part of the attribute declaration. You use ENTITIES attributes in the same way you use ENTITY attributes. You start with an element declaration and provide an ENTITIES attribute declaration, such as:

```
<!ELEMENT top_menu EMPTY>
<!ATTLIST top_menu source ENTITIES #REQUIRED>
```

Then you create the necessary entity and notation declarations, such as:

```
<!ENTITY corp_logo SYSTEM "../images/corp_logo.gif" NDATA gif>
<!ENTITY back SYSTEM "../images/back.gif" NDATA gif>
<!ENTITY next SYSTEM "../images/next.gif" NDATA gif>
<!ENTITY home SYSTEM "../images/home.gif" NDATA gif>
<!NOTATION gif SYSTEM "image/gif">
```

Because the source attribute is defined as an ENTITIES attribute, you can enter multiple entity references as part of the attribute value of the related element. The key is that each reference must be separated by a space, such as:

```
<top_menu source="corp_logo back home next" />
```

Otherwise, ENTITIES attributes are the same as ENTITY attributes. This means you can declare them as #IMPLIED, #REQUIRED, or #FIXED. You could also set a literal default value if you like.

To declare an ENTITIES attribute to reference unparsed content, follow these steps:

1. In the DTD, make the entity and notation assignments as specified in the "Declaring External Unparsed General Entities" section of this chapter. Afterward, define the element that will contain the attribute used to reference the unparsed content.
2. Type **<!ATTLIST** and then specify the name of the element declared in Step 1.
3. Enter the name of the attribute. The name must be a valid XML name as specified in Chapter 2.
4. Type **ENTITIES** to indicate that this attribute can contain references to unparsed contents.
5. Optionally, set the default usage as #IMPLIED, #FIXED, or #REQUIRED.
6. If you didn't specify an implied or required type, enter a literal value in quotation marks that will serve as the default.
7. Complete the assignment by typing >.

The result should follow this format:

```
<!ATTLIST element_name attrib_name ENTITIES usage>
```

You can then embed the content in a document by adding the attribute to the related element. The steps you follow to add the entity attribute to an element are as follows:

1. After the name of the element in the opening tag and before the closing >, type ***attribute=***, where *attribute* is the name of the entity attribute you're adding to the tag.
2. Specify the value for the attribute using either single or double quotation marks. If you're entering multiple values, separate each value with a space, such as "value1 value2 value3" or 'value1 value2 value3'.

The result should look like this:

```
<element_name attrib_name="value1 value2 ... valueN">
</element_name>
```

or

```
<element_name attrib_name="value1 value2 ... valueN" />
```

Working with Parameter Entities in DTDs

You can use two types of parameter entities: internal or external. Both types of entities act as shortcut references to DTD subsets and are always parsed. There are no unparsed parameter entities.

Using Internal Parameter Entities

When you create DTDs, you'll often find that elements have common attributes or content. Although you could handle this by repeating the content as necessary throughout the DTD, this makes the DTD larger and more complex than necessary—and larger, more complex DTDs are more difficult to maintain and implement than smaller, less complex DTDs.

Instead of repeating parts of a DTD, you can create internal parameter entities that represent the common or shared sections and then reference the entities in the places where you'd otherwise repeat the values. You now have one location to make changes to common or repeated elements—the parameter entity declaration—and can more easily maintain and implement the DTD.

To see how internal parameter entities could be used, consider the case where you're defining elements to handle contact information as part of a purchase order system. In this DTD you could have the following declarations for businesses, contacts, and persons:

```
<!ELEMENT business (name, street_address, city, state,
 zip, phone*, email*, web*, other*)>

<!ELEMENT contact (name, street_address, city, state,
 zip, phone*, email*, web*, other*)>

<!ELEMENT person (name, street_address, city, state,
 zip, phone*, email*, web*, other*)>
```

What the business, contact, and person elements have in common is that they all have names and addresses as well as other possible information, such as phone numbers and e-mail addresses, which is optional. Because you could have many other classifications of contacts, it doesn't make sense to keep repeating the common aspects of these elements. Instead, you could declare internal parameter entities that could be used to reference this information.

You declare internal parameter entities much like internal general entities. The key difference is that you place a percent sign (%) between the ENTITY keyword and the entity name. The following example defines one entity for standard contact information and another for optional contact information:

```
<!ENTITY % contact_info "name, street_address, city, state, zip">
<!ENTITY % opt_info "phone*, email*, web*, other*">
```

Once you've made these declarations, you can use the entities in the DTD. To do this, you precede entity name with a percent sign (%) and add a semicolon (;) to the end of the entity name. For example, you could rewrite the business, contact, and person element definitions like this:

```
<!ELEMENT business (%contact_info;, %opt_info;)>
<!ELEMENT contact (%contact_info;, %opt_info;)>
<!ELEMENT person (%contact_info;, %opt_info;)>
```

You can also use internal parameter entities for attribute contents. When an XML parser reads the entity declaration in a DTD, the entity reference is replaced by its actual value. Because you're replacing only part of a declaration, the DTD must be declared externally, however, and not be part of the actual internal DTD subset of a document. An external DTD is one that's defined in a separate document and is imported into the document in which it's used.

With internal DTD subsets, internal parameter entities are used to replace complete declarations—not just a part of a declaration. This means that the ways in which you can use internal parameter entities are very limited. The only real use for internal parameter entities within an internal DTD subset is to point to the complete markup declaration for an external parameter entity.

To define an internal parameter entity in a DTD, follow these steps:

1. Start the assignment by typing **<!ENTITY** and then specify the name of the internal parameter entity. The entity name must follow the rules for valid XML names as specified in Chapter 2.
2. Type **%**, followed by a space, and then enter the name of the entity.
3. Type the entity text, making sure to enclose the text in single or double quotation marks as appropriate.
4. Complete the assignment by typing **>**.

The result should follow this format:

```
<!ENTITY % entity_name "text">
```

To use the entity in a DTD, type a percent sign (**%**), followed by the name of the entity, and then type a semicolon. The result should follow this format:

```
%entity_name;
```

Using External Parameter Entities

External parameter entities provide shortcuts to external DTD subsets so that you can include a DTD in another DTD. You'll find that external parameter entities come in handy when you want to include a standard DTD in your organization's DTD. Unlike internal parameter entities, you can use external parameter entities with both internally and externally specified DTDs.

You declare and use external parameter entities much like internal parameter entities. The external parameter entity declaration starts with the `ENTITY` keyword and uses a percent sign (`%`). This is followed by the `SYSTEM` keyword to indicate that the entity source comes from an external file, and then you specify the URI for the file within quotation marks. The following example defines an external parameter entity called `purchase_system`:

```
<!ENTITY % purchase_system SYSTEM "http://www.microsoft.com/xml/
 ps.dtd">
```

Although the necessary DTD file in this example comes from an absolute location, a relative location could have been used as well, such as:

```
<!ENTITY % purchase_system SYSTEM "ps.dtd">
```

Once the entity declaration is made, you can use the entity reference to insert the contents of the ps.dtd file in the current DTD. To do this, you precede the entity name with a percent sign (`%`) and add a semicolon (`;`) to the end of the entity name, such as:

```
%purchase_system;
```

To define an external parameter entity in a DTD, follow these steps:

1. Start the assignment by typing **<!ENTITY** and then specify the name of the internal parameter entity. The entity name must follow the rules for valid XML names as specified in Chapter 2.
2. Type **%**, followed by a space, and then enter the name of the entity.
3. Type **SYSTEM** and then specify the location of the DTD file. Be sure to enclose the file location in quotation marks.
4. Complete the assignment by typing >.

The result should follow this format:

```
<!ENTITY % entity_name SYSTEM "URI">
```

To use the entity in a DTD, type a percent sign (%), followed by the name of the entity, and then type a semicolon. The result should follow this format:

```
%entity_Name;
```

Using Encoded Characters

XML supports the Unicode character set, which has nearly 50,000 characters, but the XML standard lets you choose the character set that will be used in a document through the encoding attribute of the document's XML declaration or other text declarations made in the document's body. If you want to use characters that aren't in the character set for the document, you have several options. The key options are to:

- Set the language for individual elements using the `xml:lang` attribute
- Use character references

Setting Language Encoding with xml:lang

You use the `xml:lang` attribute to specify the language in which the content of an element is written. This attribute is predefined for all elements defined in the XML standard. The value for the `xml:lang` attribute is a two-letter language code from International Organization for Standardization (ISO) 639-1 or a language identifier registered with the Internet Assigned Numbers Authority (IANA). The following example sets the language for the element's contents to U.S. English:

```
<data xml:lang="en">
</data>
```

You could also set the language to French:

```
<data xml:lang="fr">
</data>
```

or Greek:

```
<data xml:lang="el">
</data>
```

Declaring the xml:lang Attribute for Validated Documents

Although `xml:lang` is a predefined attribute, you must still declare it in the DTD of valid documents, and you must do so on a per element basis. The reason for this is that you must declare all attributes used with all elements for a document to be considered valid. With this in mind, you could declare the `data` element used in previous examples as follows:

```
<!ELEMENT data (#PCDATA)>
<!ATTLIST data xml:lang NMTOKEN #IMPLIED>
```

Here, the `xml:lang` attribute is declared as a name token to ensure that the attribute value follows the naming rules for valid name tokens. Among other things, this prevents using spaces in the value.

You could also declare the `xml:lang` attribute as `#FIXED`, `#REQUIRED`, or as a literal value. The following is an example of a fixed value:

```
<!ELEMENT data (#PCDATA)>
<!ATTLIST data xml:lang NMTOKEN #FIXED "fr">
```

The following is an example of a required value:

```
<!ELEMENT data (#PCDATA)>
<!ATTLIST data xml:lang NMTOKEN #REQUIRED>
```

The following is an example of a literal value:

```
<!ELEMENT data (#PCDATA)>
<!ATTLIST data xml:lang "fr">
```

Another way to declare the `xml:lang` attribute would be as an enumerated type with several predefined values and a default, such as:

```
<!ELEMENT data (#PCDATA)>
<!ATTLIST data xml:lang (en | fr | el) "en">
```

Here you could use U.S. English, French, or Greek character sets if you set the `xml:lang` attribute to `"en"`, `"fr"`, or `"el"`, respectively. Or use the default value "`en`" for U.S. English.

Specifying Character References

Once you set the encoding, you can use any characters in the related character set. For characters not in the character set you're using, XML lets you use character references to specify the character that you need.

Referencing encoded characters is similar to referencing entities. Character references specify the decimal or hexadecimal value of a particular Unicode character. To refer to characters using decimal notation, enter the Unicode character value in the form:

&#*Number*;

where Number is the decimal position of the character in the Unicode character set, such as:

```
&#246;
```

To refer to characters using hexadecimal notation, enter the Unicode character value in the form:

```
&#xHex;
```

where `Hex` is the hexadecimal position of the character in the Unicode character set, such as:

```
&#xF6;
```

You can place character references anywhere you'd place actual text values in the DTD or document body.

More Info You'll find a complete listing of the Unicode character set online at *http://www.unicode.org/charts/*.

Creating Entities to Reference Characters

If you find that you use particular characters frequently, you may want to declare the character references as actual entities and then refer to the entities. Because you set the name for these entities, the entities should be easier to remember than the values for the characters you want to use. For example, you may find that you frequently use the copyright, trademark, and registered trademark characters. If so, you could create entity references for these characters like this:

```
<!ENTITY tm "&#x2122;">
<!ENTITY copy "&#xA9;">
<!ENTITY reg "&#xAE;">
```

You could then use the entities in your XML documents just like other entities. As part of an internal DTD, these entities would be processed by both validating and nonvalidating parsers, and you can be sure that the entities will be available in the document. As part of an external DTD, you can guarantee only that a validating parser will read the externally specified DTD file. Nonvalidating parsers, however, may or may not read the external file.

Keep in mind that it's standard practice to name external DTD files that only contain entity references with the .ent file extension and then import the entities into the document using an external parameter entity reference. The following example shows a document that uses this technique:

```
<?xml version="1.0" standalone="no"?>
<!DOCTYPE purchase_order PUBLIC "-//Stanek//PO Specification//EN"
 "http://www.microsoft.com/xml/pospec.dtd">
```

(continued)

(continued)

```
[
<!ENTITY % purchase_system SYSTEM "http://www.microsoft.com/xml/
 ps.ent">
 %purchase_system;

]>

<purchase_order>
 <customer>
  <accountid>10-487</accountid>
  <name>
   <first>William</first>
   <mi>R</mi>
   <last>Stanek</last>
  </name>
 </customer>
 <data>&copy; 2002 Microsoft Corporation</data>
</purchase_order>
```

Here, the ps.ent file contains externally specified entities that are imported into the DTD with the `%purchase_system;` entity reference. Because the copy entity is declared in this file, the `©` reference is replaced with the copyright character.

More Info Standard entity subsets are freely available for many types of character sets. The W3 and Unicode Web sites at *http://www.w3.org/* and *http://www.unicode.org/* are good starting points to find these entity subsets.

Chapter 7

XML Namespaces

Namespaces are an extremely important part of XML. You use namespaces to prevent naming conflicts when like-named elements and attributes are associated with different types of data structures and are used in the same document. In this chapter you'll learn the essential concepts for working with namespaces and how you can use namespaces. You'll also learn how to use namespaces with XML structures declared in document type definition (DTDs). Namespaces can just as easily be applied to XML schemas, which I'll discuss in Chapter 8, "XML Schemas," Chapter 9, "Defining Simple Types in Schema," and Chapter 10, "Specifying Datatypes and Restrictions in Schema."

Understanding Namespaces

Whenever you combine documents that define different types of elements, you might find that like-named elements are used in different contexts and that this causes problems interpreting the documents. For example, in one section of a document you might have a `title` element that describes a book's title and in another section you might have a `title` element that describes a person's job title. Because the `title` elements have different meanings and might have different attributes as well, there's a problem in the associated documents. Validation software might not be able to validate the documents. Applications that are processing the documents might not be able to appropriately interpret the data. People reading the documents might get confused.

One solution to this problem would be to assign different names to elements wherever there's a conflict. Following this, you could change the first `name` element to `person_name` and the second `name` element to `item_name` and then look for and resolve other conflicts. Next, you'd need to update all the affected documents and DTDs in order to replace the old element names with the new element names. Afterward, you might need to modify applications and programs that work with the data to recognize the new elements. When you finish all this, you'll need to revalidate documents and processes. In short, what you'd discover as you worked through such an update process is that making changes to existing DTDs, documents, and applications is time-consuming and tedious. You'd also find that there'd be nothing that would prevent naming conflicts from reoccurring, which means that you might have to go through this process all over again whenever you integrate or work with different types of documents.

At the end of the process, you'd be asking yourself if there were a better way—and, believe me, there is—and this is where namespaces come into the picture. Namespaces help avoid naming conflicts within documents by assigning a universal prefix to elements and attributes. The namespace prefix allows XML parsers, applications, and other software processing or handling documents to distinguish like-named elements and attributes from one another. It's also used to group related elements and attributes together so that they can be handled appropriately.

Namespaces are defined in the Namespaces in XML specification, which was introduced after XML 1.0. Because of this, XML 1.0-compliant processors and applications might not be able to understand namespace structures you use in documents, and, as such, they might not be able to take advantage of the benefits offered by namespaces. In most cases, however, these noncompliant processors and applications shouldn't have problems reading documents that contain namespace definitions. Namespaces for XML was designed so that it wouldn't cause problems with existing processors and applications. The namespace prefix follows the rules for valid XML names, and the namespace qualifier (`:`) is a legal character.

Namespace-aware processors, on the other hand, fully understand the XML 1.0 and Namespaces in XML specifications. To ensure compliance with both specifications, these processors add checks to the normal well-formedness checks that XML processors perform. These checks

- Ensure that all namespace prefixes are defined appropriately. Documents that have improperly defined namespace prefixes fail the well-formedness test and are rejected.
- Ensure that all names used in XML structures follow the namespace constraints defined in the XML for Namespaces specification. These constraints define additional rules for names that are considered valid. Namespace constraints for valid names state the following:
    - Element and attribute names can't contain more than one colon.
    - Entity names, processor instruction targets, and notation names can't contain any colons.
    - Attribute values declared as type `ID`, `IDREF`, `IDREFS`, `ENTITY`, `ENTITIES`, and `NOTATION` can't contain colons. However, only validating processors will detect and report this type of naming error.
- Ensure that namespace problems are reported.

Otherwise, namespace-aware processors behave just like other XML processors. This means all the other rules for XML still apply.

Namespaces are applied in XML documents using qualified names. A qualified name is a complete name, including the colon, and has the general form:

`namespace_prefix:local_part`

As you can see from the example, a qualified name has two segments that are separated by a colon. These segments include a

- **Namespace prefix** Consists of the characters before the colon and identifies the namespace to which the element or attribute belongs
- **Local part** Consists of the characters after the colon and identifies the particular element or attribute within the designated namespace

When namespaces are used, elements and attributes have names that contain exactly one colon, such as:

- **xsl:stylesheet** An example referencing the stylesheet element in the Extensible Stylesheet Language (XSL) namespace
- **xlink:type** An example referencing the type attribute in the XLink namespace
- **fo:block** An example referencing the block element in the XSL Formatting Objects (FO) namespace

Note In practice, you'll define namespaces for elements much more frequently than you will attributes. XLink is an exception because it defines many attributes that you can use with elements you define.

Most XML documents will use namespaces when they combine markup from multiple XML applications. A document may contain XML, XLinks used for linking, and XSL used for adding style. If so, you'd want to use namespaces to differentiate between standard XML elements you've defined and XLink and XSL elements. You'd do this using namespaces.

Namespace declarations must be associated with URIs. Processors use the URI to differentiate various namespaces and to determine which language and version is being used for XML applications, such as XSL Transformations (XSLT) and XSL Formatting Objects (XSL-FO). The URI that must be used with a particular application of XML is predefined. The URI identifies the organization responsible for the language specification and provides an arbitrarily assigned path. Together these are defined using a URI that's an absolute URL, such as:

http://www.w3.org/1999/XSL/Transform

where the W3 is the organization responsible as specified using the `w3.org` domain and `1999/XSL/Transform` is an arbitrarily assigned path that's used to refer to the language specification and version being used. In this case this is the XSLT version 1.0 specification.

When you create your own namespaces, the URI you use should identify your organization's domain and provide an arbitrary path as well. For Microsoft corporation, a URI for a namespace could be:

http://www.microsoft.com/XSGData

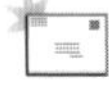

Note You don't have to use the http protocol. You could just as easily reference ftp, mailto, or gopher.

Regardless of whether the URI is for an XML application that refers to a specific implementation or is created by an organization or individual to reference a unique naming structure, the namespace URI is meant for identification only. The URI isn't meant to be the address of a Web page or to be used as a link. As such, you shouldn't expect to type the URL in a Web browser and find documentation—or any content at all, for that matter. Additionally, the URI doesn't have to point to a URL. You can use any type of URI.

Creating Namespaces

To create namespaces, you must

- Declare a namespace
- Associate the namespace with a URI
- Set\Determine the default namespace

These concepts are examined in this section.

Declaring Namespaces

You make namespace declarations by adding the appropriate namespace prefix to elements and attributes in documents. When you add the namespace prefix, you create a qualified name that follows the form:

`namespace_prefix:local_part`

where *`namespace_prefix`* is the namespace prefix being used and *`local_part`* is the name of the element or attribute you're working with. Both parts of a qualified name must follow the rules for valid XML names and must also conform to the additional constraint that they can't contain any colons—the only allowed colon is the one that separates the two name parts. This means that the following qualified name is valid:

```
myOrg:data
```

but the following qualified names are invalid:

```
my:Org:data:type
myOrg::data
```

When declaring namespaces, keep the following rules in mind:

1. Namespaces apply to the element where they're specified and to all elements within the content of that element, unless overridden by another namespace

declaration. Because of this, you could apply a single namespace declaration to a document's root element and thereby apply the namespace to the entire document.

2. Because attributes must be unique on a per element basis, you rarely need to assign namespaces to attributes. The only exception is with an application of XML, such as XLink, that defines attributes that you can use with elements. Here, you'd need to reference the xlink namespace to use the attributes that are defined in the XLink specification.

Namespace prefixes must be added uniformly. If an element has opening and closing tags, the namespace prefix must be added to both of these tags in the body of the document. The prefix must be separated from the element name with a colon, as shown in the following example:

```
<myOrg:book> Book Data </myOrg:book>
```

However, the following examples are incorrect:

```
<myOrg:book> Book Data </book>
```

```
<myOrgbook> Book Data </myOrgbook>
```

The first example doesn't use a qualified name for the closing element. The second example doesn't separate the prefix from the element name with a colon.

When you declare a namespace for an empty element, you add the namespace prefix only to the beginning of the element name, making sure to separate the prefix from the element name with a colon, such as:

```
<myOrg:image source="corp_logo" />
```

Because namespaces apply to the element where they're specified and to all elements within the content of that element, unless overridden, you can add a namespace declaration to a document's root element and thereby apply the namespace to the entire document. This means that if your original document looked like this:

```
<?xml version="1.0"?>
<book>
 <title>XHTML Pocket Consultant</title>
 <chapter number="3" title="XHTML Essentials">
 <creator>William R. Stanek</creator>
  <page> Page text.
  </page>
  <main_text> Main text.
  </main_text>
 </chapter>
</book>
```

and you wanted to add the myOrg namespace to the document, you could rewrite the document like this:

```
<?xml version="1.0"?>
<myOrg:book>
 <title>XHTML Pocket Consultant</title>
 <creator>William R. Stanek</creator>
 <chapter number="3" title="XHTML Essentials">
  <page> Page text.
  </page>
  <main_text> Main text.
  </main_text>
 </chapter>
</myOrg:book>
```

Now the myOrg namespace is the namespace for all elements in the document. Any elements or attributes that aren't in this namespace must declare a different namespace.

Note The example document doesn't associate a URI with the declared namespace. Because of this, the document can't be said to be valid. I'll add this declaration in the next section.

As explained in the previous discussion, you can declare a namespace for elements using the following technique:

1. Create the element by typing **<*prefix:element***, where *prefix* is the namespace designator you want to use and *element* is the name of the element you're creating.
2. If the namespace hasn't been defined yet, define it as specified in the "Associating URIs with Namespaces" or "Setting Default Namespaces" sections of this chapter.
3. Complete the element assignment as you normally would, making sure to end with > for an opening tag and /> for an empty tag.
4. If the element has an end tag, type **</*prefix:element*>** for the closing tag, where *prefix* is the namespace designator you want to use and *element* is the name of the element you're closing.

The result should look similar to the following:

```
<myOrg:book></myOrg:book>
```

Associating URIs with Namespaces

Every namespace that you declare in a document must have an associated URI. You associate a URI with a namespace by defining an `xmlns` attribute for prefixed elements or any parent element of a child element that uses the prefix. The `xmlns` attribute declaration specifies the namespace you're going to use and provides the URI as a quoted value, such as:

```
<xsl:stylesheet version="1.0" xmlns:xsl="http://www.w3.org/1999/
 XSL/Transform">
...
</xsl:stylesheet>
```

This declaration specifies the namespace for an XSL stylesheet that uses XSLT version 1.0. All XSLT elements in XSLT 1.0 stylesheets are associated with the `http://www.w3.org/1999/XSL/Transform` URI and use a namespace prefix of `xsl`. An XSLT processor would recognize the declared element and its child elements because the `xsl` prefix is bound to a URI defined in the XSLT 1.0 specification.

You'll find that most applications of XML, including XSLT and XSL-FO, reference a standard URI. The namespace declaration for XSL-FO looks like this:

```
<fo:root xmlns:fo="http://www.w3.org/1999/XSL/Format">
...
</fo:root>
```

This declaration specifies the namespace for an XSL-FO document that uses XSL-FO version 1.0. All XSL-FO elements in XSL-FO 1.0 documents are associated with the `http://www.w3.org/1999/XSL/Format` URI and use a namespace prefix of `fo`. An XSL-FO processor would recognize the declared element and its child elements because the `fo` prefix is bound to a URI defined in the XSL-FO 1.0 specification.

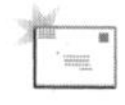

Note The URI used by applications of XML is standardized and used by processors to determine the specific application and version being used. Processors, however, don't rely on the namespace designator, and it could be any designator the document author wants to assign. That said, there are standard naming conventions for designators that are used. For example, when you use XSL, you normally use `xsl` as the namespace designator.

If you want to associate a URI with a namespace declaration, you can do this in the topmost element that uses the prefix. You can also do this in any parent element of a child element that uses the prefix, up to and including a document's root element. Here's an example that associates a URI with the `myOrg` namespace declared in earlier examples:

```
<?xml version="1.0"?>
<myOrg:book xmlns:myOrg="http://www.microsoft.com/myOrg">
 <title>XHTML Pocket Consultant</title>
 <creator>William R. Stanek</creator>
 <chapter number="3" title="XHTML Essentials">
  <page> Page text.
  </page>
  <main_text> Main text.
  </main_text>
 </chapter>
</myOrg:book>
```

You can declare multiple namespaces that will be used within a single document. You'd start by adding an additional namespace declaration and URI to the document and then adding qualified elements to the document where appropriate. Here's an example:

```
<?xml version="1.0"?>
<data:root xmlns:data="http://www.microsoft.com/Data">
 <data:header isbn="07356-0831-8"></data:header>
 <myOrg:book xmlns:myOrg="http://www.microsoft.com/myOrg">
  <title>XHTML Pocket Consultant</title>
  <creator>William R. Stanek</creator>
  <chapter number="3" title="XHTML Essentials">
   <page>XHTML Definitions
    <data:page>This is a paragraph on a page.
    </data:page>
   </page>
   <main_text>XHTML Definitions Main
    <data:main_text>This is a paragraph in the main text.
    </data:main_text>
   </main_text>
  </chapter>
 </myOrg:book>
 <data:footer>Copyright 2001 William R. Stanek</data:footer>
</data:root>
```

In the previous example, there are two elements with the same local part name but different namespace prefixes (`page/data:page` and `main_text/data:main_text`). Because these elements are in different namespaces, they can be handled and processed differently:

- A DTD describing the document could include different content models for each element. This means that `data:page` and `page` could be described differently, as could `data:main_text` and `main_text`.

- A processor handling these elements could treat them differently. This means that the element could have different styles, formatting, or transformations applied to them.
- An application making use of the elements could process the elements in different ways. For example, the application could elect to display the contents of one element but hide the contents of the other.

It's possible to redefine a namespace prefix within a document so that the prefix in one context refers to one namespace but in another context refers to a different namespace. However, this can be confusing when you or others are trying to work with the document and generally isn't a good idea. With this in mind, you should avoid redefining namespace prefixes.

You can assign the same URI to multiple elements in a document. One reason to do this is if you don't want to assign the namespace to the top-level root element in a document and have multiple immediate child elements of the root element that need namespace declarations. In this example the same namespace declaration is assigned to the `header`, `book`, and `footer` elements rather than to the `root` element:

```
<root>
  <data:header xmlns:data="http://www.microsoft.com/Data">
  The header is separate.
  </data:header>
  <data:book xmlns:data="http://www.microsoft.com/Data">
  The book contents are separate.
  </data:book>
  <data:footer xmlns:data="http://www.microsoft.com/Data">
  The footer is separate.
  </data:footer>
</root>
```

Caution Be careful when assigning the same URI several times in a document. When XML processors encounter a namespace URI, they examine the value provided on a character-by-character basis. If you use a different letter case or add an additional character, such as a space or a slash, you've created a different namespace.

As explained in the previous discussion, you can associate a URI with a namespace using the following technique:

1. In the top-level element where the namespace is used or in a parent element of this element, set an XML namespace attribute by typing **xmlns:*prefix*=** after the element name or after any existing attributes but before the end element designator >.
2. Type the URI for the namespace, making sure to enclose the namespace in quotation marks.

The result should look similar to the following:

```
<myOrg:book xmlns:myOrg="http://www.microsoft.com/myOrg">
```

Setting Default Namespaces

In addition to namespaces assigned through a namespace declaration, elements can be assigned a default namespace. As with a standard namespace, a default namespace applies to the element where it's declared and to all elements within the content of that element, unless overridden by a specific namespace declaration. Unlike standard namespaces, default namespace don't use prefixes, which makes them easier to implement.

To assign a default namespace to an element and its child elements, all you need to do is define an `xmlns` attribute that doesn't specify a prefix, such as:

```
<?xml version="1.0"?>
<book xmlns="http://www.microsoft.com/myOrg"
  title="XHTML Pocket Consultant">
 <creator>William R. Stanek</creator>
 <chapter number="3" title="XHTML Essentials">
  <page> Page text.
  </page>
  <main_text> Main text.
  </main_text>
 </chapter>
</book>
```

Here, the `book` element declares a default namespace that's associated with the `http://www.microsoft.com/myOrg` URI. Because no prefix is used for the `book` element or any other child elements, the `book`, `creator`, `chapter`, `page`, and `main_text` elements are in the default namespace.

Note Default namespace don't apply to element attributes, however. This means that the `title` attributes of the `book` and `chapter` elements aren't in any namespace.

To assign a different default namespace to a group of elements, all you need to do is assign an `xmlns` attribute to the top-level element of that group. Following this, you could rewrite the previous example to assign different default namespaces to different sections of the document, such as:

```
<?xml version="1.0"?>
<book xmlns="http://www.microsoft.com/myOrg/books"
 title="XHTML Pocket Consultant">
 <creator>William R. Stanek</creator>
 <chapter number="3" title="XHTML Essentials"
  xmlns="http://www.microsoft.com/myOrg/chapters">
```

(continued)

(continued)

```
   <page> Page text.
   </page>
   <main_text> Main text.
   </main_text>
  </chapter>
</book>
```

Here, the book and creator elements are in the http://www.microsoft.com/myOrg/books namespace and the chapter, page, and main_text elements are in the http://www.microsoft.com/myOrg/chapters namespace.

Note The title attributes for the book and chapter elements still aren't in either namespace. Attributes aren't included in default namespaces.

Documents can have specific namespaces as well as default namespaces. The following example defines a data namespace as well as a default namespace:

```
<?xml version="1.0"?>
<data:root xmlns:data="http://www.microsoft.com/Data">
 <data:header isbn="07356-0831-8"></data:header>
 <book xmlns="http://www.microsoft.com/myOrg">
  <title>XHTML Pocket Consultant</title>
  <creator>William R. Stanek</creator>
  <chapter number="3" title="XHTML Essentials">
   <page>XHTML Definitions
     <data:page>This is a paragraph on a page.
     </data:page>
   </page>
   <main_text>XHTML Definitions Main
     <data:main_text>This is a paragraph in the main text.
     </data:main_text>
   </main_text>
  </chapter>
 </book>
 <data:footer>Copyright 2001 William R. Stanek</data:footer>
</data:root>
```

Here, the book, title, creator, chapter, page, and main_text elements are in the default namespace. The data:root, data:header, data:page, data:main_text, and data:footer elements are in the http://www.microsoft.com/Data namespace.

Note The isbn attribute of the header element is part of the data namespace. When you define a specific namespace, attributes of elements in that namespace are included in that namespace.

As explained in the previous discussion, you can specify a default namespace using the following technique:

1. In the element where you want to use the default namespace or in a parent element of the element, start the default XML namespace attribute by typing **xmlns=** after the element name or after any existing attributes, but before the end element designator >.
2. Type the URI for the namespace, making sure to enclose the namespace in quotation marks.

The result should look similar to the following:

```
<book xmlns="http://www.microsoft.com/myOrg">
```

Using Namespaces with DTDs

To use namespaces with documents that you intend to validate, you must make some changes to your DTDs. The reason for this is that valid documents must declare structures in their DTD exactly as they're used in the related documents. For example, if you use an element called `data:page`, you must declare it as such in the DTD. If you use an `xmlns` attribute for an element, you must also declare an `xmlns` attribute for that element in the DTD.

Note Only the structures that use prefixes must be declared with prefixes in the DTD. This means that if an element or attribute doesn't use a namespace prefix but inherits a namespace from a parent element, you don't need to change the DTD definition for the nonprefixed child element.

Using Namespaces with Elements in DTDs

Every element that's declared with a prefix in the body of a document must have a matching declaration in the DTD in order for the document to be considered valid. Because of this, you must update element definitions that use namespace prefixes if you intend to validate documents. The steps you follow to update the element definition are as follows:

1. In the document's DTD, locate the element declaration that you want to modify. The declaration begins with `<!ELEMENT`.
2. Add the namespace prefix to the beginning of the element name and then type a colon (**:**). The result should look like the following:

   ```
   <!ELEMENT prefix:element_name (#PCDATA)>
   ```

3. Repeat this procedure for each element that uses a namespace prefix. You don't have to use this procedure for child elements that inherit the namespace or when a default namespace is defined for an element.

Using Namespaces with Attributes in DTDs

Although attributes rarely are defined using namespace prefixes, they can—and indeed, sometimes do—have namespace prefixes. If an attribute is used with a prefix in the body of the document, you must define it with the prefix in the related DTD. The steps you follow to update the attribute definition are as follows:

1. In the document's DTD, locate the attribute declaration that you want to modify. The declaration begins with `<!ATTLIST`.
2. If a namespace prefix is defined for an element, add the namespace prefix to the beginning of the element name and then type a colon (**:**). Otherwise, just type the element name.
3. Add the namespace prefix to the beginning of the attribute name and then type a colon (**:**).
4. Repeat this procedure for each attribute that uses a namespace prefix.

The result should look like the following:

```
<!ATTLIST prefix:element_describing prefix:attrib_name #IMPLIED>
```

Declaring xmlns Attributes

Anytime you specify an `xmlns` attribute for an element in a document, the `xmlns` attribute must be declared in the DTD in order for the document to be considered valid. The `xmlns` attribute for default namespaces is entered in the form:

```
xmlns="namespace_URI"
```

The `xmlns` attribute for specific namespaces is entered in the form:

```
xmlns:prefix="namespace_URI"
```

where *`prefix`* is the identifier for the namespace.

With either form of the attribute, you can declare the attribute as you would any other attribute. Typically, you'd declare the attribute as containing character data using a literal, `#IMPLIED`, `#FIXED`, or `#REQUIRED` value. In this case you could define the `xmlns` attribute in the DTD by following these steps:

1. Each element that uses the `xmlns` or an `xmlns:`*`prefix`* attribute must have a declaration for this attribute in the DTD. Start the assignment by typing **<!ATTLIST** and then enter the name of the element the attribute relates to. Don't forget the namespace prefix for the attribute if one is used.
2. Type **xmlns** for the default namespace or **xmlns:*prefix***, where *prefix* is the namespace prefix used.
3. Type **CDATA**.

4. Set the default usage as `#IMPLIED`, `#REQUIRED`, or `#FIXED`. If you use a fixed type, you must also enter a default value in quotation marks. Or simply assign a literal value as a default.
5. Complete the assignment by typing `>`. The result should follow this format:

   ```
   <!ATTLIST prefix:element_describing xmlns:prefix CDATA usage>
   ```

6. Repeat this procedure as necessary for `xmlns` attributes used with other elements.

More Info *Namespaces in XML*, eds. Tim Bray, Dave Hollander, and Andrew Layman. Textuality, Hewlett-Packard, and Microsoft. World Wide Web Consortium, 1999. Available at *http://www.w3.org/TR/REC-xml-names*.

Part III

XML Schemas

Part III focuses on the XML Schema language. XML Schemas provide an alternative way to describe the structure of XML documents in terms of the elements, attributes, and contents they can contain. The chapters in Part III discuss the XML Schema language defined by the World Wide Web Consortium (W3C) and referred to as XML Schema Definition (XSD). XSD is more advanced than early schema implementations, which are referred to as XML Data Reduced (XDR) schemas.

Chapter 8 introduces the XML Schema language and its related concepts. The chapter also discusses how namespaces are used with schemas. Chapters 9 to 11 cover the details of the XML Schema language. Chapter 12 provides a resource guide to schema declarations that's designed to clarify schema usage.

Chapter 8

XML Schemas

Like document type definitions (DTDs), XML schemas provide a way to describe the structure of XML documents in terms of the elements, attributes, and the data that they can contain. Although you define DTDs using a syntax and structure that's distinctly different from the XML language itself, an XML schema written in the XML Schema language is defined entirely in the XML language itself. This makes XML schemas much more powerful and flexible than DTDs. It also means that XML schemas can be processed with an XML processor. Schemas have other advantages over DTDs as well, especially when it comes to defining context and specifying the kind of data that can be used.

With XML schemas, elements can have either a global or a local context, which is different from DTDs, where all elements and their attributes are globally defined. A global schema definition is one that applies throughout a document. A local schema definition is one that applies in a specific context within a section of a document. This allows you to use like-named elements in different contexts.

With XML schemas you have precise control over how an element's contents are used. You could specify that the text for one element should be a valid date and that the text for another element should be a number. By adding formatting information to these values, you could further specify that the numeric value should be formatted as a U.S. postal code with five digits, followed by a dash, followed by four additional digits. In a DTD, there's no way to specify the permitted data types or formatting for content.

This chapter serves as an introduction to schemas. The focus is on the essential concepts you need to successfully implement schemas. You'll learn key concepts that'll help you get started, how to implement basic schemas, and how schemas use namespaces. Because namespaces are so important to your success with schemas, the chapter shows you how to target namespaces, how to reference components with namespaces, and how to declare schema locations.

Getting Started with Schemas

The XML Schema language defined by the World Wide Web Consortium (W3C) is also referred to as XML Schema Definition (XSD). XSD is the current standard for implementing XML schemas. XSD is more advanced than early schema implementations referred to as XML Data Reduced (XDR) schemas. You can convert existing schemas written in XDR to XSD using Microsoft's XDR-XSD Converter, which is available online for free.

As you set out to work with schemas, you'll need to learn these fundamental concepts:

- How schema content is defined using simple and complex types
- How local and global declarations are used

These concepts are discussed in the sections that follow.

More Info To find the XDR-XSD Converter, visit MSDN online at *http://msdn.microsoft.com/* and search for "XDR-XSD Converter". The converter is provided as an Extensible Stylesheet Transformations (XSLT) style sheet that transforms XDR structures to XSD.

Understanding Simple and Complex Types

With schemas, you can create documents with two different types of content:

- **Simple** Elements that contain only data are considered to be the simple type—as are all attributes—because they can contain only data values. Simple types are used to specify how the data of an element or attribute can be used.
- **Complex** Elements that contain other elements or attributes are considered to be the complex type. Complex types define the high-level elements that determine a document's structure rather than the low-level elements that contain only data.

Once you start using simple and complex types, you'll find that the type definitions become much clearer—as do the reasons that two different types are specified. On the one hand, simple types are used to define the most basic elements a document can contain and to describe their permissible values. On the other hand, complex types are used to define elements that control a document's structure.

Simple types specify the basic composition of an element or attribute value and can be used in one of three forms:

- **Atomic** Defines the exact type of data allowed for the value and allows for a single value of this type. For example, you could define an element's content as having a string, integer, or date type.
- **List** Defines a list of values having a specific type. This allows you to specify that an element's contents can contain multiple values of the same type.
- **Union** Unions are combinations of lists and atomic values that permit you to use multiple types of values. You could, for example, specify that an element can contain both date and float types.

The XML Schema language defines several dozen data types that can be used. These data types are built in and are similar to those used in programming languages like Java and C#. You'll find:

- Integer data types for working with whole numbers
- Floating-point data types for working with numbers that have decimal places
- Character data types for working with strings and character content
- Date and time data types for working with date and time values with specific formats

Although these data types are built into the XML Schema language, you can create your own custom data types as well. With custom data types, you define exactly how the content should look. You'll find detailed information on working with simple types in Chapter 9, "Defining Simple Types in Schema."

Because they contain other elements and attributes, complex elements are used to describe the structure of documents. The XML Schema language defines four complex types:

- **Simple content** Defines elements that contain only simple elements
- **Mixed content** Defines elements that contain elements and text
- **Empty content** Defines elements that are empty and have no textual contents or elements associated with them
- **Any content** Defines elements that can contain any type of content or elements

These element types are very similar to the element types that you use with DTDs. As with DTDs, each of these types allows an element to have attributes. This means you can define attributes for an empty element as well as simple, mixed, and any content elements. You'll find detailed information on working with complex types in Chapter 11, "Defining Complex Types in Schema."

Understanding Local and Global Declarations

In DTDs, every element you declare must have a unique name. The reason for this constraint is that elements have a global context. Because elements are declared globally, they can be used in multiple locations and will always have the same definition regardless of how they're used. This means that a `customer` element with a parent element of `accounts` has the same usage and declaration as a `customer` element with a parent of `shipping_info`. There is, in fact, only one `customer` element definition, which is declared globally.

Schemas handle element definitions a bit differently, however. With schemas, the context in which an element is used does matter. Schema structures, including elements and attributes, that are declared at the top level of the schema hierarchy are considered to be declared globally and can be reused in other areas of the schema. Declarations made at other levels of the schema, such as those for complex types that reference an existing global element or define a new element, are declared locally and can't be reused in other areas of the schema.

With top-level elements, the schema context doesn't affect how the element can be used in an XML document. You can explicitly declare the element anywhere in the document and it will have the meaning you've defined for the global element, provided that this meaning isn't overridden by a local context.

When you declare a local element, you set its context according to its position in the schema. Three important rules apply to local elements:

- A local element is always a child of a specific top-level element. This top-level element determines the context in which the local element is valid. Outside of this context, a local element has no meaning. With local elements, a `customer` element with a parent element of `accounts` and a `customer` element with a parent of `shipping_info` can have completely different schema definitions—both of which are valid in their local contexts and not defined otherwise.
- Local elements can have the same name as a global element. When a naming conflict occurs between a global and local element, the local context overrides that of the global context. This means that the parser processing the document uses the local definition of the element rather than the global definition.
- Local elements must have a unique name within their context. This means that local elements that share the same context can't have the same name. Because of this, you can't give identical names to local elements that have the same parent element.

You'll work with globally and locally declared elements in Chapters 9 and 11.

Working with Basic Schemas

The XML Schema language is an application of XML. This means that schemas are defined using XML and that the legal structures that schemas can use are the same as those I've discussed in other sections of this book. This means many of the concepts you learned previously apply to schemas as well.

To create and use a basic schema, you'll need to learn three important concepts:

- How to create a basic schema document
- How to associate that schema with an XML document
- How to add comments to the schema that act as documentation

These concepts are discussed in the following sections.

Creating a Basic Schema Document

A schema document is a standard XML document with a text-based format. This means you can create a schema document using a text editor or any standard word processor. As with XML documents, the name of a schema document doesn't matter. However, to follow convention, you should name the schema file with the .xsd extension to show that the file contains a schema definition.

The two basic ways to create a schema document are

- By declaring a namespace that uses the schema of schemas
- By declaring a default namespace that uses the schema of schemas

Using a Specific Namespace

Because schemas are defined using XML, a schema document can begin with a standard XML declaration, such as:

```
<?xml version="1.0" ?>
```

The declaration isn't required by processors that understand schemas, however. This means that you can omit the XML declaration if you like—as is often the case.

Next, you define the root element for the schema document and set the namespace for the schema. The standard root element is called `schema` and the standard namespace has the prefix `xsd`. Typically, the Uniform Resource Indicator (URI) that you associate with this namespace is the Schema language definition, which has the standard value of `http://www.w3.org/2001/XMLSchema`. The standard namespace is also referred to as the schema of schemas namespace. Following this, the opening and ending tags for the typical `schema` element look like this:

```
<xsd:schema xmlns:xsd="http://www.w3.org/2001/XMLSchema">
...
</xsd:schema>
```

With this in mind, a basic schema document might look like this:

```
<xsd:schema xmlns:xsd="http://www.w3.org/2001/XMLSchema">
 <xsd:element name="contact" type="ContactType" />

 <xsd:complexType name="ContactType">
  <xsd:sequence>
   <xsd:element name="customer" type="Entity" />
   <xsd:element name="organization" type="Entity" />
  </xsd:sequence>
  <xsd:attribute name="entryDate" type="xsd:date" />
 </xsd:complexType>

 <xsd:complexType name="Entity">
  <xsd:sequence>
   <xsd:element name="name" type="xsd:string" />
   <xsd:element name="street" type="xsd:string" />
   <xsd:element name="city" type="xsd:string" />
   <xsd:element name="state" type="xsd:string" />
   <xsd:element name="zip" type="xsd:decimal" />
  </xsd:sequence>
  <xsd:attribute name="country" type="xsd:NMTOKEN"
   fixed="US" />
 </xsd:complexType>

</xsd:schema>
```

This example defines a root element called `contact` and three subelements: `customer`, `organization`, and `entryDate`. The `customer` and `organization` subelements have the same definition. They're defined as the custom type `Entity` and contain `name`, `street`, `city`, `zip`, and `country` elements.

Follow these steps to create a basic schema that declares the namespace as the schema of schemas:

1. On the first line of the schema document, type **<xsd:schema**.
2. Declare the namespace as the schema of schemas by typing **xmlns:xsd= "http://www.w3.org/2001/XMLSchema"** and then complete the schema element by typing **>**.
3. Define the schema rules using simple and complex types as discussed in Chapters 9 and 10, respectively.
4. Type the closing tag for the schema element by typing **</xsd:schema>**. This completes the document.
5. Save the schema document as a text-only file with the .xsd extension. The name of the file isn't important, but it's best if it's easy to reference and remember.

The result should look like this:

```
<xsd:schema xmlns:xsd="http://www.w3.org/2001/XMLSchema">
...
</xsd:schema>
```

Using the Default Namespace

Another way to define this document would be to use the default namespace rather than a specific namespace. As discussed in Chapter 7, "XML Namespaces," when you use the default namespace, you don't use a namespace prefix. This means that the schema document definitions don't use the `xsd` prefix and that you could rewrite the previous schema document like this:

```
<schema xmlns="http://www.w3.org/2001/XMLSchema">

 <element name="contact" type="ContactType" />

 <complexType name="ContactType">
  <sequence>
   <element name="customer" type="Entity" />
   <element name="organization" type="Entity" />
  </sequence>
  <attribute name="entryDate" type="date" />
 </complexType>
```

(continued)

(continued)

```
 <complexType name="Entity">
  <sequence>
   <element name="name" type="string" />
   <element name="street" type="string" />
   <element name="city" type="string" />
   <element name="state" type="string" />
   <element name="zip" type="decimal" />
  </sequence>
  <attribute name="country" type="NMTOKEN"
   fixed="US" />
 </complexType>

</schema>
```

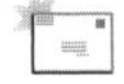

Note By itself, this schema definition isn't complete. You must add a target namespace or a prefix to make this schema complete. This schema would be fine, however, if you planned to include it in another schema.

When you use this schema, the elements and their type definitions are in the default namespace. As you'll see in examples in this and other chapters, you can define schemas that use multiple namespaces. When multiple namespaces are used, the namespace an element is in depends on its definition. Elements can be in the default namespace or in a specific namespace that's referenced by a namespace prefix.

To create a basic schema that declares a default namespace as the schema of schemas, complete the following steps:

1. On the first line of the schema document, type **<schema**.
2. Declare the namespace as the schema of schemas by typing **xmlns= "http://www.w3.org/2001/XMLSchema"** and then complete the schema element by typing **>**.
3. Define the schema rules using simple and complex types as discussed in Chapters 9 and 10 respectively.
4. Type the closing tag for the schema element by typing **</schema>**. This completes the document.
5. Save the schema document as a text-only file with the .xsd extension. The name of the file isn't important, but it's best if it's easy to reference and remember.

The result should look like this:

```
<schema xmlns="http://www.w3.org/2001/XMLSchema">
...
</schema>
```

Associating the Schema with an XML Document

After you create a basic schema, you can create XML documents that use the schema. An XML processor that understands schemas, such as MSXML Parser version 4.0, could then use the schema to validate the document. Although schemas can have namespaces associated with them, a target namespace isn't required. If you decide not to declare a specific target namespace, you specify where the schema for a document is located using the XML schema instance namespace. The XML schema instance namespace defines two key attributes for locating schemas: `noNamespaceSchemaLocation` and `schemaLocation`.

An XML schema that doesn't have a target namespace is referred to as being not namespace qualified. This means that all globally and locally declared components aren't associated with a target namespace. In contrast, a schema with a target namespace can have both qualified and unqualified components. That is, the schema can have components whose rules and structures are defined in the target namespace (meaning the components are qualified) as well as components whose rules and structures aren't defined in the target namespace (meaning the components are unqualified).

Referencing Schema Instances Using noNamespaceSchemaLocation

Using `noNamespaceSchemaLocation`, you can make a direct reference to a schema location when there's no namespace target defined for the document. In this case, you declare the XML schema instance namespace so that you can use its `schemaLocation` attribute. The value you should use for the namespace declaration is as follows:

```
xmlns:xsi="http://www.w3.org/2001/XMLSchema-instance"
```

where `xsi` is the standard prefix for an XML Schema instance namespace and `http://www.w3.org/2001/XMLSchema-instance` sets the standard URI for schema instances. The schema instance namespace provides the attributes you use to indicate schema location using the `noNamespaceSchemaLocation` attribute.

Because there's no target namespace, you can reference a specific schema location by defining a `noNamespaceSchemaLocation` attribute for the document's root element. The format for the attribute declaration is:

```
xsi:noNamespaceSchemaLocation="schema_location"
```

such as:

```
xsi:noNamespaceSchemaLocation="http://www.microsoft.com/Schema/
 contact.xsd"
```

where `http://www.microsoft.com/Schema/contact.xsd` is the Uniform Resource Locator (URL) path to the actual schema that's used. Keep in mind that the `noNamespaceSchemaLocation` attribute is defined in the `xsi` namespace.

To see how these declarations could be made in an XML document, consider the following example:

```
<?xml version="1.0"?>
<contact>
 <customer country="US">
  <name>William Stanek</name>
  <street>123 Main Street</street>
  <city>Redmond</city>
  <state>WA</state>
  <zip>98052</zip>
 </customer>
 <organization country="US">
  <name>Microsoft Corporation</name>
  <street>One Microsoft Way</street>
  <city>Redmond</city>
  <state>WA</state>
  <zip>98052</zip>
 </organization>
</contact>
```

Here, I've created an XML document that conforms to the schema defined in the previous section. The document has a root element named `contact` that defines two child elements called `customer` and `organization`. The `customer` and `organization` elements are identically structured. They have an attribute called `country` and elements called `name`, `street`, `city`, `state`, and `zip`.

As written, the document is a well-formed XML document. However, it can't be said that the document is valid. No information is provided that can be used to validate the document. To validate the document against the schema created in the previous section of the chapter, you must declare the namespace used and set a schema location. Here's an example:

```
<?xml version="1.0"?>
<contact xmlns:xsi="http://www.w3.org/2001/XMLSchema-instance"
 xsi:noNamespaceSchemaLocation="http://www.microsoft.com/
 Schema/contact.xsd">
 <customer country="US">
  <name>William Stanek</name>
  <street>123 Main Street</street>
  <city>Redmond</city>
  <state>WA</state>
  <zip>98052</zip>
 </customer>
 <organization country="US">
  <name>Microsoft Corporation</name>
  <street>One Microsoft Way</street>
  <city>Redmond</city>
  <state>WA</state>
```

(continued)

(continued)

```
  <zip>98052</zip>
 </organization>
</contact>
```

Now that the document is associated with a namespace and defines a namespace location, the document can be validated. As you might imagine, you have many other options when making these declarations. For detailed information on these options, see the "Using Targeted Namespaces with Schemas," "Referencing Components with Namespaces," and "Including and Importing Schemas" sections of this chapter.

To set a schema location when there's no namespace target defined for the document, complete the following steps:

1. In the root element of the document, set the namespace for schema instances by typing **xmlns:xsi="http://www.w3.org/2001/XMLSchema-instance"**. Once you declare the schema instance namespace, you use its attributes to indicate schema locations.
2. Type **xsi:noNamespaceSchemaLocation=** and then enter the URL to the schema, making sure to enclose the URL in quotation marks.
3. Complete the root element by typing >.
4. Define elements for the document according to the schema rules.
5. Complete the document by typing the closing tag for the root element.
6. Save the XML document as a text-only file with the .xml extension.

The result should look similar to the following:

```
<?xml version="1.0"?>
<root_element
 xmlns:xsi="http://www.w3.org/2001/XMLSchema-instance"
 xsi:noNamespaceSchemaLocation="schema_URL/file.xsd">
...
</root_element>
```

Referencing Schema Instances Using schemaLocation

Another way to make a direct reference to a schema location when there's no namespace target defined for a document is to use the `schemaLocation` attribute. Typically, you'll want to use this attribute when you set a default namespace for a schema and there's no target namespace. In this case, you'd define the default namespace for the document and then declare the XML schema instance namespace so that you can use its `schemaLocation` attribute, such as:

```
<contact
 xmlns="http://www.microsoft.com/Contact"
 xmlns:xsi="http://www.w3.org/2001/XMLSchema-instance"
>
...
</contact>
```

Afterward, you'd define the `schemaLocation` attribute using a two-part value. The first part of the value is the namespace defined for the document. The second part of the value is the URL to the schema document. In the following example, you reference the `http://www.microsoft.com/Contact` default namespace and then point to the schema document located by the URL `http://www.microsoft.com/Contact/contact.xsd`:

```
<contact
 xmlns="http://www.microsoft.com/Contact"
 xmlns:xsi="http://www.w3.org/2001/XMLSchema-instance"
 xsi:schemaLocation="http://www.microsoft.com/Contact
 http://www.microsoft.com/Contact/contact.xsd"
>
...
</contact>
```

To reference a schema location with the `schemaLocation` attribute, follow these steps:

1. In the root element of the document, set the default namespace by typing **xmlns=** and then specifying the URL for the default namespace in quotation marks.
2. Declare the XML schema instance namespace by typing **xmlns:xsi="http://www.w3.org/2001/XMLSchema-instance"**.
3. Type **xsi:schemaLocation=**. Next, enter the same value as you set for the default namespace. Type a space and then enter the URL to the schema file, making sure to enclose both values in quotation marks.
4. Complete the root element by typing **>**. You can now define elements for the document according to the schema rules.
5. Complete the document by typing the closing tag for the root element.
6. Save the XML document as a text-only file with the .xml extension.

The result should look similar to the following:

```
<?xml version="1.0"?>
<root_element xmlns="default_namespace"
 xmlns:xsi="http://www.w3.org/2001/XMLSchema-instance"
 xsi:schemaLocation="default_namespace
 schema_URL/file.xsd"
>
...
</root_element>
```

Adding Documentation to Schemas

The standard schema namespace defines three elements that you can use to add documentation to schemas. These elements are

- **annotation** A top-level element for specifying schema comments. This element is the parent of the documentation and appInfo subelements.
- **documentation** A subelement that allows you to enter text comments. These comments can be used to document the schema.
- **appInfo** A subelement that allows you to enter supplemental information for applications that process the schema.

An `annotation` element can appear at the beginning of most schema constructions to add comments that serve as inline documentation. It can have the `documentation` and `appInfo` elements as subelements. When you use the `documentation` element, you should always set the language used for the comment text using the `xml:lang` attribute. This means that most basic documentation follows this format:

```
<xsd:annotation>
 <xsd:documentation xml:lang="en">
 Documentation text
 </xsd:documentation>
</xsd:annotation>
```

Because the documentation text is enclosed by standard elements, it could be processed and extracted to create an actual documentation file or help screen. If you want to add documentation to the beginning of a schema, the `annotation` element must appear after the `xsd:schema` element. Here's an example:

```
<xsd:schema xmlns:xsd="http://www.w3.org/2001/XMLSchema">
 <xsd:annotation>
  <xsd:documentation xml:lang="en">
   Contact Schema for XML Pocket Consultant
   Copyright 2001, All Rights Reserved.
  </xsd:documentation>
 </xsd:annotation>

 <xsd:element name="contact" type="ContactType" />

 <xsd:complexType name="ContactType">
  <xsd:sequence>
   <xsd:element name="customer" type="Entity" />
   <xsd:element name="organization" type="Entity" />
  </xsd:sequence>
  <xsd:attribute name="entryDate" type="xsd:date" />
 </xsd:complexType>
```

(continued)

(continued)

```
 <xsd:complexType name="Entity">
  <xsd:sequence>
   <xsd:element name="name" type="xsd:string" />
   <xsd:element name="street" type="xsd:string" />
   <xsd:element name="city" type="xsd:string" />
   <xsd:element name="state" type="xsd:string" />
   <xsd:element name="zip" type="xsd:decimal" />
  </xsd:sequence>
  <xsd:attribute name="country" type="xsd:NMTOKEN"
   fixed="US" />
 </xsd:complexType>

</xsd:schema>
```

To add documentation to schemas, complete the following steps:

1. Immediately after the `xsd:schema` element or before the start of the schema construct, type **<xsd:annotation>** to start the annotation element.
2. Type **<xsd:documentation xml:lang="en">** to start the documentation element and then enter your text comments.

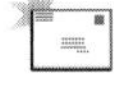

Note Be sure to set the `xml:lang` attribute of the documentation element to the appropriate value. In the text provided, "en" is for U.S. English, which may not be the language code you need.

3. Type **</xsd:documentation>** to close the documentation element and then type **</xsd:annotation>** to complete the annotation element.

The result should look similar to the following:

```
<xsd:annotation>
 <xsd:documentation xml:lang="language code">
 Your text comments.
 </xsd:documentation>
</xsd:annotation>
```

Adding Comments to Schemas

In addition to being able to add inline documentation to schemas, you can also add standard XML comments to schemas. These comments must follow the form:

```
<!-- Comment Text -->
```

Comments can appear anywhere in the schema document and are ignored by XML processors. Because of this, comments aren't available to processors and only people reading the actual text of schema files see comments.

Using Targeted Namespaces with Schemas

Schemas are designed to take advantage of all the features that namespaces offer. One of the most complex combinations of namespaces and schemas is namespace targeting within a schema. Namespace targeting allows you to specify how namespaces are used and through qualification you can specify when namespace prefixes are required.

Targeting Namespaces: The Essentials

Previous examples in this chapter have shown basic ways namespaces are used with schemas. You've seen that

- Schemas can be associated with the schema of schemas namespace (`http://www.w3.org/2001/XMLSchema`) and often use the `xsd` prefix to reference this namespace.
- Schemas can reference the XML schema instance namespace (`http://www.w3.org/2001/XMLSchema-instance`) and that this namespace typically is referred to using the `xsi` prefix.

When you declare these namespaces, you can use the schema structures defined in these namespaces. For example, if you reference the schema of schemas namespace, you can use the `annotation`, `documentation`, and `appInfo` elements to add comments to schemas. If you reference the XML schema instance namespace, you can use schema attributes to locate schema instances when target namespaces aren't used. Anytime you don't target a namespace, the schema components are said to be unqualified (which means that they aren't associated with a target namespace and don't conform to the rules of the target namespace).

In contrast, you can set a specific namespace target in a document. When you do this, all globally declared components are associated with the target namespace (meaning they're qualified) and all locally declared components are outside the target namespace (meaning they're unqualified).

The issue of whether a component belongs to a target namespace is extremely important. XML processors validating documents against schemas use the target information in the validation process. If a component is in a target namespace, its structure must follow the rules defined in the namespace. If a component isn't in a target namespace, it may be in the default namespace, the no namespace namespace (which is defined as a namespace with an empty string for a prefix), or another namespace. In any of these cases, the component may be subject to a different set of rules from a like-named component in the target namespace.

The reason schemas use this complex targeting and qualification process is that it makes it possible to reuse definitions and declarations between schemas. This means that you could refer to types in another schema with a different target namespace. The most basic example where targeting can be used is when your schema has custom type definitions that use the built-in types defined in the schema of schemas (which is the case for all the previous schema examples in this chapter). In this case, by referencing a target namespace you can define very specifically that your custom type definitions come from your organization's namespace and not from the schema of schemas. During validation, an XML processor would look in the schema document associated with your organization's namespace to validate the usage of the custom types you've defined and, as necessary, would look in the schema of schemas to validate the built-in types defined in the XML Schema language.

You can specify the target namespace for all globally declared components in a namespace by setting the `targetNamespace` attribute in the root element of your schema document so that it references this same namespace. The namespace URL can be one that you define and should be unique to a set of related documents. For example, if the namespace URL is `http://www.microsoft.com/Contact`, you could set the target namespace using the following declaration:

```
<xsd:schema xmlns:xsd="http://www.w3.org/2001/XMLSchema"
 targetNamespace="http://www.microsoft.com/Contact">
...
</xsd:schema>
```

Once you add the target namespace declaration to the schema element, you can define other rules for the schema just as you normally would. The key is to pay particular attention to which namespace a component belongs. In the following example, a target namespace has been defined with the URL `http://www.microsoft.com/Contact`:

```
<schema xmlns="http://www.w3.org/2001/XMLSchema"
 targetNamespace="http://www.microsoft.com/Contact">

<element name="contact" type="ContactType" />

 <complexType name="ContactType">
  <sequence>
   <element name="customer" type="Entity" />
   <element name="organization" type="Entity" />
  </sequence>
 </complexType>

 <complexType name="Entity">
  <sequence>
   <element name="name" type="string" />
   <element name="street" type="string" />
   <element name="city" type="string" />
   <element name="state" type="string" />
   <element name="zip" type="decimal" />
  </sequence>
  <attribute name="country" type="NMTOKEN"
   fixed="US" />
 </complexType>

</schema>
```

Because all global components in the schema are associated with the target namespace automatically, the `contact` element, the complex type `ContactType`, and the complex type `Entity` are associated with the `http://www.microsoft.com/Contact` namespace. All other components in the schema are associated with the default namespace defined as the schema of schemas.

A better way to write the previous schema would be to specify where the definition of the `Entity` type associated with the `customer` and `organization` elements is located and also to provide an association for the root element `contact`. To do this, you'd define a prefixed namespace, such as `co`, that points to the same URL used for the target namespace definition. The basic definition would look like this:

```
<schema
 xmlns="http://www.w3.org/2001/XMLSchema"
 xmlns:co="http://www.microsoft.com/Contact"
 targetNamespace="http://www.microsoft.com/Contact"
>
...
</schema>
```

You'd then associate the `Entity` type and the contact element with the `co` namespace, which would mean rewriting the schema, as shown here:

```
<schema
 xmlns="http://www.w3.org/2001/XMLSchema"
 xmlns:co="http://www.microsoft.com/Contact"
 targetNamespace="http://www.microsoft.com/Contact"
>

<element name="contact" type="co:ContactType" />

 <complexType name="ContactType">
  <sequence>
   <element name="customer" type="co:Entity" />
   <element name="organization" type="co:Entity" />
  </sequence>
 </complexType>

 <complexType name="Entity">
  <sequence>
   <element name="name" type="string" />
   <element name="street" type="string" />
   <element name="city" type="string" />
   <element name="state" type="string" />
   <element name="zip" type="decimal" />
  </sequence>
  <attribute name="country" type="NMTOKEN"
   fixed="US" />
 </complexType>

</schema>
```

Once you've made this correlation, a processor of the schema will know to look in this schema for the definition of the `Entity` type. Here's an example of a document that conforms to the schema:

```
<?xml version="1.0"?>
<xco:contact xmlns:xco="http://www.microsoft.com/Contact">
 <customer country="US">
  <name>William Stanek</name>
  <street>123 Main Street</street>
  <city>Redmond</city>
  <state>WA</state>
  <zip>98052</zip>
 </customer>
 <organization country="US">
  <name>Microsoft Corporation</name>
  <street>One Microsoft Way</street>
  <city>Redmond</city>
  <state>WA</state>
  <zip>98052</zip>
 </organization>
</xco:contact>
```

The document declared the `http://www.microsoft.com/Contact` namespace and associates a prefix of `xco` with this namespace. The prefix is used to qualify the root element for the document but isn't used for other elements. Because the namespace is the same as the target namespace in the schema document, the processor knows that it's supposed to look in the schema document for the definition of the `contact` element.

Although the `contact` element is required to be qualified, the other elements that don't use the prefix are locally declared and aren't required to be qualified. They're assumed to be in the same namespace as their parent element. This example works because only the root element is global and the other elements are local. If other elements were global, you'd need to qualify them by adding the namespace prefix.

To change the example and require that local components be qualified, you can define the `elementFormDefault` and `attributeFormDefault` attributes in the schema document. These attributes come from the XML Schema language and, as such, are defined in the schema of schemas.

By default, the `elementFormDefault` and `attributeFormDefault` attributes have the value of unqualified, which is why locally declared elements and attributes aren't required to be qualified and are instead assumed to inherit the namespace of their parent element. If you want to require that locally declared elements and attributes are qualified, you must set the value of the `elementFormDefault` and `attributeFormDefault` attributes to qualified. Here's an example:

```
<schema
 xmlns="http://www.w3.org/2001/XMLSchema"
 xmlns:co="http://www.microsoft.com/Contact"
 targetNamespace="http://www.microsoft.com/Contact"
 elementFormDefault="qualified"
 attributeFormDefault="qualified"
>

<element name="contact" type="co:ContactType" />

 <complexType name="ContactType">
  <sequence>
   <element name="customer" type="co:Entity" />
   <element name="organization" type="co:Entity" />
  </sequence>
 </complexType>

 <complexType name="Entity">
  <sequence>
   <element name="name" type="string" />
   <element name="street" type="string" />
   <element name="city" type="string" />
   <element name="state" type="string" />
   <element name="zip" type="decimal" />
  </sequence>
  <attribute name="country" type="NMTOKEN"
   fixed="US" />
 </complexType>

</schema>
```

Note It's not all or nothing when you set the `elementFormDefault` and `attributeFormDefault` attributes. You can set different values. For example, you could set `elementFormDefault` to unqualified and `attributeFormDefault` to qualified if you wanted to.

With this schema definition, you'd need to rewrite the previous example document to qualify all locally declared elements and attributes. Here, this means that you'd add `co:` to all open and close tags, such as:

```
<co:name>
</co:name>
```

And you'd add `co:` to the beginning on an attribute name, such as:

```
<co:customer co:country="US">
</co:customer>
```

Following this, the revised document would look like this:

```
<?xml version="1.0"?>
<co:contact xmlns:co="http://www.microsoft.com/Contact">
 <co:customer co:country="US">
  <co:name>William Stanek</co:name>
  <co:street>123 Main Street</co:street>
  <co:city>Redmond</co:city>
  <co:state>WA</co:state>
  <co:zip>98052</co:zip>
 </co:customer>
 <co:organization co:country="US">
  <co:name>Microsoft Corporation</co:name>
  <co:street>One Microsoft Way</co:street>
  <co:city>Redmond</co:city>
  <co:state>WA</co:state>
  <co:zip>98052</co:zip>
 </co:organization>
</co:contact>
```

You can override the qualification setting for individual components. To do this, you set the value of the form attribute to either qualified or unqualified as necessary. This attribute is defined in the XML Schema language. Here's an example that shows how you could use the `form` attribute to set the requirement that an element be qualified:

```
<element name="city" type="string" form="qualified" />
```

You can also specify that individual attributes are or aren't qualified. Here's an example:

```
<attribute name="country" type="NMTOKEN"
 fixed="US" form="qualified" />
```

Adding Elements to Target Namespaces

Only globally declared elements are associated with target namespaces by default. To specify that all locally declared elements are a part of the target namespace, add `elementFormDefault="qualified"` to the schema element. By default, all locally declared elements aren't included in the target namespace. To specify this explicitly, add `elementFormDefault="unqualified"` to the schema element. Here's an example:

```
<schema
 xmlns="http://www.w3.org/2001/XMLSchema"
 xmlns:co="http://www.microsoft.com/Contact"
 targetNamespace="http://www.microsoft.com/Contact"
 elementFormDefault="qualified"
>
...
</schema>
```

You can also qualify individual elements. To specify that an individual element is a part of the target namespace, add `form="qualified"` to the element's schema definition. To specify that an individual element isn't a part of the target namespace, add `form="unqualified"` to the element's schema definition. Here's an example:

```
<element name="street" type="string" form="unqualified" />
```

Adding Attributes to Target Namespaces

As with elements, only globally declared attributes are associated with target namespaces by default. This means that locally declared attributes aren't included in the target namespace. You can explicitly state this as well by setting the value `attributeFormDefault="unqualified"` in the schema element. To add locally declared attributes to the target namespace, add `attributeFormDefault="qualified"` to the schema attribute. Here's an example:

```
<schema
 xmlns="http://www.w3.org/2001/XMLSchema"
 xmlns:co="http://www.microsoft.com/Contact"
 targetNamespace="http://www.microsoft.com/Contact"
 attributeFormDefault="qualified"
>
...
</schema>
```

You can also qualify individual attributes. To specify that an individual attribute is a part of the target namespace, add `form="qualified"` to the attribute's schema definition. To specify that an individual attribute isn't a part of the target namespace, add `form="unqualified"` to the attribute's schema definition. Here's an example:

```
<attribute name="country" type="NMTOKEN"
 fixed="US" form="unqualified" />
```

Referencing Components with Namespaces

When multiple namespaces are used in a schema, you may need to reference the namespace component. You've seen namespace references used in many previous examples in this chapter and the previous one, so the concept of referencing namespaces should be a straightforward one. If you specify the prefix of `xsd` to reference the Schema language, you must use this prefix wherever values refer to the schema of schemas. Here's an example:

```
<xsd:schema  xmlns:xsd="http://www.w3.org/2001/XMLSchema">
 <xsd:element name="contact" type="ContactType" />
</xsd:schema>
```

A new concept is that the `type` and `ref` attributes of schema definitions may also need to use the prefix. The reason for this is that the allowed values for these attributes may be defined according to the rules of the prefixed namespace. This is true when you refer to built-in data types and you use the `xsd` prefix to refer to the schema of schemas. Consequently, definitions that would normally be written as:

```
<complexType name="Entity">
 <sequence>
  <element name="name" type="string" />
  <element name="street" type="string" />
  <element name="city" type="string" />
  <element name="state" type="string" />
  <element name="zip" type="decimal" />
 </sequence>
</complexType>
```

must be updated so that they reference the prefixed namespace for the schema of schemas each time they refer to a structure from this namespace. You'd rewrite the definitions like this:

```
<xsd:complexType name="Entity">
 <xsd:sequence>
  <xsd:element name="name" type="xsd:string" />
  <xsd:element name="street" type="xsd:string" />
  <xsd:element name="city" type="xsd:string" />
  <xsd:element name="state" type="xsd:string" />
  <xsd:element name="zip" type="xsd:decimal" />
 </xsd:sequence>
</xsd:complexType>
```

Including and Importing Schemas

The Schema language provides several techniques for making multiple schemas available for use with XML documents. This chapter has already examined some of the key techniques, including associating namespaces and using namespace prefixes and setting a specific location when no target namespace is used. Two additional methods that you may want to use are

- **Include** Used to add multiple schema files with the same target namespace to a document
- **Import** Used to add multiple schema files with different target namespaces to a document

Including Multiple Schema Files

Including schema files is handy when you want a single XML document to incorporate parts of a large schema that has been divided into several files. These schema subsets are similar to DTD subsets that are often created because files can grow very large and you don't always need the entire schema set to create and validate files.

The format for the include statement is:

```
<include schemaLocation="schema-URL/file.xsd" />
```

such as:

```
<include
 schemaLocation="http://www.microsoft.com/Contact/contact.xsd" /
>
```

The include statement brings in the definitions and declarations contained in `contact.xsd` and makes them available as part of the target namespace. If you use a namespace prefix for the schema of schemas, be sure to add this prefix to the statement, such as:

```
<xsd:include
 schemaLocation="http://www.microsoft.com/Contact/contact.xsd" />
```

With included schemas, the included files all must reference the same target namespace. If the schema target namespaces don't match, the include won't work. If a schema doesn't have a target namespace, it's assumed that the target namespace is the same as the one for the schema document in which it's being included. Here's an example schema that uses a target namespace and multiple includes:

```
<schema
 xmlns="http://www.w3.org/2001/XMLSchema"
 xmlns:co="http://www.microsoft.com/Contact"
 targetNamespace="http://www.microsoft.com/Contact"
 attributeFormDefault="qualified">
<include schemaLocation="http://www.microsoft.com/Contact/
 subset1.xsd" />
<include schemaLocation="http://www.microsoft.com/Contact/
 subset2.xsd" />
<include schemaLocation="http://www.microsoft.com/Contact/
 subset3.xsd" />
<include schemaLocation="http://www.microsoft.com/Contact/
 subset4.xsd" />
</schema>
```

Tip The document that contains the include statements that incorporate the schema subsets can be referred to as the primary or topmost schema document. Instance documents that use included schemas have to reference only the primary schema document. They don't have to reference all the schema subset documents. It's the processor's responsibility to gather all the definitions specified in the included schemas.

To include a schema in another schema, follow these steps:

1. Open the schema files that you want to work with. Check the schema files that you want to include in another schema to ensure that the target namespaces are identical. Remember that the case and punctuation of the namespace URL must be exact.
2. In the schema file to which you're adding other schemas, type **<include schemaLocation=** or **<xsd:include schemaLocation=** as appropriate and then enter the URL to the schema file that you're including. The URL must be enclosed in quotation marks.
3. End the include declaration by typing **/>**.
4. Repeat Step 2 for other schemas that you want to include in the current schema.

Importing Multiple Schema Files

Importing multiple schema files is handy when you want to reuse schema definitions from multiple schemas. By importing schemas into a document, you can combine schema definitions from multiple target namespaces so that they can be used in a single document. The import statement has the following format:

```
<import namespace="namespace-URL" />
```

such as:

```
<import namespace="http://www.microsoft.com/Contact" />
```

And you can use an optional `schemaLocation` attribute to help locate resources associated with the namespaces. This attribute is from the XML Schema Instance. Here's an example of an import statement that uses `schemaLocation`:

```
<import namespace="http://www.microsoft.com/Contact"
  xsi:schemaLocation="http://www.microsoft.com/Contact"
  http://www.microsoft.com/Contact/contact.xsd" />
```

Because the XML Schema Instance is used, you must reference it in the schema declaration, such as:

```
<schema
 xmlns="http://www.w3.org/2001/XMLSchema"
 xmlns:co="http://www.microsoft.com/Contact"
 targetNamespace="http://www.microsoft.com/Contact"
 xmlns:xsi="http://www.w3.org/2001/XMLSchema-instance">

<import namespace="http://www.microsoft.com/Inventory"
 xsi:schemaLocation="http://www.microsoft.com/Inventory"
 http://www.microsoft.com/Inventory/inv.xsd" />

</schema>
```

To guard against namespace conflicts, there are many rules for importing schemas:

- You can't import locally declared components from another schema. Only global components are imported.
- When you import schema components from multiple namespaces, each namespace must have separate import statements and these import statements must appear immediately after the schema element.
- When used in an XML document, each namespace must be associated with a unique namespace prefix that uses a standard namespace declaration. The prefix is used to qualify references to any schema components belonging to that namespace and is defined in the schema document you're importing using the `xmlns` attribute.

To import global components into a schema, follow these steps:

1. Immediately after the schema element, type **<import** or **<xsd:import** as appropriate.
2. Type **namespace=** and then enter the quotation mark-enclosed namespace URL for the schema you're importing. This namespace must be unique.
3. Optionally, relate the namespace URL with an actual file location using the xsi:schemaLocation attribute. Type **xsi:schemaLocation=**, enter the same value as you set for the default namespace followed by a space, and then enter the URL to the schema file, making sure to enclose both values in quotation marks.

Tip If you reference the `xsi:schemaLocation` attribute, you must specify this prefixed namespace in the schema element.

4. Complete the import element by typing />.
5. Repeat this process for other schemas that you want to import.

Chapter 9

Defining Simple Types in Schema

The most basic elements in a document are those that contain only data. In schema, you define these basic elements using simple types. You also define element attributes as simple types. Simple types are said to be either primitive or derived. Primitive data types are those that are built-in and are defined in the XML Schema specification. Derived data types are those that are derived from other data types.

The XML Schema language includes many built-in datatypes. These datatypes are similar to those used in many programming languages. Using the built-in datatypes, you can specify that an element can contain Booleans, Strings, Uniform Resource Indicators (URIs), date/time values, and many types of numbers. When a datatype is directly assigned, an XML processor examines the contents of an element or attribute to ensure that they meet the datatype's requirements. If they do, the element or attribute is considered to be validly formed. If they don't, the element or attribute is considered to be invalid. This means that an element defined as a number datatype could contain a series of digits but couldn't contain alphabetic characters. You could specify 1 digit, 5 digits, or 100 digits as part of the contents and it wouldn't matter as long as the datatype requirements are met.

The rules change when you apply restrictions to datatypes. A restriction says that an element must only contain the value specified and that value must be of the type prescribed. This means that you can only specify a single value of a specific type. To be able to specify multiple values when restrictions are used, you must define a list type that uses the restriction. In this way you can specify a list of values as the contents of an element or attribute.

On the other hand, if you wanted to allow multiple types of values to be used, you must define a union of multiple datatypes. With a union you could specify that an element or attribute could contain a string of a specific sequence or a numeric value, for example. The union still doesn't allow multiple values to be used—it only allows multiple datatypes to be used. To allow multiple values with multiple datatypes to be used, you'd need to combine the list and union types.

Making Simple Element and Attribute Declarations

XML Schema language defines a standard format for making element and attribute declarations. Basic declarations for simple elements and attributes are discussed in the following sections. When working with simple elements and attributes keep the following in mind:

- Simple element declarations are distinguished from other types of element declarations in that they're declared using empty XML elements. If elements have schema declarations associated with them that specify custom datatypes, they're declared as simple types and have opening and closing tags, as discussed in the "Creating Simple Types" section of this chapter. If elements have schema declarations associated with them that specify contents, such as child element or attribute definitions, they're declared as complex types and have opening and closing tags, as discussed in Chapter 11, "Defining Complex Types in Schema."
- Simple attribute declarations are distinguished from other types of attribute declarations in that they're declared using empty XML elements. If attributes have schema declarations associated with them that specify custom datatypes, they're declared as simple types and have opening and closing tags, as discussed in the "Creating Simple Types" section of this chapter. Although attributes can't contain other attributes or other elements, they can be grouped together to define sets of attributes that can be applied to multiple elements. Creating attribute groups is discussed in Chapter 11.

Note Keep in mind that all attributes are defined in schema as simple types. The reason for this is that attributes can't contain other elements or other attributes.

Declaring Simple Elements with Character Content

In XML Schema you declare elements using the element declaration, which consists of an element name followed by the element's datatype in the form:

```
<element name="element_name" type="element_type" />
```

where *element_name* is the name of the element and *element_type* specifies the datatype of the element. The datatype can be one of the predefined types or a custom type you're declaring. The following example declares an element called `street` that's a string type:

```
<element name="street" type="string" />
```

Note Because XML schemas are defined using the XML language itself, all names for schema structures must follow the rules for valid XML names. Additionally, if schema constructs use namespace prefixes, they must follow the rules for qualified names as discussed in the "Understanding Namespaces" section of Chapter 7, "XML Namespaces."

If the schema declares a separate namespace for the schema of schemas, don't forget to add the namespace prefix. For example, if the schema of schemas prefix is `xsd`, you'd modify the previous declaration, as shown in this example:

```
<xsd:element name="street" type="xsd:string" />
```

The schema prefix must be associated with the element declaration as well as the type declaration. It's incorrect to only specify the prefix for the element declaration, as shown in this example:

```
<xsd:element name="street" type="string" />
```

Elements with character content are declared at the lowest level of the schema. As such, their declarations are added to complex type definitions for higher-level elements. The following example shows the schema declaration as well as the declarations for `contact`, `customer`, and `organization` elements:

```
<schema xmlns="http://www.w3.org/2001/XMLSchema"
   targetNamespace="http://www.microsoft.com/Contact"
>

<element name="contact" type="ContactType" />

 <complexType name="ContactType">
  <sequence>
   <element name="customer" type="string" />
   <element name="organization" type="string" />
  </sequence>
 </complexType>

</schema>
```

To declare a simple element with character content in schema, follow these steps:

1. Type **<xsd:element** or **<element** as appropriate to begin the element declaration.
2. Type **name="*element_name*"**, where *element_name* is the actual name of the element you're declaring. The element name must follow the rules for valid XML names.

3. Type **type="*element_type*"**, where *element_type* is the actual type of the element you're declaring. Be sure to use the `xsd` prefix if this is defined for the schema of schemas. The basic types that are available include
   - **string** Use this value if the element will contain a string of characters.
   - **decimal** Use this value if the element will contain a decimal number.
   - **boolean** Use this value if the element will contain the values true or false. You can also use a 1 for true and a 0 for false.
   - **date** Use this value if the element will contain a date.
   - **time** Use this value if the element will contain a time of day.

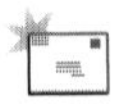

Note XML Schema has many additional data types that aren't listed here. For more information, see the "Creating Simple Types" section of this chapter.

4. Complete the declaration by typing />.

The result should look similar to the following:

```
<xsd:element name="element_name" type="xsd:element_type" />
```

Declaring Default and Fixed Values for Simple Elements

Elements can have either a default or fixed value, but not both. Default values are assigned automatically when no other value is entered in the body of the document. This means that when an XML processor encounters an element with a default value and no other value is specified in the document, the default value is inserted into the document at the appropriate location.

You assign a default value using the default attribute. In the following example the default is "USA":

```
<xsd:element name="country" type="xsd:string" default="USA" />
```

Because default values are inserted into documents when no other value is specified, an XML processor would modify the following element entry:

```
<country></country>
```

to read:

```
<country>USA</country>
```

However, if the element was defined like this:

```
<country>Unknown</country>
```

the XML processor wouldn't modify the element contents.

You assign fixed values using the fixed attribute. As with default values, fixed values are used automatically when no other value is specified. This means that the XML processor automatically inserts the element with the fixed value when it isn't used. The following example declares an element called country with a fixed value of "USA":

```
<xsd:element name="country" type="xsd:string" fixed="USA" />
```

Unlike default values that allow you to use other values, however, you can't use a value other than the specified fixed value. If you use a value that's different from the fixed value, the document is considered invalid. This means that if you declared the `country` element as shown previously and then entered a different value in the body of the document, such as:

```
<country>Unknown</country>
```

the document wouldn't be considered valid.

To add a fixed or default value to a simple element in schema, follow these steps:

1. Locate the element declaration in the schema that you want to modify. The element must not be declared as an empty element or have an existing default or fixed value.
2. To add a default value, type **default="*value*"**, where *value* is the actual text that you want to use as the default value before the end declaration designator (/>).
3. To add a fixed value, type **fixed="*value*"**, where *value* is the actual text that you want to use as the fixed value before the end declaration designator (/>).

The result should look similar to the following:

```
<xsd:element name="code" type="xsd:integer" default="100" />
```

Declaring Simple Empty Elements

As with document type definitions (DTDs), you can declare empty elements in schema. One way to do this is to specify that an element is nillable using the `nill` attribute of the XML Schema Instance namespace. By default, this attribute is false. Thus, you specify that an element can be an empty element by setting `nill` to true as shown in the following example:

```
<xsd:element name="country" type="xsd:string" xsi:nill="true" />
```

When you declare an empty element, you can't specify child elements or content for the element. You can, however, declare and use attributes for empty elements. This means that both of the following are valid empty elements:

```
<country />
```

```
<country code="190" />
```

However, the following example is incorrect:

```
<country />US</country>
```

Here, the opening tag is formatted as an empty element but a closing tag is provided, which is incorrect.

Because you reference the XML Schema instance, you must specify this namespace in your schema. Here's an example:

```
<schema
 xmlns="http://www.w3.org/2001/XMLSchema"
 xmls:co="http://www.microsoft.com/Contact"
 targetNamespace="http://www.microsoft.com/Contact"
 xmlns:xsi="http://www.w3.org/2001/XMLSchema-instance"
>
...
<co:element name="country" type="string" xsi:nill="true" />
...
</schema>
```

To declare a simple empty element in schema, follow these steps:

1. Follow Steps 1-3 in the "Declaring Simple Elements with Character Content" section of this chapter.
2. Type **xsi:nill="true"** and then complete the declaration by typing />.

The result should look similar to the following:

```
<xsd:element name="element_name" type="xsd:element_type
 xsi:nill="true" />
```

Note Another way to create an empty element is to define an element with attributes but without contents. You'll learn this technique, which uses complex types, in Chapter 11.

Declaring Simple Attributes

In XML Schema, all attributes are declared as simple types and appear as part of an element's complex type. This means that an element with attributes always has a complex type definition.

You declare attributes using the attribute declaration, which consists of an attribute name followed by the attribute's datatype in the form:

```
<attribute name="attribute_name" type="attribute_type" />
```

where *attribute_name* is the name of the attribute and *attribute_type* specifies the datatype of the attribute. The datatype can be one of the predefined types or a custom type you're declaring. The following example declares an attribute called `country` that's a string type:

```
<attribute name="country" type="string" />
```

As with elements, don't forget to add the namespace prefix for the schema of schemas if it's been declared. For example, if the schema of schemas prefix were `xsd`, you'd modify the previous declaration, as shown in this example:

```
<xsd:attribute name="country" type="xsd:string" />
```

Note that the `xsd` prefix is used with the attribute declaration and its type attribute. You must use the prefix in both locations. It's incorrect to specify only the prefix for the attribute declaration, as shown in this example:

```
<xsd:attribute name="street" type="string" />
```

As stated previously, attribute declarations always appear as part of an element's complex type definition. You'll learn about complex types in Chapter 11. To declare a simple attribute in schema, follow these steps:

1. Type **<xsd:attribute** or **<attribute** as appropriate to begin the attribute declaration.
2. Type **name= "*attribute_name*"**, where *attribute_name* is the actual name of the attribute you're declaring. The attribute name must follow the rules for valid XML names.
3. Type **type= "*attribute_type*"**, where *attribute_type* is the actual type of the attribute you're declaring. Be sure to use the xsd prefix if this is defined for the schema of schemas. The basic types that are available include
   - **string** Use this value if the attribute will contain a string of characters.
   - **decimal** Use this value if the attribute will contain a decimal number.
   - **boolean** Use this value if the attribute will contain the values true or false. You can also use a 1 for true and a 0 for false.
   - **date** Use this value if the attribute will contain a date.
   - **time** Use this value if the attribute will contain a time of day.

Note XML Schema has many additional data types that aren't listed here. For more information, see the "Creating Simple Types" section of the chapter.

4. Complete the declaration by typing />.

The result should look similar to the following:

```
<xsd:attribute name="attribute_name" type="xsd:attribute_type" />
```

Declaring Default and Fixed Values for Simple Attributes

As with elements, attributes can have either a default or fixed value. Default values are used when no other value is specified for the attribute. You assign a default value using the default attribute. In the following example the default for the `country` attribute is "USA":

```
<xsd:attribute name="country" type="xsd:string" default="USA" />
```

If this attribute were associated with an element called `organization`, the default value would be inserted into a related document any time no other value is specified. This means that an XML processor would modify the following element entry:

```
<organization>Microsoft Corp.</organization>
```

to read:

```
<organization country="USA">Microsoft Corp.</organization>
```

However, if a different value is used, the XML processor doesn't replace it with the default. This means that the following usage is legal:

```
<organization country="United States">Microsoft Corp.
</organization>
```

Tip If you wanted to ensure that only certain values could be used, the best way to do this would be to apply restrictions or to use enumeration to specify a list of values. You'll find detailed information on restrictions and enumeration in Chapter 10, "Specifying Datatypes and Restrictions in Schema."

Attributes can also have fixed values. As with default values, fixed values are used automatically when no other value is specified. This means that the XML processor automatically inserts the attribute with the fixed value when it isn't used. The following example declares an attribute called `country` with a fixed value of "USA":

```
<xsd:attribute name="country" type="xsd:string" fixed="USA" />
```

Unlike default values that allow you to use other values, however, you can't use a value other than the specified fixed value. If you use a value for a fixed attribute that's different from the fixed value, the document is considered invalid. This means that if you declared the `country` attribute for the `organization` element like this:

```
<xsd:attribute name="country" type="xsd:string" fixed="USA" />
```

the only acceptable value for the `country` attribute is "USA". If you use a different value, as shown in this example:

```
<organization country="America">Microsoft Corp.</organization>
```

the document wouldn't be considered valid.

To add a fixed or default value to a simple attribute in schema, follow these steps:

1. Locate the attribute declaration in the schema that you want to modify. The attribute must not have an existing default or fixed value.
2. To add a default value, type **default="*value*"**, where *value* is the actual text that you want to use as the default value before the end declaration designator (/>).
3. To add a fixed value, type **fixed="*value*"**, where *value* is the actual text that you want to use as the fixed value before the end declaration designator (/>).

The result should look similar to the following:

```
<xsd:attribute name="country-code" type="xsd:integer"
default="2901" />
```

Creating Optional, Required, and Prohibited Simple Attributes

All attributes are optional by default. This means that if an attribute isn't specified, the document will still be considered valid. If you want to require that an attribute be used, you must specify `use="required"` in the attribute declaration. The following example defines an attribute called `country` that's required:

```
<xsd:attribute name="country" type="xsd:string" use"="required" />
```

Because you've required that the attribute be used, documents that use this schema can only be considered valid if the attribute is used. If you want to require that an attribute be used and set to a fixed value, you can do this as well. Here's an example:

```
<xsd:attribute name="country" type="xsd:string" fixed="USA"
 use="required" />
```

You can't set the attribute usage to required when you specify a default value. The only acceptable usage with a default value is optional. This means that the following example is incorrect:

```
<xsd:attribute name="country" type="xsd:string" default="USA"
 use="required" />
```

You can also prohibit the use of an attribute by specifying `use="prohibited"`. Prohibiting the use of an attribute is useful when you want to ensure that an attribute from another schema isn't used. Although you'll learn about referencing other schema structures in Chapter 11, here's an example now:

```
<xsd:attribute ref="xml:lang" use="prohibited" />
```

This example prohibits the use of the `xml:lang` attribute from the XML Schema. As you might expect, you can't prohibit an attribute and then set a default or fixed value. This means that the following example is incorrect:

```
<xsd:attribute ref="xml:lang" use="prohibited" fixed="en" />
```

Although all attributes are optional by default, you can explicitly specify this with `use="optional"`. Here's an example:

```
<xsd:attribute ref="xml:lang" use="optional" />
```

To set the attribute usage as required or prohibited, follow these steps:

1. Locate the attribute declaration in the schema that you want to modify.
2. To require the use of the attribute, type **use="required"** before the end declaration designator (/>). Because no default value can be specified with required attributes, you'll need to delete any existing default or rethink the usage requirements.
3. To prohibit the use of the attribute, type **use="prohibited"** before the end declaration designator (/>). Because no default or fixed value can be specified with prohibited attributes, you'll need to delete any existing default or fixed value assignment.

The result should look similar to the following:

```
<xsd:attribute name="country-code" type="xsd:integer"
 use="required" />
```

Creating Simple Types

Despite their being called "simple" types, simple schema types are actually complex in the way they're structured. When you create elements or attributes using simple types, you assign a specific data type and you can add additional restrictions as necessary.

Simple types are said to be either *primitive* or *derived*. Primitive data types are those that are built-in and are defined in the XML Schema specification. Derived data types are derived from other data types. Derived data types come in several forms and are said to be

- **Derived by restriction** Data types are derived by restriction when their values are constrained.
- **Derived by list** Data types are derived by list when they come from a list of values having a specific type.
- **Derived by union** Data types are derived by union when they allow multiple types of values.

Using Values Derived by Restriction

Many derived types are built into the XML Schema language and can be defined with user-defined types as well. Knowing whether a simple type is primitive or derived is important in understanding the restrictions that apply. Primitive types have restrictions based on the type of value they accept, such as whether the values can be strings or numbers. Derived datatypes, on the other hand, have restrictions based on the datatype from which they're derived, and they can also have additional restrictions. For example, in XML Schema integers are derived from the decimal data type. They're subject to the same restrictions as decimals and have the additional restriction that they must be whole numbers without decimal values. This means that valid integers look like this:

- 1002
- 299
- -398

It also means that the following values aren't valid integers:

- 102.45
- -45.4
- 33.0

Figure 9-1 provides an overview of all the built-in datatypes. As shown, datatypes follow a specific hierarchy. Any datatype that's directly attached to the root of the hierarchy is a primitive datatype. Any datatype that's attached to another node in the hierarchy is a derived datatype. Following this, you can see that string and decimal are examples of primitive datatypes and that normalizedString and integer are examples of derived datatypes.

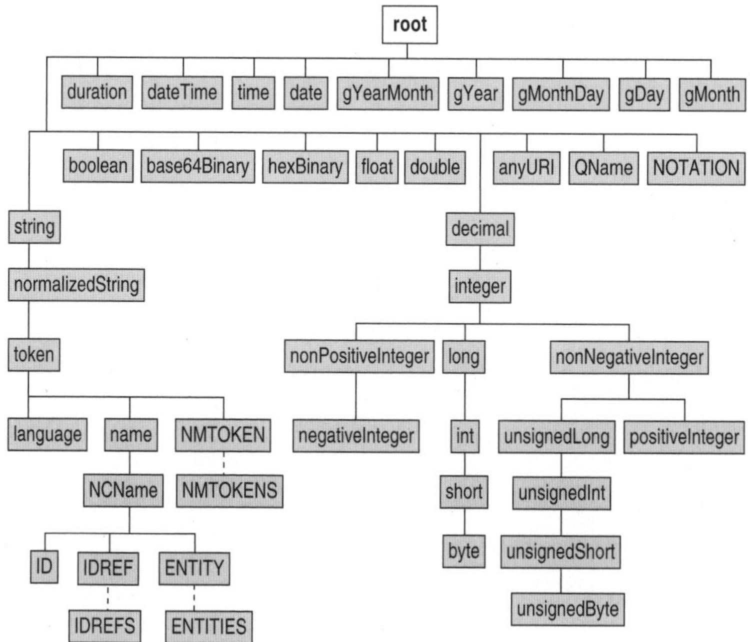

Figure 9-1. *XML Schema datatype hierarchy.*

As you set out to work with the predefined datatypes, you'll find that many different constraints can be applied. Table 9-1 provides an overview of the available constraints. You'll find examples using these constraints in this chapter and in Chapters 10 and 11.

Table 9-1. Restrictions That Can Be Applied to Datatypes

Constraint	Description
`enumeration`	Defines a list of acceptable values that are allowed.
`fractionDigits`	Sets the maximum number of decimal places allowed for datatypes derived from decimal. The value assigned must be zero or greater.
`length`	Sets the exact number of characters or list items allowed. The value assigned must be zero or greater.
`maxExclusive`	Sets the upper bounds for numeric values as less than (<) the value specified (rather than less than or equal to).
`maxInclusive`	Sets the upper bounds for numeric values as less than or equal to (<=) the value specified.
`maxLength`	Sets the maximum number of characters or list items allowed. The value assigned must be zero or greater.
`minExclusive`	Sets the lower bounds for numeric values as greater than (>) the value specified (rather than greater than or equal to).
`minInclusive`	Sets the lower bounds for numeric values as greater than or equal to (>=) the value specified.
`minLength`	Sets the minimum number of characters or list items allowed. The value assigned must be zero or greater.
`pattern`	Defines the exact sequence of characters that are acceptable using a regular expression. Regular expressions are defined in XML Schema following those used in the Perl programming language.
`totalDigits`	Sets the exact number of digits allowed for datatypes derived from decimal. The value assigned must be greater than zero.
`whiteSpace`	Determines how tabs, line feeds, carriage returns, and spaces are handled when entered in values.

Declaring Elements and Attributes with Restrictions

The way you declare a simple element or attribute depends on whether you'll use any of the restrictions listed in Table 9-1. If you don't plan to use a restriction, you can assign the type directly in the element or attribute declaration as discussed previously in the chapter, such as:

```
<xsd:element name="organization" type="xsd:string"
 default="Unknown" />
```

If you want to assign a restriction, you create a custom type for the element and then assign the restriction. The custom type can be defined in one of two ways:

- **Named** You use named custom types when you want to create a type that you can use with multiple schema constructs.

- **Anonymous** You use anonymous custom types when you plan to use a type only with a specific schema construct.

Using Named Custom Types

With a named type, you set the `type` attribute of the schema construct to a label that identifies the simple type you're creating. The name must not be the same as one of the predefined types shown in Figure 9-1. In the following example a type called `country-code` is declared for the location element:

```
<xsd:element name="location" type="country-code" />
```

After declaring a custom type, you can define the custom type using the `simpleType` declaration. The name assigned in the `simpleType` declaration must exactly match the name you used when you declared the custom type. Here's how you could declare the `country-code` simple type:

```
<xsd:simpleType name="country-code">
...
</xsd:simpleType>
```

After entering the `simpleType` declaration, you can add a restriction declaration to the simple type. The restriction declaration specifies the base datatype to use in defining the custom type and then adds individual restrictions that further constrain the base datatype. The following declarations specify that the country-code type is based on the integer datatype and has a range of allowable values from 100 to 999:

```
<xsd:simpleType name="country-code">
 <xsd:restriction base="xsd:integer">
  <xsd:minInclusive value="100" />
  <xsd:maxInclusive value="999" />
 </xsd:restriction>
</xsd:simpleType>
```

Because you're using a named custom type, the type definition doesn't have to follow the element or attribute definition in which it's declared. It can also be assigned to multiple constructs just as you'd assign one of the predefined datatypes to elements or attributes. To use the custom type with another schema construct, all you have to do is specify the custom type when you set the type of the schema construct. In the following example, the `type` attribute of the `location`, `origin`, and `destination` elements has been set to a named custom type:

```
<xsd:element name="location" type="country-code" />
<xsd:element name="origin" type="country-code" />
<xsd:element name="destination" type="country-code" />

<xsd:simpleType name="country-code">
 <xsd:restriction base="xsd:integer">
  <xsd:minInclusive value="100" />
  <xsd:maxInclusive value="999" />
 </xsd:restriction>
</xsd:simpleType>
```

To define a named custom type, follow these steps:

1. Type **<xsd:simpleType** to begin the attribute declaration.

Caution These steps assume you've declared the schema of schemas namespace using the `xsd` prefix. If you've declared it in the default namespace, don't use the prefix as indicated in these steps.

2. Type **name="*label*">**, where *label* is the actual name of the custom type you're creating. The name must follow the rules for valid XML names.
3. Begin the restriction declaration and specify the datatype on which the custom type is based by typing **<xsd:restriction base="*foundation*">**, where *foundation* is the datatype on which you're basing the custom type.
4. Set restrictions for the custom type as specified in the "Controlling Acceptable Values" section of Chapter 10.
5. Type **</xsd:restriction>** to complete the restriction definition and then type **</xsd:simpleType>** to complete the simple type definition.

The result should look similar to the following:

```
<xsd:simpleType name="label">
 <xsd:restriction base="foundation">
 ...
 </xsd:restriction>
</xsd:simpleType>
```

Using Anonymous Custom Types

Anonymous custom types are directly associated with the element or attribute to which they relate. When you use anonymous custom types, the type definition must follow the element or attribute definition in which it's declared. Further, because the anonymous type appears as part of the element or attribute declaration this declaration no longer follows the form:

```
<xsd:element name="element_name" />
```

Remember, the `/>` ends the element or attribute declaration and means that the structure has no other schema definitions associated with it. Because the anonymous type definition is considered part of the element or attribute for which it's declared, the element or attribute must be declared with an opening and ending tag. This means that a declaration for an element with an anonymous simple type follows the form:

```
<xsd:element name="element_name">
 <xsd:simpleType>
 ...
 </xsd:simpleType>
</xsd:element>
```

and that a declaration for an attribute with an anonymous simple type follows the form:

```
<xsd:attribute name="attribute_name">
 <xsd:simpleType>
 ...
 </xsd:simpleType>
</xsd:attribute>
```

With this in mind, you could define a `code` element with an anonymous simple type like this:

```
<xsd:element name="code">
 <xsd:simpleType>
  <xsd:restriction base="xsd:integer">
   <xsd:minInclusive value="100" />
   <xsd:maxInclusive value="999" />
  </xsd:restriction>
 </xsd:simpleType>
</xsd:element>
```

Unlike named custom types, which can be associated with multiple schema constructs, anonymous custom types can only be used with the element or attribute in which they're contained. To define an element or attribute with an anonymous custom type, follow these steps:

1. Begin the element or attribute declaration by typing either **<xsd:element name="*label*">** or **<xsd:attribute name="*label*">**, where *label* is the actual name of the element or attribute you're creating.

Caution These steps assume you've declared the schema of schemas namespace using the `xsd` prefix. If you've declared it in the default namespace, don't use the prefix as indicated in these steps.

2. Type **<xsd:simpleType>** to begin the simple type declaration.
3. Begin the restriction declaration and specify the datatype on which the custom type is based by typing **<xsd:restriction base="*foundation*">**, where *foundation* is the datatype on which you're basing the custom type.
4. Set restrictions for the custom type as specified in the "Controlling Acceptable Values" section of Chapter 10.
5. Type **</xsd:restriction>** to complete the restriction definition and then type **</xsd:simpleType>** to complete the simple type definition.
6. Type **</xsd:element>** or **</xsd:attribute>** as appropriate to complete the element or attribute declaration.

The result should look similar to the following:

```
<xsd:element name="element_name">
 <xsd:simpleType>
  <xsd:restriction base="foundation">
  ...
  </xsd:restriction>
 </xsd:simpleType>
</xsd:element>
```

Using Values Derived by List

In addition to being able to derive custom values by restriction, you can also derive custom values by list. Values derived by list can be part of either named or anonymous simple type definitions and can themselves be based in predefined datatypes or another custom type definition. Lists can also include union types.

Creating Lists

Standard simple type definitions only allow you to use a single value of a specific type. This means that you could define an element like this in schema:

```
<xsd:element name="code">
 <xsd:simpleType>
  <xsd:restriction base="xsd:integer">
   <xsd:minInclusive value="100" />
   <xsd:maxInclusive value="999" />
  </xsd:restriction>
 </xsd:simpleType>
</xsd:element>
```

and then use the element in the body of the document like this:

```
<code>100</code>
```

However, you couldn't assign multiple values to this element. The reason for this is that our restriction says that the value must be between 100 and 999; it doesn't say that the value can include sequences of values that meet these criteria. To define a simple type that allows you to specify sequences of values that meet certain restrictions, you must define your simple type as a list.

You can create lists using any of the available datatypes as the item type of the list, including custom types and union types. When a datatype is derived from a list type, you can use the following restrictions:

- `enumeration`
- `length`
- `maxLength`
- `minLength`
- `pattern`
- `whiteSpace`

Note For `length`, `maxLength`, and `minLength`, the unit of length is measured as the number of list items. Additionally, the `whiteSpace` restriction has a fixed value of `collapse` when used with lists. You'll learn more about these restrictions in Chapter 10.

The basic format of a list is:

```
<simpleType>
 <list itemType="dataType" />
</simpleType>
```

where *`dataType`* references the type of data the list items will contain.

You can think of a list as a sequence of white space-separated values. This means you can separate values with spaces, tabs, line feeds, or carriage returns. Thus, if you defined an element and its simple type like this:

```
<element name="values" type="valueList">

<simpleType name="valueList">
 <list itemType="integer" />
</simpleType>
```

you could use the element in a document like this:

```
<values>108 99 205 23 0 -12</values>
```

or like this:

```
<values>
108
99
205
23
0
-12
</values>
```

Understanding How Lists Use Whitespace

Lists treat whitespace differently from other datatypes. If a value type allows whitespace characters to be used, such as is the case with strings, the whitespace is still interpreted as an item separator. This means that if you defined a list like this:

```
<element name="values" type="stringList">

<simpleType name="stringList">
 <list itemType="string" />
</simpleType>
```

the following element declaration would be considered to have eight values associated with it:

```
<values>I really love working with XML! Don't you?</values>
```

and the related list items would be:

list item 1:	I
list item 2:	really
list item 3:	love
list item 4:	working
list item 5:	with
list item 6:	XML!
list item 7:	Don't
list item 8:	you?

Lists also handle tabs, line feeds, carriage returns, leading spaces, trailing spaces, and sequences of spaces a bit differently than other data types. The reason for this is that lists are defined with the whitespace restriction set to collapse. This means that XML processors

- Replace tabs, line feeds, and carriage returns with spaces wherever they occur
- Remove leading and trailing spaces
- Replace multiple spaces within strings with a single space

You'll find that the collapse value is helpful in ensuring that the list count is accurate. Without this feature, the following string would be considered to have many more list items than it actually does:

```
<values>a b c d
  e f g h
  i j k l
</values>
```

However, because the whitespace is collapsed, the XML processor modifies the contents to look like this:

```
<values>a b c d e f g h i j k l</values>
```

Now there are clearly only 12 items in the list.

Creating List Definitions in Schema

To define a list type, follow these steps:

1. Type **<xsd:simpleType** to begin the simple type declaration. If the list is a named custom type, type **name="*label*" />**, where *label* is the name of the custom type. If the list is an anonymous custom type, enter /> to complete the opening tag.

Caution These steps assume you've declared the schema of schemas namespace using the `xsd` prefix. If you've declared it in the default namespace, don't use the prefix as indicated in these steps.

2. Type **<xsd:list itemType="xsd:*dataType*" />**, where *dataType* is the actual type you want to use for the list. You can reference another custom type, one of the predefined data types, or a union type.
3. Type **</xsd:simpleType>** to complete the simple type definition.

The result should look similar to the following:

```
<xsd:simpleType name="label">
 <xsd:list itemType="xsd:dataType" />
</xsd:simpleType>
```

Using Values Derived by Union

Often you'll want to create elements or define attributes that can use multiple types of values. For example, say that you want to define an attribute that allows you to use either formatted strings or formatted numbers as values. To use both datatypes with an element or attribute, you must create a union of the simple types you want to use. The union of datatypes can be based on predefined types, custom types, or list types.

Creating Unions

Standard simple type definitions allow you to use only a single value of a specific type. However, they don't allow a single element or attribute to have multiple possible datatypes. To specify that multiple datatypes can be used with an element or attribute, you must associate the element or attribute with a union datatype.

You can create unions using any of the available datatypes or any of the list types you've defined. The basic format of a union is:

```
<simpleType>
 <union>
 ...
 </union>
</simpleType>
```

where the contents of a `union` are the simple types that you want to define as possible datatypes for the associated element or attribute.

The most basic `union` datatypes are those derived from two other simple types. In the following example the union makes it possible to use nonnegative integer values and an enumerated string as the contents for an element or attribute:

```
<simpleType>
 <union>
  <simpleType>
   <restriction base="nonNegativeInteger" />
  </simpleType>
```

(continued)

(continued)

```
  <simpleType>
   <restriction base="string">
    <enumeration value="unknown" />
    <enumeration value="invalid" />
    <enumeration value="not a number" />
   </restriction>
  </simpleType>
 </union>
</simpleType>
```

Valid values for an element or attribute that use this union datatype include

- 257
- 389
- unknown
- invalid
- not a number

But they don't include

- 0
- -27
- Hello
- Goodbye

Understanding the Order of Union Member Types

Each simple type defined as part of a union is referred to as a member type. In the previous example there were two member types. The first member type sets the rules for numbers to those of nonnegative integers. The second member type defined a list of possible values using enumeration.

The order in which member types are defined in a union is significant. When an XML processor validates a document, the union's values are validated against member types in the order in which the member types are declared. Validation stops when a match is found. In the following example values are validated according to the list of enumerated strings first, as negative integers second, and finally as positive integers:

```
<simpleType>
 <union>
  <simpleType>
   <restriction base="string">
    <enumeration value="unknown" />
    <enumeration value="invalid" />
    <enumeration value="not a number" />
   </restriction>
  </simpleType>
```

(continued)

(continued)

```
  <simpleType>
   <restriction base="negativeInteger" />
  </simpleType>
  <simpleType>
   <restriction base="positiveInteger" />
  </simpleType>
 </union>
</simpleType>
```

This means validation against a value of "27" would continue until the XML processor reached the third member in this union type but would stop at the first member for a value of "unknown". A value of "0" or "ABC", however, would fail validation.

Creating Union Definitions in Schema

To define a union type, follow these steps:

1. Type **<xsd:simpleType** to begin the simple type declaration. If the union is a named custom type, enter **name="*label*" />**, where *label* is the name of the custom union type. If the union is an anonymous custom type, enter **/>** to complete the opening tag.
2. Type **<xsd:union>** to declare the start of the union and then enter the simple type definitions that the union will contain.
3. Type **</xsd:union>** to complete the union element and then type **</xsd:simpleType>** to complete the simple type definition.

The result should look similar to the following:

```
<xsd:simpleType>
 <xsd:union>
 ...
 </xsd:union>
</xsd:simpleType>
```

More Info *XML Schema Part 2: Datatypes*, Paul V. Biron and Ashok Malhotra, eds., W3C, 2 May 2001. Available at *http://www.w3.org/TR/2001/REC-xmlschema-2-20010502/*.

Chapter 10

Specifying Datatypes and Restrictions in Schema

Many different datatypes are defined in XML Schema. The available datatypes can be divided into four general categories:

- String and name types, which include strings and other datatypes derived from strings.
- Date and time types, which include date and time values as well as duration.
- Numeric types, which include floating point and decimal values as well as values based on these datatypes.
- Miscellaneous types, which encompass all other datatypes not discussed elsewhere and include Boolean and binary values.

To control the acceptable values that can be used with datatypes, you use restrictions. You can use restrictions to assign minimum length, maximum length, or a specific length to element contents or attribute values. You can also use them to specify the acceptable format for values, the pattern to use for values, and the exact values that are permissible.

Using String and Name Datatypes

XML Schema defines many different string and name datatypes. String and name datatypes are designed for values that contain character strings. Simple types that are based on the string datatype can use the following restrictions:

- `length`
- `minLength`
- `maxLength`
- `pattern`
- `enumeration`
- `whiteSpace`

All datatypes derived from the string datatype can use the same set of restrictions. The only exceptions are `NMTOKENS`, `IDREFS`, and `ENTITIES`, which can't use patterns.

Defining a string Datatype

The base datatype for character strings is aptly named `string`. Elements and attributes with the `string` datatype can contain sequences of characters. For example, if you defined an element as the string type in schema like this:

```
<xsd:element name="owner" type="xsd:string" />
```

you could use the element in a document like this:

```
<owner>William R. Stanek</owner>
```

The string could contain tabs, multiple spaces, line feeds, and carriage returns as well, such as:

```
<owner> Owner: Unknown </owner>
```

Defining a normalizedString Datatype

If you refer to the hierarchy shown in the "Creating Simple Types" section of Chapter 9, "Defining Simple Types in Schema," you'll find `normalizedString` listed below `string` at the next level of the hierarchy. This means that `normalizedString` is derived from the `string` datatype. A `normalizedString` is a sequence of characters that doesn't contain carriage return (`#xD`), line feed (`#xA`), or tab (`#x9`) characters. The following normalized string declaration

```
<xsd:element name="owner" type="xsd:normalizedString" />
```

could be used like this in a document:

```
<owner>William R. Stanek</owner>
```

Any nonconforming whitespace in the document would be removed from the normalized string during processing. The reason for this is that the datatype definition for `normalizedString` in XML Schema looks like this:

```
<simpleType name="normalizedString">
 <restriction base="string">
 <whiteSpace value="replace">
 </restriction>
</simpleType>
```

This definition tells XML processors to replace carriage returns, line feeds, and tabs with spaces.

Defining a token Datatype

Another type of string that you might want to use is a `token`. A `token` is a normalized string that doesn't have leading or trailing spaces and doesn't have internal sequences of two or more spaces. The XML Schema definition of a `token` looks like this:

```
<simpleType name="token">
 <restriction base="string">
 <whiteSpace value="collapse">
 </restriction>
</simpleType>
```

This definition tells XML processors to remove carriage returns, line feeds, and tabs, to remove leading and trailing spaces, and to remove multiple occurrences of the space character and replace them with a single space anywhere they occur within the string. Thus, if a `token` string were defined in schema as:

```
<xsd:attribute name="currToken" type="xsd:token" />
```

and then used in a document like this:

```
<id currToken=" My Current Token " />
```

the XML processor would modify the attribute value to read:

```
<id currToken="My Current Token" />
```

Defining Other string Datatypes

Many other string and name related datatypes are available in XML Schema. A complete summary of these types is provided in Table 10-1.

Table 10-1. String and Name Datatypes

Name	Description
`ENTITIES`	A string containing a space-separated sequence of `ENTITY`s that have been declared as unparsed entities in a document type definition (DTD). Only used with schema attributes.
`ENTITY`	A string representing the `ENTITY` attribute in the XML language that has been declared as unparsed entities in a DTD. Only used with schema attributes.
`ID`	A string representing the `ID` attribute in the XML language. Only used with schema attributes.
`IDREF`	A string representing the `IDREF` attribute in the XML language. Only used with schema attributes.
`IDREFS`	A string containing a space-separated sequence of `IDREF`s. Only used with schema attributes.
`language`	A string containing a valid language identifier as specified in Request for Comments (RFC) 1766.
`Name`	A string containing a valid XML name.
`NCName`	A string that contains a valid local part name as described in the "Understanding Namespaces" section of Chapter 7, "XML Namespaces." Local part names are valid XML names that don't contain colon characters.

(continued)

Table 10-1. *(continued)*

Name	Description
`NMTOKEN`	A string representing the `NMTOKEN` attribute in the XML language. Only used with schema attributes.
`NMTOKENS`	A string containing a space-separated sequence of `NMTOKEN`s. Only used with schema attributes.
`normalizedString`	A sequence of characters that don't contain carriage return (`#xD`), line feed (`#xA`), or tab (`#x9`) characters. XML processors replace carriage returns, line feeds, and tabs with spaces.
`QName`	A string containing an XML qualified name. A qualified name has a namespace prefix followed by a colon and a local part name as described in the "Understanding Namespaces" section of Chapter 7.
`string`	A string containing sequences of characters.
`token`	A normalized string that doesn't have leading or trailing spaces and doesn't have internal sequences of two or more spaces. XML processors remove carriage returns, line feeds, tabs, leading spaces, and trailing spaces and replace multiple occurrences of the space character within the string.

`ID`, `IDREF`, `IDREFS`, `ENTITY`, `ENTITIES`, `NMTOKEN`, and `NMTOKENS` are used just like they are in DTDs. The key difference is that you're assigning these values through schema. Because of this, you declare the attribute that you want to use in schema before you use it in the related document. For example, the following declaration defines an `ID` attribute:

```
<xsd:attribute name="id" type="xsd:ID" />
```

which you could use in a document like this:

```
<owner id="d1005">William R. Stanek</owner>
```

As with DTDs, these values can be implied, fixed, or required. To do this, you'd set default or fixed values. Or you'd set `optional` or `required` usage. For example, you could make the `id` attribute required using the following declaration:

```
<xsd:attribute name="id" type="xsd:ID" use="required" />
```

Note You'll find a complete discussion of `ID`, `IDREF`, `IDREFS`, `ENTITY`, `ENTITIES`, `NMTOKEN`, and `NMTOKENS` in Chapter 5, "XML Attributes in DTDs."

Using Date and Time Datatypes

XML Schema has several predefined datatypes that can be used to represent dates and times. These datatypes can use the following restrictions:

- `enumeration`
- `maxExclusive`
- `maxInclusive`
- `minExclusive`
- `minInclusive`
- `pattern`
- `whiteSpace`

Because each `date` and `time` datatype has a slightly different usage, I'll examine each in turn, starting with `duration` and ending with `gMonth`. As you set out to work with date and time values, keep in mind that all dates are defined using Gregorian calendar dates.

Using the duration Datatype

The `duration` datatype is used to represent durations of time. You can think of a duration of time as a time interval. For example, a time interval of 1 year, 5 months and 30 days is a duration, and so is a time interval of 23 hours and 59 minutes.

Formatting duration Values

Time durations are specified in the form PnYnMnDTnHnMnS, where

- P is a required character that indicates the period.
- nY indicates the number of years. For example, to indicate five years, you'd enter 5Y.
- nM indicates the number of months. For example, to indicate six months, you'd enter 6M.
- nD indicates the number of days. For example, to indicate 15 days, you'd enter 15D.
- T indicates the start of the optional time section. Any time you use hour, minute, or second values, you must specify the start of the time section with T.
- nH indicates the number of hours. For example, to indicate 23 hours, you'd enter 23H.
- nM indicates the number of minutes. For example, to indicate 58 minutes, you'd enter 58M.
- nS indicates the number of seconds. For example, to indicate 30 seconds, you'd enter 30S.

Following this, you could indicate a duration of 1 year, 3 months, 5 days, 6 hours, 3 minutes, and 30 seconds by entering the following value:

```
P1Y3M5DT6H3M30S
```

Although the year, month, day, hour, and minute values must be entered as integers, seconds can contain a decimal place to allow for precision. This means that the following is a valid duration:

```
P1Y3M5DT6H3M30.5S
```

However, this duration is incorrect because the year value isn't an integer:

```
P1.5Y3M5DT6H3M30S
```

If the value for a position is zero, the zero and its corresponding designator can be omitted. However, don't forget the T if you enter values in the time section. This means that you could specify a duration of 30 days like this:

```
P30D
```

and you must specify a duration of 5 hours like this:

```
PT5H
```

but not like this:

```
P5H
```

You can specify a negative duration as well. When you do this, enter a minus sign (-) before the P character. The following indicates a duration of minus 30 days:

```
-P30D
```

Declaring a duration in Schema

To declare an element or attribute that uses a duration, specify the duration type when defining the schema construct, such as:

```
<xsd:element name="contract-period": type="xsd:duration" />
```

Then use it in a document like this:

```
<contract-period>P2Y6M</contract-period>
```

Don't forget that you can control the pattern used for durations (and other types of dates as well). To do this, you'd define a custom type and then set a pattern as discussed in the "Specifying Expressions for Acceptable Values" section of this chapter. In the following example, a four-digit year, two-digit month, and two-digit day is required:

```
<simpleType name='yearMonthDayInterval'>
 <restriction base='duration'>
 <pattern value='P\p{Nd}{4}Y\p{Nd}{2}M\p{Nd}{2}D' />
 </restriction>
</simpleType>
```

Because of the restriction, durations of type `yearMonthDayInterval` must look like this:

```
P2002Y05M15D
```

Using the dateTime Datatype

You use the `dateTime` datatype to reference a specific instant of time. As with durations, `dateTime` values are complex.

Formatting dateTime Values

You make specific time references in the form CCYY-MM-DDThh:mm:ss, where:

- CC represents the century, specified as two or more digits. Valid range from 00 to ...
- YY represents the year, specified as two digits. Range from 00 to 99.
- MM represents the month, specified as two digits. Range from 01 to 12.
- DD represents the day, specified as two digits. Range from 01 to 31.
- T indicates the start of the mandatory time section, specified as two digits.
- hh represents the hour, specified as two digits. Range from 00 to 23.
- mm represents the minutes, specified as two digits. Range from 00 to 59.
- ss represents the seconds, specified as two digits with an optional decimal value allowed. Range from 00 to 59.

Tip In all cases you must specify at least two digits. This means you must enter 06 instead of 6. Note also that a 24-hour clock is used, with values from 0 to 11 representing A.M. and values from 12 to 23 representing P.M. This means that the `dateTime` value 1999-11-15T08:30:05 represents the time at 5 seconds after 8:30 A.M. on November 15, 1999.

Unlike durations, all components of `dateTime` values are required. This means that you could express an exact instant in time like this:

```
1999-11-15T08:30:05
```

However, you couldn't express an instant in time like this:

```
99-11-15
```

or this:

```
11-15T08:30:05
```

Although the century is typically two digits, you can use additional digits to represent years greater than 9999. You can't, however, represent the year 0000, which is an illegal value. This means you could specify an instant in time in the year 1,000,000 like this:

```
1000000-01-01T00:00:01
```

but you couldn't specify the year 0000 like this:

```
0000-01-01T00:00:01
```

As with durations, you must represent all values as integers. The only exception is with seconds, where you can use decimal values to indicate time more precisely, such as:

```
1999-11-15T08:30:05.35
```

Setting Negative dateTime Values

All dateTime values are assumed to be A.D. and have a positive value. This means to indicate B.C. you can use a negative value, such as:

```
-0300-09-01T00:25:01
```

Here, you're indicating the year 300 B.C.

Note The year 1 A.D. is represented as 0001 and the year 1 B.C. is represented as –0001. You can't specify the year 0000, which doesn't exist in the Gregorian calendar.

Setting Time Zones

If you need to specify a time zone, you can do this in one of two ways. You can either enter your time value in UTC time (which is coordinated universal time format) or you can enter an offset from UTC time. To specify a value in UTC time, type a Z after the `dateTime` value, such as:

```
1999-11-15T08:30:05Z
```

To specify an offset from UTC time, append a positive or negative time to the `dateTime` value in the form:

```
hh:mm
```

For example, to indicate Pacific Time, which is eight hours behind UTC time, you'd add -08:00 to the end of the `dateTime` value, such as:

```
1999-11-15T08:30:05-08:00
```

Similarly, to indicate Seoul time, which is nine hours ahead of UTC time, you'd add +09:00 to the end of the `dateTime` value, such as:

```
1999-11-15T08:30:05+09:00
```

Declaring a dateTime Value in Schema

Following this discussion, you could declare an element or attribute as the `dateTime` type:

```
<xsd:attribute name="eDate": type="xsd:dateTime" />
```

then use it in a document like this:

```
<experiment number="030" eDate="1999-11-15T08:30:05-08:00" />
```

The `dateTime` value must always be exactly formatted and follow one of these conventions:

- CCYY-MM-DDThh:mm:ss
- CCYY-MM-DDThh:mm:ssZ
- CCYY-MM-DDThh:mm:ss+hh:mm
- CCYY-MM-DDThh:mm:ss-hh:mm

Using the time Datatype

The `time` datatype is used to reference a specific instant of time that occurs every day. Values of this datatype follow the exact same rules as `dateTime` values and are declared in the form hh:mm:ss. This means that hours and minutes must be specified as integer values, but seconds can use decimal values to specify an exact time. If you wanted to specify five seconds after 8:30 A.M. every day, you'd enter:

```
08:30:05
```

Caution All digits are required. You couldn't enter 8:30:05.

As with `dateTime` values, you can specify a time zone by adding a Z to indicate UTC time or you can append an offset from UTC time. Here are some examples:

```
12:15:00Z

15:45:30+9:00

01:20:15-08:00
```

To declare an element or attribute as the `time` type, you could specify the type like this:

```
<xsd:element name="dailyTask": type="xsd:time" />
```

then use the element or attribute in a document like this:

```
<dailyTask>12:00</dailyTask>
```

Using the date Datatype

You use the `date` datatype to reference a specific calendar date. Values of this datatype follow the exact same rules as `dateTime` values and are declared in the form CCYY-MM-DD. This means that

- Year, month, and date values must be specified as two-digit integers.
- Centuries must be specified with at least two digits and are also integer values.
- All dates are assumed to be A.D. unless you use the minus sign to indicate B.C. dates.

As with dateTime values, the year 0000 is illegal and you can specify additional digits for the century as needed. For example, you could specify a date in 1,000,000 B.C. like this:

```
-1000000-01-01
```

Caution All digits are required. You couldn't enter -1000000-1-1.

To declare an element or attribute as the date type, you could specify the type like this:

```
<xsd:attribute name="carbondate": type="xsd:date" />
```

then use the element or attribute in a document like this:

```
<record carbondate="-1000000-01-01">Fossil 345123</record>
```

Note You can specify a time zone with date values if necessary. Specify the time zone by adding a Z to indicate UTC time or append an offset from UTC time.

Using the gYear, gYearMonth, gMonthDay, gMonth, and gDay Datatypes

As you might expect, XML Schema lets you represent part of a date as well. These datatypes are defined as subsets of dateTime, and each individual subset type is subject to the same rules as that component in the dateTime datatype.

These dateTime subsets have the following meaning:

- gYear represents a calendar year in the form CCYY, such as 2001 for the year 2001.
- gYearMonth represents a calendar year and month in the form CCYY-MM, such as 2002-12 for the month December in the year 2002.
- gMonthDay represents a calendar month and day in the form —MM-DD, such as —12-31 for December 31 in any calendar year.
- gMonth represents a calendar month in the form —MM—, such as —12— for the month December in any calendar year.
- gDay represents a calendar day in the form —DD, such as —15 for the 15th day of any month.

As with other dateTime values, you must enter the year, month, and day as two-digit integers and you can enter the century with two or more digits. Unlike other dateTime values, only gYear and gYearMonth can be preceded by a sign to indicate B.C. instead of A.D. This means the following is a valid gYear:

```
-0300
```

However, the following is an invalid gMonth:

```
---12--
```

Note Note the extra minus sign, which is illegal for gMonth. Additionally, you can specify a time zone with any of these values if necessary. Specify the time zone by adding a Z to indicate UTC time or append an offset from UTC time.

To declare an element or attribute as the gYear, gYearMonth, gMonthDay, gMonth, or gDay type, you could specify the type like this:

```
<xsd:attribute name="year": type="xsd:gYear" />
```

Then use the element or attribute in a document like this:

```
<record year="2001">Fossil 345123</record>
```

Using Numeric Datatypes

XML Schema defines two general datatypes that can be used with numbers:

- **decimal** A numeric type that indicates the value is a number and the digits 0-9, the period (.), the plus sign (+), and the minus sign (-) are allowed as characters.
- **floats** A numeric type that indicates floating point values are allowed and follows the rules for floating point numbers specified in Institute of Electrical and Electronics Engineers (IEEE) 754-1985.

Working with the Decimal Datatype and Its Derivatives

The decimal datatype and its derivatives are the datatypes you'll use most often to represent numbers. These number types differ from floats in that they don't allow you to use scientific notation and aren't really designed to hold very large values.

The decimal datatype and its derivatives can use the following restrictions:

- enumeration
- fractionDigits
- maxExclusive
- maxInclusive
- minExclusive
- minInclusive
- pattern
- totalDigits
- whiteSpace

Defining decimal Datatypes

A `decimal` value is a number that can include an optional fractional component as well as a positive or negative number sign. This means that all of the following are valid `decimal` values:

- +3.4566
- -2.533
- 28434
- 0
- -15

You could define a `decimal` datatype in schema like this:

```
<xsd:attribute name="cost": type="xsd:decimal" />
```

then use the related element or attribute in a document like this:

```
<item cost="101.50">3 1/2" Floppy Disk Drive</item>
```

Tip The maximum number of decimal digits XML processors are required to support is 18. This means that a number could have up to 18 decimal places or a combination of digits to the right and left of the decimal place that add up to 18 but no more. If you require more digits or high precision and don't know the number of digits a processor supports, don't use values based on decimal and instead consider using floating-point values.

Defining integer Datatypes

The `decimal` datatype has a main derivative called `integer`. An integer is a decimal value that doesn't allow a fractional component. This means the following are valid integers:

- +49
- 29
- -900
- 0
- 87

However, the following are invalid integers:

- -2.5
- 3.875
- 12233.5

Table 10-2 provides a summary of `integer` values, their uses, and their valid ranges. As the table shows, datatypes that are classified as integers can be divided into three categories:

- **Range-constrained integers** A subset of integers (`nonPositiveInteger`, `nonNegativeInteger`, `positiveInteger`, and `negativeInteger`) that allow you to use whole numbers with a number sign.
- **Size-constrained integers** A subset of integers (`long`, `int`, `short`, `byte`, `unsignedLong`, `unsignedInt`, `unsignedShort`, and `unsignedByte`) with increasingly size-constrained values that are either signed or unsigned.
- **Size-constrained and sign-constrained integers** A subset of integers (`unsignedInt`, `unsignedShort`, and `unsignedByte`) with increasingly size-constrained values that are unsigned.

Table 10-2. Overview of Integer-Derived Datatypes

Integer Type	XML Datatype	Description	Range
Range-constrained	`nonPositiveInteger`	A subset of integers that includes only non-positive values	..., -2, -1, 0
	`nonNegativeInteger`	A subset of integers that includes only non-negative values	0, 1, 2, ...
	`positiveInteger`	A subset of integers that includes only positive values	1, 2, ...
	`negativeInteger`	A subset of integers that includes only negative values	...,-2, -1
Size-constrained	`byte`	A signed 8-bit integer	-2^7 to 2^7 - 1 (-128 to 127)
	`short`	A signed 16-bit integer	-2^15 to 2^15 - 1 (-32,768 to 32,767)
	`int`	A signed 32-bit integer	-2^31 to 2^31 - 1 (-2,147,483,648 to 2,147,483,647)
	`long`	A signed 64-bit integer	-2^63 to 2^63 - 1
Size- and Sign-constrained	`unsignedByte`	An unsigned 8-bit integer	0 to 2^7 -1 (0 to 127)
	`unsignedShort`	An unsigned 16-bit integer	0 to 2^15 - 1 (0 to 32,767)
	`unsignedInt`	An unsigned 32-bit integer	0 to 2^31 - 1 (0 to 2,147,483,647)
	`unsignedLong`	An unsigned 64-bit integer	0 to 2^63 - 1

As you can see from Table 10-2, `integer` datatypes have a strictly defined range. Explicit ranges ensure that the size of a datatype on one platform is the same on other platforms. This allows you to create XML schemas that are guaranteed to allow the same values on all platforms. This is important if the data within documents is to be portable and could be read on many different platforms or could be interpreted using different programming languages.

As you work with integers, you'll find that `bytes`, `ints`, and `longs` each have their uses and that `shorts` are rarely used. The `byte` datatype is useful when you work with raw binary data that might not be compatible with other built-in types. The `int` is useful when you want to create a number for counting or performing integer math. The `long` datatype is useful when you're working with large values that can't be represented as ints.

The following are examples of integer declarations in schema:

```
<xsd:attribute name="value": type="xsd:int" />

<xsd:attribute name="flagState": type="xsd:short" />

<xsd:attribute name="numExecutions":
 type="xsd:nonNegativeInteger" />
```

In order for a document to be valid, values defined using these datatypes must conform to the range of the datatype specified. For example, if you define a numeric datatype like this:

```
<xsd:attribute name="flagState": type="xsd:unsignedShort" />
```

you could specify a value for this attribute using a range from 0 to 32,767, such as:

```
<code flagState="0" />
```

or

```
<code flagState="32" />
```

However, if you specify a value outside of the acceptable range, such as:

```
<code flagState="-32" />
```

the document won't be considered valid.

Working with Floating-Point Datatypes

Floating-point datatypes are designed to represent numbers that need high precision and have decimal values. If you don't need high precision or are working with whole numbers, you should use decimal numbers or derivatives of the decimal datatype.

Using Floating-Point Values

XML Schema specifies that floating-point numbers must follow the industry standard specification as written in IEEE 754-1985. This means that floating-point values can be expressed using either standard or scientific notation. Standard notation consists of a whole number followed by a decimal point, such as 8.95, 1.393, or 3.05. Unlike the `decimal` datatype, where the decimal place is optional, the decimal place is required with floating-point values. This means that you can specify a floating-point value as 10.0 or 82.0. However, you can't specify the value as 10 or 82.

Scientific notation uses a standard notation plus a suffix that specifies a power of 10 by which the number is to be multiplied. The exponent is indicated by an e or E followed by the exponent value, which can be positive or negative, such as:

- 7.654E15
- 2.345E-04

You can't, however, use the plus sign to indicate a positive exponent. This means that the following floating-point values are invalid in XML Schema:

- 7.654E+15
- 3.3434E+3

With scientific notation, you can't have more than a single digit to the left of the decimal point and you must have at least one digit to the right of the decimal point. Additionally, leading and trailing zeroes are prohibited (except to meet the previous requirements). This means that the following scientific notations are correct:

- 7.654E15
- 3.3434E3

but these scientific notations are incorrect:

- 76.5E9
- 1E3

Note Although leading and trailing zeroes are prohibited, a value of 1.0E3 is legal. The reason for this is that there must be at least one digit to the right of the decimal point and the only way to do this with a whole number is to enter a zero.

Defining float and double Datatypes in Schema

Floating-point values in XML Schema can have two different precisions:

- Single-precision floating-point numbers consist of a 32-bit space and are designated as the `float` datatype.
- Double-precision numbers are allotted a 64-bit space and are designated as the `double` datatype.

The `float` and `double` datatypes can use the following restrictions:

- `enumeration`
- `maxExclusive`
- `maxInclusive`
- `minExclusive`
- `minInclusive`
- `pattern`
- `whiteSpace`

The largest magnitude single-precision floating-point value as defined in IEEE 754-1985 is 3.40282347e+38f, and the smallest is 1.40239846e-45f. The largest double-precision floating-point number is 1.79769313486231570e+308, and the smallest floating-point number is 4.94065645841246544e-324. However, XML Schema specifies the following noninclusive ranges that are a bit different:

- `floats` have a valid range in XML Schema from 2.3509E-38 to 3.4028E38
- `doubles` have a valid range in XML Schema from 2.2251E-308 to 8.9884E307

The float and double datatypes can also have the following special values:

- `0` Referred to as positive zero. Positive zero is greater than negative zero.
- `-0` Referred to as negative zero.
- `INF` Referred to as positive infinity. Positive infinity is greater than all other possible values (except Not-a-number).
- `-INF` Referred to as negative infinity. Negative infinity is less than all other possible values.
- `NaN` Referred to as Not-a-number. Not-a-number is equal to itself and greater than all other possible values.

Caution The `INF`, `-INF`, and `NaN` values must be specified exactly as shown. You can't change the letter case. For example, it's incorrect to set a value to `Inf` or `NAN`.

The following are examples of floating-point declarations in schema:

```
<xsd:attribute name="calculation": type="xsd:float" />
```

```
<xsd:attribute name="trajectory": type="xsd:double" />
```

In order for a document to be valid, values defined using these datatypes must conform to the range of the datatype specified. For example, if you define a numeric datatype like this:

```
<xsd:attribute name="computation": type="xsd:double" />
```

all of the following values are valid:

```
<orbit computation="0" />
<orbit computation="-0" />
<orbit computation="INF" />
<orbit computation="-INF" />
<orbit computation="NaN" />
<orbit computation="2.4521E3" />
<orbit computation="2.4521E-3" />
```

However, if you specify a value outside of the acceptable range, the document won't be considered valid. The document also won't be considered valid if the format of the number is incorrect, such as shown in this example, which has too many digits to the left of the decimal place:

```
<orbit computation="24.521E3" />
```

Using Other Datatypes

So far, we've looked at string and numeric datatypes but haven't looked at other datatypes, including `boolean`, `hexBinary`, `base64Binary`, and `anyURI`. Now let's look at each of these miscellaneous datatypes in turn.

Using boolean Datatypes

The `boolean` datatype is used to represent binary-logic values. In binary logic, a value is either `true` or `false`. In true binary format, `true` is represented as 1 and `false` is represented as 0, which is why legal values for `booleans` are `true`, `false`, 1, and `0`.

Caution You can't specify any other letter case for the true or false values. This means that True and TRUE as values for a boolean datatype are incorrect.

A `boolean` datatype can use the following restrictions:

- `pattern`
- `whiteSpace`

The following is an example of a boolean declaration in schema:

```
<xsd:attribute name="answer": type="xsd:boolean" />
```

You could then use the schema construct in a document like this:

```
<question number="5" answer="true" />
```

Using Binary Datatypes

Binary datatypes are useful if you want to define elements or attributes that can have as contents streams of data, such as the contents of a binary file. XML Schema specifies two datatypes that can be used to express binary-formatted data. These datatypes are:

- **hexBinary** Represents hexadecimal-encoded binary data, where each value is represented as a binary octet consisting of the hexadecimal digits 0-9, a-f, or A-F. For example, 13A1 is the hex encoding for the integer value 5025 (that has a binary representation of 1001110100001).
- **base64Binary** Represents Base64-encoded binary data, where each binary octet is encoded as part of a binary data stream according to the Base64 Content Transfer Encoding definition in RFC 2045.

Binary datatypes can use the following restrictions:

- `enumeration`
- `length`
- `maxLength`
- `minLength`
- `pattern`
- `whiteSpace`

The following is an example of a `hexBinary` declaration in schema:

```
<xsd:element name="blobSource": type="xsd:hexBinary"/>
```

You could then use the schema construct in a document like this:

```
<blobSource>13A113A113A113A113A113A113A113A113A113A1
</blobSource>
```

Using URI Datatypes

If you need to specify a value that's a Uniform Resource Indicator (URI) or URI subtype, such as a relative or absolute Uniform Resource Locator (URL), you can use the `anyURI` datatype. Although URI can have spaces, the use of spaces within URI values is discouraged. Instead, you should replace the space with its encoded value %20.

URI datatypes can use the following restrictions:

- `enumeration`
- `length`
- `maxLength`
- `minLength`
- `pattern`
- `whiteSpace`

The following is an example of an `anyURI` declaration in schema:

```
<xsd:attribute name="location" type="xsd:anyURI" />
```

You could then use the schema construct in a document like this:

```
<image location="http://www.microsoft.com/data.jpg" />
```

Controlling Acceptable Values

When you create custom simple types, you can control the acceptable values using restrictions. As discussed in Chapter 9, "Defining Simple Types in Schema," there are two custom types: named and anonymous. Named custom types can be used with multiple schema constructs and follow the form:

```
<xsd:simpleType name="label">
 <xsd:restriction base="xsd:foundation">
 ...
 </xsd:restriction>
</xsd:simpleType>
```

Anonymous custom types can only be used with a specific schema construct, and they have one of the following forms:

```
<xsd:element name="element_name">
 <xsd:simpleType>
 <xsd:restriction base="xsd:foundation">
 ...
 </xsd:restriction>
 </xsd:simpleType>
</xsd:element>
```

or

```
<xsd:attribute name="attribute_name">
 <xsd:simpleType>
 <xsd:restriction base="xsd:foundation">
 ...
 </xsd:restriction>
 </xsd:simpleType>
</xsd:attribute>
```

The following sections show how you can use restrictions with these custom types.

Specifying a Set of Acceptable Values

Any time you want to specify a set of acceptable values, you can use the `enumeration` restriction with your custom type. Enumerations declare a finite set of values that can be used. If a value doesn't match an item in the enumeration list, the document is considered invalid.

The basic format for an enumeration is:

```
<enumeration value="choice">
```

where *choice* is one of the acceptable values. This means that you could declare an enumeration for the continents of the world like this:

```
<xsd:simpleType name="continents">
 <xsd:restriction base="xsd:token">
 <xsd:enumeration value="Africa" />
 <xsd:enumeration value="Antarctica" />
 <xsd:enumeration value="Asia" />
 <xsd:enumeration value="Australia" />
 <xsd:enumeration value="Europe" />
 <xsd:enumeration value="North America" />
 <xsd:enumeration value="South America" />
 </xsd:restriction>
</xsd:simpleType>
```

Enumerations don't have to be declared using the format for empty elements. They could have opening and closing tags as well, such as:

```
<xsd:simpleType name="continents">
 <xsd:restriction base="xsd:token">
 <xsd:enumeration value="Africa"></xsd:enumeration>
 <xsd:enumeration value="Antarctica"></xsd:enumeration>
 <xsd:enumeration value="Asia"></xsd:enumeration>
 <xsd:enumeration value="Australia"></xsd:enumeration>
 <xsd:enumeration value="Europe"></xsd:enumeration>
 <xsd:enumeration value="North_America"></xsd:enumeration>
 <xsd:enumeration value="South_America"></xsd:enumeration>
 </xsd:restriction>
</xsd:simpleType>
```

An example of when you might use opening and closing tags with an enumeration is when you add documentation, such as:

```
<xsd:simpleType name="continents">
 <xsd:restriction base="xsd:token">
 <xsd:enumeration value="Africa">
 <xsd:annotation>
 <xsd:documentation>The second largest continent. Located
  south of Europe.</xsd:documentation>
 </xsd:annotation>
 </xsd:enumeration>
 <xsd:enumeration value="Antarctica">
 <xsd:annotation>
```

(continued)

(continued)

```
 <xsd:documentation>The continent centered in the South Pole and
  primarily located in the Antarctic Circle.</xsd:documentation>
 </xsd:annotation>
 </xsd:enumeration>
  ...
 </xsd:restriction>
</xsd:simpleType>
```

You can use enumerations with most datatypes, including strings, numbers, and date/time values. To specify an enumeration in schema, follow these steps:

1. Within the custom type definition, type **<xsd:enumeration** or **<enumeration** as appropriate.
2. Type **value="*choice*"** />, where *choice* is one of the acceptable values.
3. Repeat Steps 1 and 2 for each additional value that can be used.

The result should look like this:

```
<xsd:simpleType>
 <xsd:restriction base="xsd:baseType">
 <xsd:enumeration value="choice1" />
 <xsd:enumeration value="choice2" />
 <xsd:enumeration value="..." />
 <xsd:enumeration value="choiceN" />
 </xsd:restriction>
</xsd:simpleType>
```

Specifying Expressions for Acceptable Values

If you need to specify an exact sequence of characters that are acceptable as part of an element's or attribute's contents, you can use the pattern restriction. You construct patterns using the regular expression language defined in the Perl programming language. Regular expressions define the specific letters, numbers, and symbols that can be used, as well as the order in which those letters, numbers, and symbols should appear.

Note Because expressions are extremely complex and could fill an entire chapter by themselves, I'll focus on the essentials. For more detailed information, I recommend referring to a book that covers the Perl programming language.

Representing a Series of Values

The most basic regular expressions are those that define a series of numbers of letters that can be used. For example, if you wanted to specify a one-character string with the only valid values being the lowercase letters of the English alphabet, you could specify the expression for the pattern declaration like this:

```
<pattern value="[a-z]">
```

Now the values matching this pattern must have a single character and it must be one of the lowercase letters from a to z. To require three characters that followed this format, you'd use:

```
<pattern value="[a-z][a-z][a-z]">
```

This means that values matching this pattern include "abc", "def", and "zax" but don't include "ab", "defg", or "z". Other patterns of this type have these forms:

- **[.-.]** Represents the first and last character in a series of values of which you can use one. You could use 0-9 for the numerals 0-9, A-Z for the uppercase letters, a-zA-Z for uppercase and lowercase letters, or a-zA-Z0-9 for uppercase and lowercase letters as well as numerals.
- **[abc]** Represents a list of values of which you can use one. In this case you can use one of the letters a, b, or c.

An example using a basic expression in schema follows:

```
<simpleType name="USPostalcode">
 <restriction base="integer">
 <pattern value="[0-9][0-9][0-9][0-9][0-9]-[0-9][0-9][0-9][0-9]" />
 </restriction>
</simpleType>
```

This example provides a basic representation of the U.S. postal code values known as Zip+4. Zip+4 values are written in the form 98599-1025.

Using Groups, Occurrence Indicators, and Choices

Regular expressions provide grouping, choice, and occurrence indicators, which are identical to those used with DTDs. These indicators are

- ? for values that can occur zero or one time
- + for values that must occur one or more times
- * for values that can occur zero or more times
- ( ) for grouping sets of values
- | for specifying a list of choices

This means that you could specify that a series of characters is optional and repeatable, like this:

```
<pattern value="([a-z])*">
```

Here, the element or attribute contents can have any number of characters as long as those characters include only the lowercase letters a to z.

Similarly, you could specify a mandatory and repeatable sequence of characters like this:

```
<pattern value="([A-Z][0-9])+">
```

Here, the element or attribute contents can have multiple occurrences of an uppercase letter followed by a numeral, such as: A5B4C3 or D2E7H9.

You can also use a choice indicator (|), which has the same usage as in DTDs. For example, to specify that the value must be a or b or c, you could use the following expression:

```
<pattern value="a|b|c">
```

You could define a group of choices in schema like this:

```
<simpleType name="validAnswers">
 <restriction base="string">
 <pattern value="a|b|c|d|e|true|false" />
 </restriction>
</simpleType>
```

Using Quantity Indicators

Regular expressions also have quantity indicators, which are indicated by brackets. Here are some examples:

- `[A-Z]{5}` indicates that there must be exactly five letters in a row and those letters must be the uppercase letters A to Z.
- `[a-z]{5}` indicates that there must be at least five letters in a row and those letters must be the lowercase letters a to z.
- `[0-9]{2-4}` indicates that there must be between two and four numerals in a row.
- `(abc){5}` indicates that there must be exactly five sequences of abc in a row.

Here's an example using quantity indicators in schema:

```
<simpleType name="USPostalCode">
 <restriction base="integer">
 <pattern value="[0-9]{5}(-[0-9]{4})?" />
 </restriction>
</simpleType>
```

The example provides an improved representation of U.S. postal codes. In this example, values can be entered using five digits followed by an optional section that includes a dash and four additional digits. This means that 98599 and 98599-1025 are both legal values that match this regular expression.

Using Literal Values and Single Character Expressions

When you use regular expressions, you can also enter literal values. A literal value must appear exactly in the contents as you've entered it in the expression. To specify a literal value, simply enter the characters you want to use as they must appear in the element or attribute contents. In the following example the literal value `Dataset:` must be a part of the contents specified:

```
<pattern value="Dataset: ([0-9]){3}" />
```

You'll often use literal values with single character expressions, including

- `.` to represent that any character is allowed
- `\d` to represent that any digit character is allowed
- `\D` to represent that any nondigit character is allowed
- `\s` to represent that any whitespace character is allowed (including space, tab, new line, and carriage return)
- `\S` to represent that any character that isn't a whitespace character is allowed

For example, if your organization used purchase order numbers that followed the format:

```
INVOICE # D8000-AH
```

here are some ways you could define the pattern for the purchase order number:

- `INVOICE # ....-..` to represent that the order number could be a series of any four characters followed by a dash followed by any two characters.
- `INVOICE # .{4}-.{2}` to represent that the order number could be a series of any four characters followed by a dash followed by any two characters.
- `INVOICE # \S{4}-\S{2}` to represent that the first four and last two digits can be any non-whitespace character.
- `INVOICE # [A-Z]\d{3}-[A-Z]{2}` to represent that the first digit in the order number must be an uppercase letter, followed by three numerals, a dash, and two uppercase letters.

Now that you know how to use single character expressions, you can define more complex expressions, such as one that specifies U.K. postal codes, with the form:

```
CCD(D) DCC
```

where C is an uppercase letter and D is a digit and there's a space between the first four characters and the last three characters. One way to represent this code in schema is as follows:

```
<simpleType name="UKPostalCode">
 <restriction base="string">
 <pattern value="[A-Z]{2}\d(\d)\s\d[A-Z]{2}" />
 </restriction>
</simpleType>
```

Note In the pattern, note that the fourth character is enclosed in parentheses to indicate that it is optional. This means that both of the following are valid U.K. postal codes that conform to the specified pattern: RG7 4UZ and PO18 8UT.

Defining a Pattern for a Simple Type

You can use patterns with most datatypes, including strings, numbers, and date/time values. To specify a pattern in schema, follow these steps:

1. Within the custom type definition, type **<xsd:pattern** or **<pattern** as appropriate.
2. Type **value="*expression*"** />, where *expression* is a regular expression that uses the Perl programming language regular expression syntax.

The result should look like this:

```
<xsd:simpleType>
 <xsd:restriction base="xsd:baseType">
 <xsd:pattern value="expression" />
 </xsd:restriction>
</xsd:simpleType>
```

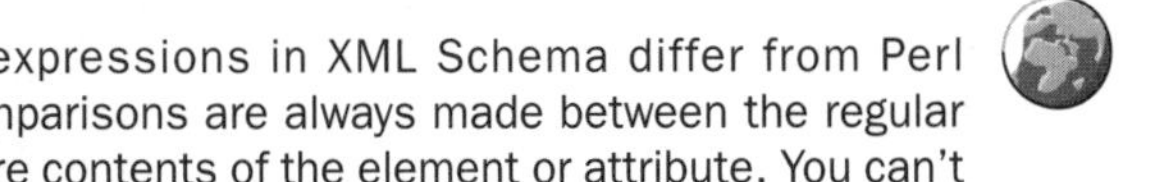
Real World Regular expressions in XML Schema differ from Perl expressions in that comparisons are always made between the regular expression and the entire contents of the element or attribute. You can't limit a match to the beginning or end of a line using ^ or $. These characters aren't available in XML Schema.

Specifying Acceptable Whitespace Characters

The `whiteSpace` restriction determines how tabs, line feeds, carriage returns, and spaces are handled when entered as values. This restriction has three possible values:

- **preserve** Ensures the string isn't normalized, meaning the XML processor replaces no whitespace characters.
- **replace** Ensures that the string is normalized, causing the XML processor to replace all tab, line feed, and carriage return characters with spaces.
- **collapse** Ensures that the string is normalized and unnecessary spaces are removed. This means all tab, line feed, and carriage return characters are replaced with spaces, leading and trailing spaces are removed, and all internal sequences of spaces are reduced to a single space.

As pointed out previously in this chapter, the `normalizedString` datatype is essentially a string that uses the whitespace restriction `replace`, and the `token` datatype is essentially a string that uses the whitespace restriction `collapse`. You could create a custom datatype that's similar to the token datatype using the following schema definition:

```
<simpleType name="modifiedString">
 <restriction base="string">
 <whiteSpace value="collapse">
 </restriction>
</simpleType>
```

You can use `whiteSpace` restrictions with most datatypes, including strings, numbers, and date/time values. To specify a `whiteSpace` restriction in schema, follow these steps:

1. Within the custom type definition, type **<xsd:whiteSpace** or **<whiteSpace** as appropriate.
2. Type **value="preserve" />**, **value="replace" />**, or **value="collapse" />** as appropriate.

The result should look like this:

```
<xsd:simpleType>
 <xsd:restriction base="xsd:baseType">
 <xsd:whiteSpace value="collapse" />
 </xsd:restriction>
</xsd:simpleType>
```

Specifying a Range of Acceptable Values

In schema, you can specify a range of inclusive or exclusive values using the following declarations:

- **maxExclusive** Sets the upper bounds for numeric values as less than (<) the value specified (rather than less than or equal to).
- **minExclusive** Sets the lower bounds for numeric values as greater than (>) the value specified (rather than greater than or equal to).
- **maxInclusive** Sets the upper bounds for numeric values as less than or equal to (<=) the value specified.
- **minInclusive** Sets the lower bounds for numeric values as greater than or equal to (>=) the value specified.

With exclusive values, consider that the value is up to or down to but not including the value specified. This means that you could define a range that included the values 100, 101, 102, 103, 104, 105, 106, 107, 108, 109, and 110 like this:

```
<xsd:simpleType name="category">
 <xsd:restriction base="xsd:integer">
 <xsd:minExclusive value="99" />
 <xsd:maxExclusive value="111" />
 </xsd:restriction>
</xsd:simpleType>
```

With an inclusive value, consider that the value is up to or down to and including the value specified. This means that you could define the range previously specified using inclusive values like this:

```
<xsd:simpleType name="category">
 <xsd:restriction base="xsd:integer">
 <xsd:minInclusive value="100" />
 <xsd:maxInclusive value="110" />
 </xsd:restriction>
</xsd:simpleType>
```

Although you could specify that a `minInclusive` range has a `maxExclusive` upper bounds or a `minExclusive` range has a `maxInclusive` upper bounds, you can't specify two minimum or two maximum values. This means that the following definitions are legal:

```
<xsd:simpleType name="category">
 <xsd:restriction base="xsd:integer">
 <xsd:minInclusive value="1" />
 <xsd:maxExclusive value="100" />
 </xsd:restriction>
</xsd:simpleType>
```

However, the following definitions are illegal:

```
<xsd:simpleType name="category">
 <xsd:restriction base="xsd:integer">
 <xsd:minInclusive value="100" />
 <xsd:minExclusive value="100" />
 <xsd:maxExclusive value="1000" />
 </xsd:restriction>
</xsd:simpleType>
```

Additionally, you don't have to specify both a lower and upper bounds for the range. You can specify only a lower or upper bounds as necessary, such as:

```
<xsd:simpleType name="category">
 <xsd:restriction base="xsd:integer">
 <xsd:minInclusive value="1" />
 </xsd:restriction>
</xsd:simpleType>
```

or

```
<xsd:simpleType name="category">
 <xsd:restriction base="xsd:positiveInteger">
 <xsd:maxInclusive value="1000" />
 </xsd:restriction>
</xsd:simpleType>
```

Ranges of values don't have to be integers. You can specify a range of values for numeric datatypes and floats as well as date and time datatypes. When you specify a range for date and time datatypes, keep the following in mind:

- A date that's greater than another must represent a later date.
- A date that's less than another must represent an earlier date.

Although you can define ranges of acceptable values for numbers and dates, you can't specify ranges for string, boolean, binary, or URI values. To specify a range of acceptable values in schema, follow these steps:

1. Within the custom type definition, set an optional lower bounds by typing **<xsd:minInclusive value="*n*" />** or **<xsd:minExclusive value="*n*" />**, where *n* is the lower bounds of the range.

2. Set an optional upper bounds by typing **<xsd:maxInclusive value="*n*" />** or **<xsd:maxExclusive value="*n*" />**, where *n* is the upper bounds of the range.

The result should look like this:

```
<xsd:simpleType>
 <xsd:restriction base="xsd:baseType">
 <xsd:minInclusive value="n" />
 <xsd:maxInclusive value="n" />
 </xsd:restriction>
</xsd:simpleType>
```

Note You can't specify a range that's outside the bounds of the base type that you're using. For example, if the base type is `positiveInteger`, you couldn't specify a minimum inclusive bounds of 0 (zero isn't a positive integer). You could, however, specify a minimum exclusive bounds of 0.

Caution These steps assume you've declared the schema of schemas namespace using the `xsd` prefix. If you've declared it in the default namespace, don't use the prefix as indicated in these steps.

Limiting the Length of Values

Any time you work with character strings, binary values, or URIs, you can limit the allowable number of characters. The restrictions you use to limit character length are:

- **length** Sets the exact number of characters or list items allowed. The value assigned must be zero or greater.
- **maxLength** Sets the maximum number of characters or list items allowed. The value assigned must be zero or greater.
- **minLength** Sets the minimum number of characters or list items allowed. The value assigned must be zero or greater.

Note With binary values, the limits apply to the number of octets. With standard ASCII characters, a single octet represents a character. In Unicode or other character sets, groups of one, two, three, or four octets are used to represent individual characters.

You could assign an exact length of eight characters to a datatype like this:

```
<xsd:simpleType>
 <xsd:restriction base="xsd:string">
 <xsd:length value="8" />
 </xsd:restriction>
</xsd:simpleType>
```

When you assign an exact length to a datatype, you can't assign a minimum or maximum length. Besides being incorrect, such an assignment doesn't make sense: a value with a specific length assignment has an implied minimum and maximum length, which is the same as the character length you defined. This means that although you could specify an exact length like this:

```
<xsd:simpleType>
 <xsd:restriction base="xsd:string">
 <xsd:minLength value="8" />
 <xsd:maxLength value="8" />
 </xsd:restriction>
</xsd:simpleType>
```

you couldn't combine `length` with `minLength` or `maxLength` assignments. Thus, the following definitions are incorrect:

```
<xsd:simpleType>
 <xsd:restriction base="xsd:string">
 <xsd:length value="8" />
 <xsd:maxLength value="12" />
 </xsd:restriction>
</xsd:simpleType>
```

As you might expect, you can assign both a minimum and maximum length to a value. However, you don't have to assign both restrictions. A value could have only a minimum requirement or only a maximum requirement.

Note The value assigned to `length`, `minLength`, and `maxLength` must be a nonnegative integer. This means you could assign a value of 0, 24, or 568 but couldn't assign a value of -1 or -18.

To specify an exact length for a value in schema, follow these steps:

1. Within the custom type definition, type **<xsd:length** or **<length** as appropriate.
2. Complete the assignment by typing **value="*n*" />**, where *n* is the exact length that must be used.

The result should look like this:

```
<xsd:simpleType>
 <xsd:restriction base="xsd:baseType">
 <xsd:length value="n" />
 </xsd:restriction>
</xsd:simpleType>
```

To specify a minimum or maximum length in schema, follow these steps:

1. Within the custom type definition, set an optional minimal length by typing **<xsd:minLength value="*n*" />** or **<minLength value="*n*" />**, where *n* is the minimum length allowed.
2. Set an optional maximum length by typing **<xsd:maxLength value="*n*" />** or **<maxLength value="*n*" />**, where *n* is the maximum length allowed.

The result should look similar to the following:

```
<xsd:simpleType>
 <xsd:restriction base="xsd:baseType">
 <xsd:minLength value="n" />
 <xsd:maxLength value="n" />
 </xsd:restriction>
</xsd:simpleType>
```

Limiting the Number of Digits

With numeric datatypes, not including float and double, you can limit the number of digits that can be specified for a number. The available restrictions are

- **totalDigits** Sets the exact number of digits allowed for datatypes derived from decimal. The value assigned must be greater than zero.
- **fractionDigits** Sets the maximum number of decimal places allowed for datatypes derived from decimal. The value assigned must be zero or greater.

With `decimal` datatypes, you'll normally use a `totalDigits` and `fractionDigits` restriction. In the following example, you limit numbers to five digits, two of which can be to the right of the decimal place:

```
<xsd:simpleType>
 <xsd:restriction base="xsd:decimal">
 <xsd:totalDigits value="5" />
 <xsd:fractionDigits value="2" />
 </xsd:restriction>
</xsd:simpleType>
```

Valid numbers that follow this format include

- 399.98
- 50025
- 5002.5

With other number types, you'll normally only use `totalDigits` restrictions. The reason for this is that all other numbers (except `float` and `double`) are derived from the integer datatype, which has no fractional component. Because of this, a restriction for an integer could look like this:

```
<xsd:simpleType>
 <xsd:restriction base="xsd:integer">
 <xsd:totalDigits value="10" />
 </xsd:restriction>
</xsd:simpleType>
```

but normally doesn't look like this:

```
<xsd:simpleType>
 <xsd:restriction base="xsd:integer">
 <xsd:totalDigits value="5" />
 <xsd:fractionDigits value="0" />
 </xsd:restriction>
</xsd:simpleType>
```

Note Keep in mind that all datatypes derived from `decimal` can use the `fractionDigits` restriction. However, this restriction normally isn't needed because the fractional digits are assumed to be zero (and can't be defined otherwise).

To restrict the number of digits in schema, follow these steps:

1. Within the custom type definition, set the number of digits allowed by typing **<xsd:totalDigits value="*n*" />** or **<totalDigits value="*n*" />**, where *n* is the number of digits allowed.
2. Set an optional fractional component by typing **<xsd:fractionDigits value="*n*" />** or **<fractionDigits value="*n*" />**, where *n* is the maximum number of decimal places allowed.

The result should look similar to the following:

```
<xsd:simpleType>
 <xsd:restriction base="xsd:baseType">
 <xsd:totalDigits value="n" />
 <xsd:fractionDigits value="n" />
 </xsd:restriction>
</xsd:simpleType>
```

Chapter 11

Defining Complex Types in Schema

In this chapter you'll learn how to define complex types in schema. If an element contains other elements or uses attributes, you'll need to define the element as the complex type in schema. Complex types follow the same basic constructs as simple types. They're defined using XML markup and have predefined sets of tags that can appear within their opening and closing tags.

You always define attributes and lower-level elements within a complex type. You can also reference globally declared elements within complex types. This is, in fact, the only way to use globally declared elements (excluding a document's root element). XML Schema also allows you to group elements and attributes and then reference those elements and attribute groups within complex types. These concepts and other concepts for working with complex types are discussed in this chapter.

Note In previous chapters, I referred to the schema of schemas namespace as using the `xsd` prefix or as part of the default namespace, meaning a prefix wasn't used. Now that you're used to working with namespaces and namespace prefixes, I'll only use constructs with the `xsd` namespace prefix. This will allow the examples to follow a more consistent format.

Working with Complex Types

The way you declare a complex type depends on how you plan to use the complex type. Complex types can be

- **Named** Named complex types allow you to create a type that you can use with multiple elements.
- **Anonymous** Anonymous complex types allow you to directly associate a type with a specific element.
- **Based On** Extensions and restrictions allow you to base a complex type on an existing complex type, thereby creating a new complex.

Declaring Elements with Named Complex Types

With a named complex type, you set the `type` attribute of the related elements to a label that identifies the complex type you're creating. The name must not be the same as one of the predefined types or an existing user-defined type. In the following example a type called `addressAttribs` is declared for the `person`, `organization`, and `contact` elements:

```
<xsd:element name="person" type="addressAttribs" />

<xsd:element name="organization" type="addressAttribs" />

<xsd:element name="contact" type="addressAttribs" />
```

After declaring the type, you can define the type using the `ecomplexType` declaration. The name assigned in the complex type declaration must exactly match the name you used when you declared the type. Here's how you could declare the `addressAttribs` type:

```
<xsd:complexType name="addressAttribs">
...
</xsd:complexType>
```

After entering the `complexType` declaration, you can add order indicators, group references, attribute definitions, or restrictions to the complex type. Order indicators are used to specify the permitted order for associated elements. Group references are used to reference existing element groups that you want to associate with the complex type. Attribute definitions specify attributes that are part of the complex type. Restrictions set constraints for element contents.

Because you're using a named custom type, the type definition doesn't have to follow the element definition in which it's declared. The reason for this is that the definition can be assigned to multiple elements just as you'd assign one of the predefined datatypes to simple elements. To define a named complex type, follow these steps:

1. Enter **<xsd:complexType** to begin the type definition.
2. Enter **name=*"label"*>**, where *label* is the actual name of the complex type you're creating. The name must follow the rules for valid XML names.
3. Enter the definitions for the body of the complex type.
4. Type **</xsd:complexType>** to complete the type definition.

The result should look similar to the following:

```
<xsd:complexType name="label">
...
</xsd:complexType>
```

Declaring Elements with Anonymous Complex Types

Anonymous complex types are directly associated with the element to which they relate and are declared as part of the element's schema definition. Because of this, the element declaration no longer follows the form

```
<xsd:element name="element_name" />
```

Instead, the element definition uses an opening and closing tag with the complex type inserted between these tags. This means that a declaration for an element with an anonymous complex type follows the form

```
<xsd:element name="element_name">
 <xsd:complexType>
 ...
 </xsd:complexType>
</xsd:element>
```

With this in mind, you could define a `person` element with an anonymous complex type like this:

```
<xsd:element name="person">
 <xsd:complexType>
 <xsd:attribute name="first" type="xsd:string" />
 <xsd:attribute name="mi" type="xsd:string" />
 <xsd:attribute name="last" type="xsd:string" />
 <xsd:attribute name="street_address" type="xsd:string" />
 <xsd:attribute name="city" type="xsd:string" />
 <xsd:attribute name="state" type="xsd:string" />
 <xsd:attribute name="zipcode" type="xsd:string" />
 </xsd:complexType>
</xsd:element>
```

Because the complex type is declared anonymously, it can only be used with the element in which it's contained. To define an element with an anonymous complex type, follow these steps:

1. Begin the element declaration by typing **<xsd:element name="*label*">**, where *label* is the actual name of the element you're creating.
2. Enter **<xsd:complexType>** to begin the complex type declaration.
3. Enter the definitions for the body of the complex type.
4. Type **</xsd:complexType>** to complete the complex type definition and then type **</xsd:element>** to complete the element definition.

The result should look similar to the following:

```
<xsd:element name="element_name">
 <xsd:complexType>
 ...
 </xsd:complexType>
</xsd:element>
```

Basing Complex Types on Complex Types

You can also base complex types on existing complex types. The new complex type inherits the definitions from the existing type and can then either extend or restrict those features. The choice as to whether to extend or restrict features is mutually exclusive. You can't perform both actions.

Extending a Complex Type Based on an Existing Complex Type

When you base a complex type on another complex type that you want to extend, the basic syntax that you follow is

```
<xsd:complexType name="new_type">
 <xsd:complexContent>
 <xsd:extension base="base_type">
 ...
 </xsd:extension>
 </xsd:complexContent>
</xsd:complexType>
```

Here, you declare the complex type as having complex content that extends the previously defined complex type. The complex type is declared as a new type and the base type for the extension is the name of the existing complex type. For example, if you declared a complex type called `ContactInfo` that contained basic attributes for describing a person, such as:

```
<xsd:complexType name="ContactInfo">
 <xsd:attribute name="first" type="xsd:string" />
 <xsd:attribute name="mi" type="xsd:string" />
 <xsd:attribute name="last" type="xsd:string" />
 <xsd:attribute name="street_address" type="xsd:string" />
 <xsd:attribute name="city" type="xsd:string" />
 <xsd:attribute name="state" type="xsd:string" />
 <xsd:attribute name="zipcode" type="xsd:string" />
</xsd:complexType>
```

you could create another complex type based on this type that provided additional attributes. The new type could be called `CompleteContactInfo` and declared as:

```
<xsd:complexType name="CompleteContactInfo">
 <xsd:complexContent>
 <xsd:extension base="ContactInfo">
 <xsd:attribute name="phone" type="phoneNumber" />
 <xsd:attribute name="fax" type="phoneNumber" />
 <xsd:attribute name="email" type="emailAddress" />
 </xsd:extension>
 </xsd:complexContent>
</xsd:complexType>
```

Because the complex type extends the `ContactInfo` type, an XML processor would interpret the definition for the type as having the following attributes:

```
<xsd:attribute name="first" type="xsd:string" />
<xsd:attribute name="mi" type="xsd:string" />
<xsd:attribute name="last" type="xsd:string" />
<xsd:attribute name="street_address" type="xsd:string" />
<xsd:attribute name="city" type="xsd:string" />
<xsd:attribute name="state" type="xsd:string" />
<xsd:attribute name="zipcode" type="xsd:string" />
<xsd:attribute name="phone" type="phoneNumber" />
<xsd:attribute name="fax" type="phoneNumber" />
<xsd:attribute name="email" type="emailAddress" />
```

To create a new complex type by extending an existing complex type, follow these steps:

1. Enter **<xsd:complexType** to begin the type definition.
2. Enter **name="*label*">**, where *label* is the actual name of the complex type you're creating. The name must follow the rules for valid XML names.
3. Enter **<xsd:complexContent>**.
4. Enter **<xsd:extension base="*existing_type*">**, where *existing_type* is the name of the type on which the complex type will be based.
5. Enter your extensions to add definitions to the new type.
6. Type **</xsd:extension>** and then type **</xsd:complexContent>**.
7. Type **</xsd:complexType>** to complete the complex type definition.

The result should look similar to the following:

```
<xsd:complexType name="label">
 <xsd:complexContent>
 <xsd:extension base="existing_type">
 ...
 </xsd:extension>
 </xsd:complexContent>
</xsd:complexType>
```

Restricting a Complex Type to a Subset of Another Type

If you want to base a new type on a restricted subset of another complex type, you define a restriction rather than an extension. Here the basic syntax that you follow is

```
<xsd:complexType name="new_type">
 <xsd:complexContent>
 <xsd:restriction base="base_type">
 ...
 </xsd:restriction>
 </xsd:complexContent>
</xsd:complexType>
```

As you can see, you declare the complex type as having a restricted set of contents from another type. The complex type is declared as a new type, and the base type for the restriction is the name of the existing complex type. Using the same `ContactInfo` type definition as before:

```
<xsd:complexType name="ContactInfo">
 <xsd:attribute name="first" type="xsd:string" />
 <xsd:attribute name="mi" type="xsd:string" />
 <xsd:attribute name="last" type="xsd:string" />
 <xsd:attribute name="street_address" type="xsd:string" />
 <xsd:attribute name="city" type="xsd:string" />
 <xsd:attribute name="state" type="xsd:string" />
 <xsd:attribute name="zipcode" type="xsd:string" />
</xsd:complexType>
```

You could now add restrictions or override the previous definitions. For example, if you wanted to ensure that the `mi` attribute was a `token` and the `zipcode` was formatted as a user-defined simple type called `USPostalCode`, you'd define the restricted type like this:

```
<xsd:complexType name="formattedContactInfo">
 <xsd:complexContent>
 <xsd:restriction base="ContactInfo">
 <xsd:attribute name="mi" type="xsd:token" />
 <xsd:attribute name="zipcode" type="USPostalCode" />
 </xsd:restriction>
 </xsd:complexContent>
</xsd:complexType>
```

Because the complex type restricts the `ContactInfo` type, an XML processor would interpret the definition for the type like this:

```
<xsd:attribute name="first" type="xsd:string" />
<xsd:attribute name="mi" type="xsd:token" />
<xsd:attribute name="last" type="xsd:string" />
<xsd:attribute name="street_address" type="xsd:string" />
<xsd:attribute name="city" type="xsd:string" />
<xsd:attribute name="state" type="xsd:string" />
<xsd:attribute name="zipcode" type="USPostalCode" />
```

To base a new complex type on a restricted subset of an existing complex type, follow these steps:

1. Enter **<xsd:complexType** to begin the type definition.
2. Enter **name="*label*">**, where *label* is the actual name of the complex type you're creating. The name must follow the rules for valid XML names.
3. Enter **<xsd:complexContent>**.
4. Enter **<xsd:restriction base="*existing_type*">**, where *existing_type* is the name of the type on which the complex type will be based.

5. Enter your restrictions, which define additional restrictions for existing definitions or override the definitions.
6. Type **</xsd:restriction>** and then type **</xsd:complexContent>**.
7. Type **</xsd:complexType>** to complete the complex type definition.

The result should look similar to the following:

```
<xsd:complexType name="label">
 <xsd:complexContent>
 <xsd:restriction base="existing_type">
 ...
 </xsd:restriction>
 </xsd:complexContent>
</xsd:complexType>
```

Defining Content for Complex Elements

Unlike simple types, complex types have several different formats and the format you use depends on the contents of the complex type. The possible formats for complex types are the same as those allowed for elements in document type definitions (DTDs). This means complex types can be defined as having

- **Standard content** Complex types with standard content have only elements or elements and attributes associated with them.
- **Text-only content** Complex types with text-only content have only character data or character data and attributes associated with them.
- **Mixed content** Complex types with mixed content have a combination of elements and text associated with them and may contain attribute definitions.
- **No content** Complex types with no content associated with them are empty, meaning they don't have, nor do they allow, content. They can, however, have attributes.

The following sections examine techniques for defining each of these complex types in schema.

Defining Complex Elements with Standard Content

Most element declarations define one or more child elements that an element must contain as its standard content. The most basic type of standard content you can define is a complex type with a sequence of child elements. In the following example the complex type must contain exactly one `customer` element and one `order` element:

```
<xsd:complexType name="orders">
 <xsd:sequence>
 <xsd:element name="customer" type="custType" />
 <xsd:element name="order" type="orderType" />
 </xsd:sequence>
</xsd:complexType>
```

Elements that implement the `orders` type must contain a single `customer` element followed by a single `order` element. Based on this declaration, elements that are defined as the `orders` type may not contain any other elements or text and may not contain multiple `customer` or `order` elements. If you associated the `orders` type with a `purchase_order` element like this:

```
<xsd:element name="purchase_order" type="orders" />
```

you could use the element in the body of the document like this:

```
<purchase_order>
 <customer>Microsoft Corp.</customer>
 <order>2002-87901</order>
</purchase_order>
```

but couldn't use the element like this:

```
<purchase_order>
 <order>2002-87901</order>
 <customer>Microsoft Corp.</customer>
</purchase_order>
```

or like this:

```
<purchase_order>
 <customer>Microsoft Corp.</customer>
 <order>2002-87901</order>
 <order>2002-87902</order>
 <order>2002-87903</order>
</purchase_order>
```

Tip To allow various formats such as these to be used, you'd have to define the orders type using a different technique. For example, you might want to define a series of child elements, relate a group of child elements with this custom type, or allow multiple child elements of a single type to be used. The schema structures needed to perform these tasks are called order, grouping, and occurrence indicators.

Although any element that contains other elements must be defined as complex, the elements declared within a complex type don't have be complex. They could be simple types as well. This means you could define the `custType` and `orderType` elements used in the previous example using either complex or simple types.

After you define the child elements for a complex type, you can define attributes or attribute groups that should appear with elements of this type. The attribute or attribute group definitions should immediately follow the element definitions, such as:

```
<xsd:complexType name="orders">
 <xsd:sequence>
 <xsd:element name="customer" type="custType" />
 <xsd:element name="order" type="orderType" />
 </xsd:sequence>
 <xsd:attribute name="current" type="xsd:boolean" />
 <xsd:attribute name="id" type="xsd:ID" />
</xsd:complexType>
```

To define a complex type with standard content, follow these steps:

1. Enter **<xsd:complexType** to begin the type definition.
2. Optionally, enter **name=*"label"*>**, where *label* is the actual name of the complex type you're creating. The name must follow the rules for valid XML names.
3. Enter **<xsd:sequence>**, enter the definitions for the child elements, and then enter **</xsd:sequence>**.

Note Usually multiple child elements are entered in the exact sequence in which they must be used. For details on sequencing and other element order indicators, see the "Structuring Complex Elements in Schemas" section of this chapter.

4. Enter the definitions for any attributes or attribute groups that will be used with elements of this type.
5. Type **</xsd:complexType>** to complete the complex type definition.

The result should look similar to the following:

```
<xsd:complexType name="label">
 <xsd:sequence>
 <xsd:element name="element_1" type="element_type" />
 <xsd:element name="element_2" type="element_type" />
 <xsd:element name="element_N" type="element_type" />
 </xsd:sequence>
 <xsd:attribute name="attrib_1" type="attrib_type" />
 <xsd:attribute name="attrib_2" type="attrib_type" />
 <xsd:attribute name="attrib_N" type="attrib_type" />
</xsd:complexType>
```

Defining Complex Elements with Mixed Content

If an element can contain both text and other elements, you'll need to declare it as allowing mixed content. The only difference between a declaration for an element with mixed content and one with standard content is that you specify `mixed="true"` as an attribute in the `complexType` definition. This means that you could rewrite the following definition:

```
<xsd:complexType name="orders">
 <xsd:sequence>
 <xsd:element name="customer" type="custType" />
 <xsd:element name="order" type="orderType" />
 </xsd:sequence>
</xsd:complexType>
```

to allow mixed content like this:

```
<xsd:complexType name="orders" mixed="true">
 <xsd:sequence>
 <xsd:element name="customer" type="custType" />
 <xsd:element name="order" type="orderType" />
 </xsd:sequence>
</xsd:complexType>
```

Now in addition to being able to use `customer` and `order` elements, you can add free-flow text to the associated element. Here's an example:

```
<purchase_order>
 <customer>Microsoft Corp.</customer>
 <order>2002-87901</order>
 The purchase order is complete.
</purchase_order>
```

The free-flow text could also come before the child elements, such as:

```
<purchase_order>
 The purchase order is complete.
 <customer>Microsoft Corp.</customer>
 <order>2002-87901</order>
</purchase_order>
```

Note The value `mixed="false"` is assumed if the mixed attribute isn't set to a specific value. The value of false means that only standard content can be used.

To define a complex type with mixed content, follow these steps:

1. Enter **<xsd:complexType** to begin the type definition.
2. Optionally, enter **name=*"label"***, where *label* is the actual name of the complex type you're creating. The name must follow the rules for valid XML names.
3. Enter **mixed="true">** to indicate that the element may contain text as well as elements and attributes.
4. Enter **<xsd:sequence>**, enter the definitions for the child elements, and then enter **</xsd:sequence>**.
5. Enter the definitions for any attributes or attribute groups that will be used with elements of this type.
6. Type **</xsd:complexType>** to complete the complex type definition.

The result should look similar to the following:

```
<xsd:complexType name="label" mixed="true">
 <xsd:sequence>
 <xsd:element name="element_1" type="element_type" />
 <xsd:element name="element_2" type="element_type" />
 <xsd:element name="element_N" type="element_type" />
 </xsd:sequence>
 <xsd:attribute name="attrib_1" type="attrib_type" />
 <xsd:attribute name="attrib_2" type="attrib_type" />
 <xsd:attribute name="attrib_N" type="attrib_type" />
</xsd:complexType>
```

Defining Complex Elements with Text-Only Content

You can define basic elements that contain only text using simple type definitions as discussed in Chapter 9, "Defining Simple Types in Schema." However, if you want to define the element as having text-only content as well as associated attributes, you must define the element using a complex type. Remember, all elements with attributes must be defined as complex types.

Complex types that contain only text and attributes follow this basic format:

```
<xsd:complexType name="label">
 <xsd:simpleContent>
 ...
 </xsd:simpleContent>
</xsd:complexType>
```

This definition says that the type contains simple content (meaning only text and attributes). When you use simple content, you must define an extension or a restriction within the `simpleContent` declaration. You use an extension when you want to expand on the base simple type for the element, and you use a restriction when you want to limit the base simple type with additional constraints. This means that the form becomes either:

```
<xsd:complexType name="label">
 <xsd:simpleContent>
 <xsd:extension base="base_type">
 ...
 </xsd:extension>
 </xsd:simpleContent>
</xsd:complexType>
```

or

```
<xsd:complexType name="label">
 <xsd:simpleContent>
 <xsd:restriction base="base_type">
 ...
 </xsd:restriction>
 </xsd:simpleContent>
</xsd:complexType>
```

Once you determine whether you want to expand or restrict the simple type on which the complex type is based, you can add any additional definitions between the opening and closing extension or restriction tags. You define the attributes associated with this type between these tags as well.

The following example defines a complex type that uses a restricted string and has attributes called `lastMod` and `entryDate`:

```
<xsd:complexType name="indicator">
 <xsd:simpleContent>
 <xsd:restriction base="xsd:string">
 <xsd:minLength value="2" />
 <xsd:maxLength value="9" />
 <xsd:attribute name="lastMod" type="xsd:dateTime" />
 <xsd:attribute name="entryDate" type="xsd:dateTime" />
 </xsd:restriction>
 </xsd:simpleContent>
</xsd:complexType>
```

If you associated the `indicator` type with a record element like this:

```
<xsd:element name="record" type="indicator" />
```

you could use the element in the body of a document like this:

```
<record entryDate= "2001-08-15T07:35:59"
 lastMod="2001-10-30T09:30:01">
2958
</record>
```

Because the attributes aren't required, you could also use the element like this:

```
<record>2958</record>
```

However, you couldn't use the element like this:

```
<record entryDate="2001-08-15T07:35:59"
 lastMod="2001-10-30T09:30:01"></record>
```

The type definition doesn't allow the textual contents to have fewer than two characters, so the previous usage is incorrect.

To define a complex type with text-only content, follow these steps:

1. Enter **<xsd:complexType** to begin the type definition.
2. Optionally, enter **name="*label*">**, where *label* is the actual name of the complex type you're creating. The name must follow the rules for valid XML names.
3. Enter **<xsd:simpleContent>**. Afterward, enter **<xsd:restriction** to define restrictions for the base simple type or enter **<xsd:extension** to extend the base simple type.
4. Enter **base="*base_type*">**, where *base_type* is the simple type on which you're basing the new complex type.
5. If you're defining restrictions, enter the constraints following the techniques discussed in Chapter 10, "Specifying Datatypes and Restrictions in Schema."
6. Declare the attributes or attribute groups that are associated with this type.
7. Complete the extension or restriction by typing **</xsd:extension>** or **</xsd:restriction>** as appropriate.
8. Type **</xsd:simpleContent>** and then type **</xsd:complexType>** to complete the type definition.

The result should look similar to the following:

```
<xsd:complexType name="label">
 <xsd:simpleContent>
 <xsd:extension base=" base_type ">
 <xsd:attribute name="attrib_1" type="attrib_type" />
 <xsd:attribute name="attrib_2" type="attrib_type" />
 <xsd:attribute name="attrib_N" type="attrib_type" />
 </xsd:extension>
 </xsd:simpleContent>
</xsd:complexType>
```

Defining Complex Elements with No Content

In Chapter 9 you learned how to create simple empty elements. Simple empty elements are elements that are nillable, which allows you to enter only an empty element tag rather than an opening and closing tag. Simple empty elements don't have contents and merely act as placeholders in their nill format. If you want an empty element to have attributes, however, you must define it as a complex element with no content.

When declaring complex elements with no content, the basic syntax that you follow is

```
<xsd:complexType name="new_type">
 <xsd:complexContent>
 <xsd:extension base="xsd:anyType">
 ...
 </xsd:extension>
 </xsd:complexContent>
</xsd:complexType>
```

Here, you declare the complex type as having complex content that is the generic base type (`anyType`). Basically, this means there's no type on which you want to base this complex type. Attribute definitions that are associated with the type must be entered between the opening and closing extension tags, such as:

```
<xsd:element name="image" type="sourceAttribs" />
<xsd:complexType name="sourceAttribs">
 <xsd:complexContent>
 <xsd:extension base="xsd:anyType">
 <xsd:attribute name="source" type="xsd:anyURI" />
 <xsd:attribute name="width" type="xsd:positiveInteger" />
 <xsd:attribute name="height" type="xsd:positiveInteger" />
 </xsd:extension>
 </xsd:complexContent>
</xsd:complexType>
```

If the following element definition were associated with the complex type:

```
<xsd:element name="image" type="sourceAttribs" />
```

you could use the element in a document like this:

```
<image source="http://www.microsoft.com/myimage.jpg"
 width="100" height="300" />
```

However, because the element can't have contents, you couldn't use the element like this:

```
<image source="http://www.microsoft.com/myimage.jpg"
 width="100" height="300">My Image</image>
```

To define an empty element that has attributes associated with it, follow these steps:

1. Enter **<xsd:complexType** to begin the type definition.
2. Optionally, enter **name=*"label"*>**, where *label* is the actual name of the complex type you're creating. The name must follow the rules for valid XML names.
3. Enter **<xsd:complexContent>** and then enter **<xsd:extension base="xsd:anyType">**.
4. Declare the attributes that are associated with the element.
5. Type **</xsd:extension>** and then type **</xsd:complexContent>**.
6. Type **</xsd:complexType>** to complete the complex type definition.

The result should look similar to the following:

```
<xsd:complexType name="label">
 <xsd:complexContent>
 <xsd:extension base="xsd:anyType">
 <xsd:attribute name="attrib_1" type="attrib_type" />
 <xsd:attribute name="attrib_2" type="attrib_type" />
 <xsd:attribute name="attrib_N" type="attrib_type" />
 </xsd:extension>
 </xsd:complexContent>
</xsd:complexType>
```

Structuring Complex Elements in Schemas

The declarations we've used so far in this chapter have had fairly basic structures. They've allowed us to define named and anonymous complex types, to define element content, and to base new complex types on existing complex types. To gain precise control over how elements are used in documents, you need to structure the element declarations using indicators.

XML Schema uses three types of indicators:

- **Order** Defines the context in which elements occur, such as whether they occur in sequence or represent choices
- **Occurrence** Defines how often elements can occur
- **Grouping** Defines related sets of elements

Unlike DTDs, where these indicators are represented with symbols, XML Schema defines these indicators using the element and attribute definitions shown in Table 11-1. Although the indicators have different structures associated with them, their basic usage is that same as with DTDs.

Table 11-1. Indicators for Elements in Schema

Type	Indicator	Description	Schema Definition
Order	`Any`	Specifies that child elements can appear in any order but each element must occur once.	`<complexType> <any>...</any> </complexType>`
	`All`	Specifies child elements that can appear in any order but must occur once and only once.	`<complexType> <all>...</all> </complexType>`
	`Choice`	Specifies that either one child element or another can occur.	`<complexType> <choice>...</choice> </complexType>`
	`Sequence`	Sets the exact sequence for elements. Elements must follow one other.	`<complexType> <sequence>... </sequence> </complexType>`
Occurrence	`minOccurs`	Sets the minimum number of times a child element can occur.	`<element minOccurs="`*n*`" />`
	`maxOccurs`	Sets the maximum number of times a child element can occur.	`<element maxOccurs="`*n*`" />`
Grouping	`Group name`	Defines a named group that can be referenced in a complex type or another group.	`<group name="`*label*`"> </group>`
	`Group reference`	References a named group within a complex type.	`<group ref="`*label*`" />`

Specifying Sequences

In XML the order of elements is often extremely important so that data can be easily interpreted or processed. Most element declarations specify that an element can contain one or more child elements. When you want the child elements to appear in a specific sequence, you enclose them in a sequence construct, which has the opening tag `<sequence>` and the closing tag `</sequence>`.

The order in which elements are defined within a sequence defines the order the elements must appear within the parent element. For example, if you wanted a parent element with complex type called `orderType` to have `customer`, `billTo`, and `shipTo` elements in that specific order, you could declare the element and the complex type as follows:

```
<xsd:element name="order" type="orderType" />

<xsd:complexType name="orderType">
 <xsd:sequence>
 <xsd:element name="customer" type="custType" />
 <xsd:element name="billTo" type="origin" />
 <xsd:element name="shipTo" type="destination" />
 </xsd:sequence>
</xsd:complexType>
```

and then use the element in a document like this:

```
<order>
 <customer> William Stanek </customer>
 <billTo> Microsoft Corp.
  One Microsoft Way
  Redmond, WA 98052-6399
 </billTo>
 <shipTo> Microsoft Corp.
  One Microsoft Way
  Redmond, WA 98052-6399
 </shipTo>
</order>
```

However, the following element usage is incorrect because the order defined in the declaration isn't followed:

```
<order>
 <billTo> Microsoft Corp.
  One Microsoft Way
  Redmond, WA 98052-6399
 </billTo>
 <shipTo> Microsoft Corp.
  One Microsoft Way
  Redmond, WA 98052-6399
 </shipTo>
 <customer> Microsoft Corporation </customer>
</order>
```

Sequences must be followed exactly as specified. You can't skip elements unless the `minOccurs` attribute is set to zero (which makes the element optional). You can't include additional elements of the same type unless the `maxOccurs` attribute is set to a value greater than 1. With a sequence, the `minOccurs` and `maxOccurs` attributes default to 1, meaning elements must appear exactly once.

Because of this, the following element example is invalid because the child element called `customer` is omitted:

```
<order>
 <billTo> Microsoft Corp.
  One Microsoft Way
  Redmond, WA 98052-6399
 </billTo>
 <shipTo> Microsoft Corp.
  One Microsoft Way
  Redmond, WA 98052-6399
 </shipTo>
</order>
```

You can't add elements that aren't in the sequence defined in the declaration either. This means the following example is incorrect because it adds an `organization` element:

```
<order>
 <customer> William Stanek </customer>
 <organization> Microsoft Corporation </organization>
 <billTo> Microsoft Corp.
  One Microsoft Way
  Redmond, WA 98052-6399
 </billTo>
 <shipTo> Microsoft Corp.
  One Microsoft Way
  Redmond, WA 98052-6399
 </shipTo>
</order>
```

To require elements to appear in a sequence, follow these steps:

1. Sequences can be inserted into `complexType` definitions or with an extension or restriction that's associated with an element's `complexContent` declaration. To indicate the beginning of the sequence, type **<xsd:sequence**.
2. By default, elements in sequence must appear once and only once. To change this behavior and allow the exact sequence of elements to be repeated multiple times, set the `minOccurs` and `maxOccurs` attributes as discussed in the "Controlling Element Occurrence" section of this chapter.
3. Type **>** to complete the opening sequence tag.
4. Declare or reference the structures that should appear in the sequence. Be sure to use the exact order in which you want the structures to appear.
5. Type **</xsd:sequence>** to complete the sequence definition.

The result should look similar to the following:

```
<xsd:sequence>
...
</xsd:sequence>
```

Specifying Choices

In addition to being able to specify that elements must occur in an exact sequence, you can also specify that an element contains one kind of child or another. When you want child elements to be choices rather than specific sequences, you enclose them in a choice construct that has the opening tag `<choice>` and the closing tag `</choice>`.

You could indicate a set of choices for a `contact` element like this:

```
<xsd:element name="contact" type="contactType" />

<xsd:complexType name="contactType">
 <xsd:choice>
 <xsd:element name="person" type="personType" />
 <xsd:element name="organization" type="orgType" />
 </xsd:choice>
</xsd:complexType>
```

Here, a `contact` element can either contain a `person` element or an `organization` element. This means you could define the element like this:

```
<contact>
 <person>William R. Stanek</person>
</contact>
```

or

```
<contact>
 <organization>Microsoft Corp.</organization>
</contact>
```

but couldn't define the element like this:

```
<contact>
 <organization>Microsoft Corp.</organization>
 <person>William R. Stanek</person>
</contact>
```

Here, the element has both an `organization` and a `person` element, which isn't allowed.

As with DTDs, schemas allow you to

- Group choices within sequences
- Specify sets of choices with specific sequences

To group choices within sequences, insert the choice definition within the sequence definition. The following example allows the `order` element to have either a `person` or an `organization` element as the first child element in the internal sequence:

```
<xsd:element name="order" type="orderType" />

<xsd:complexType name="orderType">
 <xsd:sequence>
 <xsd:choice>
 <xsd:element name="person" type="personType" />
 <xsd:element name="organization" type="orgType" />
 </xsd:choice>
 <xsd:element name="billTo" type="origin" />
 <xsd:element name="shipTo" type="destination" />
 </xsd:sequence>
</xsd:complexType>
```

This means you could define an order like this:

```
<order>
 <person> William R. Stanek </person>
 <billTo> William R. Stanek
  123 Main St.
  Anywhere, WA 98985
 </billTo>
 <shipTo> 123 Main St.
  Anywhere, WA 98985
 </shipTo>
</order>
```

or like this:

```
<order>
 <organization>Microsoft  Corp.</organization>
  <billTo> Microsoft Corporation
   One Microsoft Way
   Redmond, WA 98052
 </billTo>
 <shipTo> One Microsoft Way
   Redmond, WA 98052
 </shipTo>
</order>
```

To specify sets of choices with specific sequences, insert the sequence definition within the choice definition. Consider the following example:

```
<xsd:element name="order"     type="orderType" />

<xsd:complexType  name="orderType">
 <xsd:choice>
 <xsd:sequence>
  <xsd:element name="person" type="personType" />
  <xsd:element name="orderInfo" type="orderInfo" />
  <xsd:element name="address" type="mailingAddress" />
 </xsd:sequence>
 <xsd:sequence>
  <xsd:element name="organization" type="orgType" />
  <xsd:element name="accountNum" type="accountType" />
  <xsd:element name="orderDetails" type="orderInfo" />
  <xsd:element name="billTo" type="origin" />
  <xsd:element name="shipTo" type="destination" />
 </xsd:sequence>
 </xsd:choice>
</xsd:complexType>
```

In this example two different categories of orders are defined: those that ship to individuals and those that ship to organizations. Orders shipped to individuals could be entered in documents like this:

```
<order>
 <person> William R. Stanek </person>
 <orderInfo> Order # 2939-2. Total: $272.50 </orderInfo>
 <address> 123 Main St., Anywhere, WA 98965 </address>
</order>
```

Orders shipped to organizations could be entered in documents like this:

```
<order>
 <organization>Microsoft  Corp.</organization>
 <accountNum>A-734-B</accountNum>
 <orderDetails> Order # 2939-3. Total: $3,750.75 </orderDetails>
 <billTo> Microsoft Corporation
  One Microsoft Way
  Redmond, WA 98052
 </billTo>
 <shipTo> One Microsoft Way
  Redmond, WA 98052
 </shipTo>
</order>
```

To specify a set of choices for elements, follow these steps:

1. Choices can be inserted into `complexType` definitions or with an extension or restriction that's associated with an element's `complexContent` declaration. To indicate the beginning of the choice, type **<xsd:choice**.
2. By default, only one of the elements in choice can appear. To change this behavior and allow multiple choices to appear or for choices to be repeated, set the `minOccurs` and `maxOccurs` attributes as discussed in the "Controlling Element Occurrence" section of this chapter.
3. Type **>** to complete the opening choice tag.
4. Declare or reference the structures that should appear in the choice.
5. Type **</xsd:choice>** to complete the choice definition.

The result should look similar to the following:

```
<xsd:choice>
...
</xsd:choice>
```

Allowing Elements to Appear in Any Order

If child elements don't need to appear in a specific order, you can specify that any order is allowed using the `any` or `all` declarations. Removing the order constraint is useful when a parent element can contain different types of free-flow text. Otherwise, removing the order constraint has limited usefulness. After all, the ability to define structure and ensure that datasets follow that structure is what makes XML so powerful.

The `any` and `all` constructs have identical usages, and the difference between them is in the number of element occurrences allowed:

- `any` allows you to set the minimum number of occurrences to 0 or 1 and the maximum number of occurrences to any value between 0 and infinity (referred to as *unbounded*). The default for `minOccurs` and `maxOccurs` is 1 (meaning elements are mandatory and must occur only once).
- `all` allows you to set the minimum number of occurrences to 0 or 1 and the maximum number of occurrences can only be 1. The default for `minOccurs` and `maxOccurs` is 1 (meaning elements are mandatory and must occur only once).

This means you can use `any` to allow elements to be repeated a certain number of times, but you can't use `all` for this purpose. The `all` construct is used only to specify that elements can occur zero times or once, or must occur once. However, any constructs can be used only within choices or sequences, but all constructs can be used within complex types and groups as well as within restriction and extension constructs that appear as part of an element's complex content. This means that in most cases you'll use the `all` construct, and this is what I'll focus on in this section.

The `all` construct has the opening tag `<all>` and the closing tag `</all>`. The following example defines a complex type called `comments` that can contain free-flow text comments for support, service, and field technicians in any order:

```
<xsd:element name="callDetails" type="comments" />

<xsd:complexType  name="comments">
 <xsd:all>
 <xsd:element name="supportComments" type="textType" />
 <xsd:element name="serviceComments" type="textType" />
 <xsd:element name="fieldComments" type="textType" />
 </xsd:all>
</xsd:complexType>
```

The elements declared as part of the `all` declaration can appear once or not at all. This means that the `callDetails` element could appear like this in a document:

```
<callDetails>
 <supportComments>Received call on 10/15/01 from customer. Passed
  off to service technician.</supportComments>
 <serviceComments>Tech 805: took call from support team and
  worked to resolve issue. Sent field service tech to site.
 </serviceComments>
 <fieldComments>On site tech 912: reset systems and all is
  working.</fieldComments>
</callDetails>
```

or like this:

```
<callDetails>
 <serviceComments>Tech 805: took call from support team and
  worked to resolve issue. Sent field service tech to site.
 </serviceComments>
 <supportComments>Received call on 10/15/01 from customer. Passed
  off to service technician.</supportComments>
 <fieldComments>On site tech 912: reset systems and all is
  working.</fieldComments>
</callDetails>
```

but couldn't appear like this:

```
<callDetails>
 <serviceComments>Tech 805: took call from support team.
 </serviceComments>
 <serviceComments>Worked to resolve issue.</serviceComments>
 <serviceComments>Sent field service tech to site.
 </serviceComments>
</callDetails>
```

This example doesn't work because elements must appear once and can't be repeated. With `all` constructs, the only way to change this behavior is to set the `minOccurs` to 0, which would allow elements to appear 0 or 1 time.

To allow elements to appear in any order, follow these steps:

1. Within a complex type, group, or restriction/extension construct that appears as part of an element's complex content, start the `all` declaration by typing **<xsd:all**.
2. By default, elements in an `all` declaration must appear once and can't be repeated. To change this behavior and allow elements to be used 0 or 1 time, type **minOccurs="0"** and **maxOccurs="1"**.
3. Type **>** to complete the opening all tag.
4. Declare or reference the structures that should appear in the unordered group. Keep in mind that you don't have to declare the structures in any particular order.
5. Type **</xsd:all>** to complete the unordered group.

The result should look similar to the following:

```
<xsd:all>
...
</xsd:all>
```

Controlling Element Occurrence

XML Schema uses the `minOccurs` and `maxOccurs` attributes to specify the number of times a schema construct can appear. With `sequence`, `choice`, `any`, and `all` constructs, you've seen that elements can appear once and only once. The reason for this is that the default value for `minOccurs` and `maxOccurs` is 1.

With `minOccurs`, the following rules apply:

- Any time `minOccurs` is set to 0, the construct and its contents are optional and don't have to appear.
- Any time `minOccurs` is set to 1, the construct and its contents are mandatory and must appear at least once.
- Any time `minOccurs` is set higher than 1, the construct and its contents must be repeated at least that number of times.

With `maxOccurs`, the following rules apply:

- Any time `maxOccurs` is set to 1, the construct and its contents can appear only once.

- Any time `maxOccurs` is set higher than 1, the construct and its contents can appear only that number of times.
- Any time `minOccurs` and `maxOccurs` are set to the same value and that value is 1 or higher, the construct and its contents are mandatory and must appear exactly that many times.

Note `maxOccurs` should not be set lower than `minOccurs`. It doesn't make sense to use a lower value.

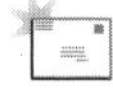

For example, if you wanted the `order` element to be able to appear between 0 and 5 times, you'd declare the element like this:

```
<xsd:element name="order" type="orderType" minOccurs="0"
 maxOccurs="5"/>
```

If you wanted the `order` element to be able to appear between 1 and 5 times, you'd declare the element like this:

```
<xsd:element name="order" type="orderType" minOccurs="1"
 maxOccurs="5"/>
```

If you wanted the `order` element to be appear once and only once, you'd declare the element like this:

```
<xsd:element name="order" type="orderType" minOccurs="1"
 maxOccurs="1"/>
```

Tip You can't use `minOccurs` and `maxOccurs` with global declarations. They're meant to be used with local declarations. If you want to specify the number of occurrences for a global element, declare a reference to it and then set the number of occurrences in the reference.

To allow any number of elements to occur, set `minOccurs` to 0 and `maxOccurs` to `unbounded;`. `unbounded` is a special keyword that indicates that a construct can be used any number of times. Here's an example:

```
<xsd:element name="order" type="orderType" minOccurs="0"
 maxOccurs="unbounded"/>
```

With this definition, the `order` element is optional and can be repeated an unlimited number of times.

Most schema constructs can be assigned occurrence values that are different from the default values. You can set the `minOccurs` and `maxOccurs` attributes for

- **Elements** With elements, you enter the `minOccurs` and `maxOccurs` attributes in the opening `element` tag. In the following example the `order` element can occur once or not at all:

  ```
  <xsd:element name="order" type="orderType" minOccurs="0"
   maxOccurs="1"/>
  ```

- **Sequences** With sequences, you enter the `minOccurs` and `maxOccurs` attributes in the opening sequence tag. In the following example the sequence of elements (`order`, `billTo`, and `shipTo`) must occur at least once and can be repeated up to three times:

  ```
  <xsd:sequence minOccurs="1" maxOccurs="3">
   <xsd:element name="order" type="orderType" />
   <xsd:element name="billTo" type="origin" />
   <xsd:element name="shipTo" type="destination" />
  </xsd:sequence>
  ```

- **Choices** With choices, you enter the `minOccurs` and `maxOccurs` attributes in the opening `choice` tag. In the following example any number of the elements in the `choice` group can be used (which is the same as using an asterisk in a DTD):

  ```
  <xsd:choice minOccurs="0" maxOccurs="unbounded">
   <xsd:element name="supportComments" type="textType" />
   <xsd:element name="serviceComments" type="textType" />
   <xsd:element name="fieldComments" type="textType" />
  </xsd:choice>
  ```

- **Unordered sets** With the `any` or `all` constructs, you enter the `minOccurs` and `maxOccurs` attributes in the opening `any` or `all` tag. In the following example any number of the elements can be used and they can appear in any order:

  ```
  <xsd:any minOccurs="0" maxOccurs="unbounded">
   <xsd:element name="supportComments" type="textType" />
   <xsd:element name="serviceComments" type="textType" />
   <xsd:element name="fieldComments" type="textType" />
  </xsd:any>
  ```

- **Group References** With references to groups, you add the `minOccurs` and `maxOccurs` attributes to the group construct. In the following example the elements in the reference group are mandatory and can't be repeated:

  ```
  <xsd:group ref="orderGroup" minOccurs="1" maxOccurs="1"/>
  ```

Tip The default value for `minOccurs` and `maxOccurs` is 1 with all of these constructs.

Using Groups and References

To enhance the reusability of schema constructs, XML Schema supports named element groups, attribute groups, and references:

- **Element groups** Define collections of elements that can be inserted by name into other groups or complex type definitions.
- **Attribute groups** Define collections of attributes that can be inserted by name into complex type definitions.
- **References** Used to refer to element or attribute groups you've defined and to refer to globally declared elements so that they can be given local context within complex type definitions.

Defining and Referencing Element Groups

You define element groups with the group declaration. The basic format for an element group is

```
<group name="groupName">
...
</group>
```

where *groupName* is the actual name of the group you're creating.

You must define an all, choice, or sequence construct within a group and then insert the element definitions within the `all`, `choice`, or `sequence` construct. The following example defines a group of elements that must occur in an exact sequence:

```
<xsd:group name="orgGroup">
 <xsd:sequence>
 <xsd:element name="organization" type="orgType" />
 <xsd:element name="accountNum" type="accountType" />
 <xsd:element name="orderDetails" type="orderInfo" />
 <xsd:element name="billTo" type="origin" />
 <xsd:element name="shipTo" type="destination" />
 </xsd:sequence>
</xsd:group>
```

You can use combinations of sequences and choices within groups as well, such as:

```
<xsd:group name="orderGroup">
 <xsd:choice>
 <xsd:sequence>
  <xsd:element name="person" type="personType" />
  <xsd:element name="orderInfo" type="orderInfo" />
  <xsd:element name="address" type="mailingAddress" />
 </xsd:sequence>
```

(continued)

(continued)

```
 <xsd:sequence>
  <xsd:element name="organization" type="orgType" />
  <xsd:element name="accountNum" type="accountType" />
  <xsd:element name="orderDetails" type="orderInfo" />
  <xsd:element name="billTo" type="origin" />
  <xsd:element name="shipTo" type="destination" />
 </xsd:sequence>
 </xsd:choice>
</xsd:group>
```

Once you've defined an element group, you can reference it in another group or in a complex type definition. The basic format for a group reference is

```
<group ref="groupName" />
```

where *groupName* is the name you previously used to identify the group. You can insert group references into other declarations like this:

```
<xsd:element name="order" type="orderType" />

<xsd:complexType name="orderType">
 <xsd:group ref="orderGroup" />
 <xsd:group ref="SummaryInfo" />
 <xsd:element name="status" type="currStatus"/>
</xsd:complexType />
```

Element groups can also be inserted into, `sequence`, `choice`, `any` and `all` constructs, such as:

```
<xsd:element name="order" type="orderType" />

<xsd:complexType name="orderType">
 <xsd:choice>
 <xsd:group ref="orderGroup" />
 <xsd:group ref="SummaryInfo" />
 </xsd:choice>
 <xsd:element name="status" type="currStatus"/>
</xsd:complexType />
```

Element groups must be declared globally at the top level of the schema. Thus, although you can reference a group from within another schema construct, you can't define a group within another construct. This means that the following declaration is incorrect:

```
<xsd:complexType name="orderType">
 <xsd:group name="orgGroup">
 <xsd:sequence>
 <xsd:element name="organization" type="orgType" />
 <xsd:element name="accountNum" type="accountType" />
```

(continued)

(continued)

```
 <xsd:element name="orderDetails" type="orderInfo" />
 <xsd:element name="billTo" type="origin" />
 <xsd:element name="shipTo" type="destination" />
 </xsd:sequence>
 </xsd:group>
</xsd:complexType >
```

To define an element group, follow these steps:

1. At the top level of the schema, type **<xsd:group**.
2. Enter **name="*label*">**, where *label* is the actual name of the group you're creating. The name must follow the rules for valid XML names.
3. Declare the sequences, choices, or unordered groups that should appear in the group.
4. Type **</xsd:group>** to complete the group definition.

The result should look similar to the following:

```
<xsd:group name="label">
 <xsd:sequence>
 ...
 </xsd:sequence>
</xsd:group>
```

After you define an element group, you can reference it by following these steps:

1. You can reference a group in `complexType`, `sequence`, `choice`, and `all` constructs as well as in other named groups. In the area of the schema where you want the elements in the group to appear, type **<xsd:group**.
2. Type **ref="*groupName*" />**, where *groupName* is the name you used to identify the group previously.

The result should look similar to the following:

```
<xsd:group ref="groupName" />
```

Defining and Referencing Attribute Groups

Attribute groups are very similar to element groups. You define attribute groups using the basic format:

```
<attributeGroup name="groupName">
...
</attributeGroup>
```

where *`groupName`* is the actual name of the group you're creating.

Attribute groups can contain attributes or references to other attribute groups. The following example declares a group of attributes called `personAttribs`:

```
<xsd:attributeGroup   name="personAttribs">
 <xsd:attribute name="first" type="xsd:string" />
 <xsd:attribute name="mi" type="xsd:string" />
 <xsd:attribute name="last" type="xsd:string" />
 <xsd:attribute name="street_address" type="xsd:string" />
 <xsd:attribute name="city" type="xsd:string" />
 <xsd:attribute name="state" type="xsd:string" />
 <xsd:attribute name="zipcode" type="xsd:string" />
</xsd:attributeGroup>
```

Once you've defined an attribute group, you can reference it in another group or in a complex type definition. The basic format for a group reference is

```
<attributeGroup ref="groupName" />
```

where *`groupName`* is the name you used to identify the group previously. You can insert attribute group references into other declarations like this:

```
<xsd:element name="person">
 <xsd:complexType>
 <xsd:attributeGroup name="personAttribs" />
 </xsd:complexType>
</xsd:element>
```

Attribute group references can be inserted in complex type definitions as well as extension and restriction definitions associated with an element's `simpleContent` or `complexContent` declarations.

As with element groups, you must declare attribute groups globally at the top level of the schema. Thus, although you can reference an attribute group from within another schema construct, you can't define an attribute group within another construct. This means that the following declaration is incorrect:

```
<xsd:element name="person">
 <xsd:complexType>
 <xsd:attributeGroup name="personAttribs">
 <xsd:attribute name="first" type="xsd:string" />
 <xsd:attribute name="mi" type="xsd:string" />
 <xsd:attribute name="last" type="xsd:string" />
 <xsd:attribute name="street_address" type="xsd:string" />
 <xsd:attribute name="city" type="xsd:string" />
 <xsd:attribute name="state" type="xsd:string" />
 <xsd:attribute name="zipcode" type="xsd:string" />
 </xsd:attributeGroup>
 </xsd:complexType>
</xsd:element>
```

To define an attribute group, follow these steps:

1. At the top level of the schema, type **<xsd:attributeGroup**.
2. Enter **name=*"label"*>**, where *label* is the actual name of the attribute group you're creating. The name must follow the rules for valid XML names.
3. Declare or reference the attributes that should appear in the group.
4. Type **</xsd:attributeGroup>** to complete the definition.

The result should look similar to the following:

```
<xsd:attributeGroup name="groupName">
...
</xsd:attributeGroup>
```

After you define an attribute group, you can reference it following these steps:

1. You can reference an attribute group in `complexType` and in other attribute groups. You can also reference attribute groups within the restriction and extension declarations associated with an element's simple and complex contents. In the area of the schema where you want the attributes in the group to appear, type **<xsd:attributeGroup**.
2. Type **ref="*groupName*" />**, where *groupName* is the name you used to identify the attribute group previously.

The result should look similar to the following:

```
<xsd:attributeGroup ref="groupName" />
```

Note It's good form to declare attributes and attribute groups at the end of the schema construct. This places the attribute or attribute group declarations after any element declarations the construct contains.

Referencing Globally Declared Elements

Any element declared at the top level of the schema is considered a global element. Unlike local elements, which have a single context, global elements can be used in multiple contexts. This allows you to reuse global element declarations.

The basic format for a global element reference is

```
<element ref="global_element_name" />
```

where *global_element_name* is the name assigned to the global element you're referencing. The following example declares three top-level elements (one is the document root and the other two are used globally):

```
<xsd:schema xmlns:xsd="http://www.w3.org/2001/XMLSchema">

 <xsd:element name="contact" type="ContactType" />

 <xsd:element name="customer" type="Entity" />
 <xsd:element name="organization" type="Entity" />

 <xsd:complexType name="ContactType">
 <xsd:element ref="customer" />
 <xsd:element ref="organization" />
 </xsd:complexType>

...

</xsd:schema>
```

Because the `customer` and `organization` elements are declared globally, they could be used in multiple contexts. In this example, they're referenced in the complex type named `ContactType`. They could be referenced in other areas of the schema as well.

After you define a global element at the top level of the schema, you can reference it by following these steps:

1. In the area of the schema where you want the elements in the element to appear, type **<xsd:element**.
2. Type **ref="*elementName*" />**, where *elementName* is the name you used to identify the element previously.

The result should look similar to the following:

```
<xsd:element ref="elementName" />
```

Chapter 12

Content Models for Schema Declarations

The XML Schema language is complex and has many nuances. After you've worked with XML Schema for a while, you'll be looking for a quick guide to the content models used by each of the various declaration types, which is exactly what this chapter provides. Content models in this chapter follow the form:

```
<schema_name
 attribute1 = type
 attribute2 = (optionA | optionB | optionC) : defaultOption
...
 attributeN = type : default
>
Content: (constructA, constructB*)
</schema_name>
```

As you can see, the first section of the content model defines the opening tag for the schema construct and the attributes it can contain. If an attribute has a default value, this will be provided as well. The content for the construct follows the opening tag. The content declaration follows the rules used with document type definitions (DTDs), which is why you'll see order indicators, qualifiers, and grouping designators. These symbols are used as defined in Table 4-1 in Chapter 4, "XML Elements in DTDs." In the example, `constructA` is required as the first item and `constructB` is an optional and repeatable item that can follow `constructA`.

Note In some content models you'll see references to `QName` and `NCName`. A `QName` is a valid XML name that includes a namespace prefix and a local name part. An `NCName` is a qualified name that doesn't include the prefix or the colon.

More Info For more information on schema content models, refer to *XML Schema Part 1: Structures*, Henry S. Thompson, David Beech, Murray Maloney, and Noah Mendelsohn, eds., W3C, 2 May 2001. Available online at *http://www.w3.org/TR/2001/REC-xmlschema-1-20010502/*.

all Definitions

The `all` declaration is defined as:

```
<all
 id = ID
 maxOccurs = 1 : 1
 minOccurs = (0 | 1) : 1
 {any attributes with non-schema namespace . . .}
>
Content: (annotation?, element*)
</all>
```

The content model shows that an `all` declaration can contain an optional `annotation` section, followed by zero or more element declarations.

annotation Definitions

The `annotation` declaration is defined as:

```
<annotation
 id = ID
 {any attributes with non-schema namespace . . .}
>
Content: (appinfo | documentation)*
</annotation>
```

The content model shows that an `annotation` declaration can contain any number of `appinfo` and `documentation` declarations.

`appinfo` is defined as:

```
<appinfo
 source = anyURI
>
Content: ({any})*
</appinfo>
```

The {any} reference in the content model means that `appinfo` can contain any free-flow text. `documentation` is defined as:

```
<documentation
 source = anyURI
 xml:lang = language
>
Content: ({any})*
</documentation>
```

The {any} reference in the content model means that `documentation` can contain any free-flow text.

any Definitions

The `any` declaration is defined as:

```
<any
 id = ID
 maxOccurs = (nonNegativeInteger | unbounded) : 1
 minOccurs = nonNegativeInteger : 1
 namespace = namespace
 processContents = (lax | skip | strict) : strict
 {any attributes with non-schema namespace . . .}
>
Content: (annotation?)
</any>
```

The content model shows that the declaration can contain an optional `annotation` section.

anyAttribute Definitions

The `anyAttribute` declaration is defined as:

```
<anyAttribute
 id = ID
 namespace = namespace
 processContents = (lax | skip | strict) : strict
 {any attributes with non-schema namespace . . .}
>
Content: (annotation?)
</anyAttribute>
```

The content model shows that the declaration can contain an optional `annotation` section.

attribute Definitions

The `attribute` declaration is defined as:

```
<attribute
 default = string
 fixed = string
 form = (qualified | unqualified)
 id = ID
 name = NCName
 ref = QName
 type = QName
 use = (optional | prohibited | required) : optional
 {any attributes with non-schema namespace . . .}
>
```

(continued)

(continued)

```
Content: (annotation?, (simpleType?))
</attribute>
```

The content model shows that an `attribute` declaration can contain an optional `annotation` section, followed by an optional simple type.

attributeGroup Definitions and References

The `attributeGroup` declaration is defined as:

```
<attributeGroup
 id = ID
 name = NCName
 {any attributes with non-schema namespace . . .}
>
Content: (annotation?, ((attribute | attributeGroup)*,
 anyAttribute?))
</attributeGroup>
```

The content model shows that an `attributeGroup` declaration can contain an optional `annotation` section, followed by zero or more `attribute` declarations or `attributeGroup` references, and ending with an optional `anyAttribute` declaration.

You reference attribute groups using the following content model:

```
<attributeGroup
 ref = QName >
</attributeGroup>
```

Because attribute group references can't contain contents, no content is specified.

choice Definitions

The `choice` declaration is defined as:

```
<choice
 id = ID
 maxOccurs = (nonNegativeInteger | unbounded) : 1
 minOccurs = nonNegativeInteger : 1
 {any attributes with non-schema namespace . . .}
>
Content: (annotation?, (element | group | choice | sequence |
 any)*)
</choice>
```

The content model shows that a choice declaration can contain an optional `annotation` section, followed by zero or more `element`, `group`, `choice`, `sequence`, or `any` declarations.

complexType Definitions

The `complexType` declaration is defined as:

```
<complexType
 abstract = boolean : false
 block = (#all | List of (extension | restriction))
 final = (#all | List of (extension | restriction))
 id = ID
 mixed = boolean : false
 name = NCName
 {any attributes with non-schema namespace . . .}
>
Content: (annotation?, (simpleContent | complexContent |
 ((group | all | choice | sequence)?, ((attribute |
 attributeGroup)*, anyAttribute?))))
</complexType>
```

The content model shows that a `complexType` declaration can contain an optional `annotation` section, followed by either `simpleContent` or `complexContent`. If the complex type doesn't have simple or complex content, it can contain a single `group`, `all`, `choice`, or `sequence` declaration followed by zero or more `attribute` declarations or `attributeGroup` references that end with an optional `anyAttribute` declaration.

Complex Type with Simple Content

When a complex type has simple content, its `simpleContent` declaration is defined as follows:

```
<simpleContent
 id = ID
 {any attributes with non-schema namespace . . .}
>
Content: (annotation?, (restriction | extension))
</simpleContent>
```

The content model shows that a `simpleContent` declaration can contain an optional `annotation` section, followed by either a `restriction` or an `extension`.

Extensions defined within simple content are used as follows:

```
<extension
 base = QName
 id = ID
 {any attributes with non-schema namespace . . .}
>
Content: (annotation?, ((attribute | attributeGroup)*,
 anyAttribute?))
</extension>
```

The content model shows that this type of extension can contain an optional `annotation` section, followed by zero or more `attribute` declarations or `attributeGroup` references that end with an optional `anyAttribute` declaration.

Restrictions defined within simple content are used as follows:

```
<restriction
 base = QName
 id = ID
 {any attributes with non-schema namespace . . .}
>
Content: (annotation?, (simpleType?, (minExclusive |
 minInclusive | maxExclusive | maxInclusive | totalDigits |
 fractionDigits | length | minLength | maxLength | enumeration |
 whiteSpace | pattern)*)?, ((attribute | attributeGroup)*,
 anyAttribute?))
</restriction>
```

The content model shows that this type of extension can contain an optional `annotation` section, followed by an optional `simpleType` and a list of repeatable `restrictions`, which is in turn followed by zero or more `attribute` declarations or `attributeGroup` references that end with an optional `anyAttribute` declaration.

Complex Type with Complex Content

When a complex type has complex content, its `complexContent` declaration is defined as follows:

```
<complexContent
 id = ID
  mixed = boolean
 {any attributes with non-schema namespace . . .}
>
Content: (annotation?, (restriction | extension))
</complexContent>
```

The content model shows that a `complexContent` declaration can contain an optional `annotation` section, followed by either a `restriction` or an `extension`.

Extensions defined within complex content are used as follows:

```
<extension
 base = QName
 id = ID
 {any attributes with non-schema namespace . . .}
>

Content: (annotation?, ((group | all | choice | sequence)?,
 ((attribute | attributeGroup)*, anyAttribute?)))
</extension>
```

The content model shows that this type of `extension` can contain an optional `annotation` section, followed by an optional `group`, `all`, `choice`, or `sequence` declaration that includes zero or more `attribute` declarations or `attributeGroup` references that end with an optional `anyAttribute` declaration.

Restrictions defined within complex content are used as follows:

```
<restriction
 base = QName
 id = ID
 {any attributes with non-schema namespace . . .}
>
Content: (annotation?, (group | all | choice | sequence)?,
 ((attribute | attributeGroup)*, anyAttribute?))
</restriction>
```

The content model shows that this type of `restriction` can contain an optional `annotation` section, followed by an optional `group`, `all`, `choice`, or `sequence` declaration that includes zero or more `attribute` declarations or `attributeGroup` references that end with an optional `anyAttribute` declaration.

element Definitions

An `element` declaration is defined as:

```
<element
 abstract = boolean : false
 block = (#all | List of (extension | restriction |
  substitution))
 default = string
 final = (#all | List of (extension | restriction))
 fixed = string
 form = (qualified | unqualified)
 id = ID
 maxOccurs = (nonNegativeInteger | unbounded) : 1
 minOccurs = nonNegativeInteger : 1
 name = NCName
 nillable = boolean : false
 ref = QName
 substitutionGroup = QName
 type = QName
 {any attributes with non-schema namespace . . .}
>
Content: (annotation?, ((simpleType | complexType)?,
 (unique | key | keyref)*))
</element>
```

The content model shows that an `element` can contain an optional `annotation` section, followed by either an optional simple type or an optional complex type. A unique constraint can be defined for the element as a `unique` id, `key`, or key reference (`keyref`).

Element group Definitions and References

Element group declarations are defined as:

```
<group
 name = NCName
>
Content: (annotation?, (all | choice | sequence))
</group>
```

The content model shows that element groups can contain an optional annotation section, followed by a mandatory all, choice, or sequence declaration. You can't repeat the all, choice, or sequence declarations.

You reference element groups using the following content model:

```
<group
 ref = QName
 maxOccurs = (nonNegativeInteger | unbounded) : 1
 minOccurs = nonNegativeInteger : 1>
</group>
```

Because element group references can't contain contents, no content is specified.

import Definitions

An import declaration is defined as:

```
<import
 id = ID
 namespace = anyURI
 schemaLocation = anyURI
 {any attributes with non-schema namespace . . .}
>
Content: (annotation?)
</import>
```

The content model shows that an import declaration has an optional annotation as its only contents.

include Definitions

An include declaration is defined as:

```
<include
 id = ID
 schemaLocation = anyURI
 {any attributes with non-schema namespace . . .}
>
Content: (annotation?)
</include>
```

The content model shows that an `include` declaration has an optional `annotation` as its only contents.

notation Definitions

The `notation` declaration is defined as:

```
<notation
 id = ID
 name = NCName
 public = anyURI
 system = anyURI
 {any attributes with non-schema namespace . . .}
>
Content: (annotation?)
</notation>
```

The content model shows that a `notation` declaration has an optional `annotation` as its only contents. You can define and use notations in schema like this:

```
<xsd:notation name="jpeg"
 public="image/jpeg" system="imageviewer.exe" />
<xsd:notation name="png"
 public="image/png" system="imageviewer.exe" />
<xsd:notation name="gif"
 public="image/gif" system="imageviewer.exe" />
<xsd:element name="image">
 <xsd:complexType>
 <xsd:simpleContent>
 <xsd:extension base="xsd:hexBinary">
 <xsd:attribute name="imageType">
 <xsd:simpleType>
  <xsd:restriction base="xsd:NOTATION">
  <xsd:enumeration value="jpeg" />
  <xsd:enumeration value="png" />
  <xsd:enumeration value="gif" />
  </xsd:restriction>
 </xsd:simpleType>
 </xsd:attribute>
 </xsd:extension>
 </xsd:simpleContent>
 </xsd:complexType>
</xsd:element>
```

You could then use the `image` element in a document like this:

```
<image imagetype="gif"></image>
```

schema Definitions

A `schema` declaration is defined as:

```
<schema
 attributeFormDefault = (qualified | unqualified) : unqualified
 blockDefault = (#all | List of (extension | restriction |
 substitution)) : ''
 elementFormDefault = (qualified | unqualified) : unqualified
 finalDefault = (#all | List of (extension | restriction)) : ''
 id = ID
 targetNamespace = anyURI
 version = token
 xml:lang = language
 {any attributes with non-schema namespace . . .}
>
Content: ((include | import | redefine | annotation)*,
 (((simpleType | complexType | group | attributeGroup) |
 element | attribute | notation), annotation*)*)
</schema>
```

The content model shows that a `schema` declaration can contain zero or more `include`, `import`, `redefine`, and `annotation` declarations followed by zero or more `simpleType`, `complexType`, `group`, `attributeGroup`, `element`, `attribute`, `notation`, and `annotation` declarations.

selector and field Definitions

Unique `id`s, `key`s, and key references use selectors and fields. The definition of a `selector` is:

```
<selector
 id = ID
 xpath = a subset of XPath expression, see below
 {any attributes with non-schema namespace . . .}
>
Content: (annotation?)
</selector>
```

The definition of a `field` is:

```
<field
 id = ID
 xpath = a subset of XPath expression, see below
 {any attributes with non-schema namespace . . .}
>
Content: (annotation?)
</field>
```

Both of these declarations can have an optional `annotation` as their only contents.

sequence Definitions

A `sequence` declaration is defined as:

```
<sequence
 id = ID
 maxOccurs = (nonNegativeInteger | unbounded) : 1
 minOccurs = nonNegativeInteger : 1
 {any attributes with non-schema namespace . . .}
>
Content: (annotation?, (element | group | choice | sequence |
 any)*)
</sequence>
```

The content model shows that a `sequence` declaration can contain an optional `annotation` section, followed by zero or more `element`, `group`, `choice`, `sequence`, or `any` declarations.

simpleType Definitions

A `simpleType` declaration is defined as:

```
<simpleType
 final = (#all | (list | union | restriction))
 id = ID
 name = NCName
 {any attributes with non-schema namespace . . .}
>
Content: (annotation?, (restriction | list | union))
</simpleType>
```

The content model shows that a `simpleType` can contain an optional `annotation` section, followed by a mandatory `restriction`, `list`, or `union`. You can use the `restriction`, `list`, or `union` only once.

Lists used within `simpleTypes` have the following content model:

```
<list
 id = ID
 itemType = QName
 {any attributes with non-schema namespace . . .}
>
Content: (annotation?, (simpleType?))
</list>
```

This content model specifies that this type of `list` can contain an optional `annotation` followed by an optional `simpleType`. Neither can be repeated.

Restrictions used within simpleTypes have the following content model:

```
<restriction
 base = QName
 id = ID
 {any attributes with non-schema namespace . . .}
>
Content: (annotation?, (simpleType?, (minExclusive |
 minInclusive| maxExclusive | maxInclusive | totalDigits |
 fractionDigits | length | minLength | maxLength |
 enumeration | whiteSpace | pattern)*))
</restriction>
```

This content model specifies that this type of restriction can contain an optional annotation followed by an optional simpleType or zero or more individual restrictions.

Unions used within simpleType have the following content model:

```
<union
 id = ID
 memberTypes = List of QName
 {any attributes with non-schema namespace . . .}
>
Content: (annotation?, (simpleType*))
</union>
```

This content model specifies that this type of union can contain an optional annotation followed by zero or more simpleTypes.

unique Constraint Definitions

Elements can have one of three types of unique constraints associated with them: a unique id, a key, or a key reference. The definition of a unique id is:

```
<unique
 id = ID
 name = NCName
 {any attributes with non-schema namespace . . .}
>
Content: (annotation?, (selector, field+))
</unique>
```

The content model shows that a unique id can contain an optional annotation section, followed by a mandatory selector with one or more defined fields.

The definition of a key is:

```
<key
 id = ID
 name = NCName
 {any attributes with non-schema namespace . . .}
>
Content: (annotation?, (selector, field+))
</key>
```

The content model shows that a key can contain an optional annotation section, followed by a mandatory selector with one or more defined fields.

The definition of a key reference is:

```
<keyref
 id = ID
 name = NCName
 refer = QName
 {any attributes with non-schema namespace . . .}
>
Content: (annotation?, (selector, field+))
</keyref>
```

The content model shows that a key reference can contain an optional annotation section, followed by a mandatory selector with one or more defined fields.

Part IV

XSLT and XPath

To round out the coverage of XML, Part IV examines techniques you can use to transform XML structures dynamically. An understanding of transformation is essential if you want to implement or support an end-to-end XML solution. Typically, you'll use transformations to structure information dynamically after extracting the information from a database.

Chapter 13 introduces XSL Transformations (XSLT) and related technologies, including XSL Formatting Objects (used to provide formatting and style) and XML Path (XPath) (used to identity parts of documents). Chapter 14 provides a detailed discussion of XPath operators and expressions that you can use to locate specific parts of XML documents. Chapter 15 examines structures that you can use to conditionally process a part of a document based on the value of an expression. As you'll learn in this chapter, XSLT implements many standard logic controls, including if-then, if-then-else, switch-case, and for-each.

Chapter 16 explores techniques you can use to pass values into templates and hold values temporarily during processing. Once you learn these techniques, you can create XSLT stylesheets that perform many advanced tasks. Chapter 17 delves into techniques you can use to manipulate the text content of elements and attributes. You'll learn how to extract substrings, convert strings to number, format strings, and much more. Chapter 18 completes the discussion of XSLT and XPath by explaining how to restructure input documents and manipulate document subsets. You'll learn how to merge documents, how to manipulate document structures, and how to define sort keys.

Chapter 13

XSL Transformations and Formatting

Extensible Stylesheet Language (XSL) defines rules that specify how to extract information from an XML document and how to format this information so that it can be viewed. XSL is divided into three parts:

- **XSL Transformations (XSLT)** A language for transforming XML documents
- **XML Path (XPath)** An expression language used by XSLT to access and refer to parts of a document
- **XSL Formatting Objects (XSL-FO)** An XML vocabulary used by XSLT to describe the formatting of text on a page

The focus of this chapter is XSLT. XSLT will remain the focus of the discussion throughout this part of the book. Chapter 14, "XPath Operators and Expressions," continues the XSLT discussion by detailing how to use XPath with XSLT. Chapter 15, "Branching and Control Functions," delves into many of the advanced features of XSLT and XPath. Chapter 16, "Variables and Parameters in XSLT," explores techniques for creating links and cross-references using XSLT.

Introducing XSLT

XSLT is a language for transforming XML documents. You use XSLT to specify the rules by which one XML document is transformed into another type of document. Although the output of the transformation process could be an XML document, it's more commonly an HTML document that's designed to be viewed by users. The output could also be a Unicode text file, a Portable Document File (PDF), a file containing programming code written in Java, Active Server Pages (ASP) or another programming language, or just about any other file type.

The typical transformation process starts with an input document that's matched against a set of one or more XSLT documents, called XSLT stylesheets. You write XSLT stylesheets to define the rules for transforming a specific type of XML document. During the transformation process, an XSLT processor analyzes the contents of the input document to match specific criteria defined in the stylesheet. These criteria are organized as templates that define actions to take when a match is found. When an XSLT processor determines that an element matches a template definition, it writes the contents of the template to an output buffer. Upon finishing the analysis, the processor might restructure the output buffer to format the document as XML, HTML, and so on.

XSLT is created to be more powerful and versatile than other stylesheet languages, such as cascading style sheets (CSS). Although you can use CSS with XML, it really isn't optimized to work with data. You can use CSS to specify font types, set margins, and position content, but you can't use CSS to perform many of the tasks you'll want to perform on data. Tasks that XSLT excels at include:

- **Sorting** Allows you to change the order of elements according to a set of criteria. For example, you could sort a list of accounts alphabetically.
- **Filtering** Allows you to remove elements that aren't applicable in a specific context. For example, you could filter out incomplete orders from an order summary to show only orders that have been completed.
- **Calculating** Allows you to perform arithmetic functions. For example, you could total the sales proceeds from multiple orders.
- **Merging** Allows you to combine multiple documents into a single document. For example, you could combine all the sales orders for the month into a single summary document called Monthly Sales.

When you need to perform any of these tasks on data or perform standard transformations going from XML to another format, XSLT should be your tool of choice. Don't worry, if you need to apply formatting to a document after it's been transformed, you can still do this—I'll show you how later in the chapter.

Because a solid understanding of the transformation process is essential to working with XSLT, let's take a more detailed look at this process, starting with the following sample input document:

```
<?xml version="1.0"?>
<document>
 XSLT is a powerful transformation language.
</document>
```

Although you can view an XML document directly in a Web browser or another application, the document isn't formatted. To format the document for viewing, you'd want to transform the document into another format, such as HTML. Here's an XSLT stylesheet that specifies how to transform the sample document:

```
<xsl:stylesheet
 xmlns:xsl="http://www.w3.org/1999/XSL/Transform"
 versioncl.0">

 <xsl:output method="html" />
```

(continued)

(continued)

```
 <xsl:template match="/">
 <xsl:apply-templates select="document" />
 </xsl:template>

 <xsl:template match="document">
 <html>
  <body>
  <p>
  <xsl:value-of select="." />
  </p>
  </body>
 </html>
 </xsl:template>

</xsl:stylesheet>
```

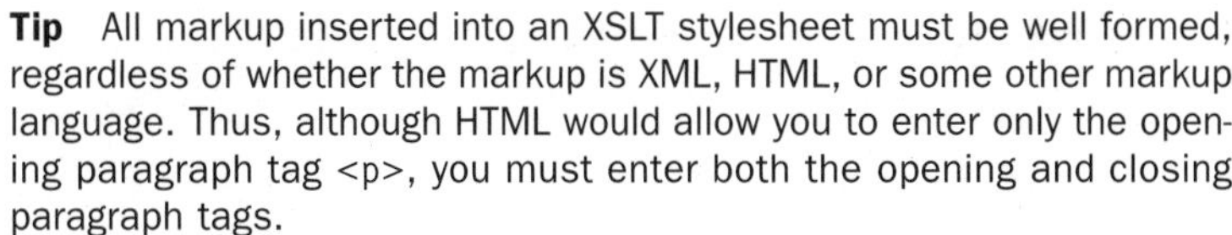

Tip All markup inserted into an XSLT stylesheet must be well formed, regardless of whether the markup is XML, HTML, or some other markup language. Thus, although HTML would allow you to enter only the opening paragraph tag `<p>`, you must enter both the opening and closing paragraph tags.

Although we'll examine XSLT stylesheets in detail shortly, let's focus on the basics for now. The first template in this stylesheet tells an XSLT processor to find the root element and apply the second template to any `document` elements in the source document. The second template replaces the begin `<document>` and end `</document>` tags with the HTML markup provided and then inserts the value of the `document` element into the HTML paragraph tag.

The result is the following HTML document:

```
<html>
<body>
<p>
 XSLT is a powerful transformation language.
</p>
</body>
</html>
```

Figure 13-1 shows the original XML document and the output document that has been transformed into HTML.

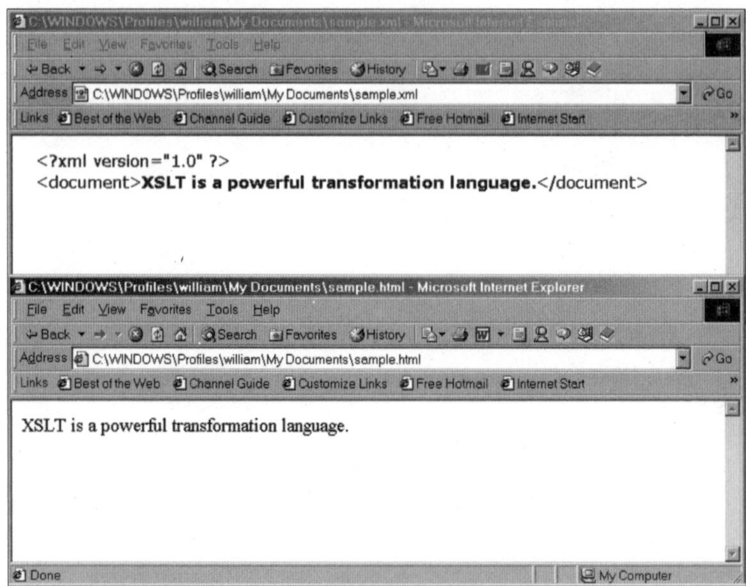

Figure 13-1. *Transforming an XML document into HTML.*

As with XML processors, you could use a number of capable XSLT processors. One of the most popular Java-based XSLT processors is Xalan from the Apache XML Project (*xml.apache.org/xalan/*). Once you've installed Java and Xalan, you use the Process class to process documents by typing:

```
java org.apache.xalan.xslt.Process -in file_in -xsl file_xsl
 -out file_out
```

where *file_in* is the input XML document, *file_xsl* is the XSL stylesheet, and *file_out* is the output file, such as:

```
java org.apache.xalan.xslt.Process -in sample.xml
 -xsl sample.xsl -out sample.html
```

Once you've transformed the file into a specific format, you can view the file in an appropriate application, such as a Web browser, to ensure that the transformation worked.

When working with XSLT, keep in mind that the only template automatically applied to any document is the template for the root node. All other templates must be invoked when a particular document structure matches a template rule. You must explicitly define expressions to determine which additional templates are applied. You do this by defining a root template that in turn invokes other templates.

Templates are always recursively processed. In this example the root template specifies that there are templates for three elements (`element1`, `element2`, and `element3`):

```
<xsl:stylesheet
 xmlns:xsl="http://www.w3.org/1999/XSL/Transform"
 version="1.0">

 <xsl:template match="/">
 <xsl:apply-templates select="element1" />
 <xsl:apply-templates select="element2" />
 <xsl:apply-templates select="element3" />
 </xsl:template>
...
</xsl:stylesheet>
```

The XSLT processor would start with the root template and then process the template for `element1`. If the rules for `element1` invoked other templates, these templates would each be processed in turn. When the processor was finished recursively processing templates associated with `element1`, the processor would start with the rules for `element2`, and so on.

Matching Document Structures to Template Rules

Recursion is a powerful aspect of XSLT. When XSLT processors analyze input documents, they see document structures as node trees, where nodes represent individual pieces of the XML document, such as elements, attributes, text, comments, and processing instructions, and the node tree itself is a hierarchical representation of the entire XML document.

At the top of the node tree is the root node, which represents a document's root element. Top-level elements in a document become branches of the tree with the low-level elements that they contain below them. Any contents or attributes of elements are broken out in the tree structure as well. This makes the node tree easy to traverse as long as the processor understands the basic parent-child-sibling concepts discussed in Chapter 2, "XML Document Structure," and knows how to locate various types of nodes using these concepts.

The actual underlying technology that enables document structures to be represented as node trees and then traversed is XPath. XPath defines a set of standard nodes and provides the functions for locating those nodes. Node types defined by XPath are

- **Root** Represents the root element in XML documents (each document has only one root node). The root node contains the entire document. Although it has no parent nodes, all top-level nodes are its children and all nodes are its descendants.

- **Element** Represents all elements in XML documents, including root nodes. This means that element nodes exist for the root element and all other elements in a document. Element nodes can have parents and children. The parent nodes are either the root node or another higher-level element node. Children nodes can include other element nodes, text nodes, comment nodes, and processing instruction nodes that occur within the element.
- **Attribute** Represents attributes in XML documents. Although element nodes are the parent of attribute nodes, attribute nodes aren't children of element nodes. This is a subtle but important semantic distinction between attribute nodes and other nodes. The reason for this distinction is that attribute nodes aren't present unless they're specifically requested. Once an attribute is requested, a node is added to the node tree and the value of the attribute can be read. This remains true if default values for attributes are defined in a document type definition (DTD) or schema but aren't explicitly specified in elements. Attributes inherited by an element from higher-level elements are also available. This applies to the `xml:lang` and `xml:space` attributes, which are applied to an element and inherited by its child elements. Keep in mind that the XML processor must be able to access external DTDs or schemas to determine that default values are defined and available. If the processor can't do this, the default values won't be available.
- **Text** Represents the text contents of elements. If any text associated with an element contains entity or character references, these references are resolved before the text node is created. `CDATA` sections in documents are represented as text nodes as well where the parent element is the element in which the `CDATA` section is defined. If the element containing the `CDATA` section is the root element, the root element will have a text node. If any element already has a text node, the contents of the `CDATA` section are added to the existing contents of the text node. This ensures that the text node contains the entire textual contents of the related element. Because references and `CDATA` sections are resolved before the text node is created, there's no way to determine that the text originally contained references or `CDATA` sections.
- **Comment** Represents comments inserted into XML documents. All comments inserted into a document become comment nodes (except for comments in a DTD or schema). The text of the comment is everything inside the comment except for the opening <!-- and closing -->, respectively.
- **Processing instruction** Represents processing instructions in XML documents. Processing instruction nodes contain two values: the name of the instruction, which can be obtained with the `name()` function, and a string containing the rest of the processing instruction, but not including the opening <? or closing ?>, respectively.
- **Namespace** Represents namespaces declared in XSLT stylesheets. Namespace nodes are used by the XSLT processor and aren't meant to be used by stylesheet developers. Namespace nodes contain the value assigned to an element's `xmlns` attribute. The `xmlns` attribute isn't represented as an attribute node.

Each of these node types has a built-in template rule associated with it that allows the node to be processed as necessary. The following sections examine these built-in template rules.

Understanding the Built-In Template for Element and Root Nodes

The built-in template for element and root nodes is used to process the root node and all of its child nodes. The template is defined as:

```
<xsl:template match="*|/">
 <xsl:apply-templates />
</xsl:template>
```

As shown, the template match value is defined as:

```
*|/
```

These characters represent an XPath expression and all have special meaning:

- * is a wildcard character, indicating that any value is allowed. In the `match` attribute, this says match any element name.
- | is a choice indicator, indicating to match either by using the asterisk (*) or the slash (/).
- / is the designator for the root node. XPath refers to the root node using this designator.

Thus, when you put these characters together, all element nodes and the root node are deemed matches for the XPath expression. The `xsl:apply-templates` statement tells the XSLT processor to apply the appropriate templates to nodes in the input document. This ensures that any node in the document can be processed, even if there are no template rules for parent nodes.

Understanding the Built-In Template for Modes

The `xsl:template` element has a mode attribute that lets you process the same set of nodes using different template rules. The built-in template that ensures modes are recognized is:

```
<xsl:template match="*|/" mode="x">
 <xsl:apply-templates mode="x" />
</xsl:template>
```

This template ensures that element and root nodes are processed regardless of the mode that's currently being used. The mode template is only invoked when you define modes in your XSLT stylesheet, and then the template only works to ensure that the various modes are recognized. You'll learn more about modes in Chapter 15.

Understanding the Built-In Template for Text and Attribute Nodes

The built-in template for text and attribute nodes ensures that these nodes can be processed regardless of their value. This template is defined as:

```
<xsl:template match="text()|@*">
 <xsl:value-of select="." />
</xsl:template>
```

As shown, the template match value is defined as:

```
text()|@*
```

These characters represent an XPath expression:

- `text()` is a reference to a function. The `text()` function is used to obtain the text contents of an element.
- | is a choice indicator, indicating to match either by using the `text()` function or the `@*` expression.
- `@*` is an expression that obtains the value of attributes.

Thus, the expression says to obtain the contents of any text or attribute node. The `value-of select="."` statement tells the XSLT processor to select these contents and copy them to the output tree. This template is only invoked when you define a template rule that attempts to access the contents of a text or attribute node, and in this case only the contents of the specified node are copied to the node tree.

Understanding Other Built-In Templates

The built-in template for comments and processing instructions is defined as:

```
<xsl:template match="comment()|processing-instruction()" />
```

This is similar to the built-in template for namespaces, which is defined as:

```
<xsl:template match="namespace()" />
```

These built-in templates define no rules for `comment`, `processing-instruction`, and `namespace` nodes. Essentially, this is the same as saying don't do anything. These templates are only invoked when you define template rules that access `comment`, `processing-instruction`, or `namespace` nodes, and then the templates only work to ensure that the nodes are recognized. If you want the contents of these nodes to be extracted, you must define specific template rules to handle this.

Structuring XSLT Stylesheets

XSLT stylesheets are used to transform XML documents into another format. To do this, stylesheets contain rules that match various parts of the input document to a template that specifies how to format that particular part of the document. Every XSLT stylesheet is itself an XML document that contains three basic structures:

- An XSLT declaration that marks the start of the stylesheet.
- An output declaration that sets the output format.
- Template rules containing declarations.

Typically, these structures are applied in the order specified. This means that you start the stylesheet with the XSLT declaration, insert an optional output declaration, and then define template rules containing declarations.

Starting the XSLT Stylesheet

Because an XSLT stylesheet is an XML document, it can start with a standard XML declaration that specifies the XML version, such as:

```
<?xml version="1.0"?>
```

However, the XML declaration isn't required and is omitted in most cases.

The optional XML declaration is followed by the <stylesheet> element, which defines the XSLT version being used and defines the namespace for XSLT definitions. The standard stylesheet declaration for XSLT version 1.0 is:

```
<xsl:stylesheet
 xmlns:xsl="http://www.w3.org/1999/XSL/Transform"
 version="1.0">
```

This declaration sets the namespace prefix as `xsl` and points to the Uniform Resource Identifier (URI) `http://www.w3.org/1999/XSL/Transform`. Different versions of XSLT use a different namespace URI and version number. For example, XSLT 1.1 uses the URI `http://www.w3.org/2001/XSL/Transform` and the version identifier 1.1.

The closing tag for the stylesheet element is </stylesheet>. This means the basic form of a stylesheet is:

```
<xsl:stylesheet
 xmlns:xsl="http://www.w3.org/1999/XSL/Transform"
 version="1.0">
...
</xsl:stylesheet>
```

For ease of reference, XSLT stylesheets normally are saved with the .xsl extension. The .xsl extension ensures that the document is easily recognized as containing XSL and that applications, such as Microsoft Internet Explorer, view the document as such.

To define an XSLT stylesheet, follow these steps:

1. To use XSLT version 1.0, type **<xsl:stylesheet xmlns:xsl="http://www.w3.org/1999/XSL/Transform" version="1.0">** to specify the namespace for the stylesheet and declare the namespace prefix as xsl.
2. To use XSLT version 1.1, type **<xsl:stylesheet xmlns:xsl="http://www.w3.org/2001/XSL/Transform" version="1.1">** to specify the namespace for the stylesheet and declare the namespace prefix as xsl.
3. Type a few blank lines where you'll later enter the body of the stylesheet.
4. Type **</xsl:stylesheet>** to complete the stylesheet.

The result should look similar to the following:

```
<xsl:stylesheet
 xmlns:xsl="http://www.w3.org/2001/XSL/Transform"
 version="1.1">
...
</xsl:stylesheet>
```

Real World Although XSLT 1.1 is the current version of XSLT, the most widely implemented and used version of XSLT at the time of this writing is 1.0. The good news is that whether you're using XSLT 1.0 or XSLT 1.1, you can use everything this book discusses. The changes from XSLT 1.0 to XSLT 1.1 aren't extensive and are primarily focused on correcting errors and deficiencies in the original 1.0 version.

Defining the Output Format

You specify the format for output documents using the output element. Although this element has no required attributes, it has many optional attributes. These attributes and their uses are discussed in the following sections.

Setting Attributes for the output Element

The primary attribute of the output element that you'll use is method, which sets the output method. The XSLT specification defines three possible output methods that processors are required to support:

- **method="xml"** Used when the output contains XML or an XML-based application, such as content formatted with XML-FO or content that uses Scalable Vector Graphics (SVG).
- **method="html"** Used when the output contains standard HTML.
- **method="text"** Used when the output contains text characters. These characters could represent standard text or the source code for a programming language.

Note Because XHTML is an XML-based application, you could set the output method to `method="xml"` when you want the output document to be formatted as XHTML. You could also set `method="html"`. If you do this, be sure to set attributes that build the appropriate XML and DOCTYPE declarations. For an example, see the "Formatting Output as XML or XML-Based Markup"section of this chapter.

The default output method is either XML or HTML, as determined by the contents of the output. If the output contains text and the root element is named `html` (in any combination of uppercase or lowercase characters), the default output method is HTML. Otherwise, the default output method is XML.

Although XSLT processors are free to implement other output methods, these are the standard output methods. The following example shows how you could set the output method to text:

```
<xsl:stylesheet
  xmlns:xsl="http://www.w3.org/1999/XSL/Transform"
 version="1.0">

<xsl:output method="text" />
...
</xsl:stylesheet>
```

Table 13-1 provides a summary of the `output` element's attributes. Example procedures using essential attributes with each of the standard output types are discussed in the following sections.

Table 13-1. Attributes of the XSLT output Element

Attribute	Description	Used with
`cdata-section-elements`	Lists elements that should be written as `CDATA` sections in the output. Processor will escape characters as necessary to ensure contents can be output.	`method="xml"`
`doctype-public`	Sets the public identifier to be used in the document type declaration.	`method="xml"` or `method="html"`
`doctype-system`	Sets the system identifier to be used in the document type declaration.	`method="xml"` or `method="html"`
`encoding`	Defines the character encoding to set in the XML or HTML declaration or the preferred encoding for text.	`method="xml"`, `method="html"` or `method="text"`
`indent`	Determines whether the processor can indent the tags in the output document. The value must be yes or no. Processors aren't required to indent.	`method="xml"` or `method="html"`

(continued)

Table 13-1. *(continued)*

Attribute	Description	Used with
`media-type`	Sets the media type (Multipurpose Internet Mail Extension [MIME] content type) of the output data.	`method="xml"`, `method="html"` or `method="text"`
`method`	Sets the output method. Typically, the value is `xml`, `html`, or `text`.	-
`omit-xml-declaration`	Determines whether the processor should omit the XML declaration in the output. The value must be `yes` or `no`.	`method="xml"`
`standalone`	Sets the standalone attribute in the XML declaration of the output document. The value must be `yes` or `no`.	`method="xml"`
`version`	Sets the version attribute of the HTML or XML declaration in the output document.	`method="xml"` or `method="html"`

Formatting Output as XML or XML-Based Markup

XML is one of the two default output formats for XSLT stylesheets. Output is formatted as XML any time the output doesn't contain a root element named `html` (in any combination of upper or lowercase characters). If you like, you can explicitly specify that the output should be formatted as XML. Simply set `method="xml"` in the `output` element of the stylesheet, as shown in this example:

```
<xsl:stylesheet
 xmlns:xsl="http://www.w3.org/1999/XSL/Transform"
 version="1.0">

<xsl:output method="xml" />
...
</xsl:stylesheet>
```

When you define the output as XML, you can set attributes that build the output document's XML declaration. The key attributes are `version`, `standalone`, and `encoding`—`version` sets the XML version being used; `standalone` specifies whether the document is a stand-alone document that doesn't use external files; `encoding` specifies the character encoding of the output document. If you don't specify values for these attributes, the XML declaration is created as:

```
<?xml version="1.0" encoding="UTF-8"?>
```

and the document is considered to be a standalone document (using the assumed default, as discussed in Chapter 2). You can modify the default values by setting explicit values. For example, if you wanted the XML declaration to look like this:

```
<?xml version="1.0" encoding="ISO-8859-1" standalone="yes"?>
```

you'd set the attributes of the output element like this:

```
<xsl:output method="xml" version="1.0" encoding="ISO-8859-1"
 standalone="yes" />
```

Any time the output is formatted using an application of XML, such as XML-FO or Scalable Vector Graphics (SVG), you should explicitly set the output method as XML and then define any additional attributes necessary to properly interpret the output document. With SVG, for example, you'll want to set the public and system identifiers so that a `DOCTYPE` declaration containing these values will be created in the output document. To do this, you set the `doctype-public` and `doctype-system` attributes of the `output` element. With SVG, the standard values for these attributes are "`-//W3C//DTD SVG 20001102//EN`" and "`http://www.w3.org/TR/2000/CR-SVG-20001102/DTD/svg-20001102.dtd`", respectively.

Note The value `EN` in the `PUBLIC` URI for SVG is the two-letter language code for U.S. English. If the document isn't formatted in U.S. English, you must change the language code to the appropriate value.

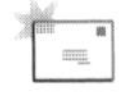

The following example shows how you could set the `doctype-public` and `doctype-system` attributes in a stylesheet:

```
<?xml version="1.0"?>
<xsl:stylesheet version="1.0"
 xmlns:xsl="http://www.w3.org/1999/XSL/Transform">

 <xsl:output method="xml"
  doctype-public="-//W3C//DTD SVG 20001102//EN"
  doctype-system="http://www.w3.org/TR/2000/CR-SVG-20001102/DTD/
   svg-20001102.dtd" />

 <xsl:template match="/">
 <svg>
 ...
 </svg>
 </xsl:template>

</xsl:stylesheet>
```

In the output document these values would be defined like this:

```
<?xml version="1.0" encoding="UTF-8"?>
<!DOCTYPE svg PUBLIC "-//W3C//DTD SVG 20001102//EN" "http://
 www.w3.org/TR/2000/CR-SVG-20001102/DTD/svg-20001102.dtd">
<svg>
...
</svg>
```

You can also use the doctype-public and doctype-system attributes when you want to format output as XHTML. With XHTML, these attributes are set to "-//W3C//DTD XHTML 1.0 Transitional//EN" and "http://www.w3.org/TR/xhtml1-transitional.dtd", respectively in most cases. This means a typical stylesheet for XHTML looks like this:

```
<?xml version="1.0"?>
<xsl:stylesheet version="1.0"
 xmlns:xsl="http://www.w3.org/1999/XSL/Transform">

 <xsl:output method="xml"
  doctype-public="-//W3C//DTD XHTML 1.0 Transitional//EN"
  doctype-system="http://www.w3.org/TR/xhtml1-transitional.dtd" />

 <xsl:template match="/">
 <html>
 ...
 </html>
 </xsl:template>
</xsl:stylesheet>
```

and these values appear in the output document like this:

```
<?xml version="1.0" encoding="UTF-8"?>
<!DOCTYPE svg PUBLIC "-//W3C//DTD XHTML 1.0 Transitional//EN"
  "http://www.w3.org/TR/xhtml1-transitional.dtd">
<html>
...
</html>
```

Note As before, the value EN in the PUBLIC URI is the two-letter language code for U.S. English. If the document isn't formatted in U.S. English, you must change the language code to the appropriate value. The PUBLIC and SYSTEM URIs also reference the transitional version of the XHTML 1.0 DTD. References to strict and frameset are also possible.

Now that you've seen basic examples, let's take a more detailed look at the conversion process. The following example defines an XSLT stylesheet that formats the example XML document used earlier in the chapter using XML-FO:

```
<?xml version="1.0"?>
<xsl:stylesheet version="1.0"
 xmlns:xsl="http://www.w3.org/1999/XSL/Transform"
 xmlns:fo="http://www.w3.org/1999/XSL/Format"
>

 <xsl:output method="xml" />
```

(continued)

(continued)

```
 <xsl:template match="/">
  <fo:root xmlns:fo="http://www.w3.org/1999/XSL/Format">

   <fo:layout-master-set>
    <fo:simple-page-master margin-right="50pt" margin-left="50pt"
      page-height="11in" page-width="8.5in"
      margin-bottom="35pt" margin-top="35pt" master-name="main">
      <fo:region-before extent="25pt" />
      <fo:region-body margin-top="50pt" margin-bottom="50pt" />
      <fo:region-after extent="25pt" />
    </fo:simple-page-master>
    <fo:page-sequence-master master-name="standard">
      <fo:repeatable-page-master-alternatives>
         <fo:conditional-page-master-reference
            master-name="main" odd-or-even="any" />
      </fo:repeatable-page-master-alternatives>
    </fo:page-sequence-master>
   </fo:layout-master-set>

   <fo:page-sequence master-name="standard">
    <fo:flow flow-name="xsl-region-body">
      <xsl:apply-templates select="document" />
    </fo:flow>
   </fo:page-sequence>
  </fo:root>
 </xsl:template>

 <xsl:template match="document">
  <fo:block line-height="16pt" font-size="12pt"
   text-align="left">
   <xsl:value-of select="." />
  </fo:block>
 </xsl:template>

</xsl:stylesheet>
```

Here, the stylesheet applies formatting to the document using XML-FO. The formatting entries set the page size to 8 ½" x 11"; define a master page layout with margins for the top, bottom, left, and right sides of the page; and then define the formatting for the body of the page. Using the Xalan XSLT processor, we could use this stylesheet to transform the sample.xml document defined earlier in the chapter. The command to do this is:

```
java org.apache.xalan.xslt.Process -in sample.xml
 -xsl sample-fo.xsl  -out sample.fo
```

The output of the transformation process is the following XML document containing formatted objects:

```
<?xml version="1.0" encoding="UTF-8"?>
<fo:root xmlns:fo="http://www.w3.org/1999/XSL/Format">
 <fo:layout-master-set>
  <fo:simple-page-master margin-right="50pt" margin-left="50pt"
   page-height="11in" page-width="8.5in"
   margin-bottom="35pt" margin-top="35pt" master-name="main">
   <fo:region-before extent="25pt" />
   <fo:region-body margin-top="50pt" margin-bottom="50pt" />
   <fo:region-after extent="25pt" />
  </fo:simple-page-master>
  <fo:page-sequence-master master-name="standard">
   <fo:repeatable-page-master-alternatives>
    <fo:conditional-page-master-reference
      master-name="main" odd-or-even="any" />
   </fo:repeatable-page-master-alternatives>
  </fo:page-sequence-master>
 </fo:layout-master-set>

 <fo:page-sequence master-name="standard">
  <fo:flow flow-name="xsl-region-body">
   <fo:block line-height="16pt" font-size="12pt" text-align="left">
    XSLT is a powerful transformation language.
   </fo:block>
  </fo:flow>
 </fo:page-sequence>
</fo:root>
```

You can easily convert documents that use XML-FO to other document formats, such as Adobe's PDF. A free tool that you can use to handle the XML-FO to PDF conversion is the Apache XML Project's FOP tool. As with Xalan, FOP is Java-based. Once you've installed FOP, you can use the `CommandLine` class to convert the XML-FO document to PDF by typing:

```
java org.apache.fop.apps.CommandLine -in file_in file_out
```

where *`file_in`* is the input XML-FO document and *`file_out`* is the output file that will be formatted using PDF. The following example converts `sample.fo` to a PDF file named `sample.pdf`:

```
java org.apache.fop.apps.CommandLine sample.fo sample.pdf
```

Once you convert the document to PDF, you could view it with Adobe Acrobat Reader.

Real World I hope you're starting to see the true power of XSLT as a document transformation powerhouse. Imagine implementing automated transformations for an e-commerce Web site. Here, you could extract data formatted as XML directly from a database and then use XSLT to transform the data into a document in any desired output format.

Formatting Output as HTML

HTML is the other default output format for XSLT stylesheets. Output is formatted as HTML any time the output contains text and has a root element named `html` (in any combination of upper or lowercase characters). If you like, you can explicitly specify that the output should be formatted as HTML. Simply set `method="html"` in the stylesheet, as shown in this example:

```
<xsl:stylesheet
 xmlns:xsl="http://www.w3.org/1999/XSL/Transform"
 version="1.0">

 <xsl:output method="html" />

 <xsl:template match="/">
 <xsl:apply-templates select="document" />
 </xsl:template>

 <xsl:template match="document">
  <html>
   <body>
    <p>
    <xsl:value-of select="." />
    </p>
   </body>
  </html>
 </xsl:template>

</xsl:stylesheet>
```

You saw this example earlier in the chapter used to convert the sample XML document to HTML. Because XSLT is so versatile, there are always additional ways to perform tasks. To create the same output document, you could have also used the following XSLT template:

```
<xsl:stylesheet
 xmlns:xsl="http://www.w3.org/1999/XSL/Transform"
 version="1.0">

 <xsl:output method="html" />
```

(continued)

(continued)

```
<xsl:template match=" /">
<html>
 <body>
  <xsl:apply-templates select="document" />
 </body>
</html>
</xsl:template>

<xsl:template match="document">
 <p>
  <xsl:value-of select="." />
 </p>
</xsl:template>

</xsl:stylesheet>
```

The subtle difference between this template and the previous template is that the `html` and `body` elements are built in the root template and only the contents of the `document` element are evaluated in the second template. This subtle change lets you easily handle the case where there are multiple `document` elements and you want to output a properly formatted document. For example, if you rewrote the sample document to contain multiple `document` elements like this:

```
<?xml version="1.0"?>
<definitions>
 <document>
  XML is a language for describing other languages.
 </document>
 <document>
  XSLT is a powerful transformation language.
 </document>
</definitions>
```

the modified stylesheet would ensure that the output document was formatted like this:

```
<html>
 <body>
  <p>
   XML is a language for describing other languages.
  </p>
  <p>
   XSLT is a powerful transformation language.
  </p>
 </body>
</html>
```

Without this change, we'd end up with a document that was incorrectly formatted and looked like this:

```
<html>
<body>
<p>
 XML is a language for describing other languages.
</p>
</body>
</html>
<html>
<body>
<p>
 XSLT is a powerful transformation language.
</p>
</body>
</html>
```

When you use HTML, you'll often want to associate the output with a cascading stylesheet or make direct style assignments. If you've worked with HTML and CSS before, defining style for an output document formatted as HTML is easy. Consider the following example output document that has two styles for paragraph tags defined:

```
<html>
 <head>
 <title>Using Classes in Style Sheets</title>
 <style type="text/css">
  <!--
   p.styleA {font: 45pt Times; color: brown}
   p.styleB {font: 30pt Arial; color: blue}
  -->
 </style>
 </head>
 <body>
 <p class="styleA"> This is a paragraph in styleA</p>
 <p class="styleB"> This is a paragraph in styleB</p>
 <body>
</html>
```

To transform an XML document into an HTML that looks like this, you'd define the XSLT stylesheet like this:

```
<xsl:stylesheet
 xmlns:xsl="http://www.w3.org/1999/XSL/Transform"
 version="1.0">

 <xsl:output method="html" />
```

(continued)

(continued)

```
 <xsl:template match="/">
 <html>
  <head>
   <title>Using Classes in Style Sheets</title>
   <style type="text/css">
    <xsl:comment>
      p.styleA {font: 45pt Times; color: brown}
      p.styleB {font: 30pt Arial; color: blue}
    </xsl:comment>
   </style>
  </head>
  <body>
   <xsl:apply-templates select="definitions/document1" />
   <xsl:apply-templates select="definitions/document2" />
  </body>
 </html>
 </xsl:template>

 <xsl:template match="document1">
  <p class="styleA">
   <xsl:value-of select="." />
  </p>
 </xsl:template>

 <xsl:template match="document2">
  <p class="styleB">
   <xsl:value-of select="." />
  </p>
 </xsl:template>

</xsl:stylesheet>
```

In this example, note that the HTML comment tags (`<!--` and `--!>`) are replaced with the `xsl:comment` tags (`<xsl:comment>` and `</xsl:comment>`) and that template matches are for elements named `document1` and `document2`, respectively. `document1` and `document2` are arbitrary names that represent elements in the input document that you want to format with either `styleA` or `styleB`. You could replace these arbitrary names with the names of any valid elements from the input document.

Although you can make internal style assignments, cascading stylesheets are more typically defined externally. In HTML, you specify the location of an external cascading stylesheet using the link element in the form:

```
<link rel="stylesheet" type="text/css" href="mystyles.css">
```

In the XSLT stylesheet that defines your output HTML document, you could insert this `link` element directly with one noteworthy exception. You'd have to define the linked stylesheet as an empty element, such as:

```
<link rel="stylesheet" type="text/css" href="mystyles.css" />
```

You could then insert the `link` element directly into the XSLT stylesheet as shown in this example:

```
<xsl:stylesheet
 xmlns:xsl="http://www.w3.org/1999/XSL/Transform"
 version="1.0">

 <xsl:output method="html" />

 <xsl:template match="/">
 <html>
  <head>
   <link rel="stylesheet" type="text/css" href="mystyles.css" />
  </head>
  <body>
   <xsl:apply-templates select="document" />
  </body>
 </html>
 </xsl:template>

 <xsl:template match="document">
  <p>
   <xsl:value-of select="." />
  </p>
 </xsl:template>

</xsl:stylesheet>
```

Formatting Output as Text or Program Source Code

Whenever you want to format the output document as text or program source code, you specify the output format as `method="text"`. Afterward, you insert the literal text or source code into `xsl:text` elements. Here's a basic example of an XSLT stylesheet that's used to output text:

```
<xsl:stylesheet
 xmlns:xsl="http://www.w3.org/1999/XSL/Transform"
 version="1.0">

 <xsl:output method="html" />

 <xsl:template match="/">
  <xsl:apply-templates select="document" />
 </xsl:template>

 <xsl:template match="document">
 <xsl:text>
  The contents of the document element are:
 </xsl:text>
 <xsl:value-of select="." />
 <xsl:text>
.
 </xsl:text>
```

(continued)

(continued)

```
 </xsl:template>

</xsl:stylesheet>
```

If the input XML document for this stylesheet looked like this:

```
<?xml version="1.0"?>
<document>
 XSLT, XML, XSL-FO
</document>
```

the output after transformation would look like this:

```
The contents of the document element are: XSLT, XML, XSL-FO.
```

With source code, the trick is to ensure that you apply templates and switch to literal text in the appropriate locations to get the exact output you desire. Consider the following Java source based on an example from my book *All-in-One Java 2 Certification Exam Guide, 3rd Edition,* (McGraw-Hill, September 2001).

```
class hello {
 public static void main(String[] args) {
  System.out.println("Hello, " + args[0] + "!");
 }
}
```

This short snippet of code writes a string to the standard output. If the program is run with the command:

```
java Hello William
```

the output string is:

```
Hello, William!
```

You could rewrite this program within an XSLT stylesheet so that the program gets its output argument from the contents of a specific element. For example, if your XML document was defined as:

```
<?xml version="1.0"?>
<name>
 Bob
</name>
```

an XSLT stylesheet that used the document with the previous Java source code would look like this:

```
<?xml version="1.0"?>
<xsl:stylesheet version="1.0"
  xmlns:xsl="http://www.w3.org/1999/XSL/Transform">

 <xsl:output method="text" />
```

(continued)

(continued)

```
  <xsl:template match="/">
   <xsl:text>
    class hello {
    public static void main(String[] args) {
   </xsl:text>
   <xsl:apply-templates select="name" />
   <xsl:text>
   }
   }
   </xsl:text>
  </xsl:template>

  <xsl:template match="name">
   <xsl:text>System.out.println("Hello, </xsl:text>
    <xsl:value-of select="." />
   <xsl:text>!");</xsl:text>
 </xsl:template>

</xsl:stylesheet>
```

Based on the contents of the input document, the output after transformation is:

```
class hello {
 public static void main(String[] args) {
  System.out.println("Hello, Bob!");
 }
}
```

Note More precisely, the output would contain a few extra spaces because of how the `name` tag is defined and used in the template. To get rid of these extra spaces, you could replace `value of select="."` with `value of select="normalize-space()"`. I'll talk about this and other available functions in upcoming chapters.

Setting the Output Format

As you've seen, you can transform XML documents in many ways using XSLT. Regardless of which output format you choose, the basic steps you follow to set the output format are the same. These steps are:

1. After the begin stylesheet element, type **<xsl:output**.
2. If you want to set a specific output method other than the default, type **method="*format*"**, where *format* sets the output format. The standard values are `xml`, `html`, and `text`.
3. Specify other attributes for the output element as necessary. For example, if you wanted to encode the document using ISO 8859 Latin 1, you'd set **encoding="ISO-8859-1"**.
4. Type /> to complete the output element.

The result should look similar to the following:

```
<xsl:output method="format" attrib1="value" attrib2="value" ...
 attribN="value" />
```

Defining Template Rules and Declarations

The processes of defining template rules and making template declarations go hand in hand. Whenever you define a template rule, you use a set of matching criteria to determine which template should be processed. The contents of the template rule are the individual declarations that you want to make. (Throughout this text, I refer to the template rule and the declarations it contains as a template.)

The following sections examine basic techniques you can use to define template rules and declarations. More advanced techniques are covered in subsequent chapters.

Creating the Root Template

As previously explained in this chapter, all templates are processed recursively, starting with the root template. This means that the root template is at the top of the execution tree and all other templates are processed after the root template. The basic format of a template rule that matches the root node is

```
<xsl:template match="/">
...
</xsl:template>
```

Although you can enter templates in any order in the XSLT stylesheet, you'll usually want the root template to be at the top of the stylesheet and other templates to follow. With this in mind, the steps you follow to create the root template are

1. After you've defined the stylesheet's start tag and output method, type **<xsl:template**.
2. Type **match="/">** to indicate that the template rule should match the root node and complete the `xsl:template` element.
3. Create template rules for other nodes in the input document as specified in the following section of this chapter, "Creating and Applying Template Rules."
4. Type **</xsl:template>** to complete the template.

Your stylesheet should now look similar to this:

```
<xsl:stylesheet
 xmlns:xsl="http://www.w3.org/1999/XSL/Transform"
 version="1.0">

 <xsl:output method="html" />

 <xsl:template match="/">
 ...
 </xsl:template>

</xsl:stylesheet>
```

Creating and Applying Template Rules

Template rules describe how a particular section of a document should be output. The basic format of a template rule is

```
<xsl:template match="pattern">
...
</xsl:template>
```

where *pattern* identifies the sections of the document to which the template should be applied. The inner section of the template rule determines what happens when a match is found. To ensure that another template rule is processed, you must use the `apply-templates` element to select the node or nodes that you want to process. The basic format of the `apply-templates` element is:

```
<xsl:apply-templates select="expression" />
```

where *expression* is an XPath expression that identifies the nodes whose templates should be applied.

To perform some other type of processing, you must specify the appropriate actions. For example, to display the value of nodes that match the template rule, you could use the `xsl:value-of` element as discussed in the following section of this chapter, "Outputting the Contents of Nodes."

Template rules are recursively processed starting with the template rule for the root node. To take advantage of recursion, you typically apply templates for top-level nodes in the root template, the next level nodes inside the templates for top-level nodes, and so on. For example, if the input document looked like this:

```
<?xml version="1.0"?>
<root>
 <elementA id="s1">
 <elementB>B1's contents
 </elementB>
 <elementC>C1's contents
 </elementC>
 <elementD>D1's contents
 </elementD>
 <elementA>

 <elementA id="s2">
 <elementB>B2's contents
 </elementB>
 <elementC>C2's contents
 </elementC>
 <elementD>D2's contents
 </elementD>
 <elementA>
</root>
```

you might define the set of template rules that processes these elements as:

```
<xsl:template match="/">
 <xsl:apply-templates select="elementA" />
</xsl:template>

<xsl:template match="elementA">
 <xsl:apply-templates select="elementB" />
 <xsl:apply-templates select="elementC" />
 <xsl:apply-templates select="elementD" />
</xsl:template>

<xsl:template match="elementB">
...
</xsl:template>

<xsl:template match="elementC">
...
</xsl:template>

<xsl:template match="elementD">
...
</xsl:template>
```

This would ensure that nodes are processed recursively in the following order:

```
root → elementA id="s1" → elementB1 → elementC1 → elementD1 →
elementA id="s2" → elementB2 → elementC2 → elementD2
```

To create a template rule that applies another template, follow these steps:

1. After you've defined the stylesheet's start tag and output method, type **<xsl:template match="*pattern*">**, where *pattern* identifies the sections of the document to which the template should be applied.
2. Type **<xsl:apply-templates select="*expression*" />**, where *expression* identifies the nodes whose templates should be applied. Repeat this step to apply other template rules.
3. Type **</xsl:template>** to complete the template.

The result should look similar to the following:

```
<xsl:template match="pattern">
 <xsl:apply-templates select="expression1" />
 <xsl:apply-templates select="expression2" />
 ...
 <xsl:apply-templates select="expressionN" />
</xsl:template>
```

Outputting the Contents of Nodes

After you define template rules for the root element and top-level elements, you'll want to define rules that apply to low-level elements that contain text. In most cases you'll want to display the value of this text in the output document. As shown in previous examples in this chapter, you can use the `xsl:value-of` element to display the contents of a particular node. The basic format of this element is:

```
<xsl:value-of select="expression" />
```

where *`expression`* identifies the node or nodes whose content should be output at the current position in the output document.

In most of the previous examples in this chapter, I've used the value . to specify that the contents of the current node should be displayed. Although you can reference the current node, you can reference any other node in the document as well. For example, you can reference the child node of the current node simply by entering the name of the child node. These values are XPath expressions called location paths, which you'll learn about in Chapter 14.

Following this discussion, you could output the contents of the current node or a child node of the current node by following these steps:

1. Within the template rule that you want to work with, type **<xsl:value-of** to begin the declaration.
2. Type **select="."** /> to specify the current node's contents or type **select="*name*"** /> to specify that the contents of the named child element of the current element should be output.

The result should be similar to the following.

```
<xsl:template match="pattern">
 <xsl:value-of select="." />
</xsl:template>
```

Chapter 14

XPath Operators and Expressions

XSL Transformations (XSLT) uses XML Path (XPath) to access and refer to parts of an input document. XPath locates various document structures by representing those structures as node trees that can be navigated using location paths. The location paths have a very specific syntax that includes operators and expressions used to locate parts of a document according to the type of structure they represent. The seven basic structures that location paths allow you to access are

- **Root nodes** Represent the root element in XML documents
- **Element nodes** Represent all elements in XML documents, including root nodes
- **Attribute nodes** Represent attributes in XML documents, including default and inherited attributes (but excluding `xmlns` attributes)
- **Text nodes** Represent the text contents of elements including any `CDATA` sections that elements might contain
- **Comment nodes** Represent the text components of comments that are inserted into XML documents
- **Processing instruction nodes** Represent processing instructions in XML documents by name and string value
- **Namespace nodes** Represent namespaces declared in XSLT stylesheets as defined in `xmlns` attributes

As you learned in Chapter 13, "XSL Transformations and Formatting," you can refer to these node types as part of match and select expressions for various XSLT elements. This allows you to create template rules that match various node types and then to specify the transformations that should be applied to those node types. The catch is that the only part of an XSLT stylesheet that's processed automatically is the template rule for a root node, which is referred to by the location path `/`. Because of this, you use template rules for root nodes to start the transformation process and typically design your XSLT stylesheets to use recursion to extract information from input documents.

Understanding Location Paths

Recursion is a powerful aspect of XSLT. It allows you to locate various structures according to their context in a document. Essentially, you work from the root context in a document to the top-level nodes, and then you explore successive levels of nodes associated with each top-level node until you've examined all the structures you want to work with in a document.

The / representing the root node is only one of the many XPath expressions you can use. Each expression follows a specific syntax and can make use of various operators to locate specific types of nodes. You can access nodes using location paths that are context-specific as well as by using paths that are context-free.

The basic difference between context-specific and context-free location paths has to do with how nodes are evaluated. With context-specific location paths, nodes are evaluated according to the context in which they appear, allowing you to match a node relative to its location in a document. With context-free location paths, nodes are evaluated directly and outside of a specific context, allowing you to locate nodes by specifying their absolute location without regard to the current context. To better understand the impact of context, consider the following XML document:

```
<?xml version="1.0" ?>
<inventory>
 <item tracking_number="459323" manufacturer="Not listed">
  <item_type>3 1/2" Floppy Disk Drive</item_type>
  <description>Standard 3 1/2" floppy drive</description>
 </item>
 <item tracking_number="459789" manufacturer="Not listed">
  <item_type>5 1/4" Floppy Disk Drive</item_type>
  <description>Standard 5 1/4" floppy drive</description>
 </item>
</inventory>
```

A basic node tree representing the elements of this document could look like this:

```
-inventory
 -item
  -item_type
  -description
 -item
  -item_type
  -description
```

Essentially, this node tree representation says that the root element, `inventory`, has two `item` elements as its only children. The `item` elements in turn have two child elements called `item_type` and `description`.

You could locate these elements using many techniques. The following example uses recursion to work with elements in a context-specific manner:

```
<xsl:template match="/">
 <html>
 <body>
   <xsl:apply-templates select="inventory/item" />
 </body>
 </html>
</xsl:template>

<xsl:template match="item">
 <xsl:apply-templates select="item_type" />
 <xsl:apply-templates select="description" />
</xsl:template>

<xsl:template match="item_type">
 <h1>
   <xsl:value-of select="." />
 </h1>
</xsl:template>

<xsl:template match="description">
 <p>
   <xsl:value-of select="." />
 </p>
</xsl:template>
```

Real World Namespaces are tracked separately by XSLT processors using namespace nodes. Every root, element, and attribute node defined in a document can have a namespace associated with it. If so, you must reference the qualified name in your XSLT stylesheets. For example, if the namespace for the inventory document were `inv`, you'd reference `inv:item`, `inv:item_type`, and `inv:description` rather than `item`, `item_type`, and `description`, respectively.

Based on this XSLT stylesheet, the inventory document is processed in the following order:

```
root → item1 → item_type → description → item2 →
item_type → description
```

and the output document would look like this:

```
<html>
<body>
 <h1>3 1/2" Floppy Disk Drive</h1>
 <p>Standard 3 1/2" floppy drive</p>
 <h1>5 1/4" Floppy Disk Drive</h1>
 <p>Standard 5 1/4" floppy drive</p>
</body>
</html>
```

When you work with the current context, XPath expressions are evaluated relative to the context node. Because expressions can match multiple nodes, the XSLT processor maintains a pointer of sorts that tracks the context position and the context size. The context position refers to the position of the node currently being processed. The context size refers to the number of nodes selected by the current expression. Together, the context position and context size allow the XSLT processor to navigate the node tree in terms of the current context.

If the inventory document contained a single `item` element whose contents we wanted to work with directly, such as:

```
<?xml version="1.0" ?>
<inventory>
 <summary>Inventory Summary for 12 - 15 - 02</summary>
 <item tracking_number="459323" manufacturer="Not listed">
  <item_type>3 1/2" Floppy Disk Drive</item_type>
  <description>Standard 3 1/2" floppy drive</description>
 </item>
 <details>No details available.</details>
</inventory>
```

we could process the `item` element directly rather than in terms of the current context. Here's an example:

```
<xsl:template match="/">
 <html>
  <body>
  <h1>
   <xsl:apply-templates select="/inventory/item/item_type" />
  </h1>

  <p>
   <xsl:apply-templates select="/inventory/item/description" />
  </p>
  </body>
 </html>
</xsl:template>
```

In this example you specify the elements you want to work with using an absolute path. Absolute paths differ from relative paths in that they're always located in terms of the root element rather than in terms of the current context. The first apply-templates declaration:

```
<xsl:apply-templates select="/inventory/item/item_type" />
```

specifies that there's a root element called `inventory` that contains an `item` element that in turn has an `item_type` element associated with it. This expression tells the XSLT processor to return all nodes that have this absolute path. In the previous document, this would mean that the processor would return the node defined as follows:

```
<item_type>3 1/2" Floppy Disk Drive</item_type>
```

The second `apply-templates` declaration:

```
<xsl:apply-templates select="/inventory/item/description" />
```

specifies that there's a root element called `inventory` that contains an `item` element that in turn has a `description` element associated with it. This expression tells the XSLT processor to return all nodes that have this absolute path. In the previous document, this would mean that the processor would return the node defined as follows:

```
<description>Standard 3 1/2" floppy drive</description>
```

Based on this, the resulting output document would look like this:

```
<html>
<body>
<h1>3 1/2" Floppy Disk Drive</h1>
<p>Standard 3 1/2" floppy drive</p>
</body>
</html>
```

Unfortunately, these XSLT expressions wouldn't work the way you intended if the document contained multiple items subsets. Remember, the processor returns all matching nodes with the specified absolute path. To allow for the case where multiple items were in the inventory document and you wanted to use absolute paths, you'd have to modify the XSLT stylesheet. The following example shows one way you could do this:

```
<xsl:template match="/">
 <html>
  <body>
  <h1>Inventory Item Summary</h1>
  <xsl:apply-templates select="/inventory/item/item_type" />
  <h1>Description Summary</h1>
  <xsl:apply-templates select="/inventory/item/description" />
  </body>
 </html>
</xsl:template>

<xsl:template match="/inventory/item/item_type">
 <p>
  <xsl:value-of select="." />
 </p>
</xsl:template>
<xsl:template match="/inventory/item/description">
 <p>
  <xsl:value-of select="." />
 </p>
</xsl:template>
```

With the original inventory document defined as:

```
<?xml version="1.0" ?>
<inventory>
 <item tracking_number="459323" manufacturer="Not listed">
  <item_type>3 1/2" Floppy Disk Drive</item_type>
  <description>Standard 3 1/2" floppy drive</description>
 </item>
 <item tracking_number="459789" manufacturer="Not listed">
  <item_type>5 1/4" Floppy Disk Drive</item_type>
  <description>Standard 5 1/4" floppy drive</description>
 </item>
</inventory>
```

the output is now:

```
<html>
<body>
<h1>Inventory Item Summary</h1>
<p>3 1/2" Floppy Disk Drive</p>
<p>5 1/4" Floppy Disk Drive</p>
<h1>Description Summary</h1>
<p>Standard 3 1/2" floppy drive</p>
<p>Standard 5 1/4" floppy drive</p>
</body>
</html>
```

As you can see from the output, the `item_type` values are listed first, followed by a list of `description` values. This output would be useful if you wanted to list the contents of various elements in separate lists. However, the output isn't optimal in this case. Here, you might want to use relative paths and rework the XSLT stylesheet accordingly.

Understanding XPath Operators and Datatypes

In this chapter and the previous one, you've seen various operators, such as `.` and `/`, used in examples. XPath defines many other operators that you can use in expressions to locate nodes. In this section I've divided these operators into three broad categories to provide a resource summary of the various operators that are available.

Table 14-1 summarizes standard XPath operators. These operators are the ones you'll use most often with XSLT and XPath.

Table 14-1. XPath Standard Operators

<table>
<tr><th>Operator Type</th><th>Operator</th><th>Description</th></tr>
<tr><td>Expression operators</td><td>/</td><td>A path separator used to indicate successive levels of the node tree hierarchy. If used at the beginning of an expression, it represents the root node.</td></tr>
<tr><td></td><td>.</td><td>Refers to the current context node.</td></tr>
<tr><td></td><td>..</td><td>Refers to the parent of the current context node.</td></tr>
<tr><td></td><td>@</td><td>Indicates an attribute reference.</td></tr>
<tr><td>Wildcard operators</td><td>*</td><td>A wildcard that selects any node of the principal node type; with element nodes, this would select or match any element node in the current context.</td></tr>
<tr><td></td><td>@*</td><td>A wildcard that selects or matches any attribute node in the current context.</td></tr>
<tr><td></td><td><code>node()</code></td><td>Selects all nodes in the current context regardless of type. (Technically, this is type of a node test that's used as a wildcard.)</td></tr>
<tr><td></td><td>//</td><td>Allows you to skip levels in the hierarchy; indicates that zero or more elements may occur between the slashes.</td></tr>
<tr><td>Other operators</td><td>[]</td><td>Predicate operator used in predicate expressions to filter a group of nodes.</td></tr>
<tr><td></td><td>|</td><td>Selects either match in a series, such as <code>match="a|b|c"</code> to match a, b, and c elements.</td></tr>
<tr><td></td><td>$</td><td>Variable operator used to indicate variable names.</td></tr>
</table>

In addition to defining standard operators, XPath defines a set of mathematical and Boolean operators. These operators are summarized in Table 14-2. Although mathematical operators evaluate expressions to specific values, Boolean operators evaluate expressions as Booleans (either true or false). Booleans are only one of the five data types that can be used with XPath. The other datatypes are:

- **node-set** Represents a set of nodes. Node sets can be empty or they can contain any number of nodes.
- **result tree fragment** A temporary tree that holds the value of a result or the value of variable assignment.
- **number** Represents a floating-point number. All floating-point numbers comply with IEEE 754 (which is the same standard used with `float` and `double` datatypes used by XML Schema). As with XML Schema, XPath and XSLT floating-point values have five special values: `0` (referred to as positive zero), `-0` (referred to as negative zero), `INF` (referred to as positive infinity), `-INF` (referred to as negative infinity), and `NaN` (referred to as not-a-number).
- **string** Represents a sequence of zero or more characters as defined in the XML specification.

Table 14-2. XPath Arithmetic Operators

Operator Type	Operator	Description
Mathematical	*	Multiplication; multiplies one number by another.
	`div`	Division; performs floating-point division on two numbers.
	`mod`	Modulus; returns the floating-point remainder of dividing one number by another.
	+	Addition; adds one number to another.
	-	Subtraction; subtracts one number from another.
Boolean	=	Equality; tests whether two expressions are equal.
	<	Less than; tests whether the first expression is less than the second.
	>	Greater than; tests whether the first expression is greater than the second.
	<=	Less than or equals; tests whether the first expression is less than or equal to the second.
	>=	Greater than or equals; tests whether the first expression is greater than or equal to the second.
	`!=`	Not equal; tests whether the two expressions aren't equal.
	`and`	Logical And; tests whether the first and the second expression are true. Both expressions must be true for the logical And to evaluate to true.
	`or`	Logical Or; tests whether one of two expressions is true. Only one expression must be true for the logical Or to evaluate to true.

Another type of operator XPath defines is an *axis*. An axis is an operator keyword that acts as a location designator. You use axes to make unabbreviated XPath references. Axes are useful when you want to use advanced techniques to locate ancestor, descendent, and sibling nodes, but they're too complex for most other uses. Table 14-3 provides a summary of the axes that are available.

Table 14-3. XPath Axes

Axis Type	Description	Usage
`ancestor`	Contains the parent of the context node, the parent's parent, and so on up to the root node (unless, of course, the context node is the root node).	`ancestor::node`, such as `ancestor::item`
`ancestor-or-self`	Contains context node, the parent of the context node, the parent's parent, and so on up to the root node.	`ancestor-or-self::node`, such as `ancestor--or-self::item`

(continued)

Table 14-3. *(continued)*

Axis Type	Description	Usage
`attribute`	Contains the attributes of the context node.	`attribute::type` or `@type`
`child`	Contains the children of the context node.	`child::node/child::node`, such as `child::item/child::item_type`.
`descendant`	Contains the children of the context node, the children's children, and so on to the lowest possible level (unless, of course, the context node is the lowest child node).	`descendant::node`, such as `descendant::item`
`descendant-or-self`	Contains context node, the children of the context node, the children's children, and so on to the lowest possible level.	`descendant-or-self::node`, such as `descendant-or-self::item`
`following`	Contains all nodes that appear after the context node in the document except descendants, attribute nodes, and namespace nodes.	`following::node`, such as `following::item`
`following-sibling`	Contains all following siblings of the context node (meaning all nodes that have the same parent as the context node and are after the context node in the current node set).	`following-sibling::node`, such as `following-sibling::item`
`namespace`	Contains all namespace nodes in the context node. If the context node isn't an element node, the axis is empty.	`namespace::node`, such as `namespace::item`
`parent`	Contains the parent of the context node.	`parent::node`, such as `parent::item`
`preceding`	Contains all nodes that appear before the context node in the document except ancestors, attribute nodes, and namespace nodes.	`preceding::node`, such as `preceding::item`
`preceding-sibling`	Contains all preceding siblings of the context node (meaning all nodes that have the same parent as the context node and are before the context node in current node set).	`preceding-sibling::node`, such as `preceding-sibling::item`
`self`	Contains the context node itself.	`self::*` or `.`

Using Relative XPath Expressions with Elements

Relative and absolute XPath expressions are similar to Uniform Resource Locators (URLs) in hypertext references in the way they're used and structured. With relative XPath expressions, you reference locations relative to the current context that the XSLT processor is working with. Relative expressions refer to:

- The current context node using a single period (`.`)
- A parent of the current node using a double period (`..`)
- A child of the current node by referencing its name directly
- A named sibling of the current node by referencing `../name`
- Nodes in other levels of the hierarchy by referencing their relative path from the current context

Techniques for working with these context-specific expressions are discussed in the following sections.

Referencing the Current Context Node

When you work with the current context, other XPath locations can be referenced relative to the current position. The XPath expression you use to reference the current node itself is a single period (`.`).

Essentially, the single period (`.`) says to use the current context node. In the following example, the contents of the current node are selected and output:

```
<xsl:template match="element">
 <html>
  <body>
   <p>
    <xsl:value-of select="." />
   </p>
  </body>
 </html>
</xsl:template>
```

Following this, if you're currently processing the node that you want to use in a select statement, you can refer to the current node by completing these steps:

1. Type a single period, as in **<xsl:value-of select=“.”** />.
2. Alternatively, specify a predicate expression that selects a subset of the current node, as discussed in the “Filtering to Match Nodes with Specific Values” section of this chapter.

Referencing a Parent Node

You can reference the parent of the current context node using a double period (`..`), such as:

```
<xsl:value-of select=".." />
```

Essentially, the double period (`..`) tells XPath to go up one level in the node tree hierarchy. For example, if the current context is processing the `item_type` elements based on this input document:

```
<?xml version="1.0" ?>
<inventory>
 <item tracking_number="459323" manufacturer="Not listed">
  <item_type>3 1/2" Floppy Disk Drive</item_type>
  <description>Standard 3 1/2" floppy drive</description>
 </item>
 <item tracking_number="459789" manufacturer="Not listed">
  <item_type>5 1/4" Floppy Disk Drive</item_type>
  <description>Standard 5 1/4" floppy drive</description>
 </item>
</inventory>
```

the parent elements referenced by `..` are the `item` elements.

You can also reference the parent of a parent node. For example, if you were working with the `description` element and wanted to access the `inventory` element (which is the parent of the parent element `item`), you could extend the parent reference so that it went two levels up the tree using the value:

```
../..
```

Tip This technique can be extended as far as necessary. If you need to go three levels up the node tree, you'd use `../../..`, for four levels up the tree you'd use `../../../..`, and so on.

You can select the parents of the current node by following these steps:

1. Type `..` to select the parent of the current context node.
2. Optionally, type `/..` to specify a parent of the parent node. Repeat this step to go farther up the hierarchy.

The result should look similar to the following:

```
<xsl:value-of select="../.."/>
```

Referencing Siblings Relative to the Current Context

Relative XPath expressions also allow you to locate nodes at the same level as the current context node. To do this, you reference the parent using double periods (`..`), enter a slash (/), and then specify the name of the sibling that you want to work with. For example, if you were working with the `item_type` element defined in the following inventory document:

```
<?xml version="1.0" ?>
<inventory>
 <item tracking_number="459323" manufacturer="Not listed">
  <item_type>3 1/2" Floppy Disk Drive</item_type>
  <description>Standard 3 1/2" floppy drive</description>
 </item>
 <item tracking_number="459789" manufacturer="Not listed">
  <item_type>5 1/4" Floppy Disk Drive</item_type>
  <description>Standard 5 1/4" floppy drive</description>
 </item>
 <summary>No summary available</summary>
</inventory>
```

you could reference the `description` element at the same level of the hierarchy using the relative path:

```
../description
```

You can select siblings of the current node by following these steps:

1. Type ***../sibling***, where *sibling* is the name of the node that's at the same level of the node tree as the current node, as in `<xsl:value-of select="../item" />`.
2. Alternatively, specify a child node of a sibling by typing ***../sibling/child***, such as `<xsl:value-of select="../item/item_type" />`.

Referencing Child Nodes

You can access child nodes of the current context node by referencing the name of the child node. The following example matches all `item_type` elements that are child nodes of the current context node:

```
<xsl:value-of select="item_type" />
```

Essentially, the direct name reference tells XPath to go to the next lower level in the node tree hierarchy. For example, if the current context is processing `item` elements based on this input document:

```
<?xml version="1.0" ?>
<inventory>
 <item tracking_number="459323" manufacturer="Not listed">
  <item_type>3 1/2" Floppy Disk Drive</item_type>
  <description>Standard 3 1/2" floppy drive</description>
 </item>
```

(continued)

(continued)

```
 <item tracking_number="459789" manufacturer="Not listed">
  <item_type>5 1/4" Floppy Disk Drive</item_type>
  <description>Standard 5 1/4" floppy drive</description>
 </item>
</inventory>
```

the elements selected by the `value-of select="item_type"` declaration are:

```
<item_type>3 1/2" Floppy Disk Drive</item_type>
```

```
<item_type>5 1/4" Floppy Disk Drive</item_type>
```

You can use relative paths that reference more than one level in the hierarchy as well. To do this, you reference the immediate child nodes that you want to work with and then separate each subsequent level of nodes below this node with a slash (/). For example, if the node tree looked like this:

```
-inventory
 -item
  -item_type
  -code
  -label
  -manufacturer
  -description
 -item
  -item_type
  -code
  -label
  -manufacturer
  -description
 -summary
```

and the current context node is an `item` node, you could reference the `code`, `label`, and `manufacturer` subnodes with the following relative paths:

```
item_type/code
item_type/label
item_type/manufacturer
```

You could use these relative paths in match or select attributes of XSLT elements, such as:

```
<xsl:template match="item">
  <tr>
  <td>
   <xsl:value-of select="item/code" />
  </td>
  <td>
   <xsl:value-of select="item/label" />
  </td>
```

(continued)

(continued)

```
  <td>
   <xsl:value-of select="item/manufacturer" />
  </td>
  </tr>
</xsl:template>
```

You can select children of the current node by following these steps:

1. Type ***child***, where *child* is the name of the node contained within the current context node.
2. Optionally, type ***/grandchild*** to specify a node set contained in the referenced child node. Repeat this step to go farther down the hierarchy.

The result should look similar to the following:

```
<xsl:value-of select="child/grandchild" />
```

Using Absolute XPath Expressions with Elements

In addition to being able to reference nodes using relative paths, you can use absolute paths as well. An absolute location path always starts with a slash, which tells the XSLT processor to start with the root element regardless of the current context and then go on to specify the exact path to the node you want to work with. For example, if the node hierarchy for a document looked like this:

```
-inventory
 -item
  -item_type
  -code
  -label
  -manufacturer
  -description
 -item
  -item_type
  -code
  -label
  -manufacturer
  -description
 -summary
```

the corresponding absolute paths to nodes in the document are

- **/inventory/item** The absolute path to top-level `item` nodes
- **/inventory/item/item_type** The absolute path to `item_type` nodes that are child nodes of the top-level node `item`
- **/inventory/item/item_type/code** The absolute path to `code` nodes that are child nodes of the `item_type` node, which in turn are child nodes of the top-level node `item`

- **/inventory/item/item_type/label** The absolute path to `label` nodes that are child nodes of the `item_type` node, which in turn are child nodes of the top-level node `item`
- **/inventory/item/item_type/manufacturer** The absolute path to `manufacturer` nodes that are child nodes of the `item_type` node, which in turn are child nodes of the top-level node `item`
- **/inventory/item/description** The absolute path to `description` nodes that are child nodes of the top-level node `item`.
- **/inventory/summary** The absolute path to top-level `summary` nodes

To disregard the current context and specify an absolute path to a node, follow these steps:

1. Type / to indicate that you're specifying an absolute path that starts at the root node.
2. Type ***root***, where *root* is the name of the root node.
3. Type /***container***, where *container* is the name of the element on the next level that contains the desired node. Repeat this step as necessary until you've specified all the ancestors of the node you're looking for.
4. Type /***element***, where *element* is the name of the element that you want to select or match.

The result should look similar to the following:

```
<xsl:value-of select="/root/container/element" />
```

Locating Attribute, Text, Comment, and Processing Instruction Nodes

XPath locations don't have to reference element nodes. They can also reference attribute, text, comment, and processing instruction nodes. Techniques for working with these node types are discussed in the following sections.

Note Don't worry, you don't have to learn a whole new syntax to locate nonelement nodes. Everything you learned about locating elements applies to attribute, text, comment, and processing instruction nodes as well.

Working with Attribute Nodes

You reference attribute nodes using the at sign (@), followed by the name of the attribute. For example, if you wanted to reference an attribute called `tracking_number`, you'd use the XPath expression:

```
@tracking_number
```

As with elements, attributes can be located using relative or absolute paths. This means you could select the current context node's `tracking_number` attribute with the following declaration:

```
<xsl:value-of select="@tracking_number" />
```

and that you could reference the relative path to another element's attribute, such as:

```
<xsl:value-of select="item/@tracking_number" />
```

Here, you reference the tracking number attribute of the `item` element that's a child of the current context node.

Following the techniques discussed earlier in the chapter, you could reference attributes of parent elements as well, such as:

```
<xsl:value-of select="../@tracking_number" />
```

and attributes of sibling elements, such as:

```
<xsl:value-of select="../item/@tracking_number" />
```

You could also reference the absolute path to another element's attribute, such as:

```
<xsl:value-of select="/inventory/item/@tracking_number" />
```

Regardless of the technique you use, the result is the same. The value of the attribute is output at the current location in the output document. For example, if the current context pointed to the `item` element that contained a `tracking_number` attribute and you wanted to display its value, you'd use the following template rule to do this:

```
<xsl:template match="item">
 <p>
  <xsl:value-of select="@tracking_number" />
 </p>
</xsl:template>
```

Of course, a rule that processes an attribute doesn't have to be the only selection in a template. You could define multiple selections as well, such as:

```
<xsl:template match="item">
 <p>
  <xsl:value-of select="@tracking_number" />,
  <xsl:value-of select="item_type"/>,
  <xsl:value-of select="description"/>
 </p>
</xsl:template>
```

or

```
<xsl:template match="item">
 <tr>
 <td>
  <xsl:value-of select="@tracking_number" />
 </td>
 <td>
  <xsl:value-of select="item_type" />
 </td>
 <td>
  <xsl:value-of select="description" />
 </td>
 </tr>
</xsl:template>
```

You could also create a separate template rule for an attribute, such as:

```
<xsl:template match="/">
 <html>
  <body>
   <xsl:apply-templates
    select="/inventory/item/item_type/@tracking_number" />
   <xsl:apply-templates select="/inventory/item/description" />
  </body>
 </html>
</xsl:template>

<xsl:template  match="/inventory/item/item_type/@tracking_number">
 <h1>
  <xsl:value-of select="." />
 </h1>
</xsl:template>

<xsl:template  match="/inventory/item/description">
 <p>
  <xsl:value-of select="." />
 </p>
</xsl:template>
```

To select a node's attribute or attributes, follow these steps:

1. Specify the absolute or relative path to the attribute that you want to select or match. If the attribute is contained in the current context node, you don't need to do this.
2. Type ***@attribute***, where *attribute* is the name of the attribute you want to work with. Or type **@*** to select all attributes of the current or specified element.

The result should look similar to the following:

```
<xsl:value-of select="element/@attribute" />
```

Working with Text Nodes

If an element contains text or `CDATA` sections, you can use the `text()` node test to select and display that text. For example, if you wanted to select the text and then do something with it, you could define a template rule like this:

```
<xsl:template match="item">
 <xsl:apply-templates select="item_type/text()" />
</xsl:template>

<xsl:template match="item_type/text()">
 <p>
 <xsl:value-of select="." />
 </p>
</xsl:template>
```

Or you could display the text directly using a `value-of` declaration like this:

```
<xsl:template match="item">
 <p>
 <xsl:value-of select="item_type/text()" />
 </p>
</xsl:template>
```

Keep in mind that the `text()` node test selects all the text-node children of the context node. This means that the result is always the concatenation of all text and `CDATA` sections that an element contains.

To display the text associated with an element, follow these steps:

1. Specify the absolute or relative path to the element that contains the text you want to select. If the text is contained in the current context node, you don't need to do this.
2. Type **text()**.

The result should look similar to the following:

```
<xsl:value-of select="element/text()" />
```

Working with Comment Nodes

To access comment nodes, you use the `comment()` node test. Working with comment nodes is similar to working with text nodes. If you wanted to access the comment node associated with an item element, you could use a relative XPath expression, such as `item/comment()`, or an absolute XPath expression, such as `/inventory/item/comment()`.

A template rule that works with a comment node could look like this:

```
<xsl:template match="item">
 <xsl:apply-templates select="item_type/comment()" />
</xsl:template>

<xsl:template match="item_type/comment()">
 <p>
 <xsl:value-of select="." />
 </p>
</xsl:template>
```

Or you could display the comment text directly using a `value-of` declaration like this:

```
<xsl:template match="item">
 <p>
 <xsl:value-of select="item_type/comment()" />
 </p>
</xsl:template>
```

The `comment()` node test selects all the comment-node children of the context node. This means that the result is always the concatenation of all comments that an element contains.

To display the comment text associated with an element, follow these steps:

1. Specify the absolute or relative path to the element that contains the comment text you want to select. If the comment text is contained in the current context node, you don't need to do this.
2. Type **comment()**.

The result should look similar to the following:

```
<xsl:value-of select="element/comment()" />
```

Working with Processing Instruction Nodes

You use the `processing-instruction()` node test to access processing instruction nodes. As with other node types, you can access processing instruction nodes using relative or absolute XPath locations, such as `../processing-instruction()` or `/inventory/item/processing-instruction()`.

By default, this node test selects the text of all processing-instruction-node children of the context node. As a result, results returned by the `processing-instruction()` node test contain the concatenation of all processing instructions that an element contains. Because processing instructions have two parts, a name and a value, you can also reference specific processing instructions by name. The format you follow is:

```
processing-instruction('name')
```

where *name* is the actual name of the processing instruction. For example, if you wanted to access the `xml-stylesheet` processing instruction, you'd use the value:

```
processing-instruction('xml-stylesheet')
```

Here, the XSLT processor would select all processing-instruction-node children of the context node that have the name xml-stylesheet.

To display the contents of processing instructions associated with an element, follow these steps:

1. Specify the absolute or relative path to the element that contains the processing instruction you want to select. If the processing instruction is contained in the current context node, you don't need to do this.
2. With named processing instructions, you can type **processing-instruction('*name*')**, where *name* is the name of the processing instruction that you want to select. Or you can select all processing instructions associated with the current or specified element by typing **processing-instruction()**.

The result should look similar to the following:

```
<xsl:value-of select="element/processing-instruction('name')" />
```

Using Namespaces with Element and Attribute Nodes

XSLT processors track namespaces using namespace nodes. Every element and attribute node defined in a document can have a namespace associated with it. Whenever a namespace is defined, you must reference the qualified name in your XSLT stylesheets. As discussed in Chapter 7, "XML Namespaces," a qualified name has two parts:

- A namespace prefix
- A local part

and follows the form:

```
namespace_prefix:local_part
```

This means that the qualified name for an `item` element in the `inv` namespace is `inv:item` and this element would be used in a document like this:

```
<inv:item>
...
</inv:item>
```

XPath defines three functions that allow you to work with element and attribute names. These functions are

- **name()** Returns the qualified name of an element or attribute. For the `inv:item` element, the function would return `inv:item`.
- **local-name()** Returns the local-part name of an element or attribute. For the `inv:item` element, the function would return `item`.
- **namespace-uri()** Returns the namespace prefix associated with an element or attribute. For the `inv:item` element, the function would return `inv`.

You can use these functions much as you use other XPath functions. Here's an example that uses these functions as part of a selection:

```
<xsl:template match="inv:item">
 <p>Qualified Name:
  <xsl:value-of select="name()" />
 </p>
 <p>Local-part Name:
  <xsl:value-of select="local-name()" />
 </p>
 <p>Namespace prefix:
  <xsl:value-of select="namespace-uri()" />
 </p>
</xsl:template>
```

To display a node's name, follow these steps:

1. Specify the absolute or relative path to the node you want to select. You don't need to do this if you want to work with the current node context.
2. To display the qualified name of the node, type **name()**. Otherwise, type **namespace-uri()** or **local-name()** to select the part of the qualified name that you want to work with.

The result should look similar to the following:

```
<xsl:value-of select="element/name()" />
```

Using Wildcards and Predicates in XPath Expressions

So far this chapter has discussed the primary expression operators but hasn't discussed wildcard or predicate operators. The following sections look at these XPath operators (with the exception of `$`, which is discussed in the next chapter).

Selecting Any Node

XPath defines three operators that can help you select multiple nodes as part of an expression. These operators are

- ***** Selects any node of the principal node type. This means that if you're working with element nodes, you can use * to select or match any element node in the current context.
- **@*** Selects any attribute node in the current context.
- **node()** Selects all nodes in the current context regardless of type.

To understand how you could use these operators, consider the following node tree representation:

```
-inventory
 -item
  @code
  @label
  @manufacturer
  -description
  -summary
 -item
  @code
  @label
  @manufacturer
  -description
  -summary
```

Here, `code`, `label`, and `manufacturer` are selected attributes of `item` and `description` and `summary` are child elements of `item`. If the `item` element is the current context node, you could create a template that selects and displays the value of `description` and `summary` child elements like this:

```
<xsl:template match="item">
 <p><xsl:value-of select="*" /></p>
</xsl:template>
```

If you wanted to select all attributes of `item`, you could change the template to read:

```
<xsl:template match="item">
 <p><xsl:value-of select="@*" /></p>
</xsl:template>
```

Or you could select all child elements and attributes using:

```
<xsl:template match="item">
 <p><xsl:value-of select="*|@*" /></p>
</xsl:template>
```

Here, the pipe symbol (|) indicates a series where either the * or the @* operator can be used in the selection. The result is that all child elements and all attributes are selected.

Still, if you wanted, you could extend the selection node set even further using `node()`, such as:

```
<xsl:template match="item">
 <p><xsl:value-of select="node()" /></p>
</xsl:template>
```

With the `node()` node test, all nodes in the current context are selected, including element, attribute, comment, and processing-instruction nodes. Of course, in an actual document you'd probably want to format the output in a more meaningful way than with simple paragraphs.

To select any node, follow these steps:

1. Specify the absolute or relative path to the nodes that you want to select or match. If the nodes are contained within the current context, you don't need to do this.
2. Specify the type of nodes to select or match:
   - Type * to match nodes of the current type. Typically, this match is for element nodes.
   - Type **@*** to select all attribute nodes of the current or specified element.
   - Type **node()** to select all nodes of any type associated with the current or specified node.

The result should look similar to the following:

```
<xsl:value-of select="element/*" />
```

Skipping Levels in the Hierarchy

The double slash operator (//) allows you to skip levels in the node tree hierarchy. This indicator tells the XSLT processor that zero or more elements may occur between the slashes and lets the XSLT processor search down the hierarchy for the node you're referencing.

To see how the double slash operator (//) works, consider the following node tree representation:

```
-inventory
 -item
  -item_type
  -description
   -code
   -label
   -manufacturer
  -summary
```

(continued)

(continued)

```
 -item
  -item_type
  -description
   -code
   -label
   -manufacturer
  -summary
```

Here the absolute paths to the lowest-level elements (`code`, `label`, and `manufacturer`) are

- `/inventory/item/item_type/description/code`
- `/inventory/item/item_type/description/label`
- `/inventory/item/item_type/description/manufacturer`

If you wanted to skip levels in the hierarchy using `//`, you could do this in several ways. Here are some examples:

- **//code** Starts from the root element and selects all `code` elements regardless of where they appear in the document
- **/inventory//code** Selects all `code` elements that are descendants of the `inventory` element
- **/inventory/item//code** Selects all `code` elements that are descendants of the top-level `item` element
- **//description/code** Selects all `code` elements that have the parent element `description`
- **.//code** Selects all `code` elements that are descendants of the current context node

Caution Although being able to skip levels in the hierarchy is very powerful, watch out! Skipping through the hierarchy requires the XSLT processor to search through the node tree for successive matches, which can be very inefficient in large documents with lots of nodes.

To select skip levels in the hierarchy, follow these steps:

1. As necessary, specify the absolute or relative path to the nodes that you want to select or match. When you get to the levels that you want to skip, type //.
2. As necessary, type the path to the nodes that you want to work with.
3. Type the name of the element node you want to select or match. Alternatively, type **@** followed by the name of the attribute node you want to select or match.

The result should look similar to the following:

```
<xsl:value-of select=".//element/@attribute" />
```

Filtering to Match Nodes with Specific Values

You use the `[]` operator to specify a predicate. Predicate expressions are used to filter a group of nodes according to their position in a node set or according to a specific match value. XSLT processors evaluate predication expressions as Boolean values, which are either true or false. If a predicate expression is true, the node is a match and is selected. Otherwise, the node isn't selected.

Predicate expressions have the basic form:

```
path[predicate]
```

where *path* is the location path to the node that contains the desired subset of nodes you want to work with and *predicate* is the predicate expression that defines your filter for this set of nodes.

If you're referencing nodes in the current context, the predicate can be used without a path. In the following example the predicate expression returns all nodes that have a `tracking_number` attribute:

```
<xsl:apply-templates select="[@tracking_number]" />
```

Numeric positions, functions, and attribute values can be referenced in predicate expressions as well. For example, the following predication expression selects the second `item` element in the current context:

```
<xsl:apply-templates select="item[2]" />
```

If the input document contains at least two `item` elements, the node set for the second `item` is returned. Otherwise, an empty node set is returned.

Using Numeric Positions in Predicates

When the current context points to a set of nodes, each node can be referred to by its position in the node set. The first element has the position 1, the second has the position 2, and so on. You can refer to the numeric position directly in the predicate expression and you can combine numeric references with other operators and expressions. For example, if you wanted to select the fifth `item` element, you could use:

```
<xsl:apply-templates select="item[5]"/>
```

In an XPath expression, the choice operator (`|`) selects either match in a series. Because nodes are processed recursively and node sets can contain multiple nodes, a value of `match="a|b|c"` says to match elements named a, b, or c. You could match numeric values in the same way. For example, if you wanted to select the second, fourth, and sixth `item` elements, you could combine the choice operator (`|`) with numeric positions, such as:

```
<xsl:apply-templates select="item[2 | 4 | 6]" />
```

or you could use:

```
<xsl:apply-templates select="item[2] | item[4] | item[6]" />
```

Using Functions in Predicates

You can also use XPath functions with predicate expressions. The most common functions you'll use are

- **last()** Returns the last node in the context subset.
- **position()** Returns the current position within the context subset. You can use this in expressions to evaluate the current position within a subset with a desired position.

Returning the last node in a set is easy. For example, if you wanted to select the last `item` element in a node set, you'd specify:

```
<xsl:apply-templates select="item[last()]" />
```

When you combine the `position()` function with arithmetic operators, you can use the resulting expressions to obtain just about any node in the context subset that you want to work with. For example, if you wanted to select the third `item` node in the node set, you'd specify:

```
<xsl:apply-templates select="item[position() = 3]" />
```

Here the equals sign is a Boolean operator. If the position of the `item` element is 3, the expression is true and the matching node is selected. Otherwise, the expression is false and a node isn't selected.

The less than (<), greater than (>), less than or equals (<=), and greater than or equals (>=) operators are useful in expressions. For example, if you wanted to select nodes 1-5 in the node set, you could specify:

```
<xsl:apply-templates select="[position() <= 5]" />
```

Another useful operator is `mod`. The `mod` operator returns the remainder after division. If you note that any value `mod 2` either returns a 0 or a value greater than 0, you can use mod to select even-numbered or odd-numbered nodes. For example, if you wanted to return only even-numbered `item` elements, you'd specify:

```
<xsl:apply-templates select="item[position() mod 2 = 0]" />
```

For only odd-numbered `item` elements, you'd specify:

```
<xsl:apply-templates select="item[position() mod 2 != 0]" />
```

Using Attribute Values in Predicates

You can also use predicate expressions to select attributes by name or by value. To see how expressions that use attributes work, consider the following XML document:

```
<?xml version="1.0" ?>
<inventory>
 <item tracking_number="459320" manufacturer="Toshiba">
  <item_type>3 1/2" Floppy Disk Drive</item_type>
  <description>Standard 3 1/2" floppy drive</description>
```

(continued)

(continued)

```
  <stock in_stock="750" orders_for="200" net_units="550"
   order="N" />
 </item>
 <item tracking_number="459323" manufacturer="Not listed">
  <item_type>3 1/2" Floppy Disk Drive</item_type>
  <description>Standard 3 1/2" floppy drive</description>
  <stock in_stock="50" orders_for="200" net_units="-150"
   order="Y" />
 </item>
 <item tracking_number="459780" manufacturer="Toshiba">
  <item_type>5 1/4" Floppy Disk Drive</item_type>
  <description>Standard 5 1/4" floppy drive</description>
  <stock in_stock="250" orders_for="200" net_units="50"
   order="Y" />
 </item>
 <item tracking_number="459789" manufacturer="Not listed">
  <item_type>5 1/4" Floppy Disk Drive</item_type>
  <description>Standard 5 1/4" floppy drive</description>
  <stock in_stock="0" orders_for="200" net_units="-200"
   order="Y" />
 </item>

...
</inventory>
```

Using this document as our input, we could work with the document's attribute nodes in several ways. If you wanted to select all `item` elements with `tracking_number` attributes, you could specify:

```
<xsl:apply-templates select="item[@tracking_number]" />
```

If you wanted to select `item` elements with specific tracking numbers, you simply specify values that represent a match. In this example, items with tracking numbers 459780 and 459789 are selected:

```
<xsl:apply-templates select="item[@tracking_number='459780' |
 @tracking_number='459789']" />
```

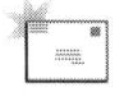

Note It's important to note that in this example double quotation marks are used to contain the entire selection and single quotation marks are used for attribute values. You could have also used single quotation marks to contain the selection and double quotation marks for attribute values. However, you couldn't use the same type of quotation marks to contain the selection and designate the attribute values. Further, you can't start a selection with double quotation marks and end it with single quotation marks.

Now imagine that this document contained hundreds of items but the user viewing the document only cared about certain items: those that didn't list a manufacturer (representing an entry error) and those that that had an order flag value of "Y" (indicating items that needed to be ordered to meet current demand). If this were the case, you could create predicate expressions that matched these values:

- `item_type/[@manufacturer='Not listed']`
- `item_type/[@order="Y"]`

Then use the expressions in select and match statements to obtain the desired results. The following XSLT stylesheet shows a partial example:

```
<xsl:template match="/">
 <html>
  <body>
   <xsl:apply-templates select="inventory/item" />
  </body>
 </html>
</xsl:template>

<xsl:template match="item">
 <xsl:apply-templates  select="item_type/[@manufacturer='Not
  listed']" />
 <xsl:apply-templates select="item_type/[@order='Y']" />
</xsl:template>

<xsl:template match="item_type/[@manufacturer='Not listed']">
...
</xsl:template>

<xsl:template match="item_type/[@order='Y']">
...
</xsl:template>
```

Specifying the Node Subset in a Stylesheet

Now that you've seen how predicates are used, you can use predicates in your XSLT stylesheets anywhere you want to filter a group of nodes and specify a node subset.

To select any node, follow these steps:

1. Specify the absolute or relative path to the node that contains the desired subset of nodes. If you want to work with a subset of nodes in the current context, you don't have to specify a path.
2. Type **[*expression*]**, where *expression* represents the predicate expression that you want to use to select the node subset.

The result should look similar to the following:

```
<xsl:value-of select="element/[expression]" />
```

Chapter 15

Branching and Control Functions

As with any sophisticated programming language, the XSL Transformations (XSLT) language defines structures that you can use to add branching and control logic to stylesheets. You use branching and control functions to conditionally process nodes based on the value of an expression. XSLT implements most of the classic branching and control functions, including

- **if-then** Specifies what processing should occur if a value matches an expression. In XSLT, if-then structures are implemented using the `xsl:if` element.
- **if-then-else** Specifies what processing should occur when a value matches an expression and when a value doesn't match an expression. In XSLT, if-then-else structures are implemented using the `xsl:choose` and `xsl:otherwise` elements.
- **switch-case** Specifies a set of values that should be matched and what should happen in the case of each match. You can also specify what happens when no match is found. In XSLT switch-case structures are implemented using the `xsl:choose` and `xsl:when` elements, and the case for no match is handled with the `xsl:otherwise` element.
- **for-each** Specifies what processing should occur for each value in a set of values. In XSLT this concept allows you to process all nodes in a set of nodes iteratively and the element you use to do this is the `xsl:for-each` element.

In this chapter you'll learn how to use these branching and control functions. You'll also learn how to control which templates are called, included, or imported.

Processing Nodes Conditionally with if Statements

With `if` statements, you can specify what processing should occur if a value matches an expression. The XSLT structure that you use to define an `if` statement is the `xsl:if` element. This element has a single attribute, called `test`, that's used to specify the expression that you want to match. If `test` evaluates to the

Boolean value true, the statements between the opening tag `<xsl:if>` and the closing tag `</xsl:if>` are processed.

The basic format of an `if` statement is then:

```
<xsl:if test="expression">
...
</xsl:if>
```

where *`expression`* is an XML Path (XPath) expression defining what you want to test. Following this basic format, you could define an `if` statement to test the value of an expression, like this:

```
<xsl:if test="stock/[@order='Y']">
 <p>Please order, stock number:
  <xsl:value-of select="@tracking_number" />
 </p>
</xsl:if>
```

Here, you define an expression that checks the `order` attribute of the `stock` element, which is a child of the current context node. If the value of the attribute is Y, the value of the `tracking_number` attribute of the node being processed is output as part of an HTML paragraph, such as:

```
<p>Please order, stock number: 459323</p>
```

The `if` statement could appear anywhere within the template you're defining. Here's an example:

```
<xsl:template match="/">
 <html>
  <body>
   <xsl:apply-templates select="inventory/item" />
  </body>
 </html>
</xsl:template>

<xsl:template match="item">
 <xsl:if test="stock/[@order= 'Y']">
 <p>Please order, stock number:
  <xsl:value-of select="@tracking_number" />
 </p>
 </xsl:if>
</xsl:template>
```

Tip The most important thing to keep in mind when working with `xsl:if` is that every expression evaluates to a Boolean value that's either true or false—there's no exception.

You'll find that if statements are useful when you want to perform basic value tests, such as determining whether a value is a number or a string. Here's a brief summary that details how datatypes are converted to Boolean values:

- **node-set** If a node-set contains one or more nodes, the node-set test evaluates to true. Otherwise, the node-set test evaluates to false. Examples follow:

  <xsl:if test="item/item_type"> If the current context contains one or more item elements that in turn contain one or more item_type elements, this test evaluates to true. Otherwise, the test is false.

  <xsl:if test=".//@tracking_number"> If the current context contains one or more descendants that have a tracking_number attribute, this test evaluates to true. Otherwise, the test is false.

- **number** If a number is greater than or less than zero, the number test evaluates to true. If the number is positive zero, negative zero, or not-a-number, the number test evaluates to false.

  <xsl:if test="count(item/item_type) >= 5"> If the current context contains one or more item elements that in turn contain five or more item_type elements, this test evaluates to true. Otherwise, the test is false.

Real World When you use <, <=, >, or >= as part of an attribute value, you should escape the < or > sign to ensure that the XSLT processor interprets the operator correctly. This means you should enter < for <, <= for <=, > for >, and >= for >=.

  <xsl:if test="number(@total_sales)"> If the current context element has an attribute called total_sales that's a valid number, this test evaluates to true. Otherwise, the test is false. For example, if the attribute has string value, such as "Hello", the test would evaluate to false.

- **string** If a string contains one or more characters, the string test evaluates to true. Otherwise, the string test evaluates to false.

  <xsl:if test="string(@manufacturer)"> If the current context element has an attribute called manufacturer that's a valid string, this test evaluates to true. Otherwise, the test is false.

  <xsl:if test="$x"> If the variable contains a value that meets the criteria for its respective datatype (either string, number or node-set), this test evaluates to true. Otherwise, the test is false. For example, if the variable represented a number and contained the value 0, the test would evaluate to false. However, if the variable represented a number and contained the value 25, the test would evaluate to true.

You can implement if statements in XSLT stylesheets by completing the following steps:

1. Within a template rule, type **<xsl:if test="*expression*">**, where *expression* is an XPath expression defining what you want to test.
2. Specify what should happen if the expression evaluates to true.
3. Type **</xsl:if>**.

Processing Nodes Conditionally with choose-when and choose-when-otherwise Statements

XSLT defines elements that you can use to specify a set of values that should be matched and what should happen in the case of a match. You can also specify what happens when no match is found. These elements are:

- **xsl:choose** Used to enclose a set of choices. The opening tag `<xsl:choose>` marks the beginning of the choices that you want to match and the closing tag `</xsl:choose>` marks the ending of those choices.
- **xsl:when** Used to specify the test expression that you want to match and to enclose the set of statements that should be processed in case of a match. An `xsl:when` element has the same syntax as an `xsl:if` element, complete with a test attribute.
- **xsl:otherwise** Used to specify what should happen when no match is found in the list of when choices.

The basic format of a choose-when structure is:

```
<xsl:choose>
 <xsl:when test="expression1">
 ...
 </xsl:when>
 <xsl:when test="expression2">
 ...
 </xsl:when>
 <xsl:when test="expressionN">
 ...
 </xsl:when>
</xsl:choose>
```

where *`expression1`*, *`expression2`*, *`...`*, *`expressionN`* are the expressions you want to test. Only the statements associated with the first match found are processed.

You can extend choose-when to include a default choice that's used when no match is found. You implement the default choice using the `xsl:otherwise` element. The basic format of a choose-when-otherwise structure is:

```
<xsl:choose>
 <xsl:when test="expression1">
 ...
 </xsl:when>
 <xsl:when test="expression2">
 ...
 </xsl:when>
 <xsl:when test="expressionN">
 ...
 </xsl:when>
 <xsl:otherwise>
 ...
 </xsl:otherwise >
</xsl:choose>
```

To see how choices use expressions, consider the following example:

```
<xsl:template match="/">
 <html>
  <body>
  <xsl:apply-templates select="inventory/item" />
  </body>
 </html>
</xsl:template>

<xsl:template match="item">
 <xsl:choose>
 <xsl:when test="stock/[@order='Y']">
  <p>Please order, stock number:
  <xsl:value-of select="@tracking_number" />
  </p>
 </xsl:when>
 <xsl:when test="stock/[@order='N']">
  <p>Item <xsl:value-of select="@tracking_number" />
   doesn't need to be re-stocked at this time.</p>
 </xsl:when>
 <xsl:otherwise>
  <p>INVALID ORDER INDICATOR FOR ITEM:
  <xsl:value-of select="@tracking_number" />
  </p>
 </xsl:otherwise>
 </xsl:choose>
</xsl:template>
```

In this example you define expressions that check the `order` attribute of the `stock` element, which is a child of the current context node. If the value of the `order` attribute is Y, the first when statement is a match for the expression and, as a result, the output specifies that the item should be ordered. If the value of the `order` attribute is N, the second when statement is a match for the expression, and, as a result, the output specifies that the item doesn't need to be ordered. On the other hand, if the `order` attribute doesn't contain a Y or N, an error indicator is output.

You can use choose-when and choose-when-otherwise in XSLT stylesheets by completing the following steps:

1. Within a template rule, type **<xsl:choose>** to mark the beginning of the choice set.
2. Type **<xsl:when test="*expression*">**, where *expression* is an XPath expression defining what you want to test.
3. Specify what should happen if the expression evaluates to true.
4. Type **</xsl:when>**.
5. Repeat Steps 2-4 for each condition.
6. If you want to specify an option to be used if no match is found, type **<xsl:otherwise>**, specify what should happen if none of the previously specified conditions are true, and then type **</xsl:otherwise>**.
7. Type **</xsl:choose>** to complete the choice set.

Caution The first match (and only the first match) is used. All other conditions that follow a match are ignored. This differs from switch-case implementations in most programming languages where a break statement is required to drop out of the switch-case construct.

Processing Multiple Nodes with for-each Statements

If you want to process all nodes that match a certain criteria, you can use the `xsl:for-each` element. This element lets you specify a set of nodes with a select attribute and then perform iterative processing on each node in the node set.

The basic format of a for-each statement is:

```
<xsl:for-each select="expression">
...
</xsl:for-each>
```

where *`expression`* is an XPath expression that returns a node set.

To see how `for-each` statements work, consider the following input document:

```
<?xml version="1.0" ?>
<inventory>
 <item tracking_number="459320" manufacturer="Toshiba">
  <item_type>3 1/2" Floppy Disk Drive</item_type>
  <description>Standard 3 1/2" floppy drive</description>
  <stock in_stock="750" orders_for="200" net_units="550"
    order="N" />
 </item>
 <item tracking_number="459323" manufacturer="Not listed">
  <item_type>3 1/2" Floppy Disk Drive</item_type>
  <description>Standard 3 1/2" floppy drive</description>
  <stock in_stock="50" orders_for="200" net_units="-150"
    order="Y" />
 </item>
 <item tracking_number="459780" manufacturer="Toshiba">
  <item_type>5 1/4" Floppy Disk Drive</item_type>
  <description>Standard 5 1/4" floppy drive</description>
  <stock in_stock="250" orders_for="200" net_units="50"
    order="Y" />
 </item>
 <item tracking_number="459789" manufacturer="Not listed">
  <item_type>5 1/4" Floppy Disk Drive</item_type>
  <description>Standard 5 1/4" floppy drive</description>
  <stock in_stock="0" orders_for="200" net_units="-200"
    order="Y" />
 </item>
</inventory>
```

This document contains a list of inventory items. Although there are currently only four items in the document, you can imagine a case where there are dozens, hundreds, or thousands of items that you want to process in some way. You could define a stylesheet that processes these elements in the traditional recursive manner, such as:

```
<xsl:template match="/">
 <html>
  <body>
   <xsl:apply-templates select="inventory/item" />
  </body>
 </html>
</xsl:template>

<xsl:template match="item">
 <xsl:apply-templates select="item_type" />
 <xsl:apply-templates select="description" />
 <xsl:apply-templates select="stock" />
</xsl:template>
```

(continued)

(continued)

```
<xsl:template match="item_type">
...
</xsl:template>

<xsl:template match="description">
...
</xsl:template>

<xsl:template match="stock">
...
</xsl:template>
```

However, the structure of the inventory document is such that you could also iteratively process the document at the `item` element level to obtain all the necessary information. You might prefer iterative processing if you simply want to extract and display the values associated with the child elements `item_type`, `description`, and `stock`.

One way to iteratively process the inventory document using for-each statements follows:

```
<xsl:template match="/">
 <html>
  <body>
  <table>
   <tr>
    <th>Inv Number</th>
    <th>Item</th>
    <th>Manufacturer</th>
    <th>Current</th>
    <th>Orders</th>
    <th>Remaining</th>
   </tr>
   <xsl:for-each select="inventory/item">
   <tr>
    <td><xsl:value-of select="@tracking_number" /></td>
    <td><xsl:value-of select="item_type" /></td>
    <td><xsl:value-of select="@manufacturer" /></td>
    <td><xsl:value-of select="stock/@in_stock" /></td>
    <td><xsl:value-of select="stock/@orders_for" /></td>
    <td><xsl:value-of select="stock/@net_units" /></td>
   </tr>
   </xsl:for-each>
  </table>
  </body>
 </html>
</xsl:template>
```

In this example the root node is the context node that you're working with. Each time the XSLT processor encounters a child node of the root node that's an `item` element, the select expression in the `for-each` statement is matched. The body of the `for-each` statement builds a table row that contains values that you want to output. The result is the following HTML document:

```
<html>
 <body>
 <table>
  <tr>
  <th>Inv Number</th>
  <th>Item</th>
  <th>Manufacturer</th>
  <th>Current</th>
  <th>Orders</th>
  <th>Remaining</th>
  </tr>
  <tr>
  <td>459320</td>
  <td>3 1/2" Floppy Disk Drive</td>
  <td>Toshiba</td>
  <td>750</td>
  <td>200</td>
  <td>550</td>
  </tr>
  <tr>
  <td>459323</td>
  <td>3 1/2" Floppy Disk Drive</td>
  <td>Not listed</td>
  <td>50</td>
  <td>200</td>
  <td>-150</td>
  </tr>
  <tr>
  <td>459780</td>
  <td>5 1/4" Floppy Disk Drive</td>
  <td>Toshiba</td>
  <td>250</td>
  <td>200</td>
  <td>50</td>
  </tr>
  <tr>
  <td>459789</td>
  <td>5 1/4" Floppy Disk Drive</td>
  <td>Not listed</td>
  <td>0</td>
  <td>200</td>
  <td>-200</td>
  </tr>
 </table>
 </body>
</html>
```

You can use `for-each` statements in XSLT stylesheets by completing the following steps:

1. Within a template rule, type **<xsl:for-each select="*expression*">**, where *expression* is an XPath expression that returns a node set.
2. Specify what should happen, the processing that should occur, for each matching node.
3. Type **</xsl:for-each>**.

Invoking, Including, and Importing Templates

So far we've always assumed that the template rules you want to work with are in the current stylesheet and that you want to recursively or iteratively process template rules. While this is true in most cases, sometimes you'll want to

- Include or import templates from one stylesheet in another stylesheet
- Call templates directly by name
- Define multiple template rules that can be applied to the same set of nodes

Techniques for performing these tasks are examined in the sections that follow.

Including and Importing Templates

When you want to work with templates defined in other stylesheets, you can include or import the stylesheets containing those templates. The elements you use to include or import stylesheets are `xsl:include` and `xsl:import`, respectively.

Defining Include Statements

You define an `include` statement like this:

```
<xsl:include href="URLpath/filename" />
```

where *`URLpath/filename`* is the actual URL and filename of the stylesheet you want to include, such as:

```
<xsl:include href="../mystyles.xsl" />
```

With an `include` statement, you can insert the template rules defined in another stylesheet anywhere in the contents of the current stylesheet. Because the template rules in the included stylesheet have the same priority as template rules in the original stylesheet, any conflicts are resolved according to the order in which the template rules are entered in the merged stylesheet (essentially, the XSLT processor uses the first template rule with a name that matches the select value of the `apply-templates` declaration).

In most cases you'll use included stylesheets when you want to define template rules containing standard markup elements, such as those for the header and footer of an HTML document. To see how this would work, consider the following example:

```
<xsl:stylesheet
 xmlns:xsl="http://www.w3.org/1999/XSL/Transform"
 version="1.0">

 <xsl:output method="html" />

<xsl:template match="/">
 <html>
  <body>
   <xsl:apply-templates
    select="/inventory/item/item_type/@tracking_number" />
   <xsl:apply-templates select="/inventory/item/description" />
  </body>
 </html>
</xsl:template>

 <xsl:include href="inventory.xsl" />

</xsl:stylesheet>
```

Here you have the definition of the original stylesheet that has an `include` statement for a stylesheet named inventory.xsl. If the contents of the inventory.xsl stylesheet are:

```
<xsl:stylesheet
 xmlns:xsl="http://www.w3.org/1999/XSL/Transform"
 version="1.0">

<xsl:template match="/inventory/item/item_type/@tracking_number">
 <h1>
  <xsl:value-of select="." />
 </h1>
</xsl:template>

<xsl:template match="/inventory/item/description">
 <p>
  <xsl:value-of select="." />
 </p>
</xsl:template>

</xsl:stylesheet>
```

the result of the include is a stylesheet that XSLT processors interpret as:

```
<xsl:stylesheet
 xmlns:xsl="http://www.w3.org/1999/XSL/Transform"
 version="1.0">

 <xsl:output method="html" />

<xsl:template match="/">
 <html>
  <body>
   <xsl:apply-templates
    select="/inventory/item/item_type/@tracking_number" />
   <xsl:apply-templates select="/inventory/item/description" />
  </body>
 </html>

</xsl:template>

<xsl:template match="/inventory/item/item_type/@tracking_number">
 <h1>
  <xsl:value-of select="." />
 </h1>
</xsl:template>

<xsl:template match="/inventory/item/description">
 <p>
  <xsl:value-of select="." />
 </p>
</xsl:template>

</xsl:stylesheet>
```

You can include a stylesheet in another stylesheet by completing these steps:

1. Compare the stylesheet(s) that you want to include in another stylesheet, looking for possible conflicts where template rules have the same match expression. If you find possible conflicts, be sure to pay particular attention to the location in which you insert the stylesheet.
2. At the point in the original stylesheet where you want to include another stylesheet, type **<xsl:include href=*"URLpath/filename"* />**, where *URLpath/filename* is the actual URL and filename of the stylesheet you want to include.
3. Repeat Steps 1 and 2 for other stylesheets that you want to include.

Defining Import Statements

You define an import statement like this:

```
<xsl:import href="URLpath/filename" />
```

where *URLpath/filename* is the actual URL and filename of the stylesheet you want to import, such as:

```
<xsl:import href="../mystyles.xsl" />
```

Unlike include statements, import statements must appear at the beginning of a stylesheet, immediately following the `xsl:stylesheet` element. Additionally, the imported template rules have a lower priority than rules in the current stylesheet. This means that rules in the current stylesheet always have precedence over rules in an imported stylesheet.

You can import a stylesheet into another stylesheet by completing these steps:

1. Locate the opening stylesheet tag in the original stylesheet. This tag follows the form `<xsl:stylesheet>`.
2. After the opening stylesheet tag, type **<xsl:import href="*URLpath/filename*" />**, where *URLpath/filename* is the actual URL and filename of the stylesheet you want to import.
3. If you want to import additional stylesheets, enter each new import declaration after the existing import declaration(s).

Calling Templates by Name

Although recursive and iterative processing are great, sometimes you want to directly access a template no matter where you are in the stylesheet and irrespective of the current context. Don't worry, XSLT does allow you to directly access a template in the current stylesheet. To do this, you call a template by name using an `xsl:call-template` element.

Calling a template is a two-part process. First, you must define a named template. The basic format for a named template is:

```
<xsl:template name="template_name">
...
</xsl:template>
```

where *template_name* is the name you'll use to call the template.

Second, you must invoke the named template using the `xsl:call-template` element. This element has the basic form:

```
<xsl:call-template name="template_name" />
```

where *template_name* is the name of the template you want to invoke.

You'll find that template calls are handy when you define standard markup components that you want to reference regularly. For example, you could define document headers and footers using named templates and then include the stylesheet that contains these templates in other stylesheets. Afterward, you could call the templates by name to invoke them as appropriate.

To summarize, to create and then call a named template, complete the following steps:

1. Type **<xsl:template name="*template_name*">**, where *template_name* is the actual name you'll use to call the template.
2. Specify the processing that should occur when the template is called.
3. Type **</xsl:template>**.
4. In the location from which you want to call the named template, type **<xsl:call-template name="*template_name*" />**, where *template_name* is the name you previously specified for the template.

Invoking Templates by Mode

When you define multiple template rules that match individual nodes within a node set, you might want to set a mode attribute for template rules that you select. The mode attribute allows you to define different templates that work with the same elements, yet in different ways. For example, you could define a template rule with `mode="summary"` and another with `mode="detailed"`. In the first template, you could create a summary or digest of the currently selected nodes. In the second template, you could create a detailed output for the same set of nodes.

When you work with modes, you assign the mode attribute in the `xsl:apply-templates` element as well as in the `xsl:template` element. Here's an example:

```
<xsl:stylesheet
 xmlns:xsl="http://www.w3.org/1999/XSL/Transform"
 version="1.0">

 <xsl:output method="html" />

<xsl:template match="/">
 <html>
  <body>
   <xsl:apply-templates select="inventory/item" mode="summary" />
   <xsl:apply-templates select="inventory/item" mode="detailed" />
  </body>
 </html>
</xsl:template>

<xsl:template match="item" mode="summary">
...
</xsl:template>

<xsl:template match="item" mode="detailed">
...
</xsl:template>

</xsl:stylesheet>
```

In this example you specify that templates should be applied using two modes: summary and detailed. You then define two sets of template rules: one for outputting the summary and another for outputting the details. Keep in mind that the actual value of the mode attribute is an arbitrary XML name. The XSLT processor only cares that the mode attribute is set; it doesn't attempt to discern what the mode designator means. Because of this, you can set the mode designator to a value that makes sense to you and to others viewing the stylesheet. For example, if you've designed a stylesheet with multiple modes and the output in the details section doesn't look right, you can quickly track the problem to the template rule defined with `mode="detailed"`.

To specify a mode and then define a template rule that uses the mode, complete the following steps:

1. Define the template rule that uses a mode attribute by typing **<xsl:template match="*pattern*" mode="*currMode*">**, where *pattern* identifies the sections of the document to which the template should be applied and *currMode* identifies the current mode for this template rule.
2. Specify the processing that should occur when the template is called and then type **</xsl:template>** to complete the template rule.
3. In the location where you want to call this template rule, type **<xsl:apply-templates select="*expression*" mode="*currMode*" />**, where *expression* identifies the nodes whose template rules should be applied and matches the previously defined pattern and *currMode* identifies the current mode and matches the previously defined mode.

Chapter 16

Variables and Parameters in XSLT

In order to perform many advanced tasks, you'll need to be able to pass values into templates that are being processed, or hold values temporarily during processing. As in a programming language, such as Java, you use parameters and variables to perform these tasks in XSL Transformations (XSLT). As you'll learn in this chapter, parameters and variables can have either a local scope or a global scope. Unlike global parameters and variables, which can be referenced anywhere in an XSLT styles heet once they're defined, local parameters and variables have a very specific scope and can only be used in a part of the stylesheet.

Working with Parameters

XSLT defines two elements that you can use to pass parameters to a template: `xsl:param` and `xsl:with-param`. You define parameters using `xsl:param`, and you pass parameter values to templates using `xsl:with-param`.

Defining and Referencing Parameters

You define a parameter in a template using the `xsl:param` element. The `xsl:param` element has two attributes:

- **name** A required attribute that sets the name of the parameter
- **select** An optional attribute that sets the parameter to a specific value

One of the most basic ways to use a parameter is to define its values in a named template and then perform some processing based on the parameter values that you're using. Here's an example of a template that defines two parameters:

```
<xsl:template name="CircleArea">
 <xsl:param name="circumference"/>
 <xsl:param name="diameter"/>
 <xsl:value-of select="$circumference * $diameter" />
</xsl:template>
```

Note You can define parameters in standard templates with match expressions as well. Regardless of whether you use a named or unnamed template, you must specify any parameters the template will use immediately after the opening `<xsl:template>` tag.

This template defines two parameters, circumference and diameter, and outputs their product. As a result, when you call this function and pass in a circumference and diameter, the output generated is the area of the circle represented by those two values.

In the previous example, note the syntax used to reference the parameters in the `value-of` element. You must use this syntax to reference parameters after you define them. This means that a parameter reference has the form:

```
$parameter_name
```

where *parameter_name* is the name of the parameter you've defined and want to use. As long as you reference the parameter as part of an XSLT element's attribute or text, you can use this basic syntax. However, if you want to reference parameters in attributes that you want to generate as part of the output markup, you must enclose the parameter reference in curly braces, such as:

```
{$parameter_name}
```

The curly braces tell the XSLT processor to replace the referenced value with its actual value. To see how this type of reference is made, consider the following template:

```
<xsl:template name="setTableStyle">
 <xsl:param name="border_size" />
 <xsl:param name="width" />
 <xsl:param name="bg_color" />
 <table border="{$border_size}" width="{$width}"
  bgcolor="{$bg_color}">
</xsl:template>
```

Here, you define a named template called `setTableStyle` that has three parameters:

- **border_size** Sets the size of the table's border
- **width** Sets the width of the table
- **bg_color** Sets the background color for the table

After defining these parameters, you reference the parameters as part of the output markup.

Note Technically, the second style of referencing parameters is called an *attribute value template*. However, it's much easier to think of this simply as a type of parameter reference.

To define a parameter without a default value, within the template that you want to define the parameter, type **<xsl:param name="*parameter_name*"/>**, where *parameter_name* is the name you want to use for the parameter.

To reference a parameter, follow these steps:

1. If the parameter is used as part of the XSLT markup, type **$*parameter_name***, where *parameter_name* is the name of the parameter you previously defined and want to use.
2. If the parameter is used as part of the attribute in the output, type **{$*parameter_name*}**, where *parameter_name* is the name of the parameter you previously defined and want to use.

Setting Default Values for Parameters

If you like, you can define a default value for parameters. One way to do this is to assign the default value in the select attribute when you define the parameter. For example, you could set default values for the `setTableStyle` template's parameters like this:

```
<xsl:template name="setTableStyle">
 <xsl:param name="border_size" select="2" />
 <xsl:param name="width" select="800" />
 <xsl:param name="bg_color" select="'white'" />
 <table border="{$border_size}" width="{$width}"
  bgcolor="{$bg_color}">
</xsl:template>
```

The default values for the `border_size`, `width`, and `bg_color` parameters are 2, 800, and 'white', respectively. Now, if you invoke `setTableStyle` without setting values for these parameters, the default values are used and the output looks like this:

```
<table border="2" width="800" bgcolor="white">
```

Real World In the example, note that single quotation marks enclose the literal string value. Anytime you want to output a literal string as part of an attribute value, you must enclose the value in quotation marks. If you don't, the XSLT processor assumes you're referencing an element name. Here, the XSLT processor would have selected all white elements in the current context, which isn't what you wanted to do. If no white elements were in the current context, the output value would have been set to an empty string.

Another way to set the default value for a parameter is to include content within the `xsl:param` element. Here's an example:

```
<xsl:template name="setTableStyle">
 <xsl:param name="width">
  <xsl:value-of select="$widthA + $widthB + $widthC + 20">
 </xsl:param>

 <xsl:param name="border_size">
 <xsl:choose>
  <xsl:when test="$width &gt; 800">
   <xsl:text>5</xsl:text>
  </xsl:when>
  <xsl:when test="$width &lt;= 800">
   <xsl:text>2</xsl:text>
  </xsl:when>
 </xsl:choose>
 </xsl:param>

 <xsl:param name="bg_color">
  <xsl:text>white<xsl:text>
 </xsl:param>

 <table border="{$border_size}" width="{$width}
  bgcolor="{$bg_color}">

</xsl:template>
```

In this example you define the width parameter based on the value of other parameters plus a base value. Then you use the `width` value to determine the `border_size` that you want to set for the table. Finally, you set the `bg_color` to the literal text value white. As an example, widthA, widthB, and widthC could represent column widths of 200, 250, and 230 respectively, in which case the width parameter is set to 700 (200+250+230+20). Based on this value, the second when test is the one that's processed and the `border_size` is set to 2. Thus, the output in this case is:

```
<table border="2" width="700" bgcolor="white">
```

To define a parameter with a simple default value, follow these steps:

1. Within the template that you want to define the parameter, type **<xsl:param name="*parameter_name*"**, where *parameter_name* is the name you want to use for the parameter.
2. If you want to set a default value for the parameter, type **select="*parameter_value*" />**, where *parameter_value* is the default value you want to assign to the parameter. Otherwise, type **/>**.

To define a parameter with default contents, follow these steps:

1. Within the template that you want to define the parameter, type **<xsl:param name="*parameter_name*">**, where *parameter_name* is the name you want to use for the parameter.
2. Insert the contents of the parameter.
3. Type **</xsl:parameter>** to complete the parameter declaration.

Passing Parameter Values to Templates

You can pass parameter values to templates as part of an `xsl:call-template` or `xsl:apply-templates` selection. To do this, you use the `xsl:with-param` element and set the value of this element's select attribute to the value you want to pass to the template you're calling or applying.

The basic format of the `with-param` element is

```
<xsl:with-param name="parameter_name" select="parameter_value" />
```

where *`parameter_name`* is the name of the parameter you previously defined and *`parameter_value`* is the value you want to pass to this parameter. Because the select attribute is optional, you don't have to use it. However, if you don't pass in a value and a default value isn't defined, the XSLT processor uses an empty string ("") as the default value.

To see how parameter passing works, consider the following example:

```
<xsl:template name="SquareOrRectangleArea">
 <xsl:param name="width" />
 <xsl:param name="height" />
 <xsl:value-of select="$width * $height" />
</xsl:template>
```

Here, you've defined a template that computes the area of a square or rectangle based on the value of width and height parameters. If you wanted to invoke this named template, you'd use the `xsl:call-template` element to do so. As you know from Chapter 15, "Branching and Control Functions," the basic format of `xsl:call-template` is:

```
<xsl:call-template name="template_name" />
```

where *`template_name`* is the name of the template you want to invoke. This format doesn't work in this case, however. Because you need to define `xsl:with-param` elements as content of the `xsl:call-template`, you must define the element with opening and closing tags, as in:

```
<xsl:call-template name="template_name">
...
</xsl:call-template>
```

Once you do this, you can specify the parameters and parameter values you want to pass to the template. In the following example, you pass width and height parameter values to the SquareOrRectangleArea template:

```
<xsl:call-template name="SquareOrRectangleArea">
 <xsl:with-param name="width" select="10" />
 <xsl:with-param name="height" select="20 />
</xsl:call-template>
```

The resulting output from this template call is:

```
200
```

To pass a parameter value to a template, follow these steps:

1. Modify the `xsl:call-template` or `xsl:apply-templates` element so that it has an opening and closing tag, such as **<xsl:call-template name= "myTemplate"> </xsl:call-template>**.
2. Insert the following as the contents of the `xsl:call-template` or `xsl:apply-templates` element: **<xsl:with-param name="*parameter_name*" select= "*parameter_value*" />**, where *parameter_name* is the name of the parameter you previously defined and *parameter_value* is an optional value that you want to pass to this parameter.

Note If you don't pass a specific value, the default value for the parameter is used. If there's no default value, an empty string ("") is used.

Using Global Parameters

So far you've worked only with local parameters that were defined and used with specific templates. XSLT defines another type of parameter called a global parameter, which can be referenced anywhere in an XSLT stylesheet once it's defined. A global parameter is simply a parameter that's defined at the top level of the stylesheet. That is, the parameter is defined as a child of the `xsl:stylesheet` element in the same way you define `xsl:template` elements as children of the `xsl:stylesheet` element. Here's an example:

```
<xsl:stylesheet
 xmlns:xsl="http://www.w3.org/1999/XSL/Transform"
 version="1.0">

<xsl:output method="html" />

<xsl:param name="textColor" />
<xsl:param name="pageBGColor" />
<xsl:param name="tableBGColor" />
```

(continued)

(continued)

```
<xsl:template match="/">
 <html>
  <body bgcolor="{$pageBGColor}" text="{$textColor}">
  <table bgcolor="{$tableBGColor}">
   <tr>
    <th>Inv Number</th>
    <th>Item</th>
    <th>Manufacturer</th>
    <th>Current</th>
    <th>Orders</th>
    <th>Remaining</th>
   </tr>
   <xsl:for-each select="inventory/item" />
   <tr>
    <td><xsl:value-of select="@tracking_number" /></td>
    <td><xsl:value-of select="item_type" /></td>
    <td><xsl:value-of select="@manufacturer" /></td>
    <td><xsl:value-of select="stock/@in_stock" /></td>
    <td><xsl:value-of select="stock/@orders_for" /></td>
    <td><xsl:value-of select="stock/@net_units" /></td>
   </tr>
   </xsl:for-each>
  </table>
  </body>
 </html>
</xsl:template>

</xsl:stylesheet>
```

Here, you define three global parameters: `textColor`, `pageBGColor`, and `tableBGColor`. You then use the parameter values to set attributes of the `<body>` and `<table>` tags in the HTML output.

You set the value of global parameters in one of two ways. You can set a default value directly when you define the parameter, such as:

```
<xsl:param name="textColor">
 <xsl:text>black</xsl:text>
</xsl:param>
<xsl:param name="pageBGColor">
 <xsl:text>white</xsl:text>
</xsl:param>
<xsl:param name="tableBGColor">
 <xsl:text>blue</xsl:text>
</xsl:param>
```

and

```
<xsl:param name="textColor" select='black'" />
<xsl:param name="pageBGColor" select='white'" />
<xsl:param name="tableBGColor" select='blue'" />
```

Alternatively, you can set the value of the global parameter when you invoke the XSLT processor—for example, with Xalan from the Apache XML Project (*http://xml.apache.org/xalan-j/*). You specify global variable values as command line arguments:

```
java org.apache.xalan.xslt.Process -in file_in -xsl file_xsl
 -out file_out -param param1 value1 -param param2 value2
 -param paramN valueN
```

where `file_in` is the input XML document, `file_xsl` is the XSL stylesheet, `file_out` is the output file, and each `-param` flag is followed by a global parameter name and value, such as:

```
java org.apache.xalan.xslt.Process -in sample.xml -xsl sample.xsl
 -out sample.html -param textColor black -param pageBGColor white
 -param tableBGColor blue
```

XSLT processors are usually invoked from within application programs rather than from the command line. For example, if the XSLT processor you're using supports the Transformation API for XML (TrAX), you could define the global parameters prior to calling the methods that parse and process the contents of the input XML document. With TrAX, you do this using the `setParameter` method of the Transformer classes that you're using to handle the input stream, which represents the input XML document you're using as the source document. The Java source code to do this would look like this:

```
import java.io.File;
import javax.xml.transform.Transformer;
import javax.xml.transform.TransformerConfigurationException;
import javax.xml.transform.TransformerException;
import javax.xml.transform.TransformerFactory;
import javax.xml.transform.stream.StreamResult;
import javax.xml.transform.stream.StreamSource;

public class DefineGPs {

 public static void parseAndProcess(String sourceID,
  String xslID, String outputID) {

 try {

  TransformerFactory trfactory =
  TransformerFactory.newInstance();

  Transformer transformer =
  trfactory.newTransformer(new StreamSource(xslID));
```

(continued)

(continued)

```
  transformer.setParameter("textColor", "black");
  transformer.setParameter("pageBGColor", "white");
  transformer.setParameter("tableBGColor", "blue");

  transformer.transform(new StreamSource(new File(sourceID)),
      new StreamResult(new File(outputID)));
 }

 catch (TransformerConfigurationException trce) {
 }
 catch (TransformerException tre) {
 }
 }

 public static void main(String argv[])
 throws java.io.IOException, org.xml.sax.SAXException {

 DefineGPs gps = new DefineGPs();
 gps.parseAndProcess("sample.xml", "sample.xsl", "sample.html");

 }
}
```

Essentially, this source code is the equivalent of the previously defined command line instruction for the Xalan XSLT processor. You set the global parameters `textColor`, `pageBGColor`, and `tableBGColor` to black, white, and blue respectively, and then you specify that the input (or source) document as sample.xml, the XSLT stylesheet as sample.xsl, and the output document as sample.html. Thus, if the input document looked like this:

```
<?xml version="1.0" ?>
<inventory>
 <item tracking_number="459320" manufacturer="Toshiba">
  <item_type>3 1/2" Floppy Disk Drive</item_type>
  <description>Standard 3 1/2" floppy drive</description>
  <stock in_stock="750" orders_for="200" net_units="550"
   order="N" />
 </item>
 <item tracking_number="459323" manufacturer="Not listed">
  <item_type>3 1/2" Floppy Disk Drive</item_type>
  <description>Standard 3 1/2" floppy drive</description>
  <stock in_stock="50" orders_for="200" net_units="-150"
   order="Y" />
 </item>
 <item tracking_number="459780" manufacturer="Toshiba">
  <item_type>5 1/4" Floppy Disk Drive</item_type>
  <description>Standard 5 1/4" floppy drive</description>
  <stock in_stock="250" orders_for="200" net_units="50"
   order="Y" />
 </item>
```

(continued)

(continued)

```
 <item tracking_number="459789" manufacturer="Not listed">
  <item_type>5 1/4" Floppy Disk Drive</item_type>
  <description>Standard 5 1/4" floppy drive</description>
  <stock in_stock="0" orders_for="200" net_units="-200"
   order="Y" />
 </item>
</inventory>
```

and the stylesheet was the one previously defined in this section, the output document would look similar to this:

```
<html>
 <body bgcolor="black" text="white">
 <table bgcolor="blue">
  <tr>
  <th>Inv Number</th>
  <th>Item</th>
  <th>Manufacturer</th>
  <th>Current</th>
  <th>Orders</th>
  <th>Remaining</th>
  </tr>
  <tr>
  <td>459320</td>
  <td>3 1/2" Floppy Disk Drive</td>
  <td>Toshiba</td>
  <td>750</td>
  <td>200</td>
  <td>550</td>
  </tr>
  <tr>
  <td>459323</td>
  <td>3 1/2" Floppy Disk Drive</td>
  <td>Not listed</td>
  <td>50</td>
  <td>200</td>
  <td>-150</td>
  </tr>
  <tr>
  <td>459780</td>
  <td>5 1/4" Floppy Disk Drive</td>
  <td>Toshiba</td>
  <td>250</td>
  <td>200</td>
  <td>50</td>
  </tr>
```

(continued)

(continued)

```
  <tr>
  <td>459789</td>
  <td>5 1/4" Floppy Disk Drive</td>
  <td>Not listed</td>
  <td>0</td>
  <td>200</td>
  <td>-200</td>
  </tr>
 </table>
 </body>
</html>
```

To define a global parameter with a simple default value or no default value, follow these steps:

1. Immediately after the opening stylesheet tag `<xsl:stylesheet>` and any `xsl:include` or `xsl:import` declarations, type **<xsl:param name="*parameter_name*"**, where *parameter_name* is the name you want to use for the global parameter.
2. If you want to set a default value for the parameter, type **select= "*parameter_value*"** **/>**, where *parameter_value* is the default value you want to assign to the parameter. Otherwise, type **/>**.

To define a global parameter with default contents, follow these steps:

1. Immediately after the opening stylesheet tag `<xsl:stylesheet>` and any `xsl:include` or `xsl:import` declarations, type **<xsl:param name= "*parameter_name*">**, where *parameter_name* is the name you want to use for the parameter.
2. Insert the contents of the parameter.
3. Type **</xsl:parameter>** to complete the parameter declaration.

To reference a global parameter, follow these steps:

1. If the global parameter is used as part of the XSLT markup, type **$*parameter_name***, where *parameter_name* is the name of the parameter you previously defined and want to use.
2. If the parameter is used as part of the attribute in the output, type **{$*parameter_name*}**, where *parameter_name* is the name of the parameter you previously defined and want to use.

To pass a global parameter value to a template, follow these steps:

1. Modify the `xsl:call-template` or `xsl:apply-templates` element so that it has an opening and closing tag, such as `<xsl:call-template name="myTemplate"> </xsl:call-template>`.
2. As the contents of the `xsl:call-template` or `xsl:apply-templates` element, enter **<xsl:with-param name="*parameter_name*" select="*parameter_value*" />**, where *parameter_name* is the name of the parameter you previously defined and *parameter_value* is an optional value that you want to pass to this parameter.

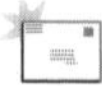

Note If you don't pass a specific value, the default value for the global parameter is used. If there's no default value, an empty string ("") is used.

Working with Variables

When you're working with XSLT, you'll often need a way to hold values temporarily during processing, and this is where you'll find that variables are extremely useful. You use variables to store values.

Defining Variables

Variables are defined using the `xsl:variable` element, which has the basic form:

```
<xsl:variable name="variable_name" select="variable_value" />
```

where *`variable_name`* is the name of the variable you're defining and *`variable_value`* is the value you're assigning to the variable. As with parameters, the `select` attribute that sets a value is optional. If you don't set a specific value, the XSLT processor assigns an empty string ("") as the default value.

This means you could define a variable called statusFlag that has the value true, like this:

```
<xsl:variable name="statusFlag" select="'true'" />
```

Note As with parameters, you must use single quotation marks to enclose literal string values. If you don't, the XSLT processor assumes you're referencing an element name.

Variables can have contents as well. This means you could also specify a literal string value for the `statusFlag` variable like this:

```
<xsl:variable name="statusFlag">
 <xsl:text>true</xsl:text>
</xsl:variable>
```

However, if you wanted to initialize the same variable to an empty string, you'd declare the variable like this:

```
<xsl:variable name="statusFlag"/>
```

Now `statusFlag` has the value "".

You can use variables in XSLT in much the same way that you can use them in programming languages. For example, if you needed to implement the following Java code in XSLT:

```
int x;
if (statusFlag > 0)
 x = 5;
else
 x = 0;
```

you could do this using the following variable declaration:

```
<xsl:variable name="x" />
 <xsl:choose>
 <xsl:when test="$statusFlag &gt; 0">
  <xsl:text>5</xsl:text>
 </xsl:when>
 <xsl:otherwise>
  <xsl:text>0</xsl:text>
 </xsl:otherwise>
 </xsl:choose>
</xsl:variable>
```

Unlike traditional programming languages, however, where you can modify the value of a variable during execution and reassign the value to the variable to modify further execution, you can't do this in XSLT. XSLT doesn't execute stylesheets—it processes them recursively or iteratively. For example, in Java you can reassign values to variables using statements like this:

```
x+=1
++x
x++
```

In Java, reassigning the value of a variable allows the language to be very dynamic. Consider the following assignments:

```
a=2;
b=++a
```

Here, the result is that the value of a is 3 and the value of b is 3. Yet if you rewrite the assignments like this:

```
a=2;
b=a++
```

The result is that the value of a is 3 and the value of b is 2.

Although Java has these types of reassignments, many less complex programming languages do not. The reason is that value reassignments are difficult to implement and track. Suffice it to say that the designers of XSLT chose not to open this Pandora's box when they defined the specification.

To define a variable with a simple default value or no default value, follow these steps:

1. Within the template that you want to define the variable, type **<xsl:variable name="*variable_name*"**, where *variable_name* is the name you want to use for the variable.
2. If you want to set a default value for the variable, type **select= "*variable_value*" />**, where variable_value is the default value you want to assign to the variable. Otherwise, type **/>**.

To define a variable with default contents, follow these steps:

1. Within the template that you want to define the variable, type **<xsl:variable name="*variable_name*">**, where *variable_name* is the name you want to use for the variable.
2. Insert the contents of the variable.
3. Type **</xsl:variable>** to complete the variable declaration.

Referencing Variables

You reference variables in the same way you reference parameters. This means a variable reference has the form:

```
$variable_name
```

where *variable_name* is the name of the variable you've defined and want to use. As long as you reference the variable as part of an XSLT element's attribute or text, you can use this basic syntax. Here's an example:

```
<xsl:template match="/">
 <html>
  <body>
  <xsl:apply-templates select="inventory/item" />
  </body>
 </html>
</xsl:template>

<xsl:template match="item">
 <xsl:choose>
 <xsl:when test="$statusFlag = 0">
 <p>Please order, stock number:
  <xsl:value-of select="@tracking_number" />
 </p>
 </xsl:when>
```

(continued)

(continued)

```
 <xsl:when test="$statusFlag = 1">
  <p>Item <xsl:value-of select="@tracking_number" />
   doesn't need to be re-stocked at this time.</p>
 </xsl:when>
 <xsl:otherwise>
 <p>INVALID ORDER INDICATOR FOR ITEM:
  <xsl:value-of select="@tracking_number" />
 </p>
 </xsl:otherwise >
 </xsl:choose>
</xsl:template>
```

In this example a variable called `statusFlag` is used to determine whether items should be ordered. If `statusFlag` is set to 0, the item should be ordered. If `statusFlag` is set to 1, the item doesn't need to be ordered. If `statusFlag` has a different value, some error occurred during processing and you should check the item order status.

If you want to reference variables in attributes that you want to generate as part of the output markup, you must enclose the variable reference in curly braces, such as:

```
{$variable_name}
```

As with parameters, the curly braces tell the XSLT processor to replace the referenced value with its actual value.

To reference a variable, follow these steps:

1. If the variable is used as part of the XSLT markup, type ***$variable_name***, where *variable_name* is the name of the variable you previously defined and want to use.
2. If the variable is used as part of the attribute in the output, type **{*$variable_name*}**, where *variable_name* is the name of the variable you previously defined and want to use.

Using Global Variables

Like parameters, variables can have a global or local scope. You define global variables at the top level of the stylesheet and their values are accessible anywhere in the stylesheet. On the other hand, you define local variables as part of a specific template and their values are only available in that template.

The following example defines four global variables (`statusFlag`, `x`, `y`, and `z`):

```
<xsl:stylesheet
 xmlns:xsl="http://www.w3.org/1999/XSL/Transform"
 version="1.0">

<xsl:output method="html" />
```

(continued)

(continued)

```
<xsl:variable name="statusFlag" />
<xsl:variable name="x" />
<xsl:variable name="y" />
<xsl:variable name="z" />

<xsl:template match="/">
...
</xsl:template">

</xsl:stylesheet>
```

Caution If you define a local variable with the same name as a global variable, the local variable overrides the global variable. This means that the value of the local variable is used instead of the global variable with the same name.

To define a global variable with a simple default value or no default value, follow these steps:

1. After the opening stylesheet tag `<xsl:stylesheet>` and any `xsl:include`, `xsl:import`, or `xsl:param` declarations, type **<xsl:variable name= "*variable_name*"**, where *variable_name* is the name you want to use for the global variable.
2. If you want to set a default value for the variable, type **select="*variable_value*" />**, where *variable_value* is the default value you want to assign to the variable. Otherwise, type **/>**.

To define a global variable with default contents, follow these steps:

1. Immediately after the opening stylesheet tag `<xsl:stylesheet>` and any `xsl:include`, `xsl:import`, or `xsl:param` declarations, type **<xsl:variable name="*variable_name*">**, where *variable_name* is the name you want to use for the variable.
2. Insert the contents of the variable.
3. Type **</xsl:variable>** to complete the variable declaration.

To reference a global variable, follow these steps:

1. If the global variable is used as part of the XSLT markup, type **$*variable_name***, where *variable_name* is the name of the variable you previously defined and want to use.
2. If the variable is used as part of the attribute in the output, type **{$*variable_name*}**, where *variable_name* is the name of the variable you previously defined and want to use.

Chapter 17

Working with Strings, Booleans, and Numbers

Previous chapters have discussed strings, Booleans, and numbers, but they haven't really discussed in detail how to manipulate these datatypes. This chapter fills that gap by explaining how to work with strings, Booleans, and numbers. Although the emphasis is on converting, sorting, extracting, and merging strings, you'll also learn how to how to format numbers and how to get the most out of Booleans.

Manipulating Strings

XSL Transformations (XSLT) and XML Path (XPath) define many functions for working with string values. You can use these functions to

- Convert numeric and Boolean values to strings
- Manage spaces within strings
- Sort and merge strings
- Extract substrings from strings
- Translate individual characters in strings

Converting Values to Strings

You use the `string()` function to convert selected values to strings. You can also use the `string()` function to convert parameter and variable values to strings.

Table 17-1 provides a summary of the string conversion rules for various types of values. As the table shows, Boolean values, integers, floats, special numeric values, and node sets are all converted in different ways.

Table 17-1. Value Conversion to Strings

Value Type	Conversion Description	Example
`Boolean`	Boolean values `true` and `false` are converted to the strings `"true"` and `"false"`, respectively.	`"true"`
`Integer`	Converted to a string representing the integer. The value won't have a decimal point or leading zeroes. If the integer is negative, it'll be preceded by a minus sign (`-`).	`"-252"`
`Floating point`	Converted to a string with at least one number before the decimal point and one number after the decimal point. If a number only has a fractional component, a zero is used to the left of the decimal point. This is only time a leading zero occurs before the decimal point.	`"0.5254245"`

`Special numeric values`	Positive zero, negative zero, positive infinity, negative infinity, and `NaN` ("not a number") are converted to string representations.	`0` becomes `"0"`
		`-0` becomes `"0"`
		`INF` becomes `"Infinity"`
		`-INF` becomes `"-Infinity"`
		`NaN` becomes `"NaN"`

`Node set`	Only the first node in a node set is converted to a string representation. Node order is determined by the order nodes are in the original document.	The first node is the node that appears prior to other nodes in the document.

Most of the time the XSLT processor will perform string conversions for you behind the scenes. For example, you can specify that you want to select the current node and output its contents like this:

```
<xsl:value-of select="." />
```

or you can explicitly convert the node's contents to a string like this:

```
<xsl:value-of select="string(.)" />
```

The `string( )` function can be useful when you're performing calculations and the result might not be a number. In this case, you might want to convert the result to a string before outputting it, such as:

```
<xsl:template name="CircleArea">
 <xsl:param name="circumference" />
 <xsl:param name="diameter" />
 <text>The area of the circle is: </text>
 <xsl:value-of select="string($circumference * $diameter)" />
</xsl:template>
```

Here, you convert the product of the `circumference` and `diameter` parameters to a string value.

To convert a value to a string, as part of a select attribute or within another function, type **string(*expression*)**, where *expression* is an XPath expression that returns a node set or an actual value that you want to convert to a string

Managing Spaces Within Strings

If you need to manage spaces within strings or the contents of a node, you'll find that `xsl:preserve-space` and `xsl:strip-space` are useful: `xsl:preserve-space` is a top-level element that specifies a list of elements for which whitespace should be preserved, while `xsl:strip-space` is a top-level element that specifies a list of elements for which whitespace should be removed.

The `xsl:preserve-space` and `xsl:strip-space` elements have nearly identical syntax. The basic form for `xsl:preserve-space` is:

```
<xsl:preserve-space elements="element1 element2 ... elementN" />
```

The basic form for `xsl:strip-space` is:

```
<xsl:strip-space elements="element1 element2 ... elementN" />
```

Both are always used as empty elements and their `elements` attribute is required.

Tip Technically, the value of the `elements` attribute for `xsl:preserve-space` and `xsl:strip-space` match element names as an XPath expression. With this in mind, you could specify `elements="*"` to match all element names.

The key thing to keep in mind when working with `xsl:preserve-space` and `xsl:strip-space` is that they don't preserve or strip all whitespace. Instead, they preserve or strip nonsignificant whitespace. Nonsignificant whitespace refers to whitespace that occurs in and around elements or is the only contents of an element's text node. In the following example, the nonsignificant whitespace for the data element is the spaces between the child elements `h` and `d`:

```
<document>
 <data>
  <h>Manufacturer</h> <d>Toshiba</d>
  <h>Inventory #</h> <d>459320</d>
  <h>Item</h> <d>3 1/2" Floppy Disk Drive</d>
  <h>Orders</h> <d>308</d>
 </data>
</document>
```

If you wanted to preserve the nonsignificant whitespace in the document to achieve output like this:

```
Manufacturer Toshiba
Inventory # 459320
Item 3 1/2" Floppy Disk Drive
Orders 308
```

you'd have to define the XSLT stylesheet so that nonsignificant whitespace is preserved for the data element. Here's an example:

```
<?xml version="1.0"?>
<xsl:stylesheet version="1.0"
 xmlns:xsl="http://www.w3.org/1999/XSL/Transform">

 <xsl:output method="text" />
 <xsl:preserve-space elements="data" />

 <xsl:template match="/">
 <xsl:for-each select="/document/data">
  <xsl:value-of select="." />
 </xsl:for-each>
 </xsl:template>

</xsl:stylesheet>
```

On the other hand, if the input data looked like this:

```
<document>
 <data>
  <h>Manufacturer:</h> <d>Toshiba</d>
  <h>Inventory #</h> <d>459320</d>
  <h>Item:</h> <d>3 1/2" Floppy Disk Drive</d>
  <h>Orders:</h> <d>308</d>
 </data>
</document>
```

and you wanted the output to look like this:

```
Manufacturer:Toshiba
Inventory #459320
Item:3 1/2" Floppy Disk Drive
Orders:308
```

you could ensure that the nonsignificant spaces weren't used by defining the stylesheet like this:

```
<?xml version="1.0"?>
<xsl:stylesheet version="1.0"
 xmlns:xsl="http://www.w3.org/1999/XSL/Transform">

 <xsl:output method="text" />
 <xsl:strip-space elements="data" />
```

(continued)

(continued)

```
 <xsl:template match="/">
 <xsl:for-each select="/document/data">
  <xsl:value-of select="." />
 </xsl:for-each>
 </xsl:template>

</xsl:stylesheet>
```

If you want to manage the use of nonsignificant whitespace, follow these steps:

1. As noted previously, define the `xsl:preserve-space` and `xsl:strip-space` elements at the top level of the stylesheet. They don't, however, need to immediately follow the opening `<xsl:stylesheet>` tag.
2. To preserve nonsignificant whitespace for an element or a group of elements, type **<xsl:preserve-space elements="*element1 element2 ... elementN*" />**, where *element1 element2 ... elementN* is a space-separated list of elements whose nonsignificant whitespace should be preserved. Or type **<xsl:preserve-space elements="*" />** to preserve nonsignificant whitespace for all elements.
3. To strip nonsignificant whitespace for an element or a group of elements, type **<xsl:strip-space elements="*element1 element2 ... elementN*" />**, where *element1 element2 ... elementN* is a space-separated list of elements whose nonsignificant whitespace should be stripped. Or type **<xsl:strip-space elements="*" />** to strip nonsignificant whitespace for all elements.

Note You can't specify the same list of elements to strip or preserve. The lists must be different.

Normalizing Space in Strings

Another useful structure for managing spaces within strings is the `normalize-space()` function. In XSLT a normalized string is similar to a token in XML Schema. This means that the `normalize-space()` function removes carriage returns, line feeds, tabs, leading spaces, and trailing spaces and replaces multiple occurrences of the space character with a single space anywhere they occur within the string.

To see how the `normalize-space()` function works, consider the following example stylesheet:

```
<?xml version="1.0"?>
<xsl:stylesheet version="1.0"
 xmlns:xsl="http://www.w3.org/1999/XSL/Transform">

 <xsl:output method="text" />
```

(continued)

(continued)

```
 <xsl:variable name="theString">
 <xsl:text>    This string
has
way
  too
  much
  whitespace.
 </xsl:text>
 </xsl:variable>

 <xsl:template match="/">
 <xsl:value-of select="normalize-space($theString)" />
 </xsl:template>

</xsl:stylesheet>
```

The output of this stylesheet is:

```
This string has way too much whitespace.
```

To normalize a string, as part of a select attribute or within another function, type **normalize-space(*expression*)**, where *expression* is an XPath expression that returns a node set or an actual value that you want to convert to a string and normalize.

Merging Values into a Single String

If you need to merge multiple values into a single string, you can do this using the `concat()` function. Any values that you merge that aren't strings are converted to strings as if you had processed them with the `string()` function.

The basic format of the `concat()` function is:

```
concat(value1, value2, ..., valueN)
```

where *`value1`*, *`value2`*, *`...`*, *`valueN`* are the values you want to concatenate.

Let's say you wanted to output a list of file names in the format filename.ext where the filename came from one variable and the extension came from a different variable. To get these values to output as a filename, you could specify:

```
<xsl:value-of select="concat($file_name,'.',$file_ext)" />
```

Thus, if the `file_name` variable has the value "data_source" and the `file_ext` variable has the value "xml", the output is the concatenated string:

```
data_source.xml
```

To merge string values, as part of a select attribute or within another function, type **concat(*value1*, *value2*, ..., *valueN*)**, where *value1*, *value2*, ..., *valueN* are the values you want to concatenate.

Examining and Manipulating String Contents

XSLT and XPath provide several functions you can use to examine the contents of strings. Table 17-2 provides a summary of the key functions.

Table 17-2. String Manipulation Functions

Function	Description	Syntax
`contains()`	Determines if the first string contains the second string. Returns true if the first string contains the second. Otherwise, returns false.	`contains(string1, string2)`
`string-length()`	Determines the number of characters in the referenced string. If no string is passed to the function, the function converts the context node to a string and returns the length of that string. Returns the number of characters in the string or context node.	`string-length(string?)`
`starts-with()`	Determines if the first string begins with the second string. Returns true if the first string starts with the second Otherwise, returns false.	`starts-with(string1, string2)`
`substring()`	Extracts a portion of a string. The function accepts three arguments: the string you want to work with, the position of the first character of the substring, and an optional number of characters from the position specified to return.	`substring(string, sub_position, num_chars?)`
`substring-after()`	Searches for a substring within a string and returns the characters that occur after the substring.	`substring-after(orig_string, search_string)`
`substring-before()`	Searches for a substring within a string and returns the characters that occur before the substring.	`substring-before(orig_string, search_string)`

Essentially, these utility functions examine an input string, which could be the contents of a node specified with an XPath expression, and do something with it, such as determining the string's length and displaying this to the output. To see how these functions work, consider the following input document:

```
<accounts>
 <customer>11285:William Stanek</customer>
 <customer>10487:William R. Stanek, Sr.</customer>
 <customer>09685:Robert W. Stanek</customer>
</accounts>
```

If you wanted to examine the contents of the `customer` element, you could work with this content in a number of ways. With `string-length()`, you could examine the number of characters in each `customer` element, such as:

```
 <xsl:variable name="newline">
<xsl:text>
</xsl:text>
 </xsl:variable>

<xsl:template match="/">
 <xsl:for-each select="customer">
 <xsl:text>String #</xsl:text>
 <xsl:value-of select="position()" />
 <xsl:text> has length: </xsl:text>
 <xsl:value-of select="string-length(.)" />
 <xsl:text>.</xsl:text>
 <xsl:value-of select="$newline" />
 </xsl:for-each>
</xsl:template>
```

The output would look like this:

```
String #1 has length: 21.
String #2 has length: 29.
String #3 has length: 23.
```

Using `starts-with()`, you could search for a particular value at the beginning of the element contents and then return the entire contents of the matching element. Here's an example:

```
<xsl:template match="/">
 <xsl:for-each select="customer">
 <xsl:value-of select="starts-with(., '10487')" />
 <xsl:text>.</xsl:text>
 <xsl:value-of select="$newline" />
 </xsl:for-each>
</xsl:template>
```

Using the previously defined input document, this template outputs:

```
10487:William R. Stanek, Sr.
```

If you want to see only account numbers, you could extract a substring from the element contents. Since the account number starts at position 1 and contains five characters, a template rule that extracted this information would look like this:

```
<xsl:template match="/">
 <xsl:for-each select="customer">
 <xsl:value-of select="substring(.,1,5)" />
 <xsl:text>.</xsl:text>
 <xsl:value-of select="$newline" />
 </xsl:for-each>
</xsl:template>
```

Now the output is:

```
11285
10487
09685
```

If you wanted only the account names instead of the account numbers, you could specify the substring that started in the sixth character position and then not specify the number of characters to return. Essentially, this declaration would say: return all characters after the fifth character in the string. The template rule to perform this task is:

```
<xsl:template match="/">
 <xsl:for-each select="customer">
 <xsl:value-of select="substring(.,6)" />
 <xsl:text>.</xsl:text>
 <xsl:value-of select="$newline" />
 </xsl:for-each>
</xsl:template>
```

The output is now:

```
William Stanek
William R. Stanek, Sr.
Robert W. Stanek
```

Because there's always another way of doing things in XSLT, you could have also used `substring-before()` and `substring-after()` to perform these tasks. Here, if you returned the substring before the first occurrence of :, you'd get the account number:

```
<xsl:template match="/">
 <xsl:for-each select="customer">
 <xsl:value-of select="substring-before(.,':')" />
 <xsl:text>.</xsl:text>
 <xsl:value-of select="$newline" />
 </xsl:for-each>
</xsl:template>
```

And if you returned the substring after the first occurrence of :, you'd get the account name:

```
<xsl:template match="/">
 <xsl:for-each select="customer">
 <xsl:value-of select="substring-after(.,':')" />
 <xsl:text>.</xsl:text>
 <xsl:value-of select="$newline" />
 </xsl:for-each>
</xsl:template>
```

To see how multiple string manipulation functions could be used together, consider the following example that implements a search and replace function using `contains()`, `substring-before()`, and `substring-after()`:

```
<xsl:stylesheet  xmlns:xsl="http://www.w3.org/1999/XSL/Transform"
 version="1.0">

 <xsl:output method="text" />

 <xsl:template match="/">
 <xsl:variable name="test">
  <xsl:call-template  name="search_replace_string">
  <xsl:with-param name="orig_string">
   <xsl:value-of select="customer" />
  </xsl:with-param>
  <xsl:with-param name="substring">
   <xsl:text>:</xsl:text>
  </xsl:with-param>
  <xsl:with-param name="replace_string">
   <xsl:text>:</xsl:text>
  </xsl:with-param>
  </xsl:call-template>
 </xsl:variable>
 <xsl:value-of select="$test" />
 </xsl:template>

 <xsl:template  name="search_replace_string">
 <xsl:param name="orig_string" />
 <xsl:param name="substring" />
 <xsl:param name="replace_string" select="''" />
 <xsl:variable name="beg_string">
  <xsl:choose>
  <xsl:when test="contains($orig_string, $substring)">
   <xsl:value-of
    select="substring-before($orig_string,$substring)"  />
  </xsl:when>
  <xsl:otherwise>
   <xsl:value-of select="$orig_string" />
  </xsl:otherwise>
  </xsl:choose>
 </xsl:variable>
 <xsl:variable name="mid_string">
  <xsl:choose>
  <xsl:when test="contains($orig_string, $substring)">
   <xsl:value-of select="$replace_string" />
  </xsl:when>
  <xsl:otherwise>
   <xsl:text></xsl:text>
  </xsl:otherwise>
  </xsl:choose>
 </xsl:variable>
```

(continued)

(continued)

```
 <xsl:variable name="end_string">
  <xsl:choose>
  <xsl:when test="contains($orig_string, $substring)">
  <xsl:choose>
   <xsl:when
    test="contains(substring-after($orig_string,$substring),
    $substring)">
   <xsl:call-template name="search_replace_string">
    <xsl:with-param name="orig_string">
     <xsl:value-of
      select="substring-after($orig_string,$substring)" />
    </xsl:with-param>
    <xsl:with-param name="substring">
     <xsl:value-of select="$substring" />
    </xsl:with-param>
    <xsl:with-param name="replace_string">
     <xsl:value-of select="$replace_string" />
    </xsl:with-param>
   </xsl:call-template>
   </xsl:when>
   <xsl:otherwise>
    <xsl:value-of
     select="substring-after($orig_string,$substring)" />
   </xsl:otherwise>
  </xsl:choose>
  </xsl:when>
  <xsl:otherwise>
   <xsl:text></xsl:text>
  </xsl:otherwise>
  </xsl:choose>
 </xsl:variable>
 <xsl:value-of
  select="concat($beg_string, $mid_string,$end_string)" />
 </xsl:template>

</xsl:stylesheet>
```

In this example, you define the element you want to search as the customer element, the substring you want to replace as "`:`", and the replacement text as a space. The result is a reformatting of the output. Instead of:

```
11285:William Stanek
10487:William R. Stanek, Sr.
09685:Robert W. Stanek
```

the output becomes:

```
11285 William Stanek
10487 William R. Stanek, Sr.
09685 Robert W. Stanek
```

The search and replace function allows you to search and replace any string value. For example, if you needed to replace occurrences of "`Robert W.`" with "`William R.`", you could have done this as well. You'd make those changes in the root template like this:

```
<xsl:template match="/">
<xsl:variable name="test">
 <xsl:call-template name="search_replace_string">
 <xsl:with-param name="orig_string">
  <xsl:value-of select="customer" />
 </xsl:with-param>
 <xsl:with-param name="substring">
  <xsl:text>Robert W.</xsl:text>
 </xsl:with-param>
 <xsl:with-param name="replace_string">
  <xsl:text>William R.</xsl:text>
 </xsl:with-param>
 </xsl:call-template>
</xsl:variable>
<xsl:value-of select="$test" />
</xsl:template>
```

Determining If a String Contains Another String

You use the `contains()` function to determine if a string contains another string. You can use the `contains()` function in your stylesheet by following these steps:

1. As part of a select attribute or within another function, type **contains(*string1*, *string2*)**, where *string1* is the string you want to examine and *string2* is the string you want to search for.
2. The function returns true if the first string contains the second. Otherwise, the function returns false.

Determining String Length

You use the `string-length()` function to determine the number of characters in the referenced string. You can use the `string-length()` function in your stylesheet by following these steps:

1. As part of a select attribute or within another function, type **string-length(*string*)**, where *string* is the string you want to examine.
2. The function returns the number of characters. If no string is passed to the function, the function converts the context node to a string and returns the length of that string.

Determining If a String Starts with Another String

You use the `starts-with()` function to determine if a string begins with another string. You can use the `starts-with()` function in your stylesheet by following these steps:

1. As part of a select attribute or within another function, type **starts-with(*string1*, *string2*)**, where *string1* is the string you want to examine and *string2* is the string you want to search for at the beginning of the first string.
2. The function returns true if the first string starts with the second. Otherwise, the function returns false.

Extracting a Substring

You use the `substring()` function to extract of portion of a string. You can use the `substring()` function in your stylesheet by following these steps:

1. As part of a select attribute or within another function, type **substring(*string*, *sub_position*, *num_chars?*)**, where *string* is the string you want to work with, *sub_position* is the position of the first character of the substring, and *num_chars* is the optional number of characters from the position specified to return.
2. The function returns the substring starting at the position specified to the end of the string or to the number of characters specified.

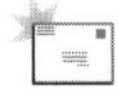

Note The position of the first character in a string is 1, which is different from many programming languages where the position of the first character in a string is 0.

Returning a Substring Before Another String

You use the `substring-before()` function to return the portion of a string that occurs before a specific substring. You can use the `substring-before()` function in your stylesheet by following these steps:

1. As part of a select attribute or within another function, type **substring-before(*orig_string*, *search_string*)**, where *orig_string* is the string you want to work with and *search_string* is the substring that you want to find within the original string.
2. The function returns the characters that occur after the specified substring. If the substring isn't found, an empty string is returned.

Returning a Substring After Another String

You use the `substring-after()` function to return the portion of a string that occurs after a specific substring. You can use the `substring-after()` function in your stylesheet by following these steps:

1. As part of a select attribute or within another function, type **substring-after(*orig_string*, *search_string*)**, where *orig_string* is the string you want to work with and *search_string* is the substring that you want to find within the original string.
2. The function returns the characters that occur after the specified substring. If the substring isn't found, an empty string is returned.

Translating Characters in Strings

Not only can you implement search and replace functions in XSLT, you can also convert individual characters in strings. The function you use to convert characters within strings is called `translate()`. This function has the basic form:

```
translate(input_string, chars_to_convert, output_chars)
```

where *`input_string`* is an actual string of the contents of a node specified with an XPath expression, *`chars_to_convert`* defines the characters in the input string that you want to convert, and *`output_chars`* defines the new character format.

Believe me, this makes much more sense when you see the `translate()` function in action. Consider the following example:

```
<xsl:value-of select="translate(. , 'abcdefghijklmnopqrstuvwxyz',
 'ABCDEFGHIJKLMNOPQRSTUVWXYZ')" />
```

This declaration says to use contents of the context node as the input string and convert any lowercase letters in those contents to an uppercase letter. Thus, if the input element looked like this:

```
<customer>10487:William R. Stanek, Sr.</customer>
```

The output would be:

```
10487:WILLIAM R. STANEK, SR.
```

Characters defined in the *`chars_to_convert`* string are compared on a character-by-character basis and matched to characters in the *`output_chars`* string. This means the character in the first position of the *`chars_to_convert`* string is matched to the first character in the *`output_chars`* string, the character in the second position of the *`chars_to_convert`* string is matched to the second character in the *`output_chars`* string, and so on.

Tip The value of characters in a specific position doesn't matter to the XSLT processor. The XSLT processor doesn't understand plain language as you and I do. If you had said to match "ABC" with "XYZ", the XSLT processor would have done this, meaning all capital A's in the input string would be translated to capital X's, capital B's to capital Y's, and capital C's to capital Z's.

If you want to translate characters on a character-by-character basis, the *`output_chars`* string should be as long as the *`chars_to_convert`* string. If the *`chars_to_convert`* string is longer than the *`output_chars`* string, there will be no translation values for some characters. As a result, the values will be omitted. Although this could cause problems in your translations, this behavior can also be useful. For example, if you wanted to remove punctuation marks (periods, colons, commas, and semicolons) from input, you could specify the following translation:

```
<xsl:value-of select="translate(., ';:.,', '')" />
```

This translation says to replace any occurrences of `;`, `:`, `.`, or `,` but doesn't provide a translation. As a result, the characters are omitted in the output string.

You use the `translation()` function in your stylesheet by following these steps:

1. As part of a select attribute or within another function, type **translate(*input_string*, *chars_to_convert*, *output_chars*)**, where *input_string* is an actual string of the contents of a node specified with an XPath expression, *chars_to_convert* defines the characters in the input string that you want to convert, and *output_chars* defines the new character format.
2. Characters are compared on a character-by-character basis. This means the character in the first position of the *chars_to_convert* string is matched to the first character in the *output_chars* string, the second character in the *chars_to_convert* string is matched to the second character in the *output_chars* string, and so on. If the *chars_to_convert* string is longer than the *output_chars* string, some characters will have no translation values.

Converting and Manipulating Boolean Values

XSLT and XPath define several functions that you can use to work with Boolean values. The main function you'll use is `boolean()`, which evaluates an expression and returns the result as a Boolean value, which is always either `true` or `false`. Consider the following example:

```
<xsl:value-of select="boolean($x > 5)" />
```

If the variable x is greater than 5, the output from the `boolean()` function is `true`. Otherwise, if x is less than or equal to 5, the result is `false`.

Note Note that XSLT processors convert the Boolean value (true or false) to a string for output. You don't need to explicitly call the `string()` function.

XSLT and XPath also include three utility functions that you can use to output Boolean values. These functions are

- **true()** Always returns the Boolean value `true`. You can use this during testing and development to test code branches and logic.
- **false()** Always returns the Boolean value `false`. You can use this during testing and development to test code branches and logic.
- **not()** Returns the negation of the expression. If the expression result isn't a Boolean value, it's converted to a `boolean()` value and then negated.

As stated, the `true()` and `false()` functions are best used during testing when you want to ensure that a branch of code is processed. For example, if you wanted to test the second `when` test in the following template:

```
<xsl:template match="item">
 <xsl:choose>
 <xsl:when test="stock/[@order='Y']">
 <p>Please order, stock number:
  <xsl:value-of select="@tracking_number" />
 </p>
 </xsl:when>
 <xsl:when test="stock/[@order='N']">
 <p>Item<xsl:value-of select="@tracking_number" />
  doesn't need to be re-stocked at this time.</p>
 </xsl:when>
 <xsl:otherwise>
 <p>INVALID ORDER INDICATOR FOR ITEM:
  <xsl:value-of select="@tracking_number" />
 </p>
 </xsl:otherwise>
 </xsl:choose>
</xsl:template>
```

you could replace the first `when` test with `false()` and the second `when` test with `true()`, like this:

```
<xsl:template match="item">
 <xsl:choose>
 <xsl:when test="false()">
 <p>Please order, stock number:
  <xsl:value-of select="@tracking_number" />
 </p>
 </xsl:when>
 <xsl:when test="true()">
 <p>Item<xsl:value-of select="@tracking_number" />
  doesn't need to be re-stocked at this time.</p>
 </xsl:when>
 <xsl:otherwise>
 <p>INVALID ORDER INDICATOR FOR ITEM:"
  <xsl:value-of select="@tracking_number" />
 </p>
 </xsl:otherwise>
 </xsl:choose>
</xsl:template>
```

Because the first `when` test evaluates to `false`, the contents of this test aren't processed. The contents of the second `when` test, however, are processed. Here, the test evaluates to `true`, which tells the processor to process the contents of this `when` test.

The `not()` function is useful when you want to convert the results of an expression to a Boolean value and then negate the results. In the following example, the value output is `false`:

```
<xsl:value-of select="not(true())" />
```

Here, you tell the processor to return the opposite of `true`, which means the output is the value `false`.

The `not()` function is useful when want to evaluate complex logical expressions, such as those that use a logical And or a logical Or. Table 17-3 provides an overview of how you can use logical And, logical Or, and the `not()` function.

Table 17-3. Using Logical Expressions

Operation	Operator	Example	Result
logical AND	`and`	(true and false)	false
logical OR	`or`	(true or false)	true
Not	`not()`	not(false)	true

Logical And tests whether the first and the second expression are true. Both expressions must be true for the logical And to evaluate to true. Logical Or, on the other hand, tests whether one of two expressions is true. Only one expression must be true for the logical Or to evaluate to true. If you wanted to return the opposite result of a Logical And or a Logical Or, you could use the `not()` function to do this, such as:

```
<xsl:value-of select="not($x and $y)" />
```

Using the true() Function

The `true()` function always returns the Boolean value `true`. To use the `true()` function in your stylesheet, as part of a select attribute or within another function, type **true()**.

Using the false() Function

The `false()` function always returns the Boolean value `false`. To use the `false()` function in your stylesheet, as part of a select attribute or within another function, type **false()**.

Using the not() Function

The `not()` function returns the negation of the expression passed as an argument. To use the `not()` function in your stylesheet, as part of a select attribute or within another function, type **not()**.

Working with Numeric Values

As with strings, XSLT and XPath define many functions you can use to work with numeric values. You can use these functions to

- Convert values to numbers
- Define formatting for numbers
- Round numbers
- Count the number of occurrences of something
- Total values

Converting Values to Numbers

You use the `number()` function to convert selected values to numbers. You can also use the `number()` function to convert parameter and variable values to numbers.

Table 17-4 provides a summary of the numeric conversion rules for various types of values. As the table shows, Boolean values, integers, floats, strings, and node sets are all converted in different ways.

Table 17-4. Value Conversion to Numbers

Value Type	Conversion Description	Example/Details
Boolean	Boolean values `true` and `false` are converted to the numbers 1 and 0, respectively.	1
Node set	The first node in a node set is converted to a string as if it were passed to the `string()` function and then the result is converted to a number as with any other string.	Converts only the contents of the first node in the node set
String	If the string contains only numeric values or a valid floating-point number that follows IEEE 754, the string is converted a floating-point value that's the nearest mathematical representation of the string. Otherwise, `NaN` is returned.	7.5425

Most of the time, the XSLT processor will perform number conversions for you behind the scenes. For example, you can specify that you want to output the product of `$x` and `$y`, which represent the variables `x` and `y` without having to explicitly convert the values to numbers, such as:

```
<xsl:value-of select="$x * $y" />
```

If `x` is "5" and `y` is "12", the result is 60, which is output as a string. You can also explicitly convert values to numbers, such as:

```
<xsl:value-of select="number(false())" />
```

Here, the output is 0, which is the numeric representation of false.

To convert a value to a number, as part of a select attribute or within another function, type **number(*expression*)**, where *expression* is an XPath expression that returns a node set or an actual value that you want to convert to a number.

Formatting Values as Numbers

XSLT and XPath define two structures that you can use to format values as numbers. These structures are

- **xsl:decimal-format** Can be used to set the default format for numbers and to define named alternative number formats
- **format-number()** Can be used to specify the exact formatting of a number and then represent it as string in the output

Techniques you can use to work with these structures are discussed in the sections that follow.

Specifying the Default and Alternative Number Formatting

You use the `xsl:decimal-format` element to define the default format for numbers as well as named formats that can be referenced from the `format-number()` function. This element is a top-level empty element that must always be used at the same level as your other top-level declarations in the stylesheet. The element has no required attributes.

Table 17-5 provides a summary of the optional attributes for the `xsl:decimal-format` element. If you don't set a format name for the element using the `name` attribute, the element is assumed to define the default number format for all output.

Table 17-5. Decimal Formatting Attributes

Attribute	Description	Example
`name`	Sets the name of the format, which can be referenced from the `format-number()` function.	`name="format-1"`
`decimal-separator`	Specifies the character used as the decimal point. With U.S. English, the decimal separator is a period (.), which is the default value. This character is used both in the format string and in the output.	`decimal-separator=","`
`grouping-separator`	Defines the character used as the thousands separator. With U.S. English, the grouping separator is a comma (,), which is the default value. This character is used both in the format string and in the output.	`grouping-separator="."`

(continued)

Table 17-5. *(continued)*

Attribute	Description	Example
`infinity`	Defines the string used to represent infinity. The string is only used in the output and has the default value `"Infinity"`.	`infinity="[out of bounds]"`
`minus-sign`	Defines the character used as the minus sign. This character is only used in the output and has a hyphen (`-`) as the default value.	`minus-sign="-"`
`NaN`	Defines the string used to represent `NaN`. The string is only used in the output and has the default value `"NaN"`.	`NaN="[not a number]"`
`percent`	Defines the character used as the percent sign. This character is only used in the output and has a hyphen (`-`) as the default value.	`percent="%"`
`per-mile`	Defines the character used as the per-mile (‰) sign. This character is used both in the format string and in the output. The default value is the Unicode per-mile character (`#x2030`).	`per-mile="‰"`
`digit`	Defines the character used in the format string to represent a digit. The default value is the number sign character (#).	`digit="#"`
`pattern-separator`	Defines the character used in the format string to separate the positive and negative subpatterns. The default value is the semi-colon character (`;`).	`pattern-separator=";"`

The following example defines a default number format and two alternative number formats:

```
<xsl:stylesheet
 xmlns:xsl="http://www.w3.org/1999/XSL/Transform"
 version="1.0">

 <xsl:output method="html" />

<xsl:decimal-format decimal-separator="." grouping-separator=","
 infinity="[out of bounds]" minus-sign="-"
 NaN="[not a number]" percent="%" per-mile="‰"
 digit="#" pattern-separator=";" />

<xsl:decimal-format name="US" decimal-separator="."
 grouping-separator="," />

<xsl:decimal-format name="UK" decimal-separator=","
 grouping-separator="." />
...
</xsl:stylesheet>
```

The default number format specifies values for all possible attributes that can be used with format and output strings. The US format specifies that the decimal separator is a period (.) and the grouping separator is a comma (,), meaning numbers look like this: 5,000,250 or 52.254. The U.K. format specifies that the decimal separator is a comma (,) and the grouping separator is a period (.), meaning numbers look like this: 5.000.250 or 52,254.

To define a default or alternative number format for a stylesheet, follow these steps:

1. At the top-level of the stylesheet, type **<xsl:decimal-format**.
2. If you want to specify a name for the number format, type **name="*format_name*"**, where *format_name* is the name you'll use to reference the number format.
3. Add any additional attributes that you want to define.
4. Complete the element declaration by typing **/>**.

Defining the Exact Number Format for Output

Whenever you want to format a number in a precise manner, you can use the `format-number()` function to handle the task. This function accepts an input value, which can be an XPath expression whose value can be converted to a number and which then formats the number using the format pattern string you define. The function also has an optional third argument that you can use to specify the name of a previously defined decimal format. If a named format isn't specified, the default decimal format is used.

The basic syntax of the `format-number()` function is:

```
format-number(number, format_pattern_string,
 named_decimal_format?)
```

where *`number`* is the number to be formatted (or an XPath expression whose value can be converted to a number), *`format_pattern_string`* is the actual format pattern string you want the processor to work with, and *`named_decimal_format`* is the optional designator for the named decimal format that you want to use to format the output.

Here's an example:

```
<xsl:value-of select="format-number(.,'$###,###.00')" />
```

This example says to format the contents of the current node using the pattern string `'$###,###.00'`. If the node contains the value "2568.5", the output is the string "$2,568.50".

Table 17-6 summarizes the characters you can use as part of the format pattern string. Keep in mind that you can customize the actual characters used for the decimal separator, grouping separator, and pattern separator. You change these characters by defining a different value in the decimal format that's applicable.

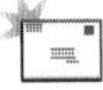

Note For a detailed example using the `format-number()` function, see the "Summing Values"section of this chapter.

Table 17-6. Characters for Format Pattern Strings

Pattern String Character	Description	Example
`#`	Represents a digit where trailing and leading zeroes aren't displayed. returns the string "51".	Formatting the value 51.0 with the pattern `"####.##"`
`0`	Represents a digit where a zero is always displayed if provided in the input string.	Formatting the value 51.0 with the pattern `"####.00"` returns the string "51.00".
`.`	Represents the decimal point. Formatting a number with too few digits to the left and right of the decimal point doesn't result in automatic truncation.	Formatting the value 51.05 with the pattern `"####.0"` returns the string "51.05".
`-`	Represents the minus sign. Typically, used as part of the negative number pattern.	The following pattern string sets a positive and negative number pattern: `"$###,###.##; -$###,###.##"`.
`,`	Represents the grouping separator.	Formatting 5005 with the pattern `"$#,###.##"` returns the string "$5,005".
`;`	Separates the positive and negative number pattern.	The following pattern string sets a positive and negative number pattern: `"0,000.00;-0,000.00"`.
`%`	Indicates that a number should be represented as a percentage. The value will be multiplied by 100 and then displayed as a percentage.	Formatting the value .51 with the pattern `"###.##%"` returns the string "51%".
`\u230`	Represents the per-mile (‰) sign. The value will be multiplied by 1000 and then displayed as a per-mile.	Formatting the value .51 with the pattern `"###.##\u230"` returns the string "510‰".

To format numbers, follow these steps:

1. As part of a select attribute or within another function, type **format(*expression*)**, where *expression* contains the number to be formatted.
2. Type **,'** (a comma followed by a single quotation mark).
3. Type the positive number pattern:
   - Type **$** if you want the value to represent dollars.
   - Type **0** for each digit that should always appear.

- Type **#** for each digit that should only appear when it isn't zero.
- Type **,** as the group separator character (or any other group separator character).
- Type **.** as the decimal separator character (or any other decimal separator character).
- Type **%** to multiply the number times 100 and display the result as a percentage.
- Type **\u230** to multiply the number times 1000 and display the result as a per-mile.

4. Optionally, if you want to specify the negative number pattern, type the number pattern separator **;** and then type **–** to indicate negative values. Use the same characters as specified in Step 2 to define the negative number pattern.
5. Type **'** (a single quotation mark) to complete the number pattern string.
6. Optionally, type the name of the previously defined number format to use. Be sure to enclose the name in single quotation marks.
7. Type **)** to close the function.

The result should look similar to the following:

```
<xsl:value-of
 select="format-number(expression,
 '$###,###.00-$###,###.00', 'format_name')" />
```

Rounding Numbers

XSLT and XPath provide three functions for rounding numbers. These functions are

- **round()** Rounds to the nearest integer. A value of .5 in the decimal position always results in the number being rounded up. For example, `round(1.5)` results in 2 being written to the output.
- **ceiling()** Rounds up to the nearest integer. Any decimal value greater than .0 is rounded up to the next nearest integer. For example, `ceiling(5.02)` results in 5 being written to the output.
- **floor()** Rounds down to the nearest integer. Any decimal value is rounded down to the next nearest integer. For example, `floor(1.92)` results in 1 being written to the output.

The usage of `round()`, `ceiling()`, and `floor()` is the same. You pass the function a value, which can be an XPath expression. If the value isn't a number, the value is converted to a number as if it had been processed by the `number()` function. If the result of the conversion can be represented as a number, the value is rounded as appropriate for the function. If the result of the conversion is `NaN`, the output of the function is `NaN`.

In the following example, you round the contents of the current context node:

```
<xsl:value-of select="round(.)" />
```

Using the round() Function

The `round()` function rounds to the nearest integer. To use the `round()` function in your stylesheet, as part of a select attribute or within another function, type **round(*number*)**, where *number* is the value that you want to round.

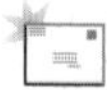

Note A value of .5 in the decimal position always results in the number being rounded up. For example, `round(100.5)` results in 101 being written to the output.

Using the ceiling() Function

The `ceiling()` function rounds up to the nearest integer. To use the `ceiling()` function in your stylesheet, as part of a select attribute or within another function, type **ceiling(*number*)**, where *number* is the value that you want to round up to the next nearest integer.

Note Any decimal value greater than .0 is rounded up to the next nearest integer. For example, `ceiling(9.15)` results in 10 being written to the output.

Using the floor() Function

The `floor()` function rounds down to the nearest integer. To use the `floor()` function in your stylesheet, as part of a select attribute or within another function, type **floor(*number*)**, where *number* is the value that you want to round down to the next nearest integer.

Note Any decimal value is rounded down to the next nearest integer. For example, `floor(8.2)` results in 8 being written to the output.

Summing Values

The most powerful yet simple function XSLT and XPath define has to be the `sum()` function. You use the `sum()` function to compute the total of all the numbers in a set of nodes. The single input argument for the function is the XPath expression that specifies the node set you want to total. If any node in the node set isn't a number, the value of the node is converted to a number as if it had been processed by the `number()` function. If the result of the conversion can be represented as a number, the value is added to the current total and the process continues. If the result of the conversion is `NaN`, the current total is set to `NaN` and the function returns this value.

The basic format of the `sum()` function is:

```
sum(expression)
```

where *`expression`* is an XPath expression that specifies the node set whose values you want to total. Following this, you could total the value of all the nodes in the current context like this:

```
<xsl:value-of select="sum(.)" />
```

To get a better understanding of how you can use the `sum()` function with other functions, consider the following input document:

```
<?xml version="1.0"?>
<report>
 <title>Annual Royalty Summary for 2001</title>
 <quarter sequence="01">
  <books-sold>8503</books-sold>
  <royalty-earned>5210</royalty-earned>
 </quarter>
 <quarter sequence="02">
  <books-sold>5008</books-sold>
  <royalty-earned>2543</royalty-earned>
 </quarter>
 <quarter sequence="03">
  <books-sold>12759</books-sold>
  <royalty-earned>8540.5</royalty-earned>
 </quarter>
 <quarter sequence="04">
  <books-sold>9567</books-sold>
  <royalty-earned>6410.25</royalty-earned>
 </quarter>
</report>
```

The document represents an annual royalty summary for a particular book. As you can see, book sales and royalty earned are totaled on a quarterly basis. If you wanted to process the input document to create a formatted output document, you might want to reformat the text to achieve output similar to the following:

```
 Quarter 1 - 8,503 books sold, $5,210.00 royalty earned.
```

The way you could do this is to examine the current sequence number and replace this value with the appropriate text designator, such as `"Quarter 1"`. To do this, you'd have to define a set of elements in the XSLT stylesheet that contained the replacement values, such as:

```
<period sequence="01">Quarter 1</period>
<period sequence="02">Quarter 2</period>
<period sequence="03">Quarter 3</period>
<period sequence="04">Quarter 4</period>
```

Then you could insert these values as appropriate in the output document using a value-of select expression like this:

```
<xsl:value-of
 select="document('')/*/period[@sequence=current()/@sequence]"  />
```

Here, you specify that you want to select the `sequence` attribute of `period` elements in the current document as specified by `document('')`, which refers to the XSLT stylesheet itself, and replace `@sequence=current()` (meaning the current value of the sequence attribute in the current context node) with the contents of the element that has the matching sequence. If the current context node is the quarter element and the sequence value of the current node is "01", the replacement value is `"Quarter 1"`.

Tip `document('')/*/period[@sequence=current()/@sequence]` may be a very complex expression, but it's still a basic predicate expression that follows the form `path[predicate]`, where *`path`* is the location path to the node that contains the desired subset of nodes you want to work with and *`predicate`* is the predicate expression that defines your filter for this set of nodes.

After you obtain the quarter designator, you can reformat the number of books sold and royalty earned values using the `number-format()` function. If you want to reformat the royalty earned for the current node in the node set, you could specify:

```
<xsl:value-of  select="format-number(royalty-earned,
 '$###,###.00')"  />
```

If you wanted to total all the royalty amounts and reformat the result, you could specify:

```
<xsl:value-of  select="format-number(sum(//royalty-
 earned),'$###,###.00')"  />
```

When you put all this together in a stylesheet, you'll end up with an .xsl file that looks like this:

```
<?xml  version="1.0"  ?>
<xsl:stylesheet  version="1.0"
 xmlns:xsl="http://www.w3.org/1999/XSL/Transform">

 <xsl:output  method="text"  />

 <xsl:variable  name="newline">
<xsl:text>
</xsl:text>
 </xsl:variable>
```

(continued)

(continued)

```
 <period sequence="01">Quarter 1</period>
 <period sequence="02">Quarter 2</period>
 <period sequence="03">Quarter 3</period>
 <period sequence="04">Quarter 4</period>

 <xsl:template match="/">

 <xsl:value-of select="/report/title" />
  <xsl:text>================================</xsl:text>
 <xsl:value-of select="$newline" />
 <xsl:value-of select="$newline" />

 <xsl:for-each select="report/quarter">
  <xsl:text> </xsl:text>
  <xsl:value-of
   select="document('')/*/period[@sequence=current()/@sequence]" />
  <xsl:text> - </xsl:text>
  <xsl:value-of select="format-number(books-sold, '###,###')" />
  <xsl:text> books sold, </xsl:text>
  <xsl:value-of select="format-number(royalty-earned,
   '$###,###.00')" />
  <xsl:text> royalty earned.</xsl:text>
  <xsl:value-of select="$newline" />
  <xsl:value-of select="$newline" />
 </xsl:for-each>
 <xsl:text> Annual Totals: </xsl:text>
  <xsl:value-of select="$newline" />
  <xsl:value-of select="$newline" />
 <xsl:value-of select="format-number(sum(//books-sold),
  '###,###')"/>
 <xsl:text> books sold, </xsl:text>
 <xsl:value-of
  select="format-number(sum(//royalty-earned),'$###,###.00')" />
 <xsl:text> royalty earned. </xsl:text>
 </xsl:template>

</xsl:stylesheet>
```

Based on this stylesheet and the previously specified input document, the output would look like this:

```
Annual Royalty Summary for 2001
===============================

 Quarter 1 - 8,503 books sold, $5,210.00 royalty earned.
 Quarter 2 - 5,008 books sold, $2,543.00 royalty earned.
 Quarter 3 - 12,759 books sold, $8,540.50 royalty earned.
 Quarter 4 - 9,567 books sold, $6,410.25 royalty earned.

 Annual Totals: 35,837 books sold, $22,703.75 royalty earned.
```

You can use the `sum()` function in your stylesheet by following these steps:

1. As part of a select attribute or within another function, type **sum(*expression*)**, where *expression* is an XPath expression that specifies the node set whose values you want to total.
2. The result is the total of the values in the specified nodes.

Note If any node in the node set isn't a number, the value of the node is converted to a number as if it had been processed by the `number()` function. If the result can't be represented as a number, the total is set to `NaN` and the function returns this value.

Chapter 18

Restructuring Input Documents and Manipulating Document Subsets

This chapter takes a detailed look at techniques you can use to work with document structures. As you'll learn, XSL Transformations (XSLT) and XML Path (XPath) define many elements and functions that you can use to manipulate document sets and subsets. You can, for example, define multiple input documents that should be merged into a single output document. You can also copy selected parts of documents and write the selections to the output.

Combining and Merging Documents

Of all the functions that XSLT and XPath define, the one function that really stands out is the `document()` function. The `document()` function is the one universal utility—the "Holy Grail"—that you'll find in all of XSLT. Simply put, you use the `document()` function to specify an external resource that you want to process in the stylesheet, and this allows you to use a stylesheet to merge multiple documents and manipulate the contents of those documents just as you do the contents of a single document.

Document Merging Essentials

The `document()` function has the basic form:

```
document(resource)
```

where *`resource`* specifies the Uniform Resource Identifier (URI) path to the resource file you want to work with. You can also specify the node set within the resource file using the form:

```
document(resource/node-set)
```

such as:

```
document(order1115-0001.xml/purchase_order)
```

The second form is the more typical usage.

To see how you can merge documents, consider the following example:

```
<?xml version="1.0" ?>

<purchase_order>
 <customer>
  <account_id>10-487</account_id>
  <name>
  <first> William </first>
  <mi> R </mi>
  <last> Stanek </last>
  </name>
 </customer>
 <inventory>
 <item tracking_number="459320" manufacturer="Toshiba">
  <item_type>3 1/2" Floppy Disk Drive</item_type>
  <description>Standard 3 1/2" floppy drive</description>
  <purchase quantity="50" unit_price="59.95" />
 </item>
 <item tracking_number="459378" manufacturer="BASF">
  <item_type>3 1/2" Floppy Disks 10-pack</item_type>
  <description>Standard 3 1/2" floppy disks</description>
  <purchase quantity="20" unit_price="7.95" />
 </item>
 </inventory>
</purchase_order>
```

Here, you've defined a purchase order in terms of a customer and the inventory items the customer is purchasing. If you had dozens or hundreds of such documents that you wanted to process, you could create a master document that referenced all the purchase orders that you wanted to work with and then use the `document()` function to process them.

The master document might look like this:

```
<master_doc>
 <title>Daily Purchase: November 15, 2001</title>
 <order filename="order1115-0001.xml" />
 <order filename="order1115-0002.xml" />
 <order filename="order1115-0003.xml" />
 <order filename="order1115-0004.xml" />
 <order filename="order1115-0005.xml" />
 <order filename="order1115-0006.xml" />
 <order filename="order1115-0007.xml" />
 <order filename="order1115-0008.xml" />
 <order filename="order1115-0009.xml" />
 <order filename="order1115-0010.xml" />
</master_doc>
```

You could then create a template rule within your stylesheet that examines the contents of each file in turn. Basically, you'd define an `xsl:for-each` element that selected the `master_doc/order` element in the master document and then called the `document()` function. The basic outline for this stylesheet would look like this:

```
<?xml version="1.0"?>
<xsl:stylesheet version="1.0"
 xmlns:xsl="http://www.w3.org/1999/XSL/Transform">

 <xsl:template match="/">
 <xsl:for-each select="/master_doc/order">
  <xsl:apply-templates
   select="document(@filename)/purchase_order" />
 </xsl:for-each>
 </xsl:template>

 <xsl:template match="purchase_order">
 ...
 </xsl:template>

</xsl:stylesheet>
```

Here, the `document()` function extracts the `filename` attribute for the `order` element and uses this value to set the URI path. Afterward, the function call specifies that the node set you want to work with is `/purchase_order`. The result is that the apply-templates selection is interpreted as:

- `order1115-0001.xml/purchase_order` on the first pass
- `order1115-0002.xml/purchase_order` on the second pass
- `order1115-0003.xml/purchase_order` on the third pass
- ...
- `order1115-0010.xml/purchase_order` on the tenth and final pass

As a result, the purchase_order template rule is called with the content node set defined as the contents of each document in turn. The really good news is that once you have a node set, you can work with it just as you do other node sets.

A key thing to note with the `document()` function is that you don't need to extract the entire contents of files. You can just as easily specify that you want to work with a subset of the document. To do this, simply specify the URI/node-set path that represents the node set that you want to work with. For example, with the previous documents, you could have processed only `customer` and `inventory` elements separately. Here's an example:

```
<?xml version="1.0" ?>
<xsl:stylesheet version="1.0"
 xmlns:xsl="http://www.w3.org/1999/XSL/Transform">
```

(continued)

(continued)

```
 <xsl:template match="/">
 <xsl:for-each select="/master_doc/order">
  <xsl:apply-templates
   select="document(@filename)/purchase_order/customer" />
 </xsl:for-each>

 <xsl:for-each select="/master_doc/order">
  <xsl:apply-templates
   select="document(@filename)/purchase_order/inventory" />
 </xsl:for-each>
 </xsl:template>

 <xsl:template match="purchase_order">
 ...
 </xsl:template>

</xsl:stylesheet>
```

Using Base Paths with the document() Function

The `document()` function has an additional form that you can use if you want to specify a base URI path to work with and then specify relative paths for the remaining resources. Here, you use the `document()` function with two arguments:

```
document(baseURI, resource)
```

where *baseURI* is the base URI path that you want to use and *resource* references the relative path to the resource that you want to work with. The relative path can include an XPath expression that specifies the node set within the resource as well.

To see how this additional form of the `document()` function works, let's continue the previous example where we want to merge multiple documents and then work with their contents. The master document could have been defined to specify the absolute path to the documents you wanted to work with, such as:

```
<master_doc>
 <title>Daily Purchase: November 15, 2001</title>
 <order filename="http://www.microsoft.com/data/
  order1115-0001.xml" />
 <order filename="http://www.microsoft.com/data/
  order1115-0002.xml" />
 <order filename="http://www.microsoft.com/data/
  order1115-0003.xml" />
 <order filename="http://www.microsoft.com/data/
  order1115-0004.xml" />
 <order filename="http://www.microsoft.com/data/
  order1115-0005.xml" />
 <order filename="http://www.microsoft.com/data/
  order1115-0006.xml" />
```

(continued)

(continued)

```
 <order filename="http://www.microsoft.com/data/
  order1115-0007.xml" />
 <order filename="http://www.microsoft.com/data/
  order1115-0008.xml" />
 <order filename="http://www.microsoft.com/data/
  order1115-0009.xml" />
 <order filename="http://www.microsoft.com/data/
  order1115-0010.xml" />
</master_doc>
```

More commonly, however, you might want to specify a base location for the documents and then use relative URLs, such as:

```
<master_doc>
 <title>Daily Purchase: November 15, 2001</title>
 <base_loc location="http://www.microsoft.com/data/" />
 <order filename="order1115-0001.xml" />
 <order filename="order1115-0002.xml" />
 <order filename="order1115-0003.xml" />
 <order filename="order1115-0004.xml" />
 <order filename="order1115-0005.xml" />
 <order filename="order1115-0006.xml" />
 <order filename="order1115-0007.xml" />
 <order filename="order1115-0008.xml" />
 <order filename="order1115-0009.xml" />
 <order filename="order1115-0010.xml" />
</master_doc>
```

If there's a base location referenced in the master document, you could reference this value when calling the `document()` function. Here's an example:

```
<?xml version="1.0"?>
<xsl:stylesheet version="1.0" xmlns:xsl="http://www.w3.org/
 1999/XSL/Transform">

 <xsl:template match="/">

 <xsl:for-each select="/master_doc/order">
  <xsl:apply-templates select="document(/master_doc/
   base_loc/@location, @filename)/purchase_order" />

 </xsl:for-each>
 </xsl:template>

 <xsl:template match="purchase_order">
 ...
 </xsl:template>

</xsl:stylesheet>
```

In this example you obtain the base URI by obtaining the value of the location attribute in the master document's `base_loc` element.

Using the document() Function To Process the Stylesheet Itself

You can use the `document()` function to process elements declared in the XSLT stylesheet using the form:

```
document('')
```

In the "Summing Values" section of Chapter 17, "Working with Strings, Booleans, and Numbers," you saw an example of this reference. There, an input document was defined like this:

```
<?xml version="1.0"?>
<report>
 <title>Annual Royalty Summary for 2001</title>
 <quarter sequence="01">
  <books-sold>8503</books-sold>
  <royalty-earned>5210</royalty-earned>
 </quarter>
 <quarter sequence="02">
  <books-sold>5008</books-sold>
  <royalty-earned>2543</royalty-earned>
 </quarter>
 <quarter sequence="03">
  <books-sold>12759</books-sold>
  <royalty-earned>8540.5</royalty-earned>
 </quarter>
 <quarter sequence="04">
  <books-sold>9567</books-sold>
  <royalty-earned>6410.25</royalty-earned>
 </quarter>
</report>
```

and you needed to define elements in the stylesheet to act as translation values for the sequence attributes that the input document declared. These elements were defined as:

```
<period sequence="01">Quarter 1</period>
<period sequence="02">Quarter 2</period>
<period sequence="03">Quarter 3</period>
<period sequence="04">Quarter 4</period>
```

You then used an empty path reference for the `document()` function to allow the elements to be processed. The reference looked like this:

```
<xsl:value-of
 select="document('')/*/period[@sequence=current()/@sequence]" />
```

If you used this declaration in a minimal stylesheet like this:

```
<?xml version="1.0" ?>
<xsl:stylesheet version="1.0"
 xmlns:xsl="http://www.w3.org/1999/XSL/Transform">

 <xsl:output method="text" />

 <period sequence="01">Quarter 1</period>
 <period sequence="02">Quarter 2</period>
 <period sequence="03">Quarter 3</period>
 <period sequence="04">Quarter 4</period>

 <xsl:template match="/">
 <xsl:for-each select="report/quarter">
  <xsl:value-of
   select="document('')/*/period[@sequence=current()/@sequence]" />
  <xsl:text>
</xsl:text>
 </xsl:for-each>
 </xsl:template>

</xsl:stylesheet>
```

the output of processing the input document is:

```
Quarter 1
Quarter 2
Quarter 3
Quarter 4
```

Here, the sequence values in the input document are replaced with the contents of the `period` elements defined in the stylesheet.

Declaring the document() Function in a Stylesheet

Now that you know a bit about the `document()` function, you're probably ready to use it in your own stylesheets. To do that, follow these steps:

1. As part of a select attribute or within another function, type **document(*resource*)** or **document(*baseURI resource*)**, where *baseURI* is the base URI path that you want to use and *resource* references the relative path to the resource that you want to work with. The relative path can include an XPath expression that specifies the node set within the resource as well.
2. The function returns the node set within the specified document that you referenced.

Manipulating Document Structures

XSLT and XPath define many additional constructs that you can use to manipulate document structures. The key constructs are

- `xsl:copy`
- `xsl:copy-of`
- `xsl:element`
- `xsl:attribute`
- `xsl:attribute-set`

Techniques you can use to work with these elements are discussed in the following sections.

Creating Copies of Node Sets

The `xsl:copy` element copies the current node and its namespace nodes to the output tree. It doesn't copy attribute nodes or any text nodes of the current node. You can think of this as a shallow copy. To see how this works, consider the following XSLT stylesheet that makes a copy of all the elements in the input document:

```
<xsl:stylesheet version="1.0"
  xmlns:xsl="http://www.w3.org/1999/XSL/Transform">

 <xsl:output method="xml" />

 <xsl:template match="*">
 <xsl:copy>
  <xsl:apply-templates />
 </xsl:copy>
 </xsl:template>

</xsl:stylesheet>
```

If this is the input document:

```
<?xml version="1.0" ?>
<inventory>
 <item tracking_number="459320" manufacturer="Toshiba">
  <item_type>3 1/2" Floppy Disk Drive</item_type>
  <description>Standard 3 1/2" floppy drive</description>
  <stock in_stock="750" orders_for="200" net_units="550"
   order="N" />
 </item>
 <item tracking_number="459323" manufacturer="Not listed">
  <item_type>3 1/2" Floppy Disk Drive</item_type>
  <description>Standard 3 1/2" floppy drive</description>
  <stock in_stock="50" orders_for="200" net_units="-150"
   order="Y" />
 </item>
```

(continued)

(continued)

```
  <item tracking_number="459780" manufacturer="Toshiba">
   <item_type>5 1/4" Floppy Disk Drive</item_type>
   <description>Standard 5 1/4" floppy drive</description>
   <stock in_stock="250" orders_for="200" net_units="50"
    order="Y" />
  </item>
  <item tracking_number="459789" manufacturer="Not listed">
   <item_type>5 1/4" Floppy Disk Drive</item_type>
   <description>Standard 5 1/4" floppy drive</description>
   <stock in_stock="0" orders_for="200" net_units="-200"
    order="Y" />
  </item>
</inventory>
```

the resulting output document looks like this:

```
<?xml version="1.0" encoding="UTF-8"?>
<inventory>
 <item>
  <item_type>3 1/2" Floppy Disk Drive</item_type>
  <description>Standard 3 1/2" floppy drive</description>
  <stock />
 </item>
 <item>
  <item_type>3 1/2" Floppy Disk Drive</item_type>
  <description>Standard 3 1/2" floppy drive</description>
  <stock />
 </item>
 <item>
  <item_type>5 1/4" Floppy Disk Drive</item_type>
  <description>Standard 5 1/4" floppy drive</description>
  <stock />
 </item>
 <item>
  <item_type>5 1/4" Floppy Disk Drive</item_type>
  <description>Standard 5 1/4" floppy drive</description>
  <stock />
 </item>
</inventory>
```

Essentially, the document is stripped of all nodes except for element and namespace nodes. The `xsl:copy` element has an optional attribute called `use-attribute-sets` that allows you to define a list of one or more attribute sets that the `xsl:copy` element should use to add attributes to the selected output elements. If you used this attribute with the previously defined stylesheet, you'd have to copy elements individually and then apply the appropriate attribute set to the element. However, it would probably be easier to just use the `xsl:copy-of` element to perform this task. The `xsl:copy-of` element copies a selected node and all its associated nodes to the output tree.

The `select` attribute is the only attribute that you can use with `xsl:copy-of` element. `select` is a required attribute that defines the XPath expression that you want to match. This means that if you defined the following template for the same input document:

```
<xsl:stylesheet version="1.0"
 xmlns:xsl="http://www.w3.org/1999/XSL/Transform">

 <xsl:output method="xml" />
 <xsl:template match=" /">
  <new_root>
   <xsl:copy-of select="item">
  </new_root>
 </xsl:template>

</xsl:stylesheet>
```

the resulting output would look like this:

```
<?xml version="1.0" encoding="UTF-8"?>
<new_root>
 <item tracking_number="459320" manufacturer="Toshiba">
  <item_type>3 1/2" Floppy Disk Drive</item_type>
  <description>Standard 3 1/2" floppy drive</description>
  <stock in_stock="750" orders_for="200" net_units="550"
   order="N" />
 </item>
 <item tracking_number="459323" manufacturer="Not listed">
  <item_type>3 1/2" Floppy Disk Drive</item_type>
  <description>Standard 3 1/2" floppy drive</description>
  <stock in_stock="50" orders_for="200" net_units="-150"
   order="Y" />
 </item>
 <item tracking_number="459780" manufacturer="Toshiba">
  <item_type>5 1/4" Floppy Disk Drive</item_type>
  <description>Standard 5 1/4" floppy drive</description>
  <stock in_stock="250" orders_for="200" net_units="50"
   order="Y" />
 </item>
 <item tracking_number="459789" manufacturer="Not listed">
  <item_type>5 1/4" Floppy Disk Drive</item_type>
  <description>Standard 5 1/4" floppy drive</description>
  <stock in_stock="0" orders_for="200" net_units="-200"
   order="Y" />
 </item>
</new_root>
```

To perform a shallow copy of a node set, follow these steps:

1. Type **<xsl:copy>**.
2. Type **<xsl:apply-templates select="*expression*" />**, where *expression* identifies the node that you want to copy.

3. Type **</xsl:copy>**.
4. The contents of the specified node and any child element nodes it contains are copied to the output tree. Although copies are also made of namespace nodes, attribute, text, comment, and processing-instruction nodes aren't copied.

To perform a deep copy of a node set, follow these steps:

1. Type **<xsl:copy-of select="*expression*" />**, where *expression* identifies the node that you want to copy in its entirety.
2. The contents of the specified node and all child nodes it contains are copied to the output tree.

Generating Elements and Attributes in the Output

Anytime you want to generate elements or attributes in an output document, you'll use `xsl:element`, `xsl:attribute`, and `xsl:attribute-set` to handle the task.

Using xsl:element

The three attributes of `xsl:element` are:

- **name** A required attribute that sets the name of the element you want to generate.
- **namespace** An optional attribute that sets the namespace for the element.
- **use-attribute-sets** An optional attribute that defines a list of one or more attribute sets that should be used with elements of this type. Each attribute set name must be separated with a space.

You'll often use `xsl:element` to define a new name for an existing element or to extract data from multiple sources and put it into a single element. To see how this works, consider the following example:

```
<item_type>3 1/2" Floppy Disk Drive</item_type>
<description>Standard 3 1/2" floppy drive</description>
<stock in_stock="50" orders_for="200" net_units="-150"
 order="Y" />
```

Here we have three separate elements definitions. If you wanted to create a single element that contained all this data, you could specify:

```
<xsl:template match="item | description | stock">
 <xsl:element name="data">
  <xsl:value-of select".|@*" />
  <xsl:text>;</xsl:text>
 </xsl:element>
</xsl:template>
```

The output is now formatted as an element with a list of values separated by semicolons:

```
<data>3 1/2" Floppy Disk Drive;Standard 3 1/2" floppy drive;
 50;200;-150;Y</data>
```

One of the most common uses of `xsl:element` is to convert all attributes in an input document to elements in an output document. A stylesheet that handles this task looks like this:

```
<?xml version="1.0"?>
<xsl:stylesheet version="1.0"
 xmlns:xsl="http://www.w3.org/1999/XSL/Transform">

 <xsl:output method="xml" />

 <xsl:template match="*">
 <xsl:element name="{name()}">
  <xsl:for-each select="@*">
   <xsl:element name="{name()}">
    <xsl:value-of select="." />
   </xsl:element>
  </xsl:for-each>
  <xsl:apply-templates select="*|text()" />
 </xsl:element>
 </xsl:template>

</xsl:stylesheet>
```

This stylesheet processes every element in the input document. Each element in the input document is examined in turn. If the element has attributes, an element with the same name as the attribute is created with its value set to the attribute's current value. After processing the element's attributes, the stylesheet processes any child or text nodes that the element contains. Following this, if the input document looked like this:

```
<?xml version="1.0" ?>
<inventory>
 <item tracking_number="459320" manufacturer="Toshiba">
  <item_type>3 1/2" Floppy Disk Drive</item_type>
  <description>Standard 3 1/2" floppy drive</description>
  <stock in_stock="750" orders_for="200" net_units="550"
   order="N" />
 </item>
</inventory>
```

the output using the stylesheet would look similar to this:

```
<?xml version="1.0" encoding="UTF-8"?>
<inventory>
 <item>
  <tracking_number>459320</tracking_number>
  <manufacturer>Toshiba</manufacturer>
  <item_type>3 1/2" Floppy Disk Drive</item_type>
  <description>Standard 3 1/2" floppy drive</description>
  <stock>
   <in_stock>750</in_stock>
   <orders_for>200</orders_for>
   <net_units>550</net_units>
   <order>N</order>
  </stock>
 </item>
</inventory>
```

To generate an element in the output, complete the following steps:

1. In the template rule that you want to use to output the element, type **<xsl:element name="*element_name*"**, where *element_name* is the actual name of the element you want to create.
2. Optionally, type **namespace="*namespace*"**, where *namespace* references the element's namespace prefix.
3. Optionally, type **use-attribute-sets="*attribsSet*"**, where *attribsSet* is a space-separated list of one or more attribute sets that should be used with elements of this type.
4. As necessary, enter any declarations that set the element's contents.
5. Type **</xsl:element>**.

The result should look similar to the following:

```
<xsl:element name="element_name">
...
</xsl:element>
```

Using xsl:attribute-set and xsl:attribute

You use `xsl:attribute-set` to define a set of attributes that you want to add to elements that you're generating. The basic form of an attribute set is:

```
<xsl:attribute-set name="attribute_set_name">
 <xsl:attribute name="attribute1_name">value1</xsl:attribute>
 <xsl:attribute name="attribute2_name">value2</xsl:attribute>
 ...
 <xsl:attribute name="attributeN_name">valueN</xsl:attribute>
</xsl:attribute-set>
```

where *`attribute_set_name`* is the name of the attribute set; *`attribute1_name`*, *`attribute2_name`*, `...`, and *`attributeN_name`* are the names of the attributes you want to define; and *value1*, *value2*, *...*, *valueN* are the values for those attributes.

The basic form can be extended:

- If you want to associate another attribute set with the current attribute set, you can set the optional `use-attribute-sets` attribute. The value for this attribute is the name of the attribute set to use.
- If you need to define a namespace for the attributes, you can set the optional namespace attribute of the `xsl:attribute` element. The value of this attribute is the name you want to use.

Generating attributes is useful when you're defining new elements with fixed attribute values. For example, if you had the following input:

```
<stock>
 <stock_year>2001</stock_year>
 <company>Microsoft</company>
 <stock_for>2001</stock_for>
</stock>
```

and wanted to create output structured like this:

```
<stock stock="2001" company="Microsoft" stock_for="2001" />
```

you could define an attribute set like this:

```
<xsl:attribute-set name="stockAttribs">
  <xsl:attribute name="stock_year">2001</xsl:attribute>
  <xsl:attribute name="company">Microsoft</xsl:attribute>
  <xsl:attribute name="stock_for">2001</xsl:attribute>
</xsl:attribute-set>
```

You could then generate an element that contained these fixed value attributes, like this:

```
<xsl:element name="stock" use-attribute-set="stockAttribs" />
```

Of course, this technique only works when there are fixed values that you want to use. If the values aren't fixed, however, you'll want to generate the attributes as the elements are being processed. For example, if the typical `stock` element looked like this:

```
<stock>
  <in_stock>750</in_stock>
  <orders_for>200</orders_for>
  <net_units>550</net_units>
  <order>N</order>
</stock>
```

and you wanted to create output structured like this:

```
<stock stock="750" orders_for="200" net_units="550" order="N" />
```

you could define a template rule to transform the original element set like this:

```
<xsl:template match="stock">
 <xsl:element name="stock">
 <xsl:for-each select="*">
  <xsl:attribute name="{name()}">
  <xsl:value-of select="." />
  </xsl:attribute>
 </xsl:for-each>
 </xsl:element>
</xsl:template>
```

This template creates a new element called `stock` and processes every child element of the original `stock` element, transforming them into attributes. Each child element is created as a like-named attribute with its value set to the current value of the child element.

To define an attribute set, complete the following steps:

1. At the top-level of the stylesheet, type **<xsl:attribute-set name="*attribute_set_name*">**, where *attribute_set_name* is the actual name of the attribute set.
2. Type **<xsl:attribute name="*attribute_name*">**, where *attribute_name* sets the name of the attribute you're defining.
3. As necessary, enter any declarations that set the attribute's contents.
4. Type **</xsl:attribute>**.
5. Repeat Steps 2-4 to define other attributes for this attribute set.
6. Type **</xsl:attribute-set>** to complete the attribute set definition.

To generate individual attributes as part of an element you're defining, follow these steps:

1. In the template rule that you want to use to output the element, type **<xsl:element name="*element_name*"**, where *element_name* is the actual name of the element you want to create.
2. Optionally, type **namespace="*namespace*"**, where *namespace* references the element's namespace prefix.
3. As necessary, enter any declarations that set the element's contents.
4. Type **<xsl:attribute name="*attribute_name*">**, where *attribute_name* sets the name of the attribute you're defining.
5. As necessary, enter any declarations that set the attribute's contents.
6. Type **</xsl:attribute>**.
7. Repeat Steps 4-6 to define other attributes for this attribute set.
8. As necessary, enter any declarations that complete the element's contents.
9. Type **</xsl:element>**.

The result should look similar to the following:

```
<xsl:element name="element_name">
  ...
 <xsl:attribute name="{name()}">
   ...
 </xsl:attribute>
  ...
</xsl:element>
```

Sorting Document Structures

So far this chapter has looked at ways you can manipulate document structures and perform various tasks. Up until now, you've always worked with structures in the order in which they were defined in the original input document and used this selection order to determine what the output looked like. Earlier in the book, however, I promised you that you could use XSLT and XPath to perform many advanced tasks, including sorting alphabetically and numerically. Now it's time to discuss how sorting works.

Sorting Essentials

The XSLT structure you use to sort nodes is `xsl:sort`. The `xsl:sort` element has several attributes that you can use. These attributes are

- **select** An XPath expression that defines the node set you want to sort. The selection can include any type of node, not just element nodes. This means you could sort by attribute values or by the values of other node types.
- **data-type** Sets the sort type. Valid values include `data-type="text"` for alphabetic sorts and `data-type="number"` for numeric sorts.
- **order** Sets the sort order as either ascending or descending. The default order is `order="ascending"`.
- **case-order** Sets the letter case sort order. By default, the letter case isn't used to determine the order of the sort. This means an uppercase A and a lowercase a have the same sort value. However, if you want the processor to differentiate between uppercase and lowercase letters, you can specify the letter case sort order as `case-order="upper-first"` or `case-order="lower-first"`. With `case-order="upper-first"`, uppercase letters sort first. With `case-order="lower-first"`, lower case letters sort first.
- **lang** Sets the language of the sort keys. For example, if the language is U.S. English, you could specify `lang="us"`.

None of these attributes are required and the default sort order is a forward alphabetic sort.

The basic format of the sort element is:

```
<xsl:sort select="expression" />
```

where *expression* is an XPath expression that specifies the node set you want to sort.

You can define the `xsl:sort` element inside `xsl:for-each` and `xsl:apply-templates` elements. Within `xsl:for-each` elements, the `xsl:sort` must appear immediately after the opening tag `<xsl:for-each>`. Otherwise a processor exception occurs.

Defining Sort Keys, Order, and Type

You use the `xsl:sort` element to reorganize selected nodes alphabetically or numerically. Each `xsl:sort` that you define acts as a sort key, meaning you can have a primary sort key, a secondary sort key, a tertiary sort key, and so on. To see how powerful this can be, consider the following example:

```
<?xml version="1.0" standalone="no"?>
<!DOCTYPE purchase_order PUBLIC "-//Stanek//PO Specification//EN"
 "http://www.tvpress.com/pospec.dtd">
<accounts>
 <customer>
  <account_id>10487</account_id>
  <name>
  <first>William</first>
  <mi>R</mi>
  <last>Stanek</last>
  </name>
 </customer>
 <customer>
  <account_id>09685</account_id>
  <name>
  <first>Robert</first>
  <mi>W</mi>
  <last>Stanek</last>
  </name>
 </customer>
 <customer>
  <account_id>11285</account_id>
  <name>
  <first>William</first>
  <mi>A</mi>
  <last>Stanek</last>
  </name>
 </customer>
</accounts>
```

Here we have a list of accounts that contain the keyword "Stanek", which was returned as an XML document from the corporate database. Although there are only three customer entries in this example, you can imagine a case where there are hundreds or thousands of customer entries—perhaps the account representative entered "William" as the keyword or wanted a list of all accounts.

To make this information useful, the data needs to be sorted in a specific order. One way to sort the data would be by `account_id`. Since this is a numerical value, you'd want to sort the `account_id` as a number. Here's an example stylesheet that sorts the `accounts` by `account_id`:

```
<?xml version="1.0"?>
<xsl:stylesheet version="1.0"
 xmlns:xsl="http://www.w3.org/1999/XSL/Transform">

 <xsl:output method="text" indent="no" />
 <xsl:strip-space elements="*" />

 <xsl:variable name="newline">
<xsl:text>
</xsl:text>
 </xsl:variable>

 <xsl:template match="/">
 <xsl:for-each select="accounts/customer">
  <xsl:sort select="account_id" data-type="number" />
  <xsl:value-of select="account_id" />
  <xsl:text> : </xsl:text>
  <xsl:value-of select="name/first" />
  <xsl:text> </xsl:text>
  <xsl:value-of select="name/mi" />
  <xsl:text> . </xsl:text>
  <xsl:value-of select="name/last" />
  <xsl:value-of select="$newline" />
 </xsl:for-each>
 </xsl:template>
</xsl:stylesheet>
```

The sort is accomplished using the `xsl:sort` element with a selection by `account_id`. This means that `account_id` is the primary sort key. The data-type for the sort is set to `number`, which tells the XSLT processor to sort the values as numbers. The resulting output looks like this:

```
09685 : Robert W. Stanek
10487 : William R. Stanek
11285 : William A. Stanek
```

In this example the `xsl:sort` element is defined inside an `xsl:for-each` element. `xsl:sort` can also appear inside `xsl:apply-templates` elements. Within `xsl:for-each` elements, the `xsl:sort` must appear immediately after the opening tag `<xsl:for-each>`. Otherwise a processor exception occurs.

The default sort order is `ascending`, which you could explicitly set using:

```
<xsl:sort select="account_id" data-type="number"
 order="ascending" />
```

You could also specify `descending` order, such as:

```
<xsl:sort select="account_id" data-type="number"
 order="descending" />
```

Now the account numbers are listed from highest to lowest, such as:

```
11285 : William A. Stanek
10487 : William R. Stanek
09685 : Robert W. Stanek
```

Another way to sort a list of accounts would be to sort by last name and then by first name. This would mean the sort would have two keys: `name/last` and `name/first`. Using the same input document, you could rewrite the stylesheet to use two sort keys like this:

```
<?xml version="1.0"?>
<xsl:stylesheet version="1.0"
 xmlns:xsl="http://www.w3.org/1999/XSL/Transform">

 <xsl:output method="text" indent="no" />
 <xsl:strip-space elements="*" />

 <xsl:variable name="newline">
<xsl:text>
</xsl:text>
 </xsl:variable>

 <xsl:template match="/">
 <xsl:for-each select="accounts/customer">
  <xsl:sort select="name/last" />
  <xsl:sort select="name/first" />
  <xsl:value-of select="name/last" />
  <xsl:text>, </xsl:text>
  <xsl:value-of select="name/first" />
  <xsl:text> </xsl:text>
  <xsl:value-of select="name/mi" />
  <xsl:text>. </xsl:text>
  <xsl:value-of select="account_id" />
  <xsl:value-of select="$newline" />
 </xsl:for-each>
 </xsl:template>
</xsl:stylesheet>
```

Using the new stylesheet, the output looks like this:

```
Stanek, Robert W. 09685
Stanek, William R. 10487
Stanek, William A. 11285
```

If you were paying particular attention to this sort, you noticed that it isn't quite perfect yet. That's because William R. Stanek appears before William A. Stanek in the output. The reason for this is that that was the original order in the input document and you didn't sort the customer list by middle initial. You can resolve this problem by adding a third sort key. The new stylesheet looks like this:

```
<?xml version="1.0"?>
<xsl:stylesheet version="1.0"
 xmlns:xsl="http://www.w3.org/1999/XSL/Transform">

 <xsl:output method="text" indent="no" />
 <xsl:strip-space elements="*" />

 <xsl:variable name="newline">
<xsl:text>
</xsl:text>
 </xsl:variable>

 <xsl:template match="/">
 <xsl:for-each select="accounts/customer">
  <xsl:sort select="name/last" />
  <xsl:sort select="name/first" />
  <xsl:sort select="name/mi" />
  <xsl:value-of select="name/last" />
  <xsl:text>, </xsl:text>
  <xsl:value-of select="name/first" />
  <xsl:text> </xsl:text>
  <xsl:value-of select="name/mi" />
  <xsl:text> . </xsl:text>
  <xsl:value-of select="account_id" />
  <xsl:value-of select="$newline" />
 </xsl:for-each>
 </xsl:template>
</xsl:stylesheet>
```

And the output is exactly what is expected:

```
Stanek, Robert W. 09685
Stanek, William A. 11285
Stanek, William R. 10487
```

Forward alphabetic sorts are the default sort type, but you can also specify an alphabetical sort explicitly. Here's an example:

```
<xsl:sort select="account_id" data-type="text"
 order="ascending" />
```

As with numeric sorts, you can do reverse alphabetic sorts. Here's an example:

```
<xsl:sort select="account_id" data-type="text"
 order="descending" />
```

Sorting Nodes in a Document

Now that you know how to work with `xsl:sort`, you can specify the nodes to sort in a document by following these steps:

1. You can define the `xsl:sort` element inside `xsl:for-each` and `xsl:apply-templates` elements. Within `xsl:for-each` elements, the `xsl:sort` must appear immediately after the opening tag `<xsl:for-each>`. Otherwise a processor exception occurs.
2. Type **<xsl:sort select="*expression*"**, where *expression* is an XPath expression that specifies the node set you want to sort.
3. Optionally, type **order="descending"** to set descending order for the sort. The default value is `order="ascending"`.
4. Optionally, type **data-type="number"** to specify a numeric sort. The default is `data-type="text"` for a text sort.
5. Optionally, with a text sort, type **case-order="upper-first"** to sort uppercase letters first or type **case-order="lower-first"** to sort lowercase letters first.
6. Type /> to complete the xsl:sort element.
7. Repeat Steps 2-6 to define additional sort keys.

Note The first sort key created is the primary sort key. The second key is the secondary sort key and so on.

Counting Nodes

Any time you need to count the number of nodes in a node set, you can use the `lcount()` function to do this. For example, let's say you had an XML document that contained all the purchase orders for the day in the form:

```
<?xml version="1.0"?>
<purchase_order>
 <order>...</order>
 <order>...</order>
 <order>...</order>
 <order>...</order>
</purchase_order>
```

and you wanted to output the total number of orders in the document. You could do this by defining a `value-of` declaration in the root node that counted the number of `order` nodes, such as:

```
<xsl:template match="/">
 <text>The total number of orders is: </text>
 <xsl:value-of select="count(order)" />
 <text>.</text>
</xsl:template>
```

The output is then:

```
The total number of orders is: 4.
```

If the summary document had three different types of orders, you might want to total orders in a different way. Here, you could total individual order types and also determine the total number orders of any type. To see how this works, consider the following example XML document:

```
<?xml version="1.0"?>
<purchase_order>
 <order type="walkin">...</order>
 <order type="phone">...</order>
 <order type="web">...</order>
 <order type="walkin">...</order>
</purchase_order>
```

Here you have three order types: `walkin`, `phone`, and `web`. With this in mind, you could define a template to count these order types and to provide a total of all orders, like this:

```
 <xsl:variable name="newline">
<xsl:text>
</xsl:text>
 </xsl:variable>

<xsl:template match="/">
 <text>
Daily Order Summary
===================
</text>

 <text> Total Walk-in Orders: </text>
 <xsl:value-of select="count(order/@type='walkin')" />
 <xsl:value-of select="$newline" />

 <text> Total Phone Orders: </text>
 <xsl:value-of select="count(order/@type='phone')" />
 <xsl:value-of select="$newline" />

 <text> Total Online Orders: </text>
 <xsl:value-of select="count(order/@type='web')" />
 <xsl:value-of select="$newline" />
```

(continued)

(continued)

```
 <text>
Daily Order Total
=================

 Total orders: </text>
 <xsl:value-of select="count(order)" />
 <text>
=================</text>

</xsl:template>
```

and the output would look like this:

```
Daily Order Summary
===================

 Total Walk-in Orders: 2
 Total Phone Orders: 1
 Total Online Orders: 1

Daily Order Total
=================

 Total orders: 4
=================
```

To count nodes, complete the following steps:

1. As part of a select attribute or within another function, type **count(*expression*)**, where *expression* is an XPath expression that specifies the node set whose nodes you want to count.
2. The result is the number of nodes in the node set.

Index

Symbols

A

D

E

O

P

Q

R

S

T

U

V

W

About the Author

William R. Stanek has nearly 20 years of hands-on experience with advanced programming and development. He is a leading technology expert and an award-winning author. Over the years, his practical advice has helped programmers, developers, and network engineers all over the world. He has written more than 25 computer books, which are sold internationally and have been translated into many languages. Current or forthcoming books include *Microsoft Windows .NET Server Administrator's Pocket Consultant, Microsoft SQL Server 2000 Server Administrator's Pocket Consultant, Microsoft Windows XP Professional Administrator's Pocket Consultant, and Microsoft IIS 6.0 Administrator's Pocket Consultant*.

Mr. Stanek has been involved in the commercial Internet community since 1991. His core business and technology experience comes from over 11 years of military service. He has substantial experience in developing server technology, encryption, and Internet solutions. He has written and conducted training courses for Digital Think, Global Knowledge, and Microsoft. His training courses cover Microsoft Windows 2000, Windows .NET, XML, Microsoft SQL Server, and Microsoft Exchange Server. He has written technical white papers on XML programming, large-scale databases, and data centers. He is widely sought after as a subject matter expert.

Mr. Stanek is proud to have served in the Persian Gulf War as a combat crewmember on an electronic warfare aircraft. He flew numerous combat and combat support missions, logging over 200 combat flight hours. Additionally, he has nearly 1000 hours of flight time. In his military career, he was a two-time distinguished graduate, honor graduate, and unit technician of the year. His civilian education includes a B.S. in computer science, magna cum laude, and an M.S. in information systems with distinction from Hawaii Pacific University. His service during the Persian Gulf War earned him nine medals, including the highest U.S. flying honor, the Air Force Distinguished Flying Cross. He was awarded 17 medals in 11 years of military service, making him one of the most highly decorated veterans of the Persian Gulf War.

Currently, Mr. Stanek lives in the Pacific Northwest with his wife and children. Although his eldest daughter has ventured out into the world, he still has three small children at home.

The manuscript for this book was prepared and submitted to Microsoft Press in electronic form. Text files were prepared using Microsoft Word 2000 for Windows. Pages were composed by nSight, Inc., using Adobe PageMaker 6.5 for Windows, with text in Garamond Light and display type in ITC Franklin Gothic. Composed pages were delivered to the printer as electronic prepress files.

Cover Designer
Landor Associates

Cover Illustrator
Landor Associaters

Layout Artist
Patty Fagan

Project Manager
Erin Connaughton

Tech Editor
Toby Andrews

Copy Editor
Joseph Gustaitis

Proofreaders
Renée Cote, Rebecca Merz, Seth Morrison

Indexer
Jack Lewis

Proof of Purchase

Use this page as proof of purchase if participating in a promotion or rebate offe this title. Proof of purchase must be used in conjunction with other proof(s) c payment such as your dated sales receipt—see offer details.

XML Pocket Consultant
0-7356-1183-1

CUSTOMER NAME

Microsoft Press, PO Box 97017, Redmond, WA 98073-9830